THE
VIKING
WARS

WAR AND PEACE IN
KING ALFRED'S BRITAIN
— 789–955 —

MAX ADAMS

PEGASUS BOOKS
NEW YORK LONDON

THE VIKING WARS

Pegasus Books, Ltd.
148 West 37th Street, 13th Floor
New York, NY 10018

Copyright © 2018 by Max Adams

First Pegasus Books paperback edition December 2019
First Pegasus Books hardcover edition August 2018

All rights reserved. No part of this book may be reproduced
in whole or in part without written permission from the publisher,
except by reviewers who may quote brief excerpts in connection with a review
in a newspaper, magazine, or electronic publication; nor may any part of this
book be reproduced, stored in a retrieval system, or transmitted in any form or
by any means electronic, mechanical, photocopying, recording, or
other, without written permission from the publisher.

ISBN: 978-1-64313-254-9

10 9 8 7 6 5

Printed in the United States of America
Distributed by Simon & Schuster

For my cousins

CONTENTS

LIST OF MAPS

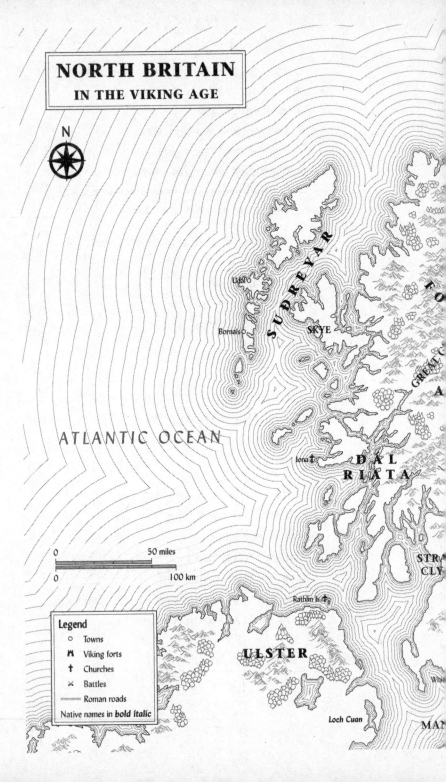

NORTH BRITAIN
IN THE VIKING AGE

N

ATLANTIC OCEAN

SUDREYAR

Udal○

Bornais○

SKYE

Iona †

DÁL RIATA

Rathlin Is.

ULSTER

Loch Cuan

STRA CLY

MAN

Whi

FO

GREAT

A

0 ——— 50 miles

0 ——— 100 km

Legend
○ Towns
ᛗ Viking forts
† Churches
✕ Battles
——— Roman roads
Native names in **bold italic**

SOUTH BRITAIN
IN THE VIKING AGE

N

IRISH SEA

CUM

AMOU

Jurby ○ Ballateare
○ Ramsey
Peel ○ **MAN**
○ The Braaid

Dublin

Brunanburh 937 ✕
Cledemuða 921 ✕

Llanbedrgoch

ANGLESEY

GWYNEDD

Buttington ⌐
POWYS

Waterford ○   Wexford ○

CEREDIGION

Wye

H

Llangorse ○ **MA**
St David's ✝   **BRYCHEINIOG**
DYFED   **YSTRAD**   **GV**
TYWI

GLYWYSING

Countisbury 877 ✕

S

WEST
WEALAS   ○ Exeter

○ Mawgan Porth
St Germans ✝

Legend

○ Towns
⌐ Viking forts
✝ Churches
✕ Battles
▦ Roman roads
— Alfred-Guthrum treaty line
Native names in **bold italic**

NORTH SEA

DEIRA

Ripon ✝
Aldwark ⚔
Wharram Percy ○
York ⚔
Tanshelf ○
Flixborough ○

LINDSEY

Torksey ⚔   Foss Dyke
Lincoln ✝

NESS

DANELAW

PECSÆTE
Derby ⚔
Repton ✝   Breedon ✝
Nottingham ⚔

THE FENS

FLEGG

EAST ANGLIA

Norwich ⚔

MERCIA
Tamworth ○
Tettenhall 910
Leicester ⚔   Stamford ⚔
✝ Medehamstede
Little Ouse
Thetford ○
Ely ✝
GYWRE
Huntingdon ⚔
Cambridge ⚔

Droitwich ○
Worcester ○
WICCE
Winchcombe ○
Gloucester ○
Cirencester ○
Brixworth ✝
Northampton ⚔
Towcester ○
Buckingham ○
Bedford
Hertford
Ipswich ○
Colchester ⚔
Maldon ○
Benfleet ⚔

ESSEX

Akeman Street
Oxford ○
Wallingford ○
Cricklade ○
Chippenham ○
Ashdown 871 ⚔
Reading ⚔
London ⚔
Kingston ○
Rochester ○
Milton
Canterbury ○

WESSEX
Edington 878 ○
Ecgberts Stone ○
Wilton 871 ⚔
Baseng 871 ⚔
Farnham 893
Acleah 851 ⚔
Winchester ○
Portway
KENT

ANDREDESWEALD
Appledore ⚔

SUSSEX
Chichester ○

Wareham ○

ENGLISH CHANNEL

0   50 miles
0   100 km

North West Europe

SHETLAND
Jarlshof

ORKNEY
Kirkwall

ATLANTIC
OCEAN

Portmahomack

PICTAVIA

Iona † DAL
RIATA
Dunottar

Rathlin Is. †
Govan
STRATH
CLYDE
Lindisfarne

Whithorn †
Hadrian's Wall
Chester le Street † Jarrow
NORTHUMBRIA

IRELAND
MAN
Kells †
Ripon †
Eoforwic

Clonmacnoise †
Meols
LINDSEY

Dublin
MERCIA

Waterford
Breedon on the Hill

St David's †
WEALAS
Medehamstede † EAST
ANGLIA Norwic
Offa's Dyke
Brixworth †
Ely †

Gipeswic

Lundenwic
Westensho
Walcheren
WEST
WEALAS
WESSEX
Domburg
Hamwic † Reculver
Fordwic

† St Bertin
Quentovic

English Channel

Rouen
FRANCI
Pitres
R. Seine Paris

BRITTANY

Irish Sea

HORDALAND

Stavanger ○ — N O R W A Y ○ Oseberg
                              ● Kaupang

Birka ●

North Sea

S W E D E N

○ Lindholm Høje

JUTLAND

D E N M A R K

Jelling ○
                    ○ Roskilde
● Ribe   SJAELLAND

Baltic Sea

Danevirke
        ● Hedeby

Lübeck ○

S A X O N I A

F R I S I A

○ Dorestad

○ Aachen

Legend

▬▬▬ Roman roads
✝ churches
● wics

| 0 | 100 | 200 | 300 km |
| 0 | 50 | 100 | 150 | 200 miles |

A BEAST OF THE IMAGINATION,
from a cross shaft at Kirk Braddan old church, Isle of Man

AUTHOR'S NOTE

THE VIKING WARS IS INTENDED AS A COMPANION volume to my previous Early Medieval histories, *The King in the North* and *In the Land of Giants*. Many of the themes, people and places encountered here refer back, one way or another, to those two books. I leave the reader to make the connections.

The word 'Viking' is problematic, and much has been written about its origins, meanings and familiarity to those who found themselves on the wrong end of a Scandinavian raid. Suffice it to say that it is safe to think of 'viking' as an activity: hence, to 'go a-Viking'. It should carry no particular ethnic or national badge—although, inevitably, it is frequently used as a convenient shorthand for a raider of Scandinavian origin. I have tried to avoid using it as an ethnic label.

A few words are required on spelling and pronunciation. I have tried as far as possible to render spellings in their original language for the sake of authenticity. In Old English, readers will come across letters like the ligature or grapheme Æ, or æ, which should be pronounced like the 'a' in 'hat' (it comes from the runic letter called æsc, or ash, after the tree with which it was associated in the runic alphabet). Less familiar, perhaps, is the thorn, written þ and pronounced with a soft 'th', as in 'think'. The eth symbol ð is a harder 'th' sound, as in 'that', and appears as Ð when it occurs at the beginning of a word. Anglo-Saxon spelling was itself inconsistent, and it is generally modernized by scholars and translators. Where I have quoted from their work, I have kept their rendering.

Old Norse has its own distinct accents and conventions. Most notably, names like Rögnvaldr have a final 'r' which is silent, and entirely absent in the possessive. So: Rögnvaldr, but Rögnvald's. In Old Irish his name is rendered Ragnall; in the Latin of the *Historia de Sancto Cuthberto* he is Regenwaldus.

The derivations of place-name forms and meanings are overwhelmingly taken from Victor Watt's magnificent *Cambridge Dictionary of English Place-Names*. All quotations from translations of the original sources are most gratefully acknowledged. To have almost all of our Early Medieval sources in fine, accessible translations is a monumental scholarly achievement. Two outstanding resources, without which the modern researcher would be stranded, are worth mentioning: the Prosopography of Anglo-Saxon England (PASE), a searchable database of all the recorded inhabitants of England up until the eleventh century; and the Electronic Sawyer, an online database of surviving charters from the Anglo-Saxon period.[1]

The Viking travel maps started as an aide-memoire to understand how Scandinavians were able to penetrate the remote corners of the island of Britain so effectively, and why it was so hard to stop them. The two versions, early and late, have proved helpful to me; I hope they are equally useful to the reader in making sense of this half-familiar, half-exotic world.

INTRODUCTION

AS THE EIGHTH CENTURY DRAWS TO ITS CLOSE, BANDS of feral men, playing by a new set of rules and bent on theft, kidnap, arson, torture and enslavement, prey on vulnerable communities. Shockwaves are felt in the royal courts of Europe, in the Holy See at Rome. The king's peace is broken. Economies are disrupted; institutions threatened. In time the state itself comes under attack from the new power in the North, a power of devastating military efficiency and suicidally apocalyptic ideology. It seems as if the End of Days is approaching. Out of the chaos come opportunities to shuffle the pack of dynastic fortune, to subjugate neighbouring states, to exploit a new economics and re-invent fossilized institutions.

The economic strengths that made Britain such an attractive target lay in the exploitation, by an organized, self-knowing élite, of abundant resources: its cattle, sheep, grain, timber, minerals and the labour to harvest and process them. The ease with which people and goods were able to move through the landscape, and the institutions which evolved to benefit from that wealth, rendered Britain uniquely wealthy, but also uniquely vulnerable. No king or counsel saw the disaster coming; only, perhaps, the wise and Venerable Bede, wagging a warning finger at the future from his writing desk in 734.[1] After the first shock, a little before the year 800, a century—four generations—passed before effective state strategies tamed the wild beast and a new European culture, vibrant, energetic and ambitious, began to take shape. Accommodations were made between native and incomer. In Britain grand projects were conceived: to unify peoples under the banners of kingdoms that came to be known as Scotland, Wales and England. It is not so clear who conceived those projects; even less so that they were successful.

The first notice of a new-dawning reality comes to us from an entry in the *Anglo-Saxon Chronicle* under the year 789. In this year, it was remembered, three ships came out of the North. Presuming them to be traders, the West Saxon king's man of business—his *portgerefa*, or port-reeve—rode to meet them somewhere on the south coast, perhaps Portland in Dorset. They slew him. Within a decade, a rash of notices recorded the sacking of monasteries along the North Sea coasts of Britain, among the Hebridean islands and as far west as Ireland. The famous attack on Lindisfarne, Holy Island, in 793 was and is seen as a marker for the start of a new European age of warfare, uncertainty and migration.

In the rich imaginations of the Scandinavian male nobility, from whose swelling ranks the sea raiders were drawn, treasure was guarded by fierce, vindictive dragons in unearthly lairs. It could only be won by guile, deceit, luck and the aid of complicit gods. Its acquisition invariably led to vengeful pursuit by jealous gods, brothers, sons. Action required reaction; warriors won honour and a place in Valhalla; death must be glorious; the pursuit of material wealth, at great personal risk, was a game every bit worth the candle.

In Britain and Ireland and on the north-western coasts of Continental Europe, where monasteries had been established under the protection of tribal warlords and founding saints across 200 years and more, treasure was guarded by prematurely balding men, sometimes by women, wearing woollen robes, unarmed and untrained in combat, living in remote communities far from the protective reach of kings' armies. Their only defensive weapons, it seemed, were the word and the cross. For any enterprising northern warrior the holy islands of Britain and Ireland were too good an opportunity to pass up.

For twenty or thirty years raiders probed the coasts and estuaries of Frisia, Saxony and Francia, Britain and Ireland, picking off the precious treasures of the church without challenging its institutional power. They set off in in their sleek longships in springtime and returned to their homelands in autumn. Dynasties rose and fell across north-west Europe, and Scandinavian entrepreneurs took a close interest in their fortunes. The middle decades of the ninth century saw more ambitious raids: scores and even hundreds of ships at a time falling on trading settlements, penetrating deep inland and occasionally, increasingly, overwintering in secure bases, their *longphuirt*,* in uncomfortable proximity to their victims.

Those military states facing the Atlantic and North Sea experimented with defensive and offensive tactics; they constructed signal stations, built fleets, dammed rivers, enforced ever-increasing military burdens on the estates of their nobles and bishops. They chased and sometimes caught the enemy, and when they were able to bring him to battle in open country they were often victorious. Much of the time they were engaged in wild goose chases across land, by river and at sea. Often and unsuccessfully they attempted bribery and sometimes they tried pitting one band of raiders against another.

In 865 the game changed: a great army landed in East Anglia, an army of conquest, precipitating a series of wars which lasted until the middle of the following century. Ælfred the West Saxon king has often been the central figure in the narrative of those conflicts—understandably, in many respects: he was an individual of rare talents, not least of which was that, like Winston Churchill, he ensured history's enduring affection by writing it himself. My purpose in writing this book is to place Ælfred's part in the story of the Viking Age in Britain in a wider cultural and geographical

---

* The singular is *longphort*.

context. The Britain encountered by the Scandinavians of the ninth and tenth centuries was one of regional diversity and self-conscious cultural identity: of Pict, Dál Riatan and Strathclyde Briton; of Bernician and Deiran, East Anglian, Mercian and West Saxon. Ancient kingdoms surviving in Kent and Cornwall, Powys, Gwynedd and Dyfed, Hwicce, Lindsey and Man had profoundly individual identities that endure, in many respects, into the present and played pivotal roles in the story of the Viking Age. The richness of those peoples' encounters with the cultures of Scandinavia, at war and in peace, cannot be captured through either a purely Ælfredan or Anglo-centric lens. A broader view brings perspective. Nor can the story of those encounters be told without offering a more nuanced portrait of the Scandinavians who both wreaked destruction and drew creative energy from their compulsion to explore and exploit the world.

The Viking Wars is a history and archaeology of the peoples of Britain, native and immigrant, during the formative century and a half between those first raids and the expulsion of a Scandinavian dynasty from York in 954. Some of the parallels that this age offers for the early twenty-first century are remarkable; disturbing, even.

> Brother will fight brother and be his slayer
> Sister's sons will violate the kinship bond
> Hard it is in the world; whoredom abounds
> Axe-age, sword-age, shields are cleft asunder
> Wind-age, wolf-age, before the world plunges headlong;
> No man will spare another.[2]

PART

I

*The tiger
in the smoke*
789–878

TIMELINE 1

789 to 878

Unless otherwise stated,
narrative source entries are from
the ASC Parker 'A' text.

ABBREVIATIONS
ASC – *Anglo-Saxon Chronicle*
Æðelweard – *Chronicon*
Alcuin Ep. – *The letters of Alcuin*
ASB – *Annals of St Bertin*
Asser – *Life of King Ælfred*
AU – *Annals of Ulster*
HSC – *Historia de Sancto Cuthberto*
LDE – *Symeon's Libellus de Exordio*
NH – *Nithard's Histories*
RFA – *Royal Frankish Annals*

789 First recorded attack by Scandinavian raiders on south coast
kills royal official named as Beauduherd (Æðelweard).

793 Lindisfarne attacked and plundered by Vikings. Famine in
Northumbria.

799 Romans capture Pope Leo, cut out his tongue, blind and ban-
ish him. He recovers and retains his see—and sight (RFA).
— First recorded Viking raid on Francia: islands off the coast
of Aquitaine (Alcuin Ep.).

807 The Iona community retreats to new monastic foundation at
Kells in Co. Meath for safety (AU).

810 King Godfrið's Danish fleet of 200 ships harries Frisian coast,
defeats Frisian forces, exacts 100 lb (45 kg) silver in tribute.
King Godfrið murdered (RFA).

814 Death of Charlemagne, aged seventy; succeeded by Louis the
Pious (RFA).

820 Approximate dendrochronology date for construction of
Oseberg ship.

825 **Battle of Ellendun**: defeat of Mercian King Beornwulf by Ecgberht, king of the West Saxons. Wessex annexes Sussex, Kent and Essex.

829 Conquest of Mercia by Ecgberht; Wiglaf exiled. Ecgberht mints coins as king in *Lundenwic*.

834 Dorestad laid waste by a raid (ASB). The beginning of a series of great Danish raids on Francia and England.

835 Heathens 'devastate Sheppey', the first great raid on an Anglo-Saxon kingdom.

839 King Ecgberht, after a series of poor harvests, tells Louis the Pious of an apocalyptic vision of darkness and heathen fleets raiding (ASB).

— Death of Ecgberht; Æðelwulf succeeds as king of Wessex; Æðelstan, his eldest son, succeeds to Kent, Surrey and Sussex.

— Large Viking raid against Fortriu in which Pictish kings are killed and the ruling dynasty is wiped out (AU).

841 Dublin becomes the principal *longphort* of the Vikings in Ireland: evidence of co-ordinated establishment of raiding bases in Ireland (AU).

— Charles the Bald becomes king of West Francia (NH).

— Cináed mac Ailpín becomes king of Alba and Pictland.

845 Paris plundered by Norse raiders (ASB).

851 350 heathen ships arrive at the mouth of the Thames; raiders attack Canterbury and London, put King Beorhtwulf of Mercia to flight. King Æðelwulf and his son Æðelbald achieve great victory over a Danish army at the **Battle of Acleah**.

855 King Æðelwulf of Wessex travels to Rome for twelve months with his youngest son Ælfred. Marries Judith, daughter of Charles the Bald (Asser).

858 Death of King Æðelwulf. Æðelbald succeeds in Wessex; Æðelberht succeeds in Kent, Essex, Sussex and Surrey.

860 King Æðelbald dies; Æðelberht succeeds to whole kingdom.

864 **Edict of Pîtres**: Charles the Bald reforms the Frankish army, forms cavalry; reforms coinage; orders construction of fortified bridges to block Viking incursions (ASB).

865 A Great Host comes to England and overwinters in East Anglia under Ívarr. East Anglians submit. Death of King Æðelberht; succeeded by his brother Æðelred (to 871).

866 Óláfr and Ásl attack Fortriu, plunder Pictland and take hostages (AU).

867 Osberht of Northumbria expelled, succeeded by Ælle. **Battle of York** against *mycel hæpen here*: city stormed by Northumbrian force.

869 **Battle of Hoxne**: Danes under Ívarr kill St Eadmund, king of East Anglia.

870 Dumbarton besieged and captured by Óláfr and Ívarr (AU); last Early Medieval mention of Dumbarton.

871 **Battle of Ashdown**. Year of nine engagements between Wessex and Danish army; King Æðelred dies (buried at Wimborne monastery); succeeded by Ælfred. Wessex makes peace with the Host.

873 The Host moves to Repton and builds a fort; King Burhred of Mercia driven overseas.

874 The Host returns to Northumbria, winters on the Tyne and 'overran that land'. The Danish army splits: one part invades Pictland and Strathclyde.

875 The southern Host evades Ælfred's forces and camps at Wareham. Hálfdan 'shares out the land of the Northumbrians' (or 876: variants of ASC).

— St Cuthbert's relics and coffin removed from Lindisfarne: beginning of the 'Seven Years' Wandering' (HSC; LDE).

876 Ælfred makes peace with the Danes on a sacred ring; they evade him by night and reach Exeter.

877 Viking army moves from Cirencester to attack Chippenham at Midwinter; occupies Wessex. Many shires submit.

878 Ælfred flees into hiding in the Somerset marshes and builds a small fort at Athelney. After Easter Ælfred decisively defeats Danes at **Battle of Edington**. Treaty with Guðrum; his baptism.

FORESPÆC*

L IKE THE PAW PRINTS OF A TIGER, THE TRACKS OF A NEW
menace stalking vulnerable coastal monasteries in the 790s
left the identity of the perpetrators in no doubt. Traders and
fishermen from the Baltic lands were no strangers; they brought
exotic furs, the tusks of walrus and narwhal, tall tales of ice and
the endless darkness of the northern winter. Their gods were recognized as those whom the ancestors of the Anglo-Saxons had
revered in these islands more than three centuries previously.
Their speech was exotic, but comprehensible.

Since no contemporary account tells of the Viking Age from
a Scandinavian point of view, historians and archaeologists must
piece their story together from fragments. Those fragments reveal
the stark, brutal realties of inglorious contact with native populations—and recent archaeological discoveries allow us to paint an
increasingly detailed picture of the crime scene. That picture begs
the question: why did they come?

The social and economic forces that propelled these maritime entrepreneurs to take up arms and go a-Viking, to engage
in theft, arson, enslavement and murder, may have been opaque
even to the raiders themselves. We can say that the inexorable
growth of the Christian Frankish empire under Charlemagne
led to a fateful clash of cultures between the inheritors of Rome
and the Northern world, and that the tribal chiefdoms of Denmark, Sweden and Norway saw the Holy Roman Emperor as
a threat. We can also suggest that the limited cultivable lands
of Scandinavia were insufficient to provide for a growing,

* *Forespæc*: An Old English word meaning 'preface'.

outward-looking population needing land to farm and on which to raise a family.

We know, too, that by the year 800 something like perfection had been achieved in the Scandinavian art of shipbuilding, the boatyards of its rivers and fjords producing fast, oceangoing vessels superbly adapted to coastal trade, deep-sea fishing, exploration and raiding. And we can point to the inherently inward-looking conservatism of the kingdoms of the British Isles: intently focused on the domestic agricultural cycle of the seasons, on a rigid caste system and on the competitive relations between a well-established church and centuries-old kingdoms. Ritualized warfare and the ancient rules of overlordship maintained a comfortable status quo among their warrior élites. The Vikings, then, had means, motive and opportunity to strike at the vulnerable fringes of the Atlantic islands. But that does not in itself explain the Viking Age: an unstoppable movement of peoples overseas in search of new lands to conquer and settle.

For the first quarter of the ninth century the interests and preoccupations of Insular* kings remained primarily domestic. The death of King Offa of Mercia, the greatest of the eighth-century Anglo-Saxon warlords, reopened a struggle with the West Saxon kings for superiority over southern Britain. They fought for the right to control the archiepiscopal see of Canterbury; for rights to trade along the River Thames and, in particular, for the financial perks generated by a thriving riverside trading settlement at *Lundenwic*. By the late 830s the dynasty of King Ecgberht of Wessex was able to assert *imperium* over many of the Anglo-Saxon, and some of the Welsh, kingdoms while, further north, the Gaelic kings of Dál Riata were beginning to exercise an ultimately successful claim to subdue the kings of Pictland and obliterate their culture.

---

* Insular, as an adjective, meaning 'of the Atlantic islands of Britain and Ireland'.

Across the Irish Sea a Norse dynasty established itself in a settlement that became Dublin on the River Liffey and founded pirate bases, the *longphuirt*, elsewhere. From these bases they raided across the Irish Sea with apparent impunity; and a hybrid Norse–Irish culture established the towns that would underpin the wealth and power of medieval Ireland. The Norse conquered Man and left an indelible legacy of settlement, art and language there. In the Hebrides, and further north in Orkney and Shetland, Norse raiders-cum-farmers found much to please them: after subduing or marrying into native communities they built a great diaspora which has profoundly influenced life in the islands over all the centuries since.

By the end of the first quarter of the ninth century monastic communities had been devastated by Viking raids across a whole generation. From the 830s onwards those raids began to be felt more widely and, if they did not yet threaten the state, they began to affect the relations between states and to weaken the institution of the church, already in decline under pressures from a secularizing state. Their effect was also felt on the wealth and productivity of the land: trade routes were disrupted; silver supplies choked off; treasure was stolen, never to be recovered; productive farms and trading settlements went into terminal decline.

The tiger may have left its prints all over the scene of the crime; but a predator that ghosted in on the dawn tide and was gone at dusk, who could penetrate Britain's rivers and ride fast along its Roman roads, presented a threat that could not, at first, be countered. It took long and bitter experience, another generation, before the Insular states began to both resist and accommodate their unwelcome visitors. The arrival of a Great Host, crossing from Francia in hundreds of ships, turned raiding into conquest in the 860s.

As it happens, the two decades of greatest threat coincided with the emergence of Ælfred, the only English king to have earned himself the epithet 'Great'. In the sixteenth and seventeenth centuries his reputation as a highly competent and religious—if perhaps unpopular—king was reforged into that of a republican hero. In the nineteenth century statues were raised to another sort of Ælfred of Wessex by Whig protestant imperialists who saw him as a bulwark against barbarism: a noble, moustachioed savage who gave England (and therefore the British Empire) its supposed legal and educational superiority.

The real Ælfred was a man of his age, obliged to fight in battle at the head of his *fyrd*,* the summoned levies of his people, the West Saxons. He was the survivor of four older brothers, all of them kings in Wessex before him. He learned, through defeat, disloyalty and the humiliation of flight, to counter the apocalyptic threat facing his kingdom. He saw how to exploit adversity to enhance the power of the Anglo-Saxon state: to professionalize it. But Ælfred was also something more: a soldier-philosopher in the mould, perhaps, of Marcus Aurelius; an administrative reformer whose experience with the Great Host taught him the art of the possible; a passionate educator and expert in the deployment of his powers of patronage to initiate his own renaissance. We are lucky enough to have Ælfred's own words to demonstrate the value he placed on wisdom. From a disastrous defeat that must have seemed as though the End of Days was come, he staged a brilliant fightback and, at Edington in 878, was able to tame the tiger in the smoke.†

---

* The levies of the Anglo-Saxon kingdoms. For its complexities and development see Richard Abels's excellent *Lordship and Military Obligation in Anglo-Saxon England* (1988).

† *The Tiger in the Smoke* is the title of a wonderfully atmospheric thriller by Margery Allingham set in the London fogs of the late 1940s and published in 1952.

LANDSCAPE WITH FIGURES

A CLASH OF WORLDS — SCANDINAVIAN SOCIETY — THE FIRST RAIDS — THE FATE OF THE MONASTERIES — MERCIAN POWER — POLITICS AND THE CHURCH — THE RISE OF WESSEX

1

I N THE 799TH YEAR FROM THE CHRISTIAN incarnation, according to contemporary chroniclers, Pope Leo III was ambushed while riding on horseback from his basilica at the Lateran to St Lawrence's church in Rome. His tongue was cut out and he was blinded. He escaped, though, and was taken to safety by envoys of Charlemagne, king of the Franks. In the same year, Charlemagne's Northumbrian scholar Alcuin recorded the first raid by heathen pirates in Francia, on islands off the coast of Aquitaine. The following year, the first of a new century, raiders were said to have destroyed the monasteries at Hartness and Tynemouth on Britain's North Sea coast;* a certain Godfrið became king in Norðmannia (i.e. Denmark); and on Christmas Day Charlemagne was crowned Emperor of the Romans by Pope Leo, now restored to power, if not health.

In the year 801 Archbishop Æðelheard of Canterbury journeyed to Rome, spending time on the way with the scholar Alcuin in his abbey at St Josse, near the trading port of *Quentovic* at the

---

* Hartness, later Hartlepool; see endnote 4.

1. THE DAWN OF THE VIKING AGE: sunrise at Stromness, Orkney.

mouth of the River Canche in Picardy. He may have arrived in Rome in time to witness part of the basilica of St Peter's collapse during an earthquake. The same year a serious fire swept through *Lundenwic*, the trading settlement on the River Thames, and a small, insignificant war broke out between Mercia and Northumbria.

In 802 Beorhtric, king of Wessex, died and was succeeded by Ecgberht, son of Ealhmund; a great battle was fought between the Men of Hwicce and the Men of *Wilsæte*, or Wiltshire; the island monastery of Iona, the foundation of Colm Cille, or St Columba, was burned by heathens; and Harun al-Rashid, Abbasid caliph in Baghdad, sent to his friend Charlemagne a gift in the shape of an elephant called Abul-Abbas.[1]

These chronicle entries, sometimes laconically brief, sometimes viscerally detailed, are a narrow window on a world tense with conflict, dynamically interconnected and full of wonder, terror, politics and, above all, populated by tangible people, actors on a grand stage. We know the names of an astonishing 11,000 men and nearly 800 women who lived in Anglo-Saxon England before the year 1041.[2] A probably comparable, possibly larger, number of names survives in Irish sources, many fewer in contemporary Welsh and Scottish materials. These are accidents of record and curation, no guide at all to numbers of real people living in the landscape and even less to the sorts of lives they led through those centuries of upheaval. But their survival is a thread joining us to a very real, if remote, past.

Fleshing out the crude sketches of the chronicles requires some imaginative use of evidence from charters, saints' lives, genealogies, archaeology and place names. Increasingly, these sources allow us to trace a subtler, richer narrative. After that, the unchanging rules of politics and patronage, jealousy, ambition and greed come into play. We can follow the fortunes of popes and kings, queens, archbishops, priests, pirate chiefs, sometimes

2. IONA ABBEY: the fragile cradle of Atlantic Christianity.

of lesser nobles and, very occasionally, of the ordinary inhabitants of farm and township and of merchants and moneyers. We can reconstruct the histories of a few places in increasingly fascinating detail, as archaeology reveals glimpses of monasteries and towns, forts and farms, the afterlife and the daily grind of *ceorl*, peasant, slave and *wifman*.* Alongside the ordinary, the rational and the inevitable lie traces of the extraordinary, the wondrous, the eccentric and the downright bizarre.

Take Charlemagne's elephant, Abul-Abbas. We cannot say whether it was male or female, African or Indian, where or when it was born. We know that in the spring of 801 Charlemagne, fresh from his coronation as Holy Roman Emperor by a grateful Pope Leo, was at Ravenna on the north-east coast of Italy when word came to him that envoys from Harun al-Rashid had arrived at the port of Pisa. They brought news that Charlemagne's own

---

* *Ceorl*: pronounced churl; a 'free' farmer subject to the lordship of a *thegn* or *dreng*. *Wifman*: literally a female man; a housewife.

mission, sent to the caliph four years earlier, was returning with extravagant gifts; or rather, one of his envoys, Isaac the Jew, was returning; the other members of the party had died. Now Charlemagne learned that one of Harun al-Rashid's gifts was an elephant (another was an astonishing brass water clock in which mechanical knights emerged from little windows and the hours were marked by bronze balls dropping onto tiny cymbals).[3] Returning to his court at Aachen, Charlemagne dispatched a fleet from Liguria to receive the gifts. That autumn, Isaac landed at Porto Venere. By now it was too late in the year to take the elephant across the Alps, so Isaac and his pachyderm spent the winter at Vercelli in Piedmont, halfway between Milan and Turin. According to the *Royal Frankish Annals*, Isaac duly delivered the elephant to his emperor at the imperial palace of Aachen in July 802.

We might speculate on the reception of this outsized marvel from the Orient in the capital of the Frankish kingdom, the crowds that must have lined the streets to gawp at its immense size; on the chances of a brave youth daring to reach out and poke its irresistible, leathery flanks; and on the elephant's own experience of the northern climate and whatever quarters and diet it was given. We would like to know more, much more, than we are told by the official Frankish chronicler.

The elephant survived eight years at the emperor's court until it died at a place called Lippeham on the River Rhine, seemingly during the advance of its master's armies to face those of the Danish King Godfrið. Had Charlemagne hoped to impress his heathen foes, to intimidate them? Was Abul-Abbas a war elephant?

In this unlikely episode the Islamic Caliphate, Rome, Francia and Scandinavia are visibly linked by the presence of an exotic gift, by diplomacy, by sea power and military campaign. The elephant stands for all those less tangible threads which connected the far-flung worlds of the Early Medieval period. If elephants could travel such distances, what of the traders, priests and warriors, the pottery, books, swords, bundles of wool and precious gems whose histories are often harder to trace?

Where the annals fail, archaeology picks up the pieces. A fabulous hoard of metalwork buried by its owner on the banks of the River Ribble in Lancashire around the year 903, either for safekeeping or through fear, and unaccountably never retrieved, contains coins from Anglo-Saxon England, from Francia and the Arab lands, and silver arm rings from Ireland and the Baltic, recording the cumulative movements of nameless traders and raiders. A marginal note, written in an elegant Old English hand in a Latin Gospel book, records how it was stolen by the heathen army and ransomed from them by a wealthy ealdorman of Surrey as a pious gift to Christ Church, Canterbury. The timbers of a Viking longship, retrieved in the 1960s from the shallow waters of Roskilde Fjord in Denmark, reveal that it had been constructed not in a Scandinavian shipyard but in Ireland, on the banks of the River Liffey. A sherd of pottery from a monastery on the north-east coast of Scotland, destroyed by fire in about the year 800, came from a Roman amphora. A stone carving in a modest Cumbrian church depicts a scene from Norse legend in which the god Thor goes fishing for a sea monster, using an ox-skull for bait. As I write, the first ever example of a Viking boat burial from the British mainland has just been reported from Swordle Bay, on the remote Ardnamurchan peninsula in Scotland.[4] One day, we must suppose, archaeologists digging somewhere in the back gardens of Aachen on the Dutch–German border will find the unlikely bones of Abul-Abbas. The story of the Viking Age is as much a tale of labyrinthine connections as it is of wars and the destinies of kings.

The collision of the Frankish and Scandinavian worlds in the year of the elephant's death in 810 can, in retrospect, be seen as a catalytic moment in European history. Charlemagne had gained sole control of the kingdom of the Franks on the death of his brother Carloman in 771. He forged strong links with the papacy and with the empires of Islam and embarked on an aggressive programme of expansion, bringing neighbouring territories under his control. He successfully defeated or marginalized rival claimants to the throne. His wide-ranging and efficient diplomatic, military and cultural progress across a forty-year period was the first genuinely unifying national movement in post-Roman Europe. He exploited and encouraged trade within and beyond Francia—his correspondence with the Mercian King Offa reveals a complex and sophisticated use of economics as a political tool. He was united with the papacy in wishing to see the revival of an empire of Christians, sidelining the historical primacy of Constantinople as the legitimate successor of the late Roman state and defending Christianity against heathens of varying hue.

Early Medieval kings were ruthless. Charlemagne committed his fair share of murders and atrocities: forcibly converting heathens, massacring armies, laying waste swathes of farmland and deporting native peoples. But he also inspired a cultural renaissance in literature, art and architecture; the palatine chapel of the royal complex at Aachen survives as a unique expression of his vision. He attempted to construct a canal linking the rivers Rhine and Danube, built bridges and fortifications and laid plans for the empire to survive his death.

By 804 persistent campaigning in the lands of the Saxons between the Rhine and Elbe had extended Charlemagne's dominions almost to the base of the Jutland peninsula. In that year he is said to have deported all the Saxons living north of the Elbe and given their lands to his allies the Obodrites, whose territories flanked the Baltic coast of what is now Germany. His empire now abutted the southern border of Denmark, a country resistant to Christian missionaries and reluctant to be absorbed into Charlemagne's imperial dominion. Franks and Scandinavians were now neighbours. Danish kings were no imperialists: they had enough on their plate managing the disparate factions and communities of the western Baltic. But Charlemagne's northerly progress was a threat that could not be ignored. King Godfrið's response was to send a fleet and army to Sliesthorp, at the head of the River Schlei, almost the narrowest part of the neck joining Jutland to the Continental plain. The two kings exchanged embassies.[5] Hostilities were avoided.

Four years later, Godfrið's armies pre-emptively invaded the lands of the Obodrites on the southern shores of the Baltic Sea, rendering them tributary. Charlemagne, ageing, ill and perhaps unwilling to embark on another major military campaign, responded by sending his son Charles with an army to counter further Danish incursions. Fierce fighting depleted Godfrið's army, but he took a number of Obodrite fortresses. In what seems to have been a long campaigning summer Charles countered by building a bridge across the Elbe and ravaging the lands of those peoples who, according to the official Frankish annals, had 'defected' to Godfrið.[6]

Before returning to Denmark the Danes destroyed the trading centre at *Riric* (possibly modern Lübeck, with its vital access to Baltic trade routes). Godfrið ordered the wholesale removal of its merchants, resettling them at a new trading town on the River Schlei at a place called *Haithabu*, or Hedeby. Anticipating a response from Charlemagne, Godfrið now ordered the extension, perhaps merely the completion, of a network of defensive earthworks across the base of the Jutland peninsula, from his new town at the navigable head of the Schlei as far as the River Treene, which flows into the Eider and thence into the North Sea. The Danevirke, like Offa's Dyke, was a hugely ambitious military and cultural project of iconic national significance, stretching more than 20 miles (32 km) in its final, complex form. As late as 1864 it could still be defended, albeit unsuccessfully, against Prussian invasion.

In 809 Danish and Frankish envoys met, hostages were exchanged, and Charlemagne ordered a new fortification to be built north of the Elbe, some 30 miles (48 km) south of the Danevirke. A year later Godfrið sent a second pre-emptive force of 200 ships to invade Frisia, harrying the islands and exacting a tribute of 100 lb (45 kg) of silver. Charlemagne sent his marshals out to raise an army and arranged to rendezvous with his fleet on the Rhine at Lippeham. The death there of his prize elephant coincided with news that the Danish fleet had returned to its home base, and that Godfrið had been murdered by one of his retainers.

If Charlemagne believed that a peace signed with Godfrið's nephew Hemming, briefly emerging from a pack of likely regal contenders, would set Frankish–Danish affairs at rest, he was mistaken: Hemming was killed in 812. A bitter war of succession between Godfrið's sons and nephews broke out, lasting more than fifteen years. Charlemagne's sole remaining legitimate son,* Louis 'the Pious', succeeding his father in 814, pursued a policy sponsoring exiled pretenders to the Danish throne, part of a giant plate-spinning exercise by which he maintained ambivalent sets of relations with Spanish caliphs, popes, Byzantine emperors, Slavs, Persians and Anglo-Saxon kings, not to mention disaffected members of his own dynasty. These dynastic exiles mixed with a Carolingian court overflowing with would-be Frankish kings seeking political and material support—refugees from successful and unsuccessful coups d'état; it hosted clerics seeking sponsorship for missions to convert heathens of various persuasions, scholars like Alcuin, traders, poets, musicians, engineers and metalsmiths, all part of an increasingly complex web of patronage, ambition,

---

* Charles the Younger died after suffering a stroke in 811.

competition and vested interest. The closer one got to the beating heart of the royal court, the higher the potential rewards, the more deadly the consequences of failure or ill-fortune.

The destabilization of neighbouring states, a favourite political tool employed by Early Medieval kings, was an equally high-risk strategy. As the history of Western intervention in the Middle East shows, support for incumbent or prospective leaders by military and economic means might win friends, gain valuable influence and open economic doors, but it has a horrid tendency to unleash unforeseen forces: to backfire. The Carolingian policy of intervention in Danish affairs came to haunt the North Sea states for two centuries.

Denmark, lying outside the Latinate Christian world, had no literate chroniclers of its own. Its history, transmitted orally through the generations, flickers in and out of focus as it interacts with Francia, Britain and the lands to the east. There are stories of missionaries building churches in the trading ports of the Baltic but if, sometimes, they lived to tell the tale, they did not effect conversion where it mattered: Denmark would not have a Christian king until the middle of the tenth century. We know the names of some of its kings, the distribution of its settlements, something of its agriculture and buildings. Pagan memorials to the dead can still be seen in the countryside and two trading settlements, Ribe on the west Jutland coast and Hedeby on the River Schlei, have yielded some of the secrets of its early trading success. Some of the vessels sailed by its traders, fishermen and pirates have been recovered from its shallow coastal waters and rivers. The fact that Denmark's armies could challenge the might of Charlemagne and its fleets terrorize all Europe speaks volumes for Danish cultural wealth and sophistication, not to mention military clout.

If ninth-century Denmark is opaque, Sweden and Norway are even more obscure. We cannot know what social or environmental factors created the circumstances in which Norwegian pirate captains set out to explore the northern seas in the late eighth century with such devastating consequences for the religious communities of coast and island. Their dynastic histories in this period, when they interacted only distantly with the worlds chronicled by Latin clerics, are utterly dark. Even so, the Danish experience, and the annals, offer some clues.

Historians agree that the Scandinavian world had not yet evolved the sort of institutions that would survive the death of its kings. In the Christian states of north-west Europe the church (its archbishops, bishops, abbots and abbesses, priests, monks, nuns and clerics) enjoyed the support and protection of kings, whose gifts of land, held by ecclesiastical communities in perpetuity and often free from obligations of military service and food renders, ensured their stability and continuity. Monastic estates were able to invest the sweat-equity of labour: they built churches, mills, and the agricultural infrastructure that fostered technical innovation. They encouraged the arts and sciences and the writing of history—above all, the production of books, the accumulation of libraries of ancient works, and inquiring scholarship of the sort exemplified by Bede and Alcuin.

In return for royal patronage, the church offered living kings and their favoured successors legitimacy and the promise that their short stay on earth would, if they were virtuous, lead to everlasting tenure at God's side in the kingdom of heaven. With its strong sense of continuity, its skills in recording land transfers, laws and rights and its unifying message and language, the church acted as a self-interested civil service, maintaining the institutions of state whoever held the reins of temporal power.

The pre-Christian kingdoms of Scandinavia lacked those institutions and their useful by-products. They offered no alternative

careers for collateral family members—alternative, that is, to
fighting in the king's war band and competing for regional power.
On the kings' part, side-tracking their family rivals' secular ambitions by offering them the fruits of large ecclesiastical landholdings without royal interference—in effect, paying them off—was
not an available option.

By the turn of the ninth century a network of élite clientèle,
with all its benefits for stabilizing kingship, was deeply embedded
in the Christian kingdoms. In the pre-Christian, geographically
disparate lands of Scandinavia, the state *was* the king; with his
death it collapsed. Networks of affiliation, loyalty, gift exchange
and obligation, built up during his reign, were reset to zero. Each
new king had to re-invent his kingdom. Only customary laws,
passed down through the generations, provided rules for tribal
conduct; and the force of arms might at any time prevail. Long-
lasting, stable dynasties that succeeded in controlling succession,
without excessive internecine warfare, were rare. In that competitive climate, opportunities abounded for young, unmarried
Scandinavian men of noble or royal stock to gain glory, cash and
a reputation by fighting for an ambitious warlord. But the acquisition of land on which to settle and of a wife with whom to raise
a family was another, altogether more difficult matter. A life spent
in exile was common.

In crude terms, the dawn of the Viking Age around the year
800 can be portrayed as the extended consequence of such unsta-
ble networks coming into conflict with Christianized states whose
stability had, ironically, become a fatal liability. Monasteries, trading settlements, royal estates even, were rarely enclosed by defensive walls, palisades or ramparts: they look, in retrospect, terribly
exposed, even if they are eloquent testimony to the king's peace
and the written rule of law.

That is not to say that Scandinavian societies were in any way
primitive, or any more thuggish than their neighbours and rivals.

The Christian chroniclers, self-appointed inheritors of Roman values of universal authority, invested much ink and vellum in de-humanizing their heathen attackers, casting them as amoral, mindless barbarians. But the Scandinavian worldview was multi-dimensional. Like ancient Greeks and Romans, Scandinavians were pantheists: their gods were sometimes playful and indulgent, often vengeful, occasionally cunning and always capricious, interfering with the world of humans, Midgard,* as with play-things in a child's toy set.

Oðin the one-eyed, whom the Anglo-Saxons remembered as Woden, was the senior figure of the pantheon: often cited as the progenitor of royal lines, he had received the wisdom of the knowledge of runes by hanging himself, starving, from the world ash tree, Yggdrasil, for nine days. He rode the eight-legged Sleipnir, a flying horse, across the sky. He was a shape-shifting poet whose destiny was to receive into his hall, Valhalla, half of the warriors who died well in battle so that at the end of time, in the last great battle of Ragnarök, he might lead them to their doom. Sacrifice, wisdom, apocalypse, revenge, terrible divine power and magic lie at the heart of the Scandinavian worldview. That those same elements are also fundamental to Christianity, whose repertoire of Old and New Testament heroes was drawn from a blend of ancient Jewish royal histories and Near Eastern mysticism, is one of history's richer ironies.

It is quite possible that by the time the stories of the Scandinavian gods and their relations with mortals were written down in the twelfth and thirteenth centuries, something of Christ's story had been grafted onto those of Oðin, Thor, Loki, Freja and the rest. Scandinavians found themselves attracted to much of what Christian priests told them of their faith and its disciplines. They were impressed by the military might and

---

* *Miðgarðr* in Old Norse: Middle Earth.

organizational capabilities of the inheritors of Rome and above all, perhaps, by their skilful use of writing. Scandinavia had its literary élite too; but runes were very much an inscriptional, messaging alphabet, found on memorial stones and carved into wood, or as graffiti. Norse laws and literature, which seem to have been plentiful, were transmitted orally.

What the Scandinavian peoples found hard to comprehend was not so much that Christians should only have one God but that they should insist that believers worship no other (they had heard much the same from the Islamic world). Even so, the fatal gap between the Scandinavian psyche and that of the Romano-Christian world was not so much an incompatibility of moral philosophy as one of institution, technology and geography.

The three ship-loads of Norwegians who encountered an unsuspecting king's reeve on the south coast of Wessex in about 789 may not have been the first of their kind, even if their assault stands as the earliest recorded Viking attack on Britain, enshrined in an entry in the *Anglo-Saxon Chronicle*. A Mercian charter of 792, issued by King Offa, confirmed existing exceptions to certain church privileges in Kent (then a Mercian possession) in their obligation to provide levies against 'marauding heathens', so the idea of piratical northerners may not have been totally novel.[7] The annals that recorded their predations were partisan, their spheres of interest limited, so we must allow for unrecorded attacks of which only scant traces survive: the community of a monastery at Lyminge, a few miles inland of the south Kent coast, was granted refuge at Canterbury in the face of a real or perceived threat of raids; a Northumbrian envoy, returning home from pleading for the support of Charlemagne for the exiled King Eardwulf, was captured by pirates.

The first wave of recorded attacks has, nevertheless, a

geographical shape to it: Lindisfarne, the island monastery off the Northumbrian coast, plundered in 793; Bede's church at Jarrow, a day's sail south of Lindisfarne, a year later. Then silence until 800, when Hartness and Tynemouth, also on the Northumbrian coast, seem to have been targets. These North Sea raids might plausibly be ascribed to Danish ships, crossing the southern North Sea from their homelands, exploring, probing.

The scale of the raiding is difficult to assess: there is no doubting the ability of the Danes to send large fleets to sea, and there may have been a political dimension: Northumbria and Wessex were allies of Charlemagne; the Danes his antagonists. Danish traders must already have known the geography of Britain's east and south coasts: they conducted business at markets in East Anglia, Yorkshire, Kent and Wessex as well as at *Lundenwic* on the Thames. What we cannot say is whether the first raiders, targeting the easy pickings of coastal minsters, used intelligence gained from traders or whether they had been traders themselves. Perhaps our desire to distinguish between the two would have baffled them.

There is another, northern and western dimension to the opening of the Viking Age; and it may have begun some time before the attacks on Wessex and Northumbria. Most scholars agree that the *Annals of Ulster*, a key Irish chronicle, records attacks by pirates of Norwegian origin: the year 795, for example, saw 'the burning of *Rechru* by the heathens, and the shrine was overwhelmed and laid waste'.[8] *Rechru* is either Rathlin Island, off the northern coast of Antrim or, more likely, Lambay near Dublin. In 798 Inish Patrick, off the Dublin coast, was raided and cattle taken. In 802 one of Irish Christianity's greatest monasteries, Colm Cille's foundation on Iona, was burned. Four years later it, or one of its dependencies, was attacked again; this time sixty-eight members of the community were martyred.

Behind the clipped language of the annals lie human stories, narratives of tragedy. A remarkable drawing on slate has, in the last few years, surfaced from excavations at the island monastery of Inchmarnock, just off the west coast of Bute.[9] Dubbed the 'hostage stone', it appears to depict a ship powered by a sail and oars, and a warrior with wild hair, dressed in chainmail, leading a prisoner who seems to be carrying a box, possibly a reliquary. It reminds one, hauntingly, of the sorts of images children create when faced with the trauma of warfare.

Historians have tried to extrapolate a coherent narrative from these events. Some have seen them as part of a more substantial series of campaigns than the sources allow, as evidence of raiding armies capable of supporting themselves and overwintering on foreign soil. There have been several suggestions that Shetland and Orkney had already been partially settled by Scandinavians by the time that the Viking raids made their grand historical stage call. Orkney, after all, lies no more than three days' sailing west of Norway. Others have read the contemporary sources at face value: these were opportunistic exploratory raids by independent captains seeking cash and glory for themselves and their dependents but limited in numbers, time and space. Whatever the truth, after 806 the Irish Annals refer only fitfully to fresh attacks from across the seas until the 820s, when notices of Viking activity,

3.
THE ART OF TRAUMA:
Viking raiders appear
to abduct a monk, in
a drawing on slate from
Inchmarnock island in
the Sound of Bute.

notably in Ulster, increase dramatically. In this decade Ireland bore the brunt of pirate aggression.

Those first twenty years of raids affected Insular societies only at a very local level. The disproportionate attention they have received from chroniclers, and from historians since, has magnified their impact. There is little evidence that monasteries were destroyed as functioning settlements in that first wave of raids. Lindisfarne, Iona and others still supported monastic communities in the ninth century and beyond. It is true that there had been a general decline in standards since the seventh-century 'golden age' of monasticism, whose intellectual and artistic glories lay in the past even in Bede's day. Scholarship had given way to acquisition; strict rules had lapsed; a more secular world had encroached on the holy sanctuaries. Whether that decline began before, or as a result of, Viking raids is not nearly so certain.

There is some evidence, too, that monastic communities were not quite as unprotected as the more lurid tales suggest. At Jarrow, if historians are correct in believing that it was the monastery 'at the mouth of the River Don' recorded in the 'E' version of the *Anglo-Saxon Chronicle*, the raiders did not even get away scot-free. Their chieftain was killed (by whom—militant monks or local militia?) and a great storm sank several of their ships.[10] On the other hand there is no record at all of the fortunes of Jarrow, or its twin foundation at Wearmouth, in the ninth century; and it is true that two of Jarrow's major buildings, when excavated, proved to have been burned down and not rebuilt. But silence does not mean non-existence, and a building may burn by accident. The jury is still out.

Alcuin, the Northumbrian scholar who spent much of his career at the court of Charlemagne, wrote a letter of support to the bishop of Lindisfarne in the wake of the raid of 793, lamenting the day when 'pagans desecrated the sanctuaries of God, and poured out the blood of saints around the altar, laid waste the house of our hope, trampled on the bodies of saints in the temple of God, like shit in the street.[11] Alcuin's perspective was that of the prophet Isaiah, of God punishing the sins of the Jews. In Alcuin's view these deadly visitations were punishment for sins already committed. Archaeology has not yet been able to confirm the state of the monastery on Lindisfarne immediately after the raid;* but the community was able, in later decades when the threat was even greater and more persistent, to take with them more or less complete the incorrupt body of their holy saint Cuthbert along with the precious head of King Oswald and some of the relics of the founding bishop, Aidan. And Cuthbert's community maintained a written record of both their possessions and their relations with kings, Vikings and the wider church. That record, the *Historia de Sancto Cuthberto*, has proved to be of the highest value in illuminating the effects of two centuries of upheaval on the British monasteries.

The community on Iona, which suffered multiple raids, began a process of removing some of its treasures and monks to a new, apparently safer, location at Kells in what is now Co. Meath, from 807; but Iona still functioned, albeit in a reduced state. Its archaeology has been ill served by a succession of small-scale excavations, none of which has succeeded in piecing together that crucial period in its history. Much later destruction of its heritage was conducted in the name of the Protestant 'reformers' of the sixteenth and seventeenth centuries; even so, the abbey's excellent museum contains sculpture and other artefacts of the highest quality.

In only one case has the Viking history of an Insular monastery been comprehensively explored by excavation. The long, thin, hammerhead-shaped Tarbat peninsula, jutting out into the North Sea north of Inverness has, for much of its history, been easier to reach by sea than by land. It is a natural stopping-off

---

* As I write, much-anticipated fresh excavations have begun on the island, close to the later medieval priory ruins.

point on the east coast route to Orkney and Shetland: sheltered, with fine access inland and close to a great centre of Early Medieval power, the Pictish kingdom of Fortriu. Even today it is a four-hour drive north from Edinburgh, across or around the rocky massif of the Grampians, beyond the Great Glen and out along the northern edge of the ethereally lovely Moray Firth.

On its north-western edge, where the Tarbat peninsula forms the jutting lower mandible of the Dornoch Firth, lies a sheltered harbour called Portmahomack; as the Tarbat* name suggests, an overland portage route once connected it to the Cromarty Firth. On the south-east side of the peninsula there is direct access, via the Moray Firth, to the Great Glen and thence, with a portage between Loch Ness and Loch Oich and another into Loch Lochy, to Loch Linnhe and the western seaways: to Iona and beyond. Tarbat is on the same latitude as the southern tip of Norway, 250 miles (400 km) to the east.

Like other such liminal landscapes, the peninsula has an air of otherworldliness; but its apparent remoteness today is illusory: in the Early Christian period it was a busy place, and it lay in fertile lands. Beautifully carved cross slabs stand (or stood) at Nigg, at Shandwick and at Hilton of Cadboll, testifying to a concentration of early churches with wealthy, not to say regal, patrons. The site of a probable early bishopric lies just along the coast of the firth at Rosemarkie, and visible directly across Moray is the great royal Pictish fortress of Burghead, while the hillfort of King Bruide, ally of Colm Cille in the late sixth century, may be that which guards the entrance to the Great Glen at Craig Phadraig.

Tarbat is mostly low lying, its skyline punctured today only by the grain silos and venerable beech trees that speak of landed

---

* There are twelve Tarbat, Tarbet or Tarbert names across Scotland and two in Ireland. Each one locates a narrow strip of land, an isthmus, separating two nearby stretches of open water. Several can be demonstrated to have been the sites of historical portages.

wealth, of stability and order. But it has the same edgy sensibility as Whithorn in Wigtownshire, or Iona and Lindisfarne: close to power, remote from the secular world; half belonging to the sea. At Portmahomack a modest whitewashed chapel stands on a small rise set back from the shore and protected from the worst of the North Sea's tempers. Over the years, fragments of sculpture have been recovered from, or spotted in, the churchyard and surrounding fields. Its harbour and its ancient connectedness made this tiny village a key location on north-east Scotland's otherwise largely inaccessible coast.

Bede says that the Picts were converted by the missionary work of Colm Cille in the late sixth century. Others have suggested that St Ninian, a more dubious historical character, was responsible. Behind these two apparently contradictory traditions may lie the identities of not one but two Pictish kingdoms: Fortriu, the lands around the Moray Firth, and Atholl, south of the Grampians and centred on Strathearn and the headwaters of the River Tay.[12] Before Martin Carver's* excavations at Portmahomack, between 1995 and 2002, arguments over the origins of Pictish monasticism were, in any case, largely academic: no Pictish monastery site had been identified, let alone investigated. Only the marvellous carved stones bearing hybrid Christian and Pictish symbols that grace the Scottish landscape (and fill its museums) stood to map the geography of its early church. But an aerial photograph taken by archaeologist Barri Jones offered the first key evidence to back up the sculpture on the Tarbat peninsula: the crop mark of a telltale D-shaped enclosure ditch surrounding Portmahomack's church.†

Excavation of the interior of the redundant church and in the fields to the south and west, over several years, hit the

---

* Emeritus Professor of Archaeology at York University; he is also widely known for his campaign of excavation at Sutton Hoo.

† Circular or D-shaped enclosures are diagnostic of Early Medieval monastic sites—or of temporary Viking forts.

archaeological jackpot. Developing from a small cemetery with sculpted stonework in the sixth century, more or less contemporary with Colm Cille on Iona, a monastery flourished here in the seventh and eighth centuries. The presence of vellum and glass-making workshops, an elaborately conceived smith's hall and the exalted standards of the sculpture being produced on the peninsula, elevate Portmahomack to the first rank of ecclesiastical communities alongside Jarrow, Lindisfarne and Iona. Careful management of the local water supply allowed its monks to construct a mill for grinding corn. A metalled road serving the industrial complex must have added the final touch of sophistication. The production of vellum, a complicated series of chemical and mechanical processes requiring considerable expertise, implies the presence of a scriptorium: books were being written and produced here; there must have been a library.

Bede, had he visited, would have recognized its layout and culture, the sounds of chant, forge and lowing calves, the smells of byre, steeping tank and wax candle; the timeless magic of the eucharist and the daily hubbub and gossip of the guest house. The workshops, and the church, flourished for a century and more. It is tempting, in the historical and political context of the site, to associate Portmahomack's heyday with Nechtan mac Dargarto, the king who, in consultation with Bede, brought the Pictish church into line with Roman orthodoxy around the year 712.[13]

In uncovering this unique evidence for a thriving, wealthy Pictish monastery, the excavation team, based at the University of York, had first to remove deposits dating to later periods, constructing as they did so a narrative in reverse. The church itself, still in use well into the twentieth century, testified to Christian continuity on the site. Evidence from later phases of the monastic landscape showed that in the ninth and tenth centuries production of metalwork and crops also continued: it survived the Viking Age. But in between these phases and those of its monastic

4. THE CHURCH AT PORTMAHOMACK
on the Tarbat peninsula, Easter Ross: now a museum,
once the site of a great Pictish monastery.

pomp in the eighth century there was stark evidence of an abrupt, not to say catastrophic, event. A great carved cross slab had been smashed and burned, its charred fragments scattered over the site; layers of lurid purple, orange, pink and red soils told a story of absolute destruction by fire some time between 780 and 820, dated by C14 analysis from the abundant burnt material.*

At least one member of the community, buried in the church, had died from a sword wound to the head. It seems reasonable to conclude that seaborne raiders perpetrated the arson: the trashing of the sculpture seems particularly pointed, even vindictive. These decades are historically obscure, but it looks as though the raid on Portmahomack is only the most visible evidence of a

---

* C14, a radioactive isotope of carbon absorbed by all living things, decays at a more or less consistent rate. Charred wood, in particular, can be roughly dated by measuring the amount left in its cells after burning.

concerted campaign against Fortriu which culminated in a great raid recorded in 839: 'The heathens won a battle against the men of Fortriu and Eóganán son of Aengus… and others almost innumerable fell there.'[14] From this disaster the legendary Cináed mac Ailpín emerged.

Archaeology and history combine to paint a picture of wanton, if periodic, harassment of the most easily accessible coastal and estuarine monasteries. Even so, those communities seem largely to have survived and their sufferings, psychological and material, at first had little effect on the wider economies of the Insular kingdoms of the early ninth century, let alone on the functioning of the state. Kings on both sides of the Irish Sea and across the Channel concerned themselves with administration, with the contents of their treasuries, with noisy neighbours and troublesome nephews. Hostilities broke out periodically between Mercians, West Saxons, Welsh and East Angles; competing dynasties of Northumbrian kings deposed one another in dizzying succession. Kings in Dál Riata, Strathclyde, Fortriu and Atholl fought for primacy in North Britain and the Isles, and with the kings of North Irish kindreds for overlordship of the western seaways. The kingdoms of Wales—Gwynedd, Powys, Ceredigion, Dyfed, Glywysing, Gwent and Brycheiniog—sought to assert tributary rights over each other and defend themselves from Mercian aggression.

Bishops and abbots sought to consolidate and extend their lands, to defend their rights and privileges. Ealdormen sought preferment in the royal household; their retainers hoped for honour in the king's war band and the reward of gifts and land on which to raise families. Farmers hoped for good harvests and feared ominous portents like fiery dragons in the sky and the appearance of comets. Occasionally they suffered hunger and pestilence. There is a surprising amount of evidence in the annals for diseases in livestock, whose impacts were probably felt much more widely and over a longer period than periodic predations from across the sea.

Beneath the surface, underlying the bald record of events, swirling undercurrents can be detected. Lowland Britain's most powerful kings in the eighth century had been drawn from Mercia's stable royal dynasties. From 716, for eighty years, just three kings ruled here—and one of those for a single year.* The last of the three laid claim to overlordship of all the Anglo-Saxon kingdoms and much of Wales. King Offa's most visible monument to the strength of that regime is his dyke, built to demarcate Mercia from the Welsh kingdoms and as a testosterone cenotaph to his powers of coercion. In a reign of almost forty years he established Mercia's supremacy over Wessex, Kent and the other southern kingdoms of Britain. He controlled the valuable trading settlement at *Lundenwic* on the Thames, key to southern England's economic hinterland. He was able to appoint archbishops at Canterbury and to raise the see of Lichfield to archiepiscopal status, minting high-value silver coinage and reforming land rights. He interacted with the Frankish court, issued charters as *Rex Anglorum*, King of the English, and constructed the first fortified settlements or burhs, anticipating Ælfred by a century.

A rapprochement with Charlemagne in 796, cancelling a Frankish trade embargo and sealing a deal on safe passage for merchants and pilgrims (but not, pointedly, for Mercian traders masquerading as pilgrims), came too late for Offa. His death that year sent ripples across Britain's political pond. His son, Ecgfrith, succeeded him but died almost immediately. According to Alcuin, Ecgfrith had 'not died for his own sins; but the vengeance for the blood shed by the father has reached the son'.[15]

---

* Æðelbald (716–757); Beornred (757) and Offa (757–796).

Offa's rule, ambitious and impressive, had been that of military overlord as much as statesman. During the uncertainty of the interregnum the Kentish nobility took the opportunity to throw off Mercian rule and raised one Eadberht Praen to the throne at Canterbury. Æðelheard, a Mercian appointee to the archbishopric there, thought it wise to flee. Offa left no other sons; his throne now passed to Coenwulf, only very distantly related but seemingly enjoying the support of senior Mercian ealdormen. Coenwulf moved quickly and violently to suppress the rebellion in Kent. In 798 he seized Eadberht Praen, had him blinded and his hands cut off. He appointed his own brother, Cuðred, as a client king in Kent and restored Æðelheard to his see in Canterbury.

In the same year *Lundenwic*, the East Saxon trading centre on the banks of the Thames at Aldwych, suffered a serious fire.[16] Mercian kings had long enjoyed the fruits of its commercial success; had this been the last vengeful act of Eadberht Praen, an accident or a Scandinavian raid? Mercian power was, in any event, restored over Kent, Canterbury and the Channel ports. Normal service appeared to have resumed.

Coenwulf's chance to reinforce Mercian supremacy over his West Saxon neighbours to the south came in 802 with the passing of their king, Beorhtric. According to the *Anglo-Saxon Chronicle*, on the day of his death the Men of Hwicce (an ancient kingdom, much reduced in status, consisting broadly of Worcestershire, Gloucestershire and eastern parts of Warwickshire, and long subject to Mercian rule) crossed the Thames, the frontier river, and invaded Wiltshire. But the opportunity evaporated: the Mercian force was defeated, the leaders of both armies slain. In retrospect it was seen as a turning point in the fortunes of the two kingdoms. The new king of the West Saxons, Ecgberht was the grandfather of Ælfred.

Under King Coenwulf, Mercian control of Canterbury was maintained, at least nominally. But tensions between church and state, between Mercia and Kent, were a continuing source of conflict. Since St Augustine's mission of 597 the primate of the Anglo-Saxon kingdoms had maintained his see at Canterbury, and Kentish kings had enjoyed the political advantages of that primacy. In 735 Northumbria, then the most powerful of the English kingdoms, was granted the dignity of its own archbishop, with his throne at York close to the church built by Bishop Paulinus in the seventh century among the ruins of the Roman city. London, former capital of Roman Britain, had never had an archbishop. In 786 King Offa persuaded the pope that the senior Anglo-Saxon kingdom must be served by its own archbishop, more inclined to pursue its king's policies and preferable as a recipient of royal Mercian land grants. Lichfield became Britain's third archdiocesan see. The appointment of one of Offa's men, Æðelheard, to Canterbury in 792, inflamed Kentish sentiment against its overlord. Kent wanted a Kentish archbishop, and no competition from Lichfield.

Archbishop Æðelheard, restored to his see after the Kentish rebellion of 798, travelled to Rome in 801 and, perhaps surprisingly, put the Kentish case to the pope. On the way, we know, he stayed with Alcuin close to the trading settlement at *Quentovic* on the estuary of the River Canche, near modern Étaples.[17] He was lucky to avoid the earthquake that struck the papal basilica of St Peter's that year. He made his case to the pope, the restored Leo III, and returned to Kent in 802 or 803 with instructions that the Lichfield archdiocese be reduced to its former status. The primacy of Canterbury was restored, although with what damage to relations between the archbishop and King Coenwulf it is hard to say. Æðelheard's loyalties to Offa had, perhaps, been personal, even familial; he had become a Canterbury man.

Æðelheard's successor, Wulfred (805–832), suffered even more strained relations with the Mercian king. He set about consolidating the considerable landed assets of Christ Church, the cathedral minster at Canterbury, and began to mint his own coinage. In 814 he, like his predecessor, travelled to Rome, probably along the ancient pilgrimage route called the *Via Francigena* through Francia and Lombardy, punctuated by Christian hostels and monastic communities well used to taking in pilgrims, including kings. It was the year in which Charlemagne died and was succeeded by Louis the Pious. The two following years were tumultuous: Pope Leo was the subject of a second coup, died a year later and was followed in quick succession by Popes Stephen IV—during whose brief reign the English Quarter in Rome, the *Schola Saxonum*, burned down—and Paschal I.

Wulfred, returning from Rome, found that Coenwulf had performed what amounted to a coup against Canterbury. He had called a synod at Chelsea, on the banks of the Thames upstream from *Lundenwic*. The synod placed severe limits on Wulfred's powers; ruled that 25 December should henceforth be the day on which Christ's Mass should be celebrated; enacted episcopal, effectively secular control over the abbots and abbesses of the minster;* and sanctioned the sale or gift of monastic lands to secular lords.[18] Wulfred was sent into exile or deprived of his office for some time between 817 and 825, when a synod at the unidentified site of *Clofesho*† resolved the dispute in Canterbury's favour. By then Coenwulf was dead and his brother and successor, Ceolwulf (821–823), had been deposed in a coup by a rival dynasty. The new Mercian king, Beornwulf, attempted to follow the practice of his forebears by placing a member of his kin, Baldred, on the Kentish throne; he also set out to make peace with Canterbury.

Beornwulf (823–825) is unlikely to have been related to his two predecessors: he came from a line of the Mercian nobility

---

* Since the earliest days of the Insular church the independence of monastic houses had been challenged by the assertion of papal authority through its bishops.

† The most favoured location for this lost site is the magnificent seventh-century basilica at Brixworth in Northamptonshire.

with a penchant for giving their sons names beginning with 'B'. The heartland of their territory seems to have lain in the central Midlands, perhaps near Breedon on the Hill in Leicestershire, where a great minster stood. Its church, perched high above the surrounding countryside (and now uncomfortably close to the edge of a stone quarry), occupied the interior of an Iron Age fortress. A collection of fragments of high-quality sculpture can still be seen there, testament to its Early Medieval importance.

One of the new king's most pressing political tasks was to deal with the festering issue of Coenwulf's daughter, Cwenðryð.* The ancestral lands of the 'C' dynasty family lay around Winchcombe†

5.
A FABULOUS
BEAST
of the Viking
and Christian
imagination:
cross shaft
fragment from
Breedon
on the Hill.

---

* *Quoenðryð* in contemporary charters.
† Winchcombe, once the centre of an important and wealthy shire of the same name, is now a small town in north Gloucestershire.

in the former kingdom of the Hwicce, where Cwenðryð was abbess of a wealthy minster. Since the late seventh century kings had exploited their extensive landholdings to endow the church with estates which they placed under the control of collateral members of their family, ensuring that the land, although alienated to the church in perpetuity, could still be passed as a family asset down through successive generations. Very substantial holdings, free from many of the burdens of renders and service owed by dependent farmers and warrior nobles, had been accumulated over a century and a half. Minsters, those churches with origins as monasteries endowed with substantial estates, were big players in agriculture, trade, technology and both secular and religious politics. They commanded wealth and the powers of patronage that went with it.

Cwenðryð's possession of Winchcombe, a community founded on her family's estates, was not at issue; her control, as abbess, of two other monastic communities, at Minster-in-Thanet and at Reculver (both ancient and lucrative foundations),* was a cause of considerable resentment in Kent. These may have come into her possession in the aftermath of the unsuccessful Kentish rebellion under Eadberht Praen in 796, perhaps over a period of several years. The historian of the Anglo-Saxon church, John Blair, likens such acquisitions to 'a speculator assembling a portfolio'.[19] The breadth and value of Cwenðryð's portfolio is indicated by Thanet's possession of three trading ships, which plied the waters between the abbey and markets in Frisia, Francia and *Lundenwic*, where it benefited from the remission of port tolls.[20]

Cwenðryð's entrepreneurial spirit is cast in a much more

---

* Thanet, now part of Kent, was still an island, separated from the mainland by the Wantsum channel and the River Stour, through which ships passed between the English Channel at Richborough castle, and Reculver. Both were former Roman forts now occupied by monastic settlements, sited in key locations to exploit maritime traffic and onward trade to Kent's hinterland.

sinister light by a tradition which held that she had done away with her infant brother, Cynehelm, Coenwulf's only legitimate heir, when he was seven years old. The crime, according to William of Malmesbury—writing in the twelfth century when the story was still circulating—was revealed miraculously (a dove carried a message to the pope, who spilled the beans) and the dead boy was elevated to the status of a martyr. His shrine at Winchcombe became a popular site for pilgrimages, and his fame assured him a bit-part in the Canterbury Tales.*

A series of charters recorded between 821 and 827 show that although Cwenðryð was able to keep her lucrative abbacies, she was successively relieved of other possessions in Kent and Middlesex, part of a diplomatic initiative by King Beornwulf to pacify Archbishop Wulfred and, perhaps, to weaken the power of his own rivals.[21] Reading between the lines, it looks as though the see-saw of political initiative had tilted in favour of an independent Canterbury.

The rapid succession of four kings following the death of Coenwulf in 821 is an indication of instability in the ninth-century Mercian state.† A second indication is the speed at which King Ecgberht of the West Saxons, twenty years into his reign, was able to shake off Mercian superiority and assert his independence during the following decade. The reverse in fortunes appears sudden and dramatic. An entry in most surviving versions of the *Anglo-Saxon Chronicle* for 825 is eloquent in its laconic account:

> *þy ilcan geare gefeaht Ecgbryht cyning 7‡ Beornwulf cyning on Ellendune 7 Ecgbryht sige nam 7 þær wæs micel wæl geslægen...*

> King Ecgberht and King Beornwulf fought at Ellendun and Ecgberht was victorious and great slaughter was made there...

---

* In the *Nun's Priest's Tale*.

† Ceolwulf 821–823; Beornwulf 823–825; Ludeca 825–827; Wiglaf 827–829 and 830–839.

‡ The '7' symbol was used in manuscripts to denote 'and'.

then he sent his son, Æðelwulf, from his levies [*fyrð*]... to
Kent with a great force and they drove King Baldred north
over Thames, and the Kentishmen submitted to him, and the
men of Surrey and Sussex and Essex... And the same year the
king of the East Angles and the court turned to Ecgberht as
their protector and guardian... and the same year the East
Angles slew Beornwulf, king of the Mercians.[22]

The location of the battle at *Ellendun*, unidentified but seemingly in Wiltshire south of Swindon, suggests that Beornwulf was
the aggressor, possibly with the aim of reinforcing his own, thin
domestic credentials. Mercia's inability to maintain a stable leadership continued. An ealdorman, Ludeca, succeeded Beornwulf.
In 827 he too was slain alongside five of his ealdormen, leaders
of the shire levies. We do not know if this was West Saxon or
East Anglian aggression, or civil war, but the loss of so many
high-ranking leaders in the space of six years is the plain-speak-
ing testimony of an unfolding dynastic catastrophe. Ludeca's successor, Wiglaf, from a line whose power base seems to have lain
around Repton in modern Derbyshire (the so-called 'W' dynasty
of Mercian kings) came to the throne with his kingdom on the
ropes. In 829 he was driven out by King Ecgberht. In triumph,
the king of Wessex issued a series of silver coins from London,
with REX ECGBERHT on the obverse surrounding a cross; and
LUNDONIA CIVIT[AS] on the reverse: to the victor the economic spoils.[23] In the same year Ecgberht was able to lead his levies to Dore in what is now South Yorkshire (very likely then the
boundary between the kingdoms of Mercia and Northumbria)
and receive the submission of the North. By 830 he was claiming overlordship over parts of Wales. Offa's Mercian empire lay
shrunken and outflanked.

The compilers of the *Anglo-Saxon Chronicle*, reflecting on
these events during a peaceful interlude in King Ælfred's reign in
the early 890s, noted under the year 829 that Ecgberht was the

eighth king to enjoy the status of *Bretwalda*—that is, to wield *imperium* over all the other kingdoms of the Anglo-Saxons. It is an overtly propagandist declaration: the first seven entries on the list were taken directly from Bede, writing in 731.[24] Conveniently missing out the powerful eighth-century Mercian overlords Æðelbald and Offa, this is a self-conscious West Saxon attempt to legitimize the primacy of Ælfred's line, to draw on the golden age of the seventh century and prefigure its inevitable success in saving the Anglo-Saxon kingdoms from Viking invasion.

Historians have a way of smoothing out unsightly wrinkles. A year after what was, ostensibly, the decisive moment in the rise of Wessex, Wiglaf had been restored and was striking his own coins at London. Mercia survived, albeit with the loss of its authority over East Anglia, Kent, Sussex and Surrey.

CENTRAL PLACES

LUNDENWIC—A VIKING TRAVEL MAP—
BRITAIN'S VULNERABILITY—RAIDS INTENSIFY—
THE FRANKISH EXPERIENCE—TRADE AND
PRODUCTION—MINSTERS AND THEIR ESTATES—
VIKING SHIPS AND SEAFARING

2

A MERCHANT ARRIVING AT THE TRADING port of *Lundenwic* around 830 would sail or row upstream on the flood tide, coasting past the crumbling stone walls of the ancient Roman city where St Paul's church (*Paulesbyri* to contemporaries) and perhaps a royal residence stood—but not much else. The abutments of the Roman bridge might still have been visible, but the only crossing was by ferry. Just upstream of the mouth of the River Fleet the Thames takes a sharp southward bend towards what was once Thorney Island, for over a thousand years the site of Westminster Abbey and before that, perhaps, a Saxon minster. Between the two, along what is now the Strand, between Aldwych and Charing Cross, lay the busy wharves of Middle Saxon *Lundenwic*.

Founded by King Wulfhere of Mercia in the late 600s and described in 731 by Bede as 'an emporium for many nations who come to it by land and sea', it was not, perhaps, the great port it had once been.[1] In those days, with a population in the

6. LINDHOLM HØJE: the memorial fleet of a seagoing culture, overlooking Denmark's Limfjord.

low thousands,* it was substantially the largest settlement in the British Isles, one of only four contemporary settlements that we might recognize as something like a town with planned streets, close-set houses divided by narrow passages, warehouses, smithies, workshops, wells and all: noisy with the clang of smith's hammers and the calls of longshoremen; reeking of tanners' steeping vats and domestic waste. Its overall functioning was the responsibility of the king's *portgerefa*, the port-reeve, whose erstwhile colleague had committed such a fatal *faux pas* on the coast of Dorset in the 780s. Through his reeve, the king charged tolls on arriving cargoes and administered the sometimes complex justice and trading rights of the many interested parties who made money there: regional noblemen, bishops, the abbots and abbesses of the great minsters; Frisian, Frankish, Danish and possibly Arab merchants, not to mention its indigenous or itinerant craftsmen and those farmers who supplied the settlement with meat and other provisions.

In its eighth-century heyday *Lundenwic*, geographically part of the kingdom of the East Saxons, passed from Mercian to Kentish to West Saxon hands and back again: its value as a source of revenue and prestige and its prime location facing the Continental ports of Francia, Frisia and Denmark were constant sources of tension and opportunity. By the reign of King Offa (757–796) *Lundenwic* had already achieved its greatest wealth and extent.

The river frontage lay some 80–100 yards (73–90 m) inland from its present position; the Thames was a wider, slower river then and the Roman road running west from the city along the line of what is now Fleet Street and the Strand was set back from the river by less than 100 paces.† The main settlement lay to the

---

* Cowie and Blackmore (2012) estimate some 6,000 inhabitants. I must say I am sceptical of a figure this high; but population of any Early Medieval settlement is notoriously difficult to estimate.

† The Strand was probably at that time called *Akemennestraete*—literally, the road to

north-west of this road, densest in the area of Covent Garden and with its north-west limit somewhere in the region of today's fashionable Neal's Yard. To the south-east of the road a natural terrace led down from the Strand to the foreshore, part of it revetted with piers and wharves where deep-draughted cargo vessels might tie up, and another part no more than a beach (the strand) where shallow-draughted boats might be pulled up above the tide and where temporary markets, very much a feature of these centuries, would have been held periodically.[2] A church may have stood close to *Lundenwic's* south-west edge on the site later occupied by St-Martin-in-the-Fields, on the corner of what is now Trafalgar Square. The port's north-east corner seems to have coincided with the east side of King's College and the Temple.

The shorefront deposits of *Lundenwic* lie buried some 16 feet (5 m) beneath the modern ground surface of the Victoria Embankment, a pleasant public park whence one might, these days, catch a pleasure boat, but whose commercial wharves are long gone. Across the river, on the Surrey side, a landscape of fen and water meadow was punctuated by natural gravel islands on which isolated settlements like the minster of Bermondsey benefited from access to the arterial Thames and its Roman road links to the north, east and west.

The recovery of *Lundenwic's* past from brief passing mentions in contemporary sources,* but primarily from excavation, has been challenging and protracted. Until the 1980s scholars could not agree where Middle Saxon London stood. Archaeological investigations had concentrated on large commercial developments

---

Bath, the Roman Spa town of *Aquae Sulis*, later Aquamannia (Watts 2004). The road runs in a giant curve north-west from London towards Bicester before turning south-west.

* A very useful list of those sources mentioning not just *Lundenwic*, but also the other major trading settlements of Atlantic Europe, can be found in Hill and Cowie 2001.

within the walls of the old Roman city from where, apart from the very evident presence of a church on the site of St Paul's cathedral from its founding in 604, the seventh and eighth centuries were effectively missing. The contemporary interior of the city seems to have been largely uninhabitable marsh between natural prominences at Ludgate Hill and Cornhill along the River Walbrook.

In 1984 two archaeologists, Martin Biddle and Alan Vince, independently suggested that the Saxon town lay to the west, where place names like Aldwych (literally 'Old wic', a farm or trading site) were suggestive of a pre-Conquest presence and whence occasional fragments of Middle Saxon pottery had been retrieved over the years. Piecemeal interventions, sometimes nothing more than watching briefs undertaken as the bulldozers moved in, gradually assembled a case confirmed by the discovery in 1985 of sixth- and seventh-century burials and rubbish pits on the site of Jubilee Hall in Covent Garden.[3] Now, these fragments combine to paint a lively picture of a thriving settlement, fleshing out the notices of travellers like the missionary priest Boniface in the early eighth century, Bede's testimony, mentions in charters and coins minted here over the two centuries before Ælfred's refounding of the city in the 880s.*

Lundenwic may have owed its origins to the convenient beach, its proximity to a minster church and its location near the old Roman city. But at some point in the late seventh century it was formally reorganized, its thoroughfares relaid on a grid pattern with house and warehouse plots of equal size sharing an axial orientation at right angles to the river. The same phenomenon can be seen in Godfrið's foundation at Hedeby in Denmark, at

---

* Boniface was a West Country son of a wealthy family, educated at a monastery near Winchester. He left England in 716 to join Willibrord, the so-called apostle of the Frisians. He was famous for having felled an oak tree sacred to the indigenous pagans. He became archbishop of the newly founded German church and was killed by bandits in 764 on a last mission in Frisia (Talbot 1954).

Dorestad on the Rhine, at *Hamwic* close to Southampton and elsewhere, including Norse Dublin.

Like other trading ports *Lundenwic* lay undefended by palisade or garrison. Aside from a stream that bounded its southwest edge, *Lundenwic* lay grotesquely exposed, its weak domestic defences wholly inadequate against determined assault from the river. But its apparent decline after the end of the eighth century was not initially catastrophic, despite a series of fires from whose ashes it rose again. More likely, a range of economic factors was in play, not all of them obvious from the archaeological or historical record. West Saxon kings who managed to win control over *Lundenwic* may have promoted their own *mercimonium*,[4] or trading port, at *Hamwic* at the mouth of the River Itchen on Southampton Water, to its detriment. Subtle shifts in trading networks, in production and profit margins, may have undermined its commercial power. Charlemagne's short-lived economic blockade in the 790s cannot have helped.[5] In Francia, a civil war between Louis the Pious and his sons from the late 820s seems to have disrupted the flow of royal patronage on which the great trading ports on the Continent relied for their continued success. The European silver supply was affected by events further afield, in the Abbasid caliphate. Other, even less tangible, elements can be dimly traced in the rise of rival centres of trade and production: the minsters.

A series of major seaborne raids that began in the 830s and lasted for twenty years and more sealed the fate of the great trading sites of north-west Europe. Dorestad, *Quentovic*, *Lundenwic*, *Eoforwic* (York), *Hamwic* and others never recovered from the attentions of those Scandinavian entrepreneurs for whom the ports became the destinations *de choix* to go a-Viking. Attacks on the Thames-side settlements in 842 and 851 finished *Lundenwic*, and the former Roman capital lay more or less deserted until the early 870s.[6]

Twenty-first-century citizen and visitor alike know London's geography largely through the topological masterwork affectionately called the Tube map. People stare at it on giant posters long after they have found their destination. Thousands carry a miniature version in their pockets or bags. The Tube map is an abstraction of a vastly complex reality, in which travellers have only to orient themselves with the nearest access point that connects them to their destination: an underground railway station. No commuter much cares how deep the lines run, how they twist and turn to avoid natural streams, sewers and foundations, or how the system is maintained. Those stations, or nodes, are linked by linear routes of unvarying sequence: from *Lundenwic*'s heart, at Covent Garden, one takes a northbound train on the Piccadilly line one stop to Holborn, changes to the eastbound Central line and two stops later arrives at St Paul's, in *Londinium*.

Like a Roman itinerary, on which places of interest were marked along theoretically straight roads, the Tube map invites its users to visualize, or at least recognize, a simple set of linear sequences, one for each colour-coded branch of the network. The stylized thick blue ribbon of the River Thames is the only concession to geographical reality. Thus, the District line, which runs 30 or so miles (48 km) from Richmond in the west to Upminster in the east, serves sixty such nodes, which schoolchildren and commuters alike learn by heart: Kew Gardens, Gunnersbury, Turnham Green, Stamford Brook, Ravenscourt Park, and so on, in unvarying succession from west to east. Trains may be late, or cancelled; but Baron's Court will always come before Hammersmith. Where lines intersect, commuters transfer from one branch to another: from District line to Piccadilly, Victoria or Northern line, and so forth. Branches run far out from the centre into what purports to be bucolic countryside. The map serves a population of more than 10 million people and an area of more than 600 square miles or 384,000 acres. By contrast, *Lundenwic* covered 150 acres, less than half a square mile.

In attempting to make sense of the geography of the Viking Age, to envision how Scandinavian raiders and traders mastered a world of coast and open sea, of river and hinterland, it is worth imagining that world as a network like the Tube map (see p. 50). Consider, to begin with, Britain's complex, island- and estuary-ridden coast as a long, thin conceptual rectangular route whose inshore waters constitute something like a maritime Circle line: on the ground it traces a path very unlike a circle, but like its underground counterpart the coast acts as a continuous loop on which bored passengers might fall asleep and still conveniently arrive at their intended destination—eventually. Imagine that theoretical rectangle, the outline of British inshore waters, as a line on which vessels encounter a sequence of possible destinations and intersections: harbours, churches, river estuaries, royal fortresses. Imagine, also, the route of the River Thames (a theoretical dead-straight line running right to left, east to west) intersecting with that line at a point between Shoeburyness and Sheppey. This is a maritime/riverine interchange.

Following the Thames due west, the Early Medieval sailor would pass, like a litany of commuting stations, settlements on Sheppey itself, on Canvey Island, at Tilbury and Barking, before reaching *Lundenwic*. Travellers with business at settlements upriver (a royal residence at Kingston; minsters at Chertsey, Dorchester and beyond) need only follow its course until, after perhaps a week's passage, they reached Cricklade, deep inside what is now Wiltshire on the edge of the Cotswolds. Here, not much more than 20 miles (32 km) from the Severn estuary, they might disembark and continue to the centre of the salt trade at Droitwich along the existing Roman road network, or to Gloucester in the ancient kingdom of Hwicce. The Severn links

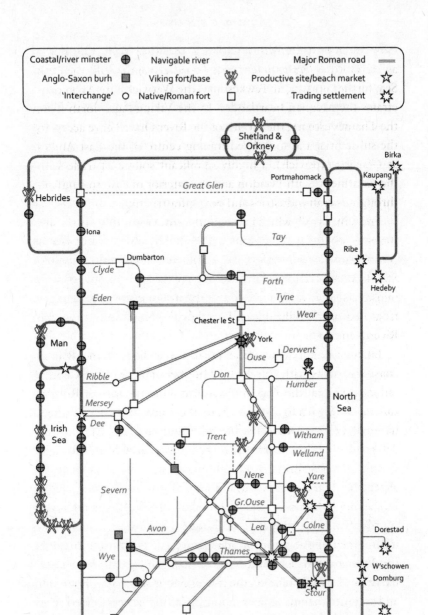

Legend

Symbol	Meaning	Symbol	Meaning	Symbol	Meaning
Coastal/river minster ⊕		Navigable river —		Major Roman road ═	
Anglo-Saxon burh ■		Viking fort/base ⚔		Productive site/beach market ★	
'Interchange' ○		Native/Roman fort ☐		Trading settlement ✶	

Shetland & Orkney

Birka
Kaupang
Portmahomack
Hebrides
Great Glen
Iona
Tay
Ribe
Dumbarton
Clyde
Forth
Hedeby
Eden
Tyne
Man
Wear
Chester le St
York
Ribble
Derwent
Ouse
Mersey
Don
Humber
Dee
North Sea
Irish Sea
Trent
Witham
Welland
Severn
Nene
Yare
Avon
Gr.Ouse
Lea
Colne
Dorestad
Wye
Thames
W'schowen
Domburg
Stour
Scillies
Exe
Itchen
Rother
Quentovic
Rouen

Viking Age travel map: British Isles c. 800–872

Gloucester with the Bristol Channel, the River Wye as far north as Hereford (*Here-path ford*: army-road crossing), and the Irish Sea; further upriver, at Tewkesbury, the Warwickshire Avon penetrates the Mercian heartlands.[7] In the Viking Age, north from the Thames estuary, the mouth of the River Orwell gave access to the substantial and long-lived trading centre of the East Angles at *Gipeswic* (Ipswich), a highly significant source of trade with the Continent, with London and the interior of eastern England through its craft industries and port infrastructure.

From the Wash, which in the ninth century was more extensive than it is today, the River Great Ouse offered a direct line of inland communication, via various tributaries and linked waterways, to Stamford, to Thetford in the kingdom of the East Angles, to great minsters at Ely and Peterborough (*Medehamstede*) and inland as far as Bedford, Cambridge and perhaps also Northampton on the River Nene.

Further north, where the great Circle line of the British coast intersects with the broad Humber estuary, vessels could sail inland along the Yorkshire Ouse as far as the former Roman *colonia* at *Eoforwic* (York) where the third of Britain's international trading ports lay in the kingdom of Northumbria. Alternatively, a sharp left turn a few miles west of the Roman ferry crossing at Brough on Humber would bring a ship south along the Trent, past a trading and production settlement at Flixborough, as far as Lincoln (via the old Roman canal known as Fossdyke), Nottingham, Derby and almost to Lichfield— itself joined to the salt-producing centre at Droitwich through the Roman road network. That network linked almost all the navigable heads of the major rivers: one giant communication and trading system. Roman administrators had conceived it as such, but also as a highway for their armies. Half a millennium later, it was to be co-opted by another race of entrepreneurial invaders.

Britain's' navigable rivers belong largely to the south, but on the west coast the Dee was navigable inland from the Irish Sea to a point beyond Chester; the Mersey as far upstream as Warrington; the Clyde perhaps as far inland as Lanark. In the east, the River Tees gave access at least as far inland as Worsall weir near Yarm; the Wear was accessible by boat as far as Chester le Street. The River Tyne gave access to monasteries at Jarrow, Monkchester, Gateshead and as far west at least as Newburn—a possible major royal residence close to Hadrian's Wall and the trans-Pennine Stanegate road between Corbridge and Carlisle. Corbridge was a significant crossroads, linking the east–west road and river route with the great north–south Dere Street, connecting *Dun Edin* (Edinburgh) and *Eoforwic*.*

In Scotland, the Tay could be navigated at least as far up stream as the royal palace at Scone, heartland of the kingdom of Atholl, while the opposed inlets of the Forth and Clyde allowed deep penetration from the North Sea and Irish Sea. The Great Glen connected east and west further north. At other points along this circular route, monasteries, royal fortresses and sheltered harbours were the pearls in a necklace of seats of learning, of spiritual (and material) enrichment: repositories of the relics of powerful saints, centres of power and craft, safe havens, markets for goods and news or, depending on one's point of view, deposits of easy cash.

Britain, thanks to its rivers, long-distance native tracks like the Icknield Way, and its Roman legacy of hard, direct, metalled roads maintained by trade and the kings' armies, was extraordinarily penetrable. The ease with which goods and people were able to move across its fertile landscapes between settlements, rivers and production centres rendered it accessible to any pirate captain capable of remembering simple sequences of directions. It is no coincidence that important churches, royal residences,

* See map on p. 322.

sites of councils and synods, battlefields, production sites and records of destructive Viking raids are all concentrated on these lines of communication: they are the key to Britain's success, and to envisioning the impact of the Viking Age on the kingdoms of Britain. Over the course of half a century of raiding and reconnaissance Scandinavian seafarers equipped themselves with a detailed mental atlas of the British Isles, a conceptual Tube map that allowed them to access, at speed, almost every significant place in Early Medieval Britain.

7.
PREHISTORIC
LEGACY
of a connected
landscape: the
ancient Berkshire
Ridgeway.

The maritime raiders from the North showed themselves equally adept at political intelligence, exploiting opportunities presented by civil war, dynastic weakness and the preoccupations of neighbouring states. The conflict that broke out between Louis the Pious and his sons in the 830s, and which must have severely compromised the Frankish state's coastal defences, provoked a rapid response from Norse opportunists. In 834 raiders laid waste the extensive trading settlement at Dorestad, sited on an old course of the River Rhine south-east of Utrecht in Frisia. A year later the first large-scale raid on an Anglo-Saxon kingdom was recorded, at Sheppey in the mouth of the Thames estuary. In 836 King Ecgberht of Wessex fought twenty-five pirate ships off Carhampton on the north coast of Somerset and was defeated, while the monks of the monastery of Noirmoutier at the mouth of the Loire, first attacked in 799, abandoned their island, taking the relics of St Philibert to safety at Tournus in Burgundy. A year later, in 837, the *Annals of St Bertin* noted a great Viking raid on the trading settlement of Domburg on Walcheren Island at the mouth of the River Scheldt. The picture, if incomplete, is clear: in the political vacuum created by Frankish civil war, Viking pirates roamed at will along the southern part of the North Sea and the English Channel. No contemporary force was able to defend the approaches to the coastal trading settlements.

In 839 King Ecgberht, ageing and tired after thirty-seven years on the throne of Wessex and having produced a viable, grown-up son to succeed him, wrote to Louis the Pious, tenuously restored to power and concentrating on bolstering his coastal defences. Might he, Ecgberht, pass through Louis's kingdom on pilgrimage to Rome—in what was, effectively, an abdication?* In the same

---

* Ecgberht had been exiled in Francia in his youth by Offa and by his predecessor Beorhtric (*ASC* 839). He may well have known Louis personally.

letter Ecgberht related a vision that had achieved widespread notoriety in England. It had been revealed to a priest that, in a certain church, boys (to be interpreted as the souls of grieving saints) could be seen writing down in blood all the sins that the English had committed. The priest was warned that if God's sinners did not repent their sins and attend to the Christian feast days:

> A great and crushing disaster will swiftly come upon them: for three days and nights a very dense fog will spread over their land, and then all of a sudden pagan men will lay waste with fire and sword most of the people and land of the Christians along with all they possess.[8]

As if to confirm God's wrath a terrible flood killed more than 2,000 people across Frisia; Ecgberht was also dead within the year, having failed to achieve his ambition of reaching Rome but having rescued the ailing fortunes of his kingdom. In the same year Fortriu, the kingdom of the Northern Picts, suffered a devastating Viking raid in which its ruling dynasty was wiped out. Louis the Pious died, too, a year later, his empire split and factionalized.[9] Overwhelming disaster must indeed have seemed imminent.

The raids continued, becoming more intense. Ireland's suffering at the hands of Norwegian pirates, almost continuous for the first two decades of the ninth century, was exacerbated by Norse raiders establishing long-term bases, the *longphuirt*, at convenient coastal locations. By 841 the principal of these had been built on the south bank of the River Liffey at a place called *Baile Átha Cliath*, the 'place at the ford of the hurdles' close to the black pool, *Dubh Lind*, which gives Ireland's capital its modern English name. Dublin's Viking past has been sensationally revealed by a series of excavations that show a sophisticated, well-organized trading town developing over the course of the ninth century.[10] Other *longphuirt* were established at Wexford, Waterford, Limerick and Cork: Ireland's celebrated medieval towns owe their origins to piracy.

The *Anglo-Saxon Chronicle* relates that in 842 there was slaughter at three trading settlements: *Lundenwic*, *Hamwic* and *Norðunnwig* (probably Norwich). It was as if an immense raiding orgy had been planned and executed in the sure knowledge that Atlantic Europe, suffering an acute vacuum of effective military power, was theirs for the taking. Ecgberht's successor as West Saxon king, his son Æðelwulf, fought against a large Scandinavian fleet off Carhampton and, like his father before him, was defeated. For the next five years the *Anglo-Saxon Chronicle* is blank.

Viking attentions returned, during these years, to Francia. The three sons of Louis the Pious disputed the succession in a series of campaigns that lasted from 840 to 843. A bloody battle was fought at Fontenoy on the River Yonne, an eastern tributary of the Seine, in 841. Raiders took the opportunity to burn the port at Rouen. The following year Nantes and *Quentovic* were attacked; raiders overwintered on the monastic island of Noirmoutier at the mouth of the Loire. Embassies passed to and fro between the rival Frankish dynasts. In 843 peace was signed at Verdun, giving West Francia to Charles *Calvus* 'the Bald', East Francia to Louis 'the German' and Middle Francia, including the Rhineland, Frisia and Lombardy, to Lothair.

It is hard to tell how much institutional damage was sustained by the Frankish states in these years: the best evidence comes from the behaviour of the raiders themselves. In 845 the first substantial raid on the Île de la Cité in Paris on the Seine, deep inside northern Francia's heartland, showed how dangerously exposed the soft underbelly of Charlemagne's former empire had become. Paris was no mere riverside trading village; it had been a Roman city, *Lutetia*, with a grand basilica, St Etienne, two splendid bridges and an iconic island location: the former capital of Clovis, first king of a united Francia, from 508. Its port controlled trade along the Seine and its tributary the Marne. If Viking raiders, wasting and pillaging as they sailed and rowed upstream, could penetrate so far into Frankish territory, the arteries of the empire lay open.

The razing of the trading ports was a commercial nuisance; the attacks on monasteries had been local, highly personal, psychological disasters whose effects on the greater institutions of the church were, initially, low key. Buildings were trashed; lives lost; labour taken into slavery; material wealth stolen. But landed property and rights had not yet been appropriated by the executive arm of the heathen Northern menace; refugees were not on the move in large numbers, so far as we can tell. The attack on Paris showed, for the first time, that Scandinavian raiders might threaten to tear the essential fabric of the Christian state.

Charlemagne's, now Lothair's, capital lay to the north, at Aachen (in French, Aix-la-Chapelle), between the Rivers Meuse and Rhine. During the year in which Paris was attacked his new kingdom was assaulted by a huge fleet, said to comprise 600 ships, sent from Denmark by King Horik along the Elbe. Lothair managed to defeat them and, in the following year, was able to sign a peace agreement with Horik. The interests of Charles the Bald, focused primarily on Aquitaine and the South, were divided by necessity: a war with Brittany, asserting its independence; rebellions on the Spanish border and a bold Viking raid along the Garonne as far inland as Toulouse.[11] Paris lay at the edge of his radar. His pragmatic response was to pay the raiders off with a treasure of 7,000 livres of silver,* the first of thirteen such 'Danegelds' extracted from Frankish kings.

Historians debate the merits of ransoms paid to raiders, of the dangers of setting such precedents, with the benefit of hindsight. But Charles was inventing a Viking policy on the hoof; the kings of Atlantic Europe would watch and learn from his mistakes and successes over the next three decades and, often, adopt similar

---

* A rough equivalent, perhaps, to the *wergild* or head-price of a hundred ealdormen.

expedient solutions. Those same raiders, sailing down the Seine with their ships full of bullion, had sufficient space and nerve to fill their boots on their way home, laying waste the coastal communities of the Channel; they might well have asked themselves how often they could repeat such profitable exercises.

The Frankish and Anglo-Saxon kingdoms survived Viking assaults on their trading ports because the essential wealth of north-west Europe lay in its agricultural and industrial surplus and internal trade, not in its economic relations with the rest of the Continent. Merchants had succeeded in evolving emporia from beach markets, often located on the boundaries between kingdoms, and had done very nicely out of them. Kings, too, had seen the potential for raising cash at such sites, through tolls on imports and by recycling and minting silver, hiving off a percentage. Sometimes they allowed powerful clergymen and women to trade free of tolls and to mint their own coinage in such places. The richer minsters, and bishops, possessed their own warehouses at some of these sites. Nevertheless, the economies of Atlantic Europe succeeded because they produced sufficient cattle and grain to support kings, armies and minsters, and such regionally distinct and specialized surpluses as salt, lead, cloth, pottery, furs, antler, glass and iron to largely satisfy domestic consumption.

Since the end of the Roman imperial state, which had operated under a command economy, emergent kingdoms had succeeded by a combination of cash-raising through warfare and the imposition of customary renders: goods and services owed by units of land to lords higher up the chain of rank, from *ceorls* to thegns to ealdormen to kings. Those renders were collected at vills and on royal estates, where they were consumed by peripatetic lords and kings on an unending cycle through whose mechanisms they also dispensed justice and distributed wealth and favours, ensuring a smooth bilateral flow of patronage and reciprocal obligation. The alienation of estate lands from the king's portfolio to the church, a gradual process beginning in the first half of the seventh century, affected this system significantly, and increasingly. Minsters, those churches established and maintained by communities of monks, nuns and their unfree tenants, were static institutions whose legacy was a form of sustained capital. They were able to invest in agriculture and manufacture because the fruits of their labours were inherited directly by the community, in an unmoving location with fixed estate boundaries. When we hear about St Cuthbert acquiring land and negotiating with kings long after his death, we have to envision the saint operating from beyond the grave as the symbolic embodiment of those who survived him and continued to function as his community.

Abbots and abbesses were both physical and spiritual manifestations of the community's heritage and privileges. Kings, their right to rule legitimized by the church, liked to believe themselves the inheritors of the same functions with regard to the state; but still they were obliged to travel through their lands consuming food, managing the services of their warrior élites: putting it about. The only personal wealth that they could retain was portable treasure in the form of bullion. The estates, with their arable and meadow lands, rivers, quarries and woodlands, were the kingdom's infrastructure. Public projects, so far as we can tell, were confined to the construction of dykes and bridges and occasional repairs to Roman roads.

Increasingly, from the late seventh century, minster communities were able to invest in the construction and maintenance of mills, forges and workshops for the crafting of vellum, antler, horn, metalwork, grain and cloth. They began to enclose fields and specialize production.* The larger establishments gradually

---

* Hence such commonplace Middle Saxon place names as Goswick (goose farm); Keswick (cheese farm); Berwick (barley farm), and so on.

became centres for the gathering of surplus raw materials and the conversion of that surplus into products that might be traded— for books; for craftsmen expert in masonry, sculpture and glazing; for wines, dyes and oils imported from the Continent. Their surpluses included grain, increasingly of the valuable bread wheat varieties; wool and woollen cloth; timber; ironwork; ale; books where the skills existed to create them; honey; wax for candles; and livestock bred specially for markets such as the trading ports. At what point some of the greater minsters began to look like trading settlements, even towns, is a moot question.

The evolution of minsters as central places is also, and perhaps even more significantly, traced in their secularization. Originally founded either under royal patronage or by ascetics and charismatic holy persons, minsters were aristocratic institutions, often ruled by collateral members of royal kindreds and increasingly divorced from the spiritual fervour which had led to their foundation between about 635 and 700. By the second quarter of the eighth century Bede was already complaining that royal estates were being given over, with their highly valuable freehold, to persons unsuited to the strict rule of monastic life. He was, in effect, accusing lay aristocrats of taking monastic vows simply in order to avoid the burdens of military service and food render, and so as to be able to bequeath land to their heirs.[12]

By the beginning of the ninth century, as the cases of Cwenðryð and others show, minster estates might be acquired as a means of expanding the property portfolios of the landed élite, sometimes in a calculated effort to acquire key resources such as salt, lead, iron and timber. Monastic lands and privileges began to change hands for cash on an open market in which bishops and archbishops were active. The tensions that grew up between those minsters whose communities were substantially composed of monks and nuns in holy orders, and those controlled largely by secular canons, were played out very publicly during and beyond the Viking Age. They form a parallel, equally compelling and significant narrative to the more obvious headline acts of raiding and settling.

The sorts of transactions by which such monastic estates changed hands can be traced through the increasing use of charters to 'book' those lands and by subsequent attempts to alter, forge and invent such titles or the privileges and lands that went with them. Charter donations were often recorded during ceremonies at great assemblies; sometimes, if not always, the transfer was tangibly confirmed by the placement of the enacting parchment and a sod of earth from the land in question on to the altar of the recipient church.[13] The *Historia de Sancto Cuthberto* is highly instructive in this context. It was likely compiled in the tenth century by the community of the venerable Northumbrian holy man, bishop and abbot of Lindisfarne, whose disinterment as an uncorrupted corpse in 698, eleven years after his death, assured his celebrity as the greatest saint of northern England. The *Historia* purports to record the history of that community, especially in those years after it fled Lindisfarne in the face of Viking attacks; its relations with kings; and the means by which it lost or came into possession of its estates.[14]

The original gift of land, by King Oswald in 635, consisted of two royal estates, Islandshire and Norhamshire, close to what is now the Scottish border with Northumberland; others followed under Oswald's successors.[15] Over the next two centuries further estates were acquired, and we are afforded a unique glimpse of the mechanisms by which the early minster portfolios were accumulated. During St Cuthbert's lifetime Lindisfarne received a royal grant of lands at Crayke, near York, so that the holy man might have somewhere to stay when travelling to that city, and at Carlisle, in the formerly independent British kingdom of Rheged—both, it seems, as part of a deal in which Cuthbert would leave contemplative retirement on Inner Farne to take on the politically critical and onerous bishopric of Northumbria at a time of key church reforms.

The same king, Ecgfrith, later gave the community lands at Cartmel and Gilling, after Cuthbert raised a boy from the dead.* In 679 Cuthbert was granted an estate at Carham on the banks of the River Tweed because his prayers for the king's victory against Mercia in a battle on the River Trent had been successful. King Ceolwulf of Northumbria, the dedicatee of Bede's *Ecclesiastical History*, abdicated in 737 and, retiring to Lindisfarne, brought with him the gift of a substantial royal estate at Warkworth on the Northumbrian coast;[16] and so it went on. Later kings, notably Osberht,† 'stole' some of these estates and recycled them to the royal portfolio although, almost needless to say, he was divinely punished for the offence.‡ Behind these donations lie political realities: a king's need for ecclesiastical and divine support; the hope of sins expiated and of assured entry into the everlasting joys of heaven; the need to liquidate assets in a time of crisis.

No Early Medieval minster site can be reconstructed in its entirety: almost all of them lie beneath later churches and towns and we are only ever afforded glimpses of their layout and workings. Our model minster is a compilation of hard-won fragments: a church, perhaps two churches; monks' cells, a guest house; an enclosing *vallum* or ditched enclosure. Mills, a key marker of stability and technical innovation, have been excavated at Tamworth, Wareham, Barking and Ebbsfleet in England (all associated with minster complexes) and, most extensively, close by the island monastery of Nendrum at the head of Strangford Lough in Northern Ireland.[17] Many others, such as that identified by the excavators of Portmahomack, must have stood among the several hundred minsters in existence in the eighth and ninth

* Cartmel, on the South Cumbrian coast; Gilling in Yorkshire.
† Died 867; possibly reigning from 849.
‡ See below, pp. 101–2; he was killed in battle against the heathens.

centuries. At the same Pictish site vellum was produced at an industrial complex which required expertise to construct, manage and maintain it. The smiths' hall at Portmahomack also shows how much infrastructure was required for the iron-working industry; and a seventh-century charter survives which records the gift of an iron mine in the Kentish Weald to the abbey of St Augustine in Canterbury.[18] Rights to deposits of lead ore and to stone quarries which fed monastic sculpture workshops were similarly granted to and traded by ecclesiastical communities. The larger establishments, such as the twin monasteries of Jarrow and Wearmouth in Northumbria, boasted nearly 600 *fratres*, or brothers (effectively their supply of cheap manual labour) in the early eighth century.[19] Their minster complexes, with lofty stone buildings, stained glass windows and the craftsmen to maintain them, were the most sophisticated institutions of their day.

If the smaller minsters, whose existence can often only be inferred, relied mostly on their food renders for survival, the greater establishments were able, with their large labour forces and extensive estates, to operate as sustained economic enterprises. Some minsters seem to have evolved relationships with outlying farms that either supplied their provisions while the minster intensified production of particular livestock, grain or manufactured goods, or supplied specialist materials to them. Archaeologist Duncan Wright calls them 'home farms'.[20] Often these seem to have been situated upstream from minsters on rivers so that their produce might be floated conveniently downstream. Lands were not acquired randomly, but to supply key resources or to fill niches in a minster's portfolio, like woodland for coppice or marsh for reeds and waterfowl.

The minster of St Peter at *Medehamstede*, later known as Peterborough, is unusually well documented. Although its surviving founding charter is a later forgery, analysis shows that its core lands were formed out of a small defunct Anglian fenland kingdom, North Gyrwe, in the seventh century.[21] These lands were rich in riverine resources, enjoying access through inland rivers to the Wash and to unknown numbers of island communities, amounting to around 600 hides—that is, the render expected from the estate was worth that of 600 family farms. The minster of St Peter was no minor foundation. Its original estate was donated by King Wulfhere of Mercia from about 674, later enhanced by generous lands across the East Midlands, whose inclusion in its portfolio must have reflected the need for the minster to be supported by more than just the grazing, fishing and fowling of the fens.

An entry in the *Anglo-Saxon Chronicle* for the year 852 records the leasing by the abbot of *Medehamstede* of an estate at Sempringham, some 30 miles (48 km) away in Lincolnshire, providing that the estate still rendered annually to the minster sixty waggon-loads of wood, twelve of brushwood, six of faggots and sundry other items. Sempringham, it seems, rendered to the minster its requirement for timber and firewood—nearly 80 tons of it a year. Such were the functionings of the monastic economy. Minsters at Brixworth in Northamptonshire, Yarnton in Oxfordshire and Ely in the Cambridgeshire fens were focal points for densely clustering settlements, interacting with them economically and, we might suggest, socially.[22] King Wulfhere's apparent role in the foundation of both *Medehamstede* and the trading port of *Lundenwic* is suggestive of increased royal interest in trade and exchange; and that interest seems also to have driven a dramatic increase in the administration and quantity of coinage at the same period.

If this sounds as though a small industrial revolution were taking place in parts of Britain, the historian and archaeologist must exercise caution: this is not a full-blown medieval manorial system but a series of local and regional responses to opportunity. Even so, minsters produced and traded goods because they had become centres of consumption, not as a coherent strategy to stimulate the economies of their kingdoms. Their unique advantages, in privileges and international connections to a Europe-wide web of Latinate, educated, capital-intensive centres of social and economic excellence, loaded trade in their favour, and they exploited it to the full.

However, although there is a broad consensus that minsters evolved during the eighth century as central places with a range of social, economic and spiritual functions (including burial) the picture has to be pieced together from disparate sources. Such evidence as exists shows a dramatic rise in trade after about 725. The phenomenon is easiest to detect in East Anglia, where the first post-Roman industrial manufacture of wheel-finished, kiln-fired pottery at the trading port and production site of *Gipeswic* (Ipswich) seems to have been stimulated by an influx of Flemish potters from the Continent in the 720s. Fragments of Ipswich ware turn up in excavations across the region, with small quantities reaching as far south as London and Kent, inland along the Thames corridor, through Lincolnshire and as far north as York.[23] A single sherd has been recovered from excavations at *Hamwic* on the south coast.

The distinguished ceramicist Paul Blinkhorn believes that the pottery, often retrieved from sites with ecclesiastical associations, reflects a rapid expansion of internal trading networks across the kingdom of East Anglia, just as finds from the trading ports of the east and south coasts echo international production and exchange in high-value luxury goods.[24] Evidence from excavated rural settlements, both secular and ecclesiastical, seems to show that this expansion in trade coincided roughly with physical structural alterations: re-alignments of buildings; construction of rectangular enclosures—suggestive of intensive, specialized farming. In East Anglia the new type of pottery, showing a limited range of forms, is found almost exclusive of any other local wares: it became a badge, almost, of regional identity.

Widespread gifting of royal estates to the church over 200 years across the kingdoms of Britain and Ireland fostered dynamic, productive economies which those of Scandinavia could not match. In Norway, Denmark and Sweden opportunities for the forms of patronage and exploitation evolving in partnership with the church and a compliant, not to say enthusiastic, warrior élite, were extremely limited: fertile land was scarce and confined to narrow coastal plains. Shifting alliances and groupings of warrior kindreds, often armed to the teeth and with vengeance in their hearts, were not easy even for the most formidable kings to control.

The agricultural, industrial and political expertise of the Insular peoples, in part indigenous and in part learned from the Romanized Frankish empire, was largely absent from the loose-held kingdoms of Scandinavia. They did not enjoy the legacy of an Imperial road system or the protection of its ruined forts. Their seafaring, mercantile and boat-building skills were, however, highly advanced. With those skills Scandinavian raiders were able both to relieve the western Christian kingdoms of some of their material wealth and to observe at close quarters the sophistication of their economies. They admired much of what they saw. The price which Bede had foreseen the Anglo-Saxon kingdoms paying, in their enthusiastic patronage of the church, was that, economic miracles and statehood notwithstanding, they surrendered something of the military prowess with which they had amalgamated the small kingdoms of the post-Roman tribal reshuffle.

The Insular psyche saw its world in terms of produce, labour, patronage, lordship and regional bragging rights, tied to the soil. The poor, unlanded, unfree cottar travelled to the *ceorl*'s farmstead with his or her waggon-load of wood, eggs or wool; the *ceorl* to his lord's vill to render his services to a thegn; thegn travelled to ealdorman or to abbot and might occasionally fight with the men of his shire against their neighbours. Ealdormen travelled through the lands of their shires dispensing justice in disputes over boundaries, livestock, theft, murder and the return of escaped slaves. They led their levies into battle against their, or the king's, enemies and, like the bishops, attended royal assemblies. Kings concerned themselves with exacting tribute and toll; with planning and plotting their succession; with their wills and with treasure chests full of scrap metal and precious objects; with the activities and ambitions of rivals at home and abroad; with the distribution of gifts and favours; with the movements and provisioning of their warriors and the probity or otherwise of their moneyers.

It is hard to exaggerate the psychological unpreparedness of the Insular states against a fast-moving, water-based, entrepreneurial enemy with nothing to lose but their skins, playing by a new set of rules and uncaring of retribution, their wives and children safe at home waiting for son, brother, husband to return home from what amounted to a hunting expedition, with bounty to supplement their meagre living from fishing, farming and domestic crafts.

Scandinavia was uniquely blessed with a tradition of excellence in shipbuilding, with ample supplies of slow-grown, straight-grained wood, supreme skills in carpentry and a seaward-facing culture. Long experience, experimentation and competition for naval supremacy led, by the middle of the ninth century, to something like perfection in the construction of a wide variety of vessels capable of deep-sea sailing, coastal trading, raiding, and the penetration of navigable rivers. Ships were more than merely transportation: in Scandinavian culture they carried a symbolic role greater even than that of Britain's eighteenth-century 'wooden walls': they were named, famed, celebrated in song and verse as sea steeds riding the whale road.

On the north bank of Limfjord in northern Jutland, close to an important ancient crossing point, lies the Viking period cemetery of Lindholm Høje.* Hundreds of graves, the cremated remains of villagers and traders, are marked by placements of stones in the unmistakeable shapes of boats. The gently sloping hillside looks like nothing so much as a grassy harbour crowded with jostling stone ships, a flotilla of memorials tying Danish culture to the sea and to boats. Ship burials are known from Orkney, the Hebrides, the Isle of Man, mainland Scotland and England, most famously the monumental burial of King Rædwald at Sutton Hoo over-looking the River Deben in Suffolk—the legacy of Scandinavian contact before and during the Viking Age. In Scandinavia they occur, as at Sutton Hoo, in association with royal cult sites. At Lindholm Høje a more subtle rendering of maritime sensibility is displayed; no ships were buried here, but the cemetery's inhabit-ants saw themselves as peoples of the sea, cremated on pyres, like Beowulf, before being, as it were, launched on to the breeze-ruf-fled waters of the afterlife.

The famous Norwegian ship burial at Oseberg,† excavated in 1904, was no abstraction of salty sentiment; no mere model. The length of a cricket pitch, 22 yards (20 m), the Oseberg vessel, clinker-built of oak planks, had been buried in a huge trench and, to ensure that it stayed put, it had been 'moored' to a large boul-der. This was the last resting place of two royal women, interred with their waggons, sleighs, weaving equipment, horses, dogs and treasure, as well as provisions and equipment for their last journey. Constructed in about 820, the Oseberg ship lies three quarters of the way along the evolutionary path towards the perfect Viking

---

* A splendid museum nearby tells the story of the settlement, its graves and excava-tions. Danish archaeology has a long and distinguished tradition of excellence in excavation, publication and display.

† Oseberg lies 30 miles (48 km) or so due south of Oslo in Vestfold, Norway. The Gokstad vessel comes from a site just 10 miles (16 km) further south.

vessel, represented by another Norwegian burial: the Gokstad ship. Their clean, refined lines, their high carved prows, shallow draught and rakish low freeboard, are predatory refinement: these were fast, light war machines with no concession to comfort, designed for attack and a quick getaway. The Oseberg ship had served her time on inshore waters for more than a decade before being sacrificed to the otherworldly needs of her queenly owners.

For a deeper understanding of Scandinavian shipbuilding craft and the brilliance of its technologies, one must travel to Roskilde at the head of a long, narrow fjord on Sjælland, the largest island

8. CARSTEN HVID, skipper of the *Sea Stallion of Glendalough*, in the rope works at Roskilde ship museum, Denmark.

of the Danish archipelago.* Here you can see longships and their more modest cargo-carrying cousins being built and sailed, and talk to the craftsmen and sailors who study, construct and crew them. At some time in the eleventh century Roskilde Fjord was blocked, 15 miles (24 km) north of the city, at a place called Skuldelev, by five ships deliberately scuttled to prevent attack from the sea—Scandinavian states were as vulnerable to Viking predation as the rest of north-west Europe.

In 1962 the five vessels were excavated from inside a temporary coffer dam and their remains form the core displays of the Roskilde Ship Museum. An admirable programme of research has led, first, to the reconstruction of these vessels in order to understand their capabilities, technologies and materials and, second, to the development of expertise in the shipbuilding techniques of the Viking Age. The Skuldelev ships offer a hint of the wide range of vessel designs belonging to the regional repertoire, from the small inshore two-bench rowing boats called *færings*, to medium range cargo vessels (the *knarrs*), to larger deep-sea trading ships; from small warships of the *snekkja* type right up to the cruisers of their day, represented by Skuldelev 2, a longship 100 feet (30 m) long and 12 feet (3.8 m) wide, designed for a crew of sixty, with a mast and square sailing rig.

In 2007 Skuldelev 2, reconstructed as the *Sea Stallion of Glendalough*, was sailed and rowed to and from Dublin, at an impressive maximum speed of 15 knots. The voyage commemorated Viking links with Ireland, especially poignant because Skuldelev 2 had been built on the banks of the Liffey in the middle of the eleventh century.

Scandinavian ships had many design features in common: all were clinker-built with overlapping strakes; all were equipped

---

* Denmark consists of the northern two thirds of the Jutland peninsula and more than 400 islands. At its closest point the largest island, Sjaelland, is less than 2 miles (3 km) across the Oresund from the coast of Sweden at Helsingborg.

9. THE *SEA STALLION OF GLENDALOUGH*, a reconstruction of Skuldelev 2, which sailed from Roskilde Fjord to Dublin in 2007.

with oars, many also with a single mast that bore a square, woollen sail for use when the wind lay aft. Unlike Mediterranean and Frankish vessels, they were plank- rather than frame-built. The earliest ships were built up from a keel plank rather than a true keel, to which the first strakes, or hull planks, were attached on either side. Each successive plank was fastened in order to fashion the basic shape of the hull; internal framing, a keelson* and mast step were added to stiffen the hull later. Strakes were generally attached using clench nails (effectively large iron rivets), their joints caulked with moss, tar and wool.

Aside from the larger cargo vessels, broad in the beam and relatively deep-draughted, ships were designed to sail in shallow water, often as little as 2 feet (60 cm) deep, and so that they could be pulled up on to a sloping beach or drawn overland on skids. The lack of a true keel until, for example, the Oseberg and Gokstad

---

* A keelson was a member running from stem to stern to attach internal framing to the keel below.

ships of the ninth century, meant that at sea ships made substantial leeway: they slid sideways and downwind of their intended course. The exaggerated leeway meant, in turn, that with their square-rigged sails they could not make rapid progress to windward except by rowing. Steering was accomplished with a side-rudder so that the clean, sweeping leaf-shaped lines of the vessel, and her stiffness, should not be compromised by a stern transom.*

The experimental ships built at Roskilde and elsewhere have demonstrated without doubt their virtues of speed, manoeuvrability and seaworthiness. Their design allowed them to flex like fish in heavy seas, and the subtly perfect form of the stem, or prow, ensured that high waves were swept beneath the hull: these ships planed over waves rather than plunging into them. That the tools used in their construction were so simple (for the most part axes, adzes, chisels and augers) and that the techniques used in their construction were so refined, is the unwritten testimony of more than a thousand years of seagoing tradition, of a culture umbilically joined to the waters of the Baltic and the north-east Atlantic.

Much scholarship has been devoted to the question of Viking navigation. First-hand knowledge of inshore waters developed by generations of sailors, traders, fishermen and raiders contributed to the construction of a mental marine chart, the Viking Age 'Tube map' described earlier in this chapter. Out of sight of land, greater skill was required to navigate safely. Compasses were unknown in northern waters in the Viking Age, but knowledge of the positions of the sun, moon and stars, the behaviour of waves and cloud formations, of marine animals and birds, and 'dead-reckoning' (calculating one's position by estimating speed and direction over a long period) must all have been employed. The jury is, as yet, out on the possibility that Scandinavian deep-water skippers made use of crystals such as Icelandic spar,

* Transom: a transverse, flat stern, as if the natural leaf shape curve towards a point has been cut off.

whose properties include polarizing light, to find the direction of
the sun beneath cloud.*

The geography of north-west Europe offered its own characteristic advantages for navigators: sailing west from Norway the
north–south alignment of Shetland's islands and the position of
Orkney close to the Scottish mainland meant that landfall was difficult to miss. Those navigating the Outer Hebrides enjoyed similar fortune: one island led south-west towards the next. Britain's
intricate, complex coastlines, with their distinctive headlands,
bays and estuaries, were an unfolding chart to the experienced
sailor. Local currents, tides and landmarks must all have become
part of the conscious repertoire of the seafaring skipper and, as
Scandinavian captains and their crews explored increasingly distant waters, their confidence grew.

It is also a convenient truth that in springtime North Sea
currents allow relatively easy passage west despite the prevailing
westerlies of these latitudes; and in autumn, both currents and
winds provide a reliable passage back to home waters. By the
dawn of the ninth century no part of the British coastline was
unexplored by Scandinavian seafarers. Orkney and Shetland may
even, by 800, have undergone a first phase of Norse settlement.

A much later source, the thirteenth-century *Orkneyinga Saga*
or *History of the Earls of Orkney*, gives us an idealized picture
of the dedicated Viking life, one dominated by agriculture but
infused with the wandering spirit of the seafarer, as convincing a
portrait as any written of the archetypal eighteenth-century frig-
ate captain by a long-suffering grass widow. Of Svein Asleifarson
we hear that:

> Winter he would spend at home on Gairsay, where he enter-
> tained some eighty men at his own expense. His drinking hall

---

* Sunlight is refracted by the rare crystal in such a way that, in northern latitudes,
weak polarization of sunlight can be detected by an observer looking through it in
the direction of the sun even on a cloudy day.

was so big, there was nothing in Orkney to compare with it. In the spring he had more than enough to occupy him, with a great deal of seed to sow which he saw to carefully himself. Then, when that job was done, he would go off plundering in the Hebrides and in Ireland on what he called his 'spring trip', then back home just after midsummer, where he stayed until the cornfields had been reaped and the grain was safely in. After that he would go off raiding again, and never came back till the first month of winter was ended. This he used to call his 'autumn trip'.[25]

The Roskilde collection allows us to picture the range of ships owned and deployed by these farmer-pirates. We might envision Svein Asleifarson's vessel as a small longship like Skuldelev 5, 18 yards (16 m) long with twenty-six oars, a crew of thirty men and a maximum speed of 15 knots. Its draught, at just 2 feet (60 cm), allowed it to penetrate the shallowest waters and navigable rivers. But it is possible that he used something more modest; the sort of fishing boat represented by Skuldelev 6, carrying a crew of just fifteen or so. We must, I think, allow for a wide variety of regional and functional types, of traditional style and personal preference; and, indeed, as the Skuldelev vessels show, for conversion, upgrade and modification.

British and Irish seagoing communities had their distinctive vessels too: there may have been dozens of local and regional forms, from the simple woven lath coracle to a modest skiff rather like the two-bench *færing*, to the seven-bench assault vessel inferred from the Dál Riatan *Senchus fer nAlban*.[26] The Irish currach, in its many forms, survives as a uniquely adapted boat-building tradition, and a variety of other types is suggested by references in contemporary sources such as Adomnán's *Vita Colombae*.

Only one Insular Viking Age vessel has been recovered by excavation, to tell of an otherwise entirely lost shipbuilding tradition. The Graveney boat, recovered from a muddy channel in Kent in 1970, was a small trading vessel, not unlike a *færing* in size. When sunk, by accident or design, she was carrying hops and Rhineland quern stones, and must have been typical of boats engaged in small-scale cross-Channel trade in the ninth century. No warship from Irish, Scottish, Welsh or Anglo-Saxon fleets has yet been found intact.

King Ælfred seems to have been the first to establish something like a strategic fleet for naval defence, although the Franks evidently had substantial numbers of vessels under royal control. For the Insular kingdoms, facing inwards to their rich arable lands and pastures, ships were for trading and fishing, or for small-scale transportation of warriors. With the exception, perhaps, of Dál Riata, they had no overseas ambitions. Their ships were no match for a determined marine assault. Nevertheless, in a naval engagement recorded by the *Anglo-Saxon Chronicle* under the year 850, Ealdorman Ealhhere and the Kentish regent Æðelstan, eldest son of Æðelwulf, king of Wessex, fought against a Viking fleet at Sandwich in Kent and were able to capture nine ships. That speaks of competence, built up over the previous two generations, to deal with small- and medium-sized fleets.

If the summer raiding season and the homebound wind were such reliable aids to those skippers who took their men a-Viking, the Atlantic kingdoms must have enjoyed some respite during the months of darkness, storm and ice. At least, that is, until the winter of the year 850 when, for the first time, a Scandinavian fleet, perhaps the remnants of that defeated off Sandwich, made its decision to overwinter on the Isle of Thanet: the prelude to 100 years of invasion, conquest, response and integration.

THE INCOMING TIDE

3

WHILE ÆÐELSTAN, ÆÐELWULF'S REGENT in Kent, was considering how to deal with unwelcome winter visitors, the coastal communities of the Irish Sea and the Western Isles counted the human cost of Viking raids. Our most assiduous informants for these events are the monks whose accounts of the lives of saints, in an age when the first flush of monastic fervour had faded, came alive again with the threat of apocalypse and the promise of eternal glory. Martyrdom, the End of Days, miraculous deliverance from the evil heathen, divine punishment for sins: these themes resonate through contemporary literature, from Alcuin's letters admonishing his peers to the annals of the senior Irish monastic houses. The hagiographers, experiencing the horrors of piracy and destruction at second hand, deployed a full palette of literary and theological imagery to enrich the portraits of their holy men.

St Findan was a famous ascetic of Rheinau Abbey, founded on an island in the upper reaches of the Rhine, who died around 879 having voluntarily spent the last twenty-odd years of his life

10. MENACE ON THE HORIZON:
the annals record a litany of attacks
on coastal communities.

as a walled-in hermit under circumstances of extreme privation.[1]
His improbable life was told prosaically, and with absolute conviction, by those who had known him. He was born in Ireland,
in the province of Leinster, in a generation whose parents had
become accustomed to the predations of Scandinavian raiders
and slave-traders and were hardened to the violence of feud and
raiding among rival kindreds.

> This man's sister, among other women, became a captive of the
> foreigners who go by the name of Norðmanni, in the course
> of destructive raids which they made on many parts of the
> Irish island which is also known as Hibernia. Then the father
> instructed his son Findan to take a sum of money, ransom his
> sister and bring her back to him. Accordingly, taking with him
> some followers and an interpreter he sought eagerly to carry
> out a father's instructions and obey the urgings of a brother's
> affectionate heart. But early in the course of this mission, he
> was waylaid by the foreigners, cast into chains and, as was to
> be expected, brought straight away to their ships which were
> moored off the nearby shore.[2]

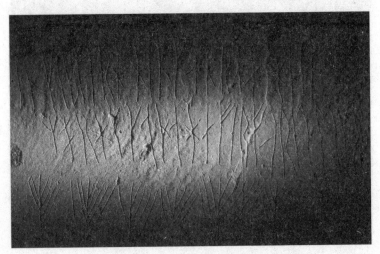

11. NORSE RUNES carved into the walls
of the Neolithic passage grave at Maes Howe,
Mainland, Orkney.

Findan was bound in chains and left without food or drink. So far his story is conventional: a tale of the indiscriminate inhumanity of terrorism. But his captors, discussing his fate, decided that it was unreasonable to enslave a man who had brought ransom. They let him go, although, we surmise, they kept his money and his sister.

For a second time, fate conspired against the Irishman. His father's clan became embroiled in the sort of blood feud that dogged the small kingdoms of Ireland just as it did the disparate tribes of Scandinavia. Its prevalence in Early Medieval society is told in the law codes that proscribe feuding (often in vain, one suspects) and define the values of all classes of men so that their families might claim blood price from the families of perpetrators, instead of perpetuating cycles of violence. In Findan's case, his father killed a warrior belonging to a rival clan. The chief of his enemies sent a war band to exact revenge, surrounding Findan's father's hall, setting fire to it and murdering him as he fled. Findan's brother was also slaughtered; Findan, enjoying the divine protection which had favoured him before, escaped.

Peace was eventually restored; compensation paid. But such feuds were not easily laid to rest. Findan's enemies now conspired to lure him to a feast from which, by prior arrangement, a band of Norse slave-traders kidnapped him. Like common merchandise he was passed from one trader to another before finding himself on board a vessel heading north in company with other raiding parties: north beyond Ireland towards the Minch and Cape Wrath: the cape of storms.

The western seaways must have bristled with ships during the ninth and tenth centuries. The Hebrides were in the process of being settled by significant numbers of Norse; traders, raiders and fishermen plied the seas during the summer months between Ireland and Norway in increasingly large fleets, raiding for slaves and church relics, fishing, sealing and whaling in the rich waters and trading with settlers in furs, antler, steatite (soapstone) and wool. The sheltered east coasts of Uist, Harris and Lewis provided harbours in which to establish *longphuirt*; the machair* of the west offered fertile, frost-free farming; perhaps also freedom from stifling overlordship.

The convoy carrying Findan and his fellow slaves now encountered another fleet of Norse. They parleyed; a fight broke out and became deadly serious. Findan, shackled, nevertheless acquitted himself with distinction in the ensuing pandemonium and was rewarded by having his shackles removed. So it came about that when the fleet reached Orkney the pirates went ashore to rest and take on fresh water and Findan was given his parole until such time as favourable winds might carry them eastwards, and home.

In an episode reminiscent of David Balfour's Hebridean adventure in Robert Louis Stevenson's Highland novel *Kidnapped*, Findan found a boulder by the shore beneath which he might hide. Between the tide-washed rock and his Norse captors, he chose exposure, hunger and the risk of drowning; after two days the pirates sailed away, having failed to discover his cave. Like David Balfour, on exploring his new world he found that he was marooned on an island—Hoy, probably—with no human habitation and with no food to sustain him. Eventually, near starving and casting his lot in with sea monsters and dolphins, he leapt into the perilous waters of Hoy Sound and was miraculously carried by the tides (the tidal races around Orkney are among the fiercest in the world) to Mainland, where he found sanctuary with a Christian bishop who happened to speak the Irish language.[†]

---

* Machair: low-lying grassy coastal plains formed by the wind-borne accumulation of sand and shells.

† Some historians have argued that there could have been no bishop in Orkney in the mid-ninth century and that, therefore, the whole story is incredible. I find the detail convincing; and that the Orkneys should have a Gaelic-speaking Christian community at this time seems to be gaining credence. See Woolf 2009 for a précis of the argument.

12. 'A FOREIGN ARMY sat in York's crumbling ruins':
the fourth-century remains of the emperor Constantine's tower.

The *Annals of Ulster* offer a more laconic but chilling account of events: a litany of destruction. Under the year 825, for example, are listed *Mag Bile* (Movilla in Co. Down), burning with its oratories; the plundering of *Inis Daimle* and *Dún Lethglaise*; a great pestilence across Ireland; and a rout inflicted by the Ulaid* on the heathen—they did not always have it their own way. The last entry for that year, written as if in bland disgust at such a comprehensive butcher's bill, recounts 'the violent death of Blamac son of Flann at the hands of the heathen in Í Coluim Cille': Iona. Walafrid Strabo, Carolingian court scholar and abbot of the island monastery of Reichenau on Lake Constance, must have felt a special affinity with his brothers far away on Iona, most celebrated of the western monasteries. A fascinating, if grisly, story of Viking predation is contained in a poem he composed about Abbot Blamac (or Blathmac), who, he wrote, had come to Iona 'wishing to endure Christ's scars, because there many a pagan horde of Danes is wont to land, armed with malignant greed'.³

Blathmac was blessed, if that is the right word, with foresight of an impending attack, sensing that 'the approaching wolves were hastening' towards the island. Many of the brethren scattered, taking footpaths to the remotest parts of Iona where they might hide; but Blathmac stayed behind, praying in Colm Cille's church. The pirates (historians generally agree that they were probably Norwegians rather than Danes) burst into the abbey buildings, slaying those who had remained to celebrate mass with their abbot.† The intruders now demanded that Blathmac surrender the shrine of Colm Cille, with its precious relics. Many of Iona's treasures must already have been plundered or taken to safety at Kells in Ireland; what remained on the island had been buried by

---

* A historic tribal confederation of north-eastern Ireland covering roughly the modern counties of Antrim and Down.

† Blathmac seems to have been, as was the custom with Ionan abbots, a descendant of the same branch of the Úi Neill dynasty as its founder, Colm Cille.

the monks in a barrow beneath a pile of turfs, according to Strabo. Blathmac's refusal to give up the shrine ensured his martyrdom, 'torn limb from limb' by the impious barbarians, and he became a glorious exemplar for the faithful of those troubled times, his story travelling the length and breadth of Christian Europe.

The fortunes of the secular Scottish kingdoms in the ninth century,* and of the vast bulk of small, rural settlements whose labour supported them, are more difficult to track than the fates of the martyrs. Few indigenous annals survive: there is no remotely contemporary Pictish text nor any from the kingdom of Strathclyde, and only one from Dál Riata.† Partial genealogies of kings, surviving in later material, allow historians to reconstruct a few fragments of a lost narrative. For the most part, Scottish kingdoms feature only when Irish or Northumbrian interests there drew the attention of their annalists, or when much later Norse sagas wrote down the creation myths of their own kind. But the enigmatic art of Pictland is still a very active focus for research and, now and then, a 'new' sculpture turns up. Historical geography yields fresh perspectives on landscape, territory and political developments from the analysis of existing material. Only archaeology can produce substantial new material, and its wheels grind slowly, if sometimes spectacularly.

Early Scottish history is a flimsy bridge constructed between the two banks of a river: projecting tentatively forward from the Roman period (rebellious, half-seen tribes partially subdued by Roman generals but ultimately left to their own devices and never a full part of the Imperial project) and back from the medieval

---

* 'Scottish' and 'Scotland' are anachronistic terms; I adopt them here, where convenient, to refer to the kingdoms later absorbed into the medieval state.
† The *Senchus Fer nAlban*, an apparent census of military service, among other things. See Bannerman 1974 for the text.

(steeped in nationalist myth and cultural smoked glass). Studies of Scottish history were, for a long time, diverted from the sorts of questions being asked of contemporary kingdoms further south and west by both a lack of secular sources and the apparent enigma of the Picts, evident from the distinct and opaque symbolism of their stone sculpture and odd references apparently implying that they were an archaic race, unrelated to the so-called Celts.

Scholarship has moved on. The Pictish kingdoms are now recognized as having belonged culturally and linguistically to the greater indigenous group to which the Irish and Welsh belong. Their language was a form of 'Q' Celtic, with similarities to Irish, Manx and Scots Gaelic. The ideology of their social and political élites is harder to reconstruct, except insofar as they shared affinities with other Christian tribal states. But the wonderfully carved symbols of their self-conscious psyches—bulls, fabulous marine monsters, hunting parties, hounds, mirrors, birds of prey—pictured with or without crosses, saints and apostles, shows their élite to have enjoyed a rich cultural hinterland somewhat obsessed with expressions of rank, with animist totems, warfare, noble pursuits and religious symbolism. Portmahomack, as nowhere else, shows the Picts to have been proficient farmers, engineers and craftspeople.

By the end of the seventh century much of what is now Scotland south of the Forth–Clyde isthmus lay under Northumbrian influence. Argyll and the southern Hebrides were the Gaelic-speaking lands of Dál Riata, with strong historic ties to Ulster. Looming over the River Clyde, Dumbarton Rock, more properly *Alclud*, was the fortress capital of Strathclyde: British in language and culture, periodically powerful and, in later centuries, resurgent, able to rule over south-west Scotland and Cumbria.

The distribution of so-called Pictish art, of early churches, of fortresses, suggests that two kingdoms dominated the east of what would become Scotland: Atholl, centred on Strathearn and the watershed of the River Tay, with a capital at Forteviot and a sacral 'hill of destiny' at Scone; and Fortriu, centred on the equally fertile lands around the Moray Firth and north Aberdeenshire.* North of the Great Glen there seems to have been a separate entity called *Cait*, which became Caithness, and it is possible that *Fib*, or Fife, retained a status as an independent kingdom; but these are murky waters.

The political geography of these kingdoms can be mapped in terms of what are known as cultural core lands, after the phrase proposed by the eminent historical geographer Brian Roberts.[4] In the Early Medieval period fertile lowland plains, the drainage basins of navigable rivers, offered both rich lands for exploitation and coherent territorial units, often ruled over by chieftains whose descendants became their kings. The land of the Hwicce around the Severn and Warwickshire Avon was one; the Bernicia of the River Tyne another, each one offering a range of riverine, arable, pastoral and other natural resources, the river its unifying thread. The name Strathclyde, meaning the broad valley of the River Clyde, neatly encapsulates the type.

Significant features of such core lands include royal palaces: Craig Phadraig, perhaps, near Inverness, and Forteviot in Strathearn; inauguration sites like Scone; fringe zones of less favourable land where grants of estates were made to establish 'royal' minsters. These latter are usually identified by the frequent occurrence of sophisticated, decorative sculpture, such as one finds at Meigle in Strathmore and on the Tarbat peninsula, displays of élite patronage of important cult sites. Secular settlements characterized by specialized production and large-scale consumption, which ought to go with such core lands, have not yet been found in eastern Scotland: do they lie in wait, or were

---

* Historians have argued for decades about the locations and existence of these two kingdoms, but a seminal paper by the Early Medieval historian Alex Woolf seems definitively to have sorted out the mess; see Woolf 2006.

these lands simply not sufficiently productive or developed for them to exist? Archaeology will eventually have its say; and the smart money says they will be found.

Pictish settlements have still not been excavated in sufficient numbers to construct a robust economic and social narrative for them. The classic type-site of the so-called Pictish longhouse, a timber and turf dwelling whose walls have distinctively rounded corners, is Pitcarmick in north-east Perthshire; another small complex has recently been excavated in Glenshee in the same county. Frustratingly, the latter has produced Pitcarmick-type structures that, perversely, did not contain hearths; and without a hearth, what is a dwelling? The longhouses at Lairn in Glenshee sit in a landscape of roundhouses which are often assumed, on thin grounds, to be 'prehistoric' in date. Archaeologists continue to scratch their heads. Other Pictish sites are associated with souterrains, the enigmatic underground structures also found in Ireland, which look as though they were food storage complexes (not the dwellings of hobbit-like Picts, as popular fancy would have it).

On many Scottish lochs, crannogs (pile-built circular dwellings lying just offshore, reached by wooden causeways) seem to have belonged to transhumant* élites, perhaps the summer residences of chiefs and petty kings. It remains to be seen if the bulk of the northern post-Roman peoples lived in as yet unidentified settlements not visible to archaeology (perhaps lying beneath contemporary farms and villages); or if they were still living at sites traditionally identified with the late Iron Age; hillforts and brochs, for example. A comprehensive programme of Early Medieval field archaeology, especially excavation, is required in mainland Scotland. Portmahomack proves that the evidence is there, even if acidic upland soils have often degraded it severely.†

---

* Transhumant: seasonal migration between lowland or coastal winter settlements and high summer pastures.

† Metalwork, bone, even pottery, are susceptible to destruction in soils that go

Alex Woolf, author of the most authoritative recent history of Scotland in this period,[5] in unpicking the complexities of its early dynasties, proposes that in the early ninth century the northern kingdoms were dominated by King Constantín, son of Wrguist, ruling Fortriu and Atholl together for thirty years and probably, by the end of his life in 820, overlord of all the lands north of the Forth; then by his brother Onuist, who succeeded him for fourteen years until 834; and by Constantín's son Domnall, who ruled Dál Riata in the west for twenty-four years until 835. The deaths of two powerful kings in such a short space of time unsurprisingly left the northern kingdoms vulnerable. Scandinavian entrepreneurs had keen eyes and ears, their sensitivity to the weakness of their potential prey as acute as stalking tigers. Four years later a Norse invasion triggered the series of events that would lead to the emergence of a kingdom of Alba.

Under the year 839 (the year in which King Ecgberht of Wessex died) the *Annals of Ulster* record that 'the heathens won a battle against the men of Fortriu, and Eóganán son of Aengus, Bran son of Óengus, Aed son of Boanta, and others almost innumerable fell there'. These were the short-lived successors to the dynast Constantín. Historians used to make much of an entry, in the Irish *Annals of the Four Masters* under the year 835 (but corrected to 839, the same year as the devastating raid on Fortriu), in which an Irish chief went to Dál Riata with a war band in support of one Cináed, son of Ailpín. From such trivial entries are national myths born. Kenneth McAlpin, Cináed mac Ailpín, has become Scotland's Ælfred, its royal dynastic founder and unifier. He sits at the head of a genealogy preserved in a work known as

---

through severe wet-dry and freeze-thaw cycles, and are acidic. Exceptionally, and this is often the case with crannogs, waterlogged sites such as those covered by peat or submerged on lake beds provide anaerobic conditions offering very high levels of preservation of material culture and what is flippantly known as bio-swag: seeds, charred wood, micro-fossils and industrial waste, of the highest value to the archaeologist.

the *Chronicle of the Kings of Alba* (*CKA*) whose credibility for this period is seriously in doubt and whose complexity makes it very difficult to interpret with confidence.[6] In the *Chronicle*, essentially an expanded king list, Cináed is credited with conquering and then absorbing Pictavia from a base in his Dál Riatan homeland; with founding Alba as a single entity, just as Ælfred is frequently credited with seeing off the Vikings single-handed and creating a kingdom called England.

The chronicler of the *CKA* would have us believe that Cináed ruled Dál Riata and Pictavia for the next sixteen years before dying at a date calculated as 858; that he attacked Dunbar and the monastery of Melrose in north Northumbria and transferred the relics of Colm Cille from Iona* to a new church (assumed to be Dunkeld in Strathtay: *Dún Chaillean*, the Fort of the Caledonii). During his reign, the chronicler records, *Danari* (a generic for Norse) wasted Pictavia as far east as Clunie and Dunkeld.

Cináed, then, was later remembered to have ruled over both Picts and Dál Riatan Scots. He was not the first; and we cannot even be sure of his geographical origins, so from those points of view his career is noteworthy rather than spectacular. From his reign, it is true, Pictavia and Dál Riata lost their individual identities so far as the chroniclers were concerned; they are simply not mentioned again after the middle of the ninth century. But as a founding dynast Cináed must be demoted; only in the reign of his grandson, Constantín mac Áeda, can we confidently begin to describe the emergence of a coherent kingdom of all Scotland outside Strathclyde and the Scandinavian settlements: of a state called Alba.

No more detailed history of this key period in northern history is ever likely to be drawn. But if we cannot identify the reign

---

* In a contrasting narrative, the *Annals of Ulster* record, under 849, that relics of the saint were taken to Ireland. Many members of Colm Cille's community had fled to Kells on the Irish mainland as far back as 807.

of Cináed as the founding event of Alba, we can at least say that the intervention of Norsemen, and their future domination of the western part of Scotland, had forced a decisive shift in the orientation of Scottish politics towards the east.

The kingdoms of Early Medieval Scotland had been Christian, at least nominally, since the seventh century. In common with other early kingdoms their economies were coinless (coins were circulated as bullion, but not minted north of York) and based on food and service renders; their social structures hierarchical, with slaves at the base and kings at the top. Warrior élites were supported by groupings of households whose economic geographies cannot have looked much different from the shires of Northumbria or the small territorial kingdoms and cantrefi* of Ireland and Wales: miniature cultural core lands, if you like. The sophistication of the monastic settlement at Portmahomack and the overwhelming evidence of surviving Pictish art reveal a highly politicized, self-conscious culture, actively connected to its neighbours by linguistic, historical and intellectual ties. Had the works of its scholars and genealogists survived, as they did in Northumbria, we would be able to paint every bit as rich a picture of Pictavia and the other Scottish kingdoms.

In the lands north of the Forth and Clyde the impact of Viking raids and settlement was felt earlier and more profoundly than in the kingdoms of the Anglo-Saxons and Welsh. Rival dynasties took advantage of the instability caused by this new, third-party intruder, to make war on their neighbours and ancient rivals, to annex, render tribute, even conquer. If Cináed is to fit credibly into Scottish history, it is as one of many opportunists of the Viking Age, one whose dynastic legacy assured him a permanent place in history as a nation's progenitor.

While history and archaeology let us down in the Early

---

* The cantref, literally 'a hundred townships', is a very rough equivalent of the Northumbrian shire. See below, Chapter 12.

Medieval North, at least the latter has been much more productive in the island communities of Shetland, Orkney and the Western Isles. This is itself a matter of historical and geographical chance. Many coastal island sites, buried by windblown sand over the millennia, have been revealed by the same sorts of storms that buried them; in sand their structural integrity and material culture—drystone walling, domestic utensils, hearths, bed-settings, decorative items and containers—have been preserved. They are treasure chests.

In the isles, the distinctive forms of so-called Pictish wheelhouse and Norse longhouse, with their dramatic and tightly-managed internal layouts, beautifully constructed walls and wide distribution, have allowed archaeologists to map the settlement of Scandinavian communities from the late eighth and ninth centuries onwards, far into the medieval period when the Lords of the Isles were overtly Norse in culture, language and affiliation; to map, also, the crucial period when native populations co-existed with or were driven out, enslaved or oppressed by the incomers.

Attention was first drawn to the possibility of such cultural conflict by the romantic re-emergence of the Shetland site that became known as Jarlshof (christened by Walter Scott on a visit there in 1814). Excavated between the 1930s and the 1950s, it revealed a sequence of occupation that stretched as far back as the Neolithic (roughly 4000 BCE to 2000 BCE) and was represented in all subsequent periods. Its Norse longhouses, the first to be excavated in Britain, were found to have been continuously occupied until the fourteenth century.

In Orkney substantial excavation campaigns have allowed archaeologists to reconstruct highly detailed sequences of settlements at Brough of Birsay on the west coast of Mainland, and elsewhere. Burials of Scandinavian appearance, including boat burials, now have distribution maps all their own, and a number of settlements of the Norse period are currently under excavation in the Western Isles. The material clues to a century and more of human contact, tension and survival, of clashes of religion, belief and language, are slowly being teased from the sands of the Atlantic shores.

Like Western Scotland, Wales shared affinities and vulnerabilities with the coastal communities of Ireland; its land borders were zones of periodic tension and conflict with ambitious Anglo-Saxon neighbours; its mountainous heart gave Welsh political geography a regional, north–south axis. But its history and archaeology in the early part of the Viking Age are frustratingly obscure.

In earlier periods kings of Powys and Gwynedd dominated the north and the border zone with Mercia. At the beginning of the ninth century a new dynasty, perhaps originating in the Isle of Man and apparently seeking new horizons under pressure from Scandinavian piracy and settlement, came to control the ancient kingdom of Gwynedd from its heartland in Anglesey, or Môn. In 825, that tumultuous year recorded in the *Anglo-Saxon Chronicle* and the *Annals of Ulster*, Merfyn Frych acquired the crown of Gwynedd from the supposed last king of the line of Cunedda, Hywel ap Rhodri Molwynog. His son Rhodri Mawr (the 'Great') annexed Powys sometime around 856 and the southern kingdom of Seisyllwg* in about 871. In 876 he was defeated in a battle on Môn by a Viking force; he died in 878, killed by a king of Mercia after having won mastery of most of modern Wales. His sons, like those of Cináed and of Æðelwulf of Wessex, were rulers of successful houses themselves; the dynasty would produce a celebrated overlord, law-maker and friend of the West Saxons, Hywel Dda, the 'Good'.

Just as Northumbria had its precious Cuthbert and Dál Riata its Colm Cille, so the Welsh church had as its cult hero St David,

* Comprising roughly Ceredigion and Ystrad Tywi.

a tough, uncompromising sixth-century bishop and monastic entrepreneur whose relics were said to be held in the cathedral of the city that bears his name.[7] The *Annales Cambriae* or Welsh Annals, preserved in the historical miscellany known as 'Nennius', seem to have been compiled here in the middle of the ninth century. Uniquely, David's shrine was not despoiled by Viking pirates during the ninth or tenth centuries, despite several raids on the community; indeed Wales as a whole, Anglesey apart, seems to have been affected more by the tides of the Viking Age than by direct attack.*

The geography of Wales, as its engineers know only too well, does not favour communications. Only the Rivers Dee, Severn, Wye and Cleddau offer substantial navigable waterways, mostly along its eastern borders (and each of them was penetrated by raids during the ninth century). The legacy of Roman roads is unimpressive: routes through the valleys have been hard won. Its great natural harbours are confined to the south-west, on Milford Haven, and the south coast and Severn estuary. The features that most hinder its economic development are precisely those that protected it from the worst attentions of the Vikings.

The first overwintering of a Scandinavian fleet, on Sheppey in 850, was followed by the arrival of an immense naval force at the mouth of the Thames in the spring or summer of 851. A fleet of 350 ships, if true, is a step-change in ambition: this was not raiding but state-sponsored invasion. The *hæðnum herige* or 'heathen army' attacked Canterbury, perhaps the closest thing to a town in any of the Anglo-Saxon kingdoms and vulnerable to marine assault by virtue of the River Stour. In the ninth century the river may have been navigable as far inland as the trading settlement at

---

* But see below in Chapter 7 for a treatment of excavations at Llanbedrgoch.

Fordwich, just 2 miles (3 km) from the Roman *civitas** capital of the Cantiaci and from Christ Church. It is far from clear whether the Scandinavian forces had a coherent plan or whether, on arriving in the Thames estuary in convoy, they split up to pursue their own predatory ambitions. Coin production in Canterbury and London seems to have been disrupted for some time afterwards and no Kentish charters survive from the years immediately after the great raid.

Part of the fleet, at least, penetrated the Thames valley: King Beorhtwulf of Mercia was put to flight, his levies defeated, his fate unrecorded. The heathen army crossed the Thames into Surrey, where they faced stiffer resistance. Æðelwulf, king of Wessex, with the levies of his second son Æðelbald, met the invading force at an unidentified place called *Acleah* and 'there made the greatest slaughter of a heathen host that we have heard tell of up to the present day, and there won the victory'.[8] In spite of their very evident vulnerability to coastal attacks, the kings of the Anglo-Saxons, fighting on their own territory with experienced shire musters and a well-trained and armed warrior élite, were more than a match for a Viking force reliant on raiding for supplies and isolated from its ships. In 851 the economic and social machinery of the Anglo-Saxon states may have been bruised, but their existence was not yet threatened.

Mercia's new king, Burghred,† now sought to establish himself and revive the waning fortunes of a once-great kingdom. In 853 he won support from Æðelwulf in pressing historical claims against Powys, his western neighbour. He married Æðelwulf's daughter Æðelswið in a ceremony at the royal West Saxon town-

---

* *Civitates* were tribal entities recognized by the Romans and maintained as administrative units through the Empire and beyond. Their capitals, including Canterbury, Carlisle and Exeter, often emerged in later centuries as shire towns.

† The name suggests alliteratively that he was related to Beorhtwulf, who must by now have died, perhaps of wounds sustained in battle.

ship of Chippenham (*Cippanhamme*: Cippa's promontory') in Wiltshire: a seal of both alliance and submission. By 857 he was able to issue a charter granting a house and commercial rights in *Lundenwic* to the bishop of Winchester.[9]

The shuffling pack of Insular dynastic succession produced new cards in this decade. Cyngen, the Powysian king who built the famous Pillar of Eliseg in memory of a great ancestor, perhaps under pressure from both Mercian ambitions to the east and a newly aggressive kingdom of Gwynedd in the north, abdicated and travelled to Rome, where he died in 854. The following years saw Viking raids deep into the Welsh marches among the dwellers of the Wrekin and on Môn.[10] In 856 Powys was annexed by Rhodri Mawr (who impressed the Irish annalists by killing a Viking chieftain called Orm in the same year) and absorbed into a greater Gwynedd.[11] King Æðelweard of East Anglia, an obscure figure, died and was succeeded by the more famous Eadmund. In Northumbria, the death of a King Eanred was followed by a number of short reigns and depositions, the fruits of ancient rivalries, and the once-great kingdom descended into factional warfare. In Pictavia, in 858, Cináed died and was succeeded by his brother Domnall.

Æðelwulf, whose father, Ecgberht, had ruled from 802 to 839, had five sons (Æðelstan, Æðelbald, Æðelberht, Æðelred and Ælfred) and may have felt sufficiently secure—or old—by 855 to undertake his own pilgrimage to Rome, taking with him his youngest child Ælfred and, on his return a year later, bringing home a new bride: Judith, the daughter of Charles the Bald. The king of the West Saxons now enjoyed sufficient prestige to dine at Europe's high table.

The king's eldest son, Æðelstan, his regent in Kent, must by now have died. Like Charlemagne in Francia, Æðelwulf tried by agreement and treaty to ensure a peaceful succession by the division of the kingdom in his will. At least one of his sons now pre-empted that will, perhaps fearing that his new, very young Frankish stepmother might produce rival heirs. The *Anglo-Saxon Chronicle* is diplomatically silent on the matter; but Ælfred's Welsh biographer, Bishop Asser, recorded that on Æðelwulf's return from Rome and Francia in 855–856, Æðelbald relegated him to the subordinate throne of Kent and Sussex. After his father's death in 858 Æðelbald married his stepmother Judith, much to the disgust of the church.[12] As Æðelstan had ruled in Kent as a *subregulus*, so Æðelbald deployed his next brother Æðelberht in the same role; but after Æðelbald's own untimely death in 860 Æðelberht came to rule over all the southern kingdoms.

A disputed succession that might have metastasized into dynastic war, as it had in Francia, was resolved by Æðelbald's death and by that of his brother Æðelberht five years later in 865. The fourth son, Æðelred, succeeded to a united Wessex, Kent and Sussex. His only surviving brother, Ælfred, was just sixteen.* Æðelred could not have chosen a more unpropitious time. The leaders of a fleet laid up menacingly on Thanet through the winter of 864–865 negotiated a large tribute from the Kentishmen and then, in secret and by night, left their camp and plundered eastern Kent. Worse was to come:

> *þy ilcan geare cuom micel here on Angelcynnes lond.*
>
> The same year a great host came to the land of the Angles.

The year 865 marks a pivotal moment in the Viking Age: when raiders became conquerors. From this year, Scandinavian kings ruled parts of Britain, through fluctuating fortunes, for almost a century. The arrival of the *mycel hæþen here*,† the Great Heathen Host, shocked contemporaries. It may have been no more than a great raid that morphed into a longer campaign, with no initial strategy other than the winning of booty and slaves. But it altered

---

* Æðelred first witnessed one of his father's charters in 864.

† From the 'B' version of the *Anglo-Saxon Chronicle*, under 867.

British history irrevocably and, in a connected world, it has a political and geographical context that requires some explaining. South-eastern Britain, facing the Continent and familiar to generations of Scandinavian traders and raiders, was a soft target; even so, it would help if we knew where the Great Host had been before it arrived on the shores of East Anglia.

One might see, in the death of King Horik in Denmark a dozen years previously, the collapse of Danish royal authority and in its aftermath the sort of political chaos that propels ambitious rivals to try their hand abroad. Here the evidence of the *Historia de Sancto Cuthberto* offers a clue: the invaders of 865 were, it says, led by one Ubba, leader of a Frisian contingent, and Hálfdan, a Danish king; and together the Host is referred to as *Scaldingi*.[13] The *Scaldingi* might be the Scyldings of *Beowulf*, as argued by Colin Chase: that is to say, Danes, for whom this is a generic term.[14] Alex Woolf has suggested, however, that they were identified as *Scaldingi* because they had recently crossed the Channel from the mouth of the River Scheldt, where they had established a *longphort* and trading centre on the island of Walcheren. In the Anglo-Saxon kingdoms, the term *Deniscan*,* Danes, was later used to denote Scandinavians who had crossed from Continental Europe, as opposed to the *Norðmannum*, 'Northmen', who came from either Norway or Ireland.

To add to the possible confusion, the absence of a great Norse chief, the celebrated Ívarr, from Irish annals at this time might suggest that he was seeking new territorial conquests: he is named as a leader of the Great Host by the late tenth-century chronicler Æðelweard† and in the Norse saga *Knutsdrápa*.[15] In

---

* Pronounced 'Denishan'.

† Æðelweard was a descendant of Ælfred's immediately older brother Æðelred. His *Chronicle*, written in a style archaic even for his own time, occasionally includes material derived from otherwise unknown sources, perhaps even orally transmitted to him at court. The manuscript survives in a single, fire-damaged copy. The best modern edition is that of Campbell (1962).

the Irish records he appears, fighting with and against Irish kings, alongside Óláfr and Ásl from a base in Dublin, and one source describes them as brothers.[16] The *Anglo-Saxon Chronicle* records that he was a brother of Hálfdan.[17] Ívarr, sometimes called Ivar 'the Boneless', is much discussed by historians because he spawned three generations of formidable leaders—the so-called *Uí Ímair* —among the kingdoms of Ireland and Britain. If so, he stands alongside the Ailpín dynasty of Alba, the Ecgberhtings of Wessex and the descendants of Merfyn Frych in Wales as a founding dynast of medieval Britain.

It is quite plausible that several sons of a powerful family might seek their fortunes beyond the seas and, at some point, agree to combine in a grand expedition of conquest; or that they should fix on the Insular kingdoms, weakened by internal rivalries, to try their hand. The *Annals of Ulster* record that Óláfr and Ásl plundered Fortriu in 866,* initiating a series of campaigns in the North with profound implications for the future of Alba.

To understand the timing of the Great Host's arrival in East Anglia it is worth looking across the Channel again, to events in Francia. Charles the Bald may have been seeking allies to assist in his defence against Viking raids when he gave his daughter Judith to Æðelwulf in 855. Western Francia, an enormous territory with a very long and exposed coastline, had been subject to many damaging raids during previous decades. Pippin of Aquitaine, another grandson of Charlemagne, went so far as to conspire with . Viking raiders on the River Loire after escaping from enforced monastic retirement and together, in 857, they sacked Poitiers in Aquitaine. A year later Charles's brother Louis the German invaded West Francia and Charles was forced to flee to Burgundy.

---

* The route into Fortriu from the Atlantic seems to have been that used by earlier generations of missionaries like Colm Cille: by boat and overland portage along the Great Glen; further south, it is arguable whether portages existed between the Rivers Forth and Clyde, allowing passage between the Irish Sea and the North Sea.

In 859, according to the *Annals of St Bertin*, the Danes 'ravaged the places beyond the Scheldt'—that is to say, the Frisian coastline. The monastery at St Valery sur Somme in Picardy was laid waste, as were the *civitas* of Amiens and the island of Betuwe in the River Rhine. In Paris, the monks of St Denis removed the relics of their great saint to a safe place, as previously the community of Colm Cille had taken their saint's shrine to safety.

Charles's restoration in 860 signalled an outbreak of fragile internal peace in Francia; even so, large and numerous bands of increasingly confident pirates were able to penetrate the great waterways of northern and eastern Francia at will. Like an unquenchable forest fire, the extinguishing or paying off of one band simply invited the arrival or return of another. In 861 a Viking fleet attacked and burned Paris. Another fleet, lately returned from an attack on England (an entry in the *Anglo-Saxon Chronicle* records the sacking of Winchester in that year), sailed up the Seine with 200 ships, besieging a 'Norse' fortification on the island of Oissel, south of present-day Rouen.

In 862 Charles won a small but significant victory in his attempt to frustrate the pirates. They had penetrated his defences along the River Marne, burning a bridge at a place called Trilbardou. Charles responded rapidly, following 'indispensable advice', as the chronicler of St Bertin put it, rebuilding the bridge while the pirate vessels were upstream and trapping them. The raiders were forced to come to terms. Charles, seizing the moment, called a great assembly at Pîtres on the Seine in Normandy, just upstream from Rouen, and ordered defensive bridges to be built all along the Seine, reasoning that physical barriers *across* rivers might act as both a disincentive to piracy and as a means of concentrating and manoeuvring his own forces in rapid response to intelligence.*

---

* The historian Simon Coupland argues that only two bridges were actually fortified, one each on the Seine and Loire. Coupland 1991.

Two years later, in 864, Charles reconvened the assembly at
Pîtres and issued thirty-seven edicts which have taken their place
in French history as *Magna Carta* has in England. Like that charter, his edicts' role as founding documents of French statehood
might be overstated. What we can say is that they represented
an attempt by Charles, following in the footsteps of the late
Roman codices, to impose universal military burdens, to revalue
and reform coinage, to reorganize the army and create a rapid-
response cavalry unit; to ban the sale of weapons to 'foreigners'
and expand the provision of strategic bridges. In strengthening
the economic and military defences of West Francia, Charles cannily increased both his personal power and that of the state. In
adversity lay opportunity.[18] The *mycel here* landed in East Anglia a
year after the edicts issued at Pîtres; it is not certain that invasion
was a direct reaction to the frustration of their Frankish ambitions, but it seems very likely. They overwintered there, perhaps in
the secure, watery fastnesses of Flegg, north of Great Yarmouth.*
King Eadmund sued for peace and gave them horses. From this
point onwards, the *Anglo-Saxon Chronicle* follows their fortunes
in detail:

> *Her for se here of Eastenglum ofer Humbre muþan to Eoforwic-
> ceastre on Norþhymbre…*
>
> In this year the host went from East Anglia over the mouth of
> the Humber to York in Northumbria… and there was great
> dissension of the people among themselves; and they had
> repudiated their king Osberht and accepted Ælle, a king not
> of royal birth; and it was late in the year when they set about
> making war against the host.[19]

At the end of 866, then, Northumbria appears to have been in
a state of civil war, and lay fatally exposed. If the *Historia* of St
Cuthbert is right in saying that the two kings were brothers,

* See below, p. 193.

they must have been rivals from an ancient Deiran dynasty, its ancestral heartlands in East Yorkshire, from which King Edwin had risen in the seventh century to the heights of *imperium* over almost all the Anglo-Saxon kingdoms. Edwin had built his first church in the ruins of the Emperor Constantine's city of *Eboracum*: *Eoforwicceastre* to the Anglo-Saxons; *Jorvik* to the Vikings, modern York. We should not be surprised if the leaders of the Scandinavian Host were aware of the military potential for decapitating the brittle ruling house of southern Northumbria and seizing the weakened kingdom for themselves. All the evidence suggests that their intelligence-gathering was effective. But they did not, to begin with, have it all their own way.

The various sources recording Northumbria's conquest combine to paint a vivid picture of swinging fortunes and much spilt blood.[20] In November the *mycel here* captured the ancient Roman legionary fortress at York and wasted the surrounding area.[21] The bulk of the invading army may have travelled by ship from East Anglia along the coast of Lindsey and thence into the Humber, past its confluence with the Trent and followed the Ouse north. But the Host had acquired horses in East Anglia, so it seems more likely that fleet and land army agreed a rendezvous; and two points suggest themselves. If the fleet sailed up the Yorkshire Ouse to its confluence with the River Wharfe and thence to Tadcaster, where it bisects the Roman road, they could have met a rapidly moving mounted force arriving there overland. With the support of the main force in ships, the Host might then advance on York, lying exposed a mere 5 miles (8 km) away.

The military risk attached to this route was its necessarily passing through the heart of Mercia, where an attempt to engage it on home territory by King Burghred posed dangers. More likely, I think, the fleet first met and ferried the army across the Humber, where Ermine Street runs north from Lincoln; then the mounted force continued to York by road through territory lacking organized military control, while the fleet arrived on the Ouse in support shortly afterwards.

Early in 867 the two Northumbrian rivals put aside their differences and combined to attack the Danish Host, who retreated behind what was left of the Roman walls of the city, on the northeast bank of the only-too-navigable River Great Ouse. But the attack on the Host besieged in the city failed. In a bloody pitched battle inside the walls both sides suffered heavy casualties; but the Northumbrian army was destroyed, the two rival kings killed, and 'the remnant' made peace with the invaders.* Recalling those events the community of Cuthbert regarded Osberht's and Ælle's fate as divine punishment for having 'stolen' between them six *vills* from St Cuthbert and for having 'hated' the saint.[22] No chronicler recorded the devastating and permanent loss of York's great library and monastic school, where Alcuin had acquired his scholarship in the previous century. The city's subsequent flowering under Scandinavian influence would be industrial and commercial, rather than intellectual. Coin evidence suggests a vacuum in political control in the immediate aftermath of the battle for York; and the trading centre that lay at the confluence of the Rivers Great Ouse and Foss beneath medieval Fishergate, excavated in the 1980s, all but ceased to function. We do not know under whose direct administration York, or the kingdom, fell. The twelfth-century chronicler Symeon of Durham understood that one Ecgberht was set up as a puppet king north of the River Tyne, in Bernicia.

A foreign army sat in York's crumbling ruins, feeding off its hinterland by whatever direct form of taxation it saw fit to impose and dispensing justice by right of arms. Northumbria, it seems, split into its ancient components, Bernicia and Deira. It is a salutary fact that north of the River Tees, perhaps an ancient

---

* Lurid stories about a blood feud between Ívarr and Ælle, recorded in a late Scandinavian poem, resulting in Ælle's ritual evisceration, might just be true; but most historians treat the story, and the punishment, with scepticism.

boundary between the two Northumbrian kingdoms, there are virtually no Scandinavian place names, so common in Yorkshire. The descendants of the great seventh-century Bernician over-lords may not have been able to expel the foreigners from the lands south of the Tees; but the dynasty that emerges as the Reeves of Bamburgh and later Earls of Northumbria does seem to have been able to halt the *mycel here* on the line of the Tyne.

The Host did not stay long in York to rule it directly. Towards the middle or end of 867 they turned south and, again, their des-tination suggests a co-ordination of land and water forces, this time at a point where Roman road and navigable river met on the River Trent in Mercia. They took winter quarters at Nottingham, if nothing else a statement of intent that could not be ignored by King Burghred. The *Anglo-Saxon Chronicle* entry for 867 records that the Mercians 'begged' for help from King Æðelred and his young brother Ælfred, a partisan entry that can be read, more neutrally, as a formal request for military alliance against a common enemy. One might speculate that the Mercian queen, Æðelswið, was the intermediary between her husband and her brothers in Wessex.

Wessex responded, and the combined army came on the *mycel here* in their newly fortified river-front camp early in 868. The *Chronicle* records that despite a siege there was 'no serious engagement' and that the Mercians 'made peace with the Host'. They were, it seems, given money to go away. Confronted with a large, if not superior, enemy and an apparently united front the Host returned to York and stayed there for a year, more or less secure in the knowledge that no Northumbrian force could engage them on equal terms.

If nothing else this early encounter between an invading Scandinavian force and the combined armies of two Anglo-Saxon kingdoms shows that the Host, from long practice on the Continent, could rapidly construct a defensive camp capable of withstanding a siege; and that the latter had no means of breaching such defences. Siege warfare was in its infancy; the initiative lay with the invaders: mobile, battle hardened and alive to every opportunity to divide and rule, or raid and vanish.

The seriousness of the threat posed by the *mycel here* to the southern kingdoms was by no means underestimated, even in its earliest phases. The impromptu alliance of 868 was cemented in the same year by the marriage of a Mercian ealdorman's daughter, one Ælswið, to the ætheling of Wessex, Ælfred. Ælfred was nineteen years old. He had been born on a royal estate at Wantage, now in Berkshire, in the year 849, the youngest of five brothers.* Stories recorded by Bishop Asser from Ælfred's childhood—of illness, of his eagerness to learn his letters, of his comely appearance and piety, of his two journeys to Rome (one in company with his father in 855)—belong to the irreducible canon of English legend. He can have grown up with little or no expectation of becoming king after his father Æðewulf and four older brothers.

Ælfred has played a central role in narratives of the Viking Age in England for three perfectly good reasons. Firstly, his gifts in military strategy, administration, learning and Christian philosophy were considerable, perhaps unrivalled in his age; secondly, because he is the first Englishman whose life we know in the sort of detail that allows biographers to write convincingly, and at length, about his character, achievements and failures; and, lastly, because his heirs and successors cemented his legacy and constructed a superbly powerful state on the foundations that he and his forbears laid. Part of that legacy was the retrospective creation of what we might call the grand unification project—an idea of 'England'.

---

* Ælfred also had an older sister, Æðelswið. See above pp. 93 and 102 and below, p. 125.

The detail of Ælfred's life comes, to begin with, from a species of contemporary biography, Bishop Asser's *Life of King Ælfred*. Asser came from south-west Wales to Ælfred's court in 885 during a period of relative political calm. Just as Charlemagne had brought scholars into his imperial court, so Ælfred picked men of intellect and vision to help him with his grand educational and institutional ambitions. The *Life* was composed, or finished, in about 893, a year which was anything but calm in the realm of Wessex. Whatever its historical and literary merits, it opens a dramatic window on the machinery of the West Saxon court, on the legacy that Ælfred wished to build, and on many of his personal and political struggles. It must, naturally, be read with caution.

One of Ælfred's most significant historical achievements was the compilation at his instigation of the *Anglo-Saxon Chronicle*, which supplies a parallel, and sometimes identical, account of the wars of his reign and much more besides. Like the *Royal Frankish Annals* it is partisan, sometimes blatantly so; but in its various versions it offers historians sufficient shades of grey to unpick some of its claims; to look back at earlier material incorporated into it, and to hear voices from outside the West Saxon court which found their way into Mercian and Northern variants. As the battle for Britain enters its first phase in the late 860s, the historian takes up arms: Asser, the Irish Annals, the *Historia* and the *Chronicle* in one hand; archaeology, coins and charter evidence in the other. The game is afoot.

The year that the *mycel here* spent unmolested in York allowed them to set up some sort of administrative framework for ruling by proxy; to plan their next campaign and to draw supplies from York's dependent settlements. A Viking camp, recently identified by fieldwork, lying some 14 miles (23 km) upstream from York at Aldwark, may yet tell us much about the make-up and activities of the *mycel here* at this time.[23] How many of their countrymen joined them at this stage to settle, fabricate, trade and farm, is impossible to say. What we can say is that possession of York was not enough to satisfy their ambitions; not by a long shot. During 869 they returned, this time moving unchallenged across Mercia, to East Anglia: to *Đeodford* (Thetford), where they overwintered.

A day's journey downstream from Thetford on the River Little Ouse, at Brandon, lay a thriving settlement on a sand island in the river, looking out onto the vast peatlands of the fens to the west. Probably the lowest natural crossing point of the river, it had grown from seventh-century origins as a sort of miniature trading settlement and industrial complex. In the twenty-first century, lying on the edge of Thetford forest in Breckland, many miles from the sea, it is no more than a modest town, the odd pleasure boat moored on the river and a small railway station to

13.
GRIM'S DITCH
near Ashampstead,
Berkshire.

connect it to the outside world. Excavations immediately west of the town during the 1980s revealed that in its eighth-century heyday the inhabitants manufactured textiles, dyeing and bleaching flax in buildings along the riverside.[24] They built earth-fast houses and workshops of upright timber posts clad with planks or, perhaps, the weatherboard so distinctive of the region. They were buried in two cemeteries, one either side of a three-cell church, also built in wood. A causeway joined the island to dry land. One wonders if, like some of the Continental trading communities, Brandon was rather exclusive, perhaps even founded by Frisian artisans or traders whose presence is known at York and elsewhere.

The people of Brandon were profligate in their accumulation of rubbish, discarding large quantities of pottery (more than 24,000 sherds of Ipswich ware and of Frankish imports) and animal bone. They lost, or discarded, an incomparably rich inventory of finds indicating that they were literate, wealthy and connected to international trading networks. They imported window glass and glass vessels for drinking; they had acquired a Coptic bowl and a gold plaque of St John the Evangelist. They ate rye bread, beans and plums, mutton and beef and large quantities of fish and oysters. The presence of writing styli alongside evidence of conspicuous consumption inclines the archaeologist to believe that Brandon was a minster complex, increasingly shedding its austere monastic traditions in favour of production and the enjoyment of the fruits of its wealth. Brandon did not survive the third quarter of the ninth century in its original form, although it was eventually rebuilt on the site of the present town. Whether its demise and relocation can be laid at the door of the Host of 868 is impossible to say.

In 869 King Eadmund of the East Angles summoned his levies and came to fight the *mycel here* at an unknown location. One version of the *Chronicle* records that the Host's leaders, Kings

Ubba and 'Ingwar' (the latter better known from his Norse name Ívarr) were directly responsible for Eadmund's death.[25] Later tradition has it that Eadmund was shot with arrows and beheaded at a place called *Hægelisdun* after he refused to renounce Christ—but the episode is conventional in form and bears suspicious resemblance to the deaths of earlier martyrs like St Sebastian; one is sceptical.[26] It is true, though, that later Viking rulers of East Anglia, who converted to Christianity, expressed penitence over his killing and that a cult centre developed at the Suffolk town that bears his name. For twenty years after 895 coins were minted in East Anglia (and perhaps in Eastern Mercia) bearing the legend SCE EADMVNDE REX—'O St Eadmund the King'.[27] But in the immediate aftermath of Eadmund's fall, according to the *Chronicle*, the *mycel here* overran East Anglia, destroying all the monasteries they found. They slew the abbot of the great minster at *Medehamstede*, burned it down, killed the monks and 'reduced it to nothing'.[28] Now they were ready to turn their attentions to Wessex.

Asser's description of the arrival of the *mycel here* in West Saxon territory early in 871 contains the sort of detail that suggests he had access to first-hand accounts from someone who had fought there—possibly Ælfred himself or one of his veteran commanders—which eventually found their way into the *Chronicle*. In the middle of that winter the Viking army left East Anglia and came to a *villa regia* at Reading on the south bank of the River Thames, where it runs east to west for a few miles just before a sharp turn to the north, cutting a gorge between the Berkshire Downs and the Chiltern hills at Goring. The Thames here, some 60 miles (95 km) upstream from the now terminally-in-decline trading settlement at *Lundenwic*, was the frontier between Wessex and Mercia.

The location strongly suggests, once again, a rendezvous between overland force and supporting fleet. The overland army would travel by way of the Roman road network to London and march or ride west towards what is now Staines (*Stána*: 'the Stones'), where a crossing of the Thames took it onto the Silchester road a little south of Reading.* The precision with which the invaders seem to have been able to identify and meet at such targets demonstrates the sophistication of their knowledge of river and road systems in lowland Britain: that mental Tube map again. The river is broad and strong here, and in the Anglo-Saxon period it was not merely the boundary between Wessex and Mercia but also a great trading artery of the southern kingdoms: barges plied up and down to and from *Lundenwic* and the Kentish ports, as far upstream at least as Lechlade in Gloucestershire. Any fleet venturing this far inland must negotiate fish traps and flash weirs† by the score, water mills tapping the river's power; riverside minsters, farms, hamlets and ancient ferry crossings. With the open sea and a homeward passage left further and further behind, penetration of the soft underbelly of the south was a risky game played for high rewards. Rowing upstream on these waters, whose moody gods can quickly switch between the benign and the vengeful, and passing through the densely wooded gorge at Goring with the hills tumbling down on either side, one can easily believe oneself to be venturing into England's own heart of darkness.

That Reading was a royal estate, where food renders were collected from the townships all around, implies that the Host's leaders were already aware of its potential for re-supplying them. It lay open to attack. We know of no *villae regiae* in this period defended by substantial earthworks or palisades, although there is some evidence that King Offa instituted a number of fortified

---

* John Peddie, who has made a study of military tactics in this period, suggests the possibility that they came south-west along the ancient Icknield Way and crossed the Thames at Goring, a few miles north of Reading. Peddie 1999, 79.

† Flash weir: an arrangement of vertical planks slotted through a beam. The planks could be temporarily removed to allow passage of boats up and down river.

settlements in Mercia in the eighth century. That may have changed in the years leading up to 871; but in any case the Host had no difficulty in taking Reading. Asser's informant told him that on the third day after their arrival, they rode out to plunder the district under two of their jarls. The remainder threw up a defensive rampart between the Rivers Kennet and Thames, where they converge on the east edge of the modern town.* The occupation of defended confluences, and the D-shaped enclosure on a river bank, were to become the classic *modi operandi* of the Viking armies, allowing them to break out into open country in fighting or foraging formations and to retreat to their boats if necessary, or be re-supplied by river.

Five miles (8 km) to the west the ealdorman of Berkshire, Æðelwulf, caught up with the foraging party at Englefield (*Englafelda*) and engaged them, killing one of their jarls; the rest retired to the new defensive position on the Thames. It took four days for King Æðelred and his young brother to muster their main forces and invest the fort. On their arrival some of the Host's soldiers were caught unprepared outside the gates of their new camp and cut down; but those inside burst out 'like wolves', according to Asser, and fought with all their might. The West Saxon force was repulsed with serious casualties, including a fatally wounded Ealdorman Æðelwulf.

Four days later the two armies met again, this time in open country on the Berkshire Downs, which rise to about 600 feet (185 m) above sea level. Despite the combined efforts of academics and enthusiastic investigators, *Æscesdune* (Ashdown), the site of the battle, cannot be identified: place-name scholars have shown that the name applied to the whole eastern expanse of the downs at this period. The battlefield archaeologist can reconstruct many

---

* John Peddie quotes John Man, a nineteenth-century Reading historian, who identified the remnants of the earthwork as late as 1816 on land now occupied by Reading railway station. Peddie 1999, 84.

plausible scenarios, none of them particularly convincing, but the landscape offers a few hints. Close to Ashampstead, a day's march north-west of Reading, parts of a great earthwork complex called Grim's Ditch might have been constructed, or re-used, by either army. The downlands are open and gently rolling here, long given over to summer pasturing for sheep and cattle; the ancient, long-distance Ridgeway passes close by to the north.

It seems significant that the Host chose to leave its defensive position at Reading, either because its commanders believed themselves to have already struck a decisive blow and needed only to deliver the *coup de grâce*; perhaps because they had been sent an embassy demanding a showdown; or because they believed they could outflank Æðelred's army and penetrate deep into Wessex further upstream along the Thames. We cannot say.

The *mycel here* split into two forces, one commanded by its kings, the other by its jarls. They had, it seems, been in a position to choose the field of battle. The West Saxon force, responding, similarly divided itself in two. The king led one shield wall; Ælfred the other.* Asser, keen to establish Ælfred's military credentials at an early stage in his narrative, writes that the young prince arrived first on the battlefield, his brother late at prayers in his tent, and fronted the force led by the jarls—a mark, presumably, of his and their junior status. Ælfred attacked 'like a wild boar', divinely inspired and protected, according to Asser.

Battle joined, the fiercest fighting took place around a solitary thorn tree. This was no ritual testing of enemy strength: the third engagement in less than a fortnight, Ashdown was a bloody and serious affair. The West Saxons drove the Host from the field of battle, inflicting heavy casualties: a King Bacseg was killed, along with his jarls Sidroc the Older and Younger, Osbern, Fraena and

---

* Caution must be exercised by those wishing to read into Asser's account an eye-witness record of battle-dispositions and tactics. The shield wall had become something of a poetic trope by Asser's day.

14. 'ASHDOWN was a bloody and serious affair':
the Ridgeway.

Harald.* The Host retreated behind its rampart at Reading and licked its wounds.

King Æðelred's commanders may have believed that they had decisively repulsed the army that had overwhelmed Northumbria and East Anglia. But two weeks later the Host had regrouped and, at a place called *Baseng*, most obviously identifiable with the village of Old Basing just east of Basingstoke in Hampshire, they in turn drove the West Saxons from the field. The *Chronicle* claimed that 'thousands' lost their lives. Ominously, Asser recalled that 'when the battle was over, another Viking army came from overseas and attached itself to the land'.[29] Oddly, in the litany of battles, skirmishes, retreats and cross-country campaigns of the year 871, which came to be known as the year of nine engagements, Asser fails to record a battle at the unidentified *Meretun*, which the *Chronicle* places two months after the defeat at *Baseng*. The result is in some doubt: the *Chronicle* claimed a West Saxon victory but allowed that the Host held the field: a score-draw, perhaps. Shortly afterwards, at Easter, King Æðelred died, perhaps of wounds received there. Ælfred, aged twenty-two, succeeded to the kingship of Wessex in the most perilous circumstances.

A month later he was forced to fight again, this time at *Wiltun*, with what the *Chronicle* describes as a small force. Again, he is said to have won the victory but ceded the field of battle. *Wiltun* can, at least, be positively identified as Wilton on the south bank of the River Wylye, a little north and west of Salisbury, whence the partially navigable River Avon runs south towards the coast of Dorset. We know from the *Chronicle* that the engagements of that year were all fought south of the Thames. If *Meretun*, *Baseng*, and the other, unnamed, battlefields lay in the lands between Reading and Wilton, they cover a large swathe of the

---

* The surviving king is named by the *Chronicle* as Hálfdan. One wonders if Ubba had been left behind in East Anglia with part of the army, or whether he remained at York.

heartlands of Wessex. This was a campaign of conquest and of desperate defence, fought sometimes in the open in pitched battle, army against army; more often, perhaps, in skirmishes between reconnaissance parties, foragers and smaller war bands.

The enemy might appear anywhere where a river penetrated deep into the shires of Wessex; their mobility, their professionalism and long experience of raiding gave them decisive advantages over a cumbersome system of farmer-militias led by a warrior élite whose loyalties were often local, familial and agricultural. Ælfred's kingship was new, untested. The sheer pace and geographical span of the 871 campaign is breathtaking. How could a land of farms and farmers survive the onslaught of a veteran, battle-hardened raiding force able to appear and disappear at will, spawning like mushrooms in the night and evaporating like the morning mist, ghosting along inshore coasts and estuaries, ever probing, exploiting the network of major rivers and ancient roads, the legacy of Rome, to deploy at great speed? The *Chronicle* dourly draws a line under a tumultuous year:

> *7 þy geare namon Westseaxe friþ wiþ þone here*
> And in this year the West Saxons made peace with the Host.

The new West Saxon king was forced to pay off the *mycel here*, to allow his warriors and followers to return to their farms and homes, to consider how he might counter the Viking threat in the months to come. The Host moved to London (the *Chronicle* uses *Lundenbyrig*, suggesting the old walled city of *Londinium* rather than the trading settlement at *Lundenwic*) where they obtained tribute from the Mercian King Burghred and overwintered. They too had cause to reconsider their plans and count the cost of war.

THE END OF DAYS

RAGNARÖK AND THE DAY OF JUDGEMENT—
THE ANTAGONISTS—TORKSEY AND REPTON
—THE CONQUEST OF YORK—
INCOMERS—THE ATTACK ON WESSEX
—ATHELNEY—EDINGTON—

4

AND I LOOKED, AND BEHELD A PALE horse: and his name that sat on him was Death, and Hell followed with him. And power was given unto them over the fourth part of the earth, to kill with sword, and with hunger, and with death, and with the beasts of the earth...

... And, lo, there was a great earthquake; and the sun became black as sackcloth of hair, and the moon became as blood...

... And the kings of the earth, and the great men, and the rich men, and the chief captains, and the mighty men, and every bondman, and every free man, hid themselves in the dens and in the rocks of the mountains...

... For the Great Day of His wrath is come; and who shall be able to stand?[1]

Thus the *New Testament* revelation of the Day of Judgement. The Norse poem *Völuspá*, or the Seeress's Prophecy, is scarcely less apocalyptic on the subject of Ragnarök, the last battle of the

15. RAGNARÖK: the end of days.
Cross shaft fragment from St Andrew's church,
Andreas, Isle of Man.

gods. The god Heimdallr blows his great horn and Yggdrasil, the world tree, shudders and groans. The Midgard serpent writhes in anger and, in the churning of the seas that follows, the ship Naglfar, constructed from the fingernails and toenails of the dead, breaks free from its moorings; the eagle shrieks its anticipation of doom. The giants advance into battle; the armies of Muspelheim, the land of fire, are unleashed. One by one the gods of the Norse pantheon engage in deadly combat: Oðin fights the wolf, Fenrir, and is swallowed whole; his son Thor does battle with Jörmungandr, the Midgard serpent, and dies from exhaustion and his wounds, before:

> The sun turns black, land sinks into the sea
> The bright stars vanish from the sky;
> Steam rises up from the conflagration,
> Hot flame plays against heaven itself.[2]

In the decade and a half after the arrival of the *mycel here* in 865, when all but two* of the Anglo-Saxon dynasties were extinguished, it must have seemed that the end of days was come. Kings were martyred, deposed or, through civil war, failed to protect their people; houses of God were destroyed, their monks enslaved by pagans; the wealth of the land was taken overseas, treasures and heirlooms stolen. The forces of heathenism advanced inexorably. The rules by which Christian states maintained order—the bonds of lordly patronage, of oath-swearing and loyalty which held society, religious and secular, in its delicate equipoise of reciprocity—seemed cast aside. The trading settlements that underpinned an explosion in wealth in the eighth century no longer functioned; many minsters were abandoned or barely survived; royal estates were plundered.

Intolerable burdens were imposed on the free men of the shires: to fight seemingly from one end of the year to the other

---

* Historians are wont to ignore the survival of the House of Bamburgh, former kings of Bernicia and Northumbria.

in the king's host, to repair fortifications and build bridges. Even the institutional might of the church was threatened. Wærferth, Bishop of Worcester, forced to rent his lands out to pay his share of tribute to the raiders in London, bemoaned 'the pressing affliction and immense tribute of the barbarians'.* King Ælfred later lamented that south of the River Humber there was scarcely a literate priest left.[3] Scholarship and literacy, already in decline in the ninth century, plumbed such depths that at Canterbury the single active scribe had gone blind and could barely copy out a line correctly.[4]

Northumbria, once the greatest power in the north of Britain, languished in a state of apparent anarchy comparable to that which Bede, referring to the apostate year of 633, described as having been deleted by 'those who compute the dates of kings'. Hoards of coins and hacksilver† were buried and never retrieved, just as they had been during the dark days at the end of the Roman Empire. Coldingham Abbey, founded in the seventh century by Æbbe, sister of that King Oswald who had brought the Irish mission to Lindisfarne, was destroyed in a raid in 870.[5]

Further north, in that same year, the ancestral fortress of the Northern Britons, *Alclud* on Dumbarton Rock, was captured by Dublin Norse chiefs Óláfr and Ívarr after a four-month siege.[6] A year later, according to the *Annals of Ulster*, those armies returned to Dublin in 200 ships laden with immense booty and 'a great prey of Angles and Britons and Picts'. Arthal ap Dyfnwal, Dumbarton's king, was assassinated in a plot by Constantín mac Cináed the following year.[7] Gwgon ap Meurig, the last attested king of Ceredigion, was drowned, perhaps while fighting Norse

---

* A charter surviving from 872 records the lease by Bishop Wærferth of Worcester of lands for 20 mancuses of gold, to be paid as *wergeld*. A gold mancus weighed about a sixth of an ounce (4.25 g), equivalent to about 30 pence of silver. Charter S1278, of 872, translated by Whitelock 1979, 532.

† Literally, items of silver cut into scrap for reworking or as currency.

raiders.[8] In 872 the *mycel here*, joined from the Continent by another supporting army, stood poised to conquer all. Six years later almost the last Anglo-Saxon king standing, Ælfred, was left ruling no more than a few acres of fetid marsh in the Somerset levels.

This apocalyptic scenario, which conveniently sets up Ælfred as the hero of a pervasive English nationalist narrative, deserves to be balanced by the scrutiny that modern textual critique and sober archaeological witness bring to bear. If the future looked grim in 871, as it must have done, there is no evidence that Scandinavian raiders and would-be conquerors wilfully set about destroying the apparatus of the state, embarked on a campaign of ethnic cleansing, the proscription of Christian worship or, indeed, the obliteration of Insular culture. Far from it. They set no precedent for their Norman descendant William, whose Harrying of the North in 1069–70 laid waste great swathes of territory, inducing famine and economic destruction. Like earlier (and later) would-be invaders, much of their interest in the Insular kingdoms was fostered by admiration for their wealth, their administrative sophistication and cultural confidence. What they wanted was a share.

The pope in Rome may have demanded that heathens be destroyed but the spiritual antipathy felt by many Christians towards the 'gentiles', as the chroniclers called them, was not necessarily reciprocated. Scandinavians, seeing much to envy and many similarities with their own beliefs, were curious, sometimes bemused—amused, even—by Christian worship, by the swearing of oaths on holy relics and by the rites of baptism practised in Christian kingdoms. In the eschatology of the heathen North, death and the afterlife were much greater preoccupations than the beginnings of life or religious induction. They also thought it very odd, not that Christians followed the sayings of the prophet of Judea, but that they had use for only a single God, presumed to be able to control all the forces of nature and of human destiny everywhere, at once and exclusively.

British, Pictish, Anglo-Saxon and Irish élites shared many cultural affinities with Scandinavian societies in their love of martial valour and their pursuit of glory, in some cases sharing even mythological heroes like Wayland the Smith. The Irish epic tale *Táin Bó Cúailnge* (The cattle raid of Cooley), with its teenage hero Cú Chulainn, was a poetic legend with themes and motifs that any Viking could admire: a great cattle raid, proven valour in single combat, a campaign of guerrilla warfare; an animist transformation into monstrous form. And of crucial importance for the nature of their interaction over the next two centuries was that Anglo-Saxon, Dane and Norseman were, for the most part, mutually intelligible on some functional level.* Above all, the leaders of the *mycel here* came to appreciate that native respect for the institutions and offices of church and state, and the fundamental rationality of that relationship, might be turned to their advantage.

There is no evidence either that, whatever their seafaring genius, Scandinavian armies were inherently superior to those of their Insular antagonists. It is true that they were highly effective raiders, veterans of campaigns in Francia, in Ireland and at home. Their weaponry—spear, axe, shield and sword—may often have been of a very high quality. Their martial culture and the bonds which held ships' crews together as fighting units in pursuit of glory and treasure made them justly feared. Their tactical knowledge of coastal, riverine and overland routes gave them significant advantages against a slow territorial opponent, as did their fast, shallow-draughted ships. Once they had constructed

---

* The evidence that Old Norse and Old English could be mutually comprehensible comes from analysis of the way in which place names and other vocabulary hybridized during later periods of assimilation in the tenth and eleventh centuries, especially in what is now Yorkshire. See Townend 2014.

bridgeheads, and seized or bought sufficient horses to create mobile mounted forces, they were capable of striking with apparent impunity across large swathes of territory and retreating laden with booty and prisoners.

However, even if the military organization of the Insular kingdoms was flawed by its reliance on the regional muster, its part-time field capabilities and its slowness to respond to the lightning raiding tactics of the Scandinavian marine assault, there is no suggestion that the ninth-century armies of the Anglo-Saxons, Britons and Scots were poorly led, unskilled or ill equipped. In open-field encounters with the enemy they were often successful. Their ealdormen were tied by strong historical bonds of lordship and tenurial obligation downwards to the men in their *fyrð* and upwards to their own lords, the kings. Their loyalties might have been regional rather than 'national'; but that did not mean that they failed to recognize the value of mutual defence.

Inter-dynastic warfare was rife in Early Medieval Britain; no generation had forgotten how to fight. Tactical flexibility is shown in the *Chronicle* account of the battle of Ashdown and by reports of local militias taking on Viking raiders and defeating them. Indigenous forces were even able to tackle marauding fleets, although the surviving details of such encounters are negligible. Above all, perhaps, Insular armies were supported by the wealth of agricultural surplus that these fertile lands produced. If that wealth had been targeted by raiders over several decades, it had by no means been exhausted—yet.

The Insular military response was, even so, hampered by significant disadvantages. As Ryan Lavelle points out in his survey of Alfred's campaigns, generals are always guilty of fighting their last war.[9] In the days of Ecgberht and even Æðelwulf, opponents had played by the same rules. Kings' retinues met at the sorts of places where battles had traditionally been fought: river crossings on ancient routes, on borders, or sites with a bit of elbow room.

Shield walls formed, pressing for advantage; skirmishes and duels were fought; the army that held the field claimed the victory. The victors claimed tribute and bragging rights. Superiority over neighbouring territory was affirmed by raiding, by exchange of hostages and by dynastic marriage, sealing a tributary alliance. Viking armies, increasingly large, battle-hardened and effective, brought a new set of hit-and-run tactics. They came, initially, for cash and slaves, and proved perfidious in negotiations even if, on the Continent, they periodically acted as allies or auxiliaries of one or other Frankish faction.

And then, the opportunity afforded by Viking raids for Insular warlords to press their own historical claims, to kick old enemies while they were down, sometimes prevented the sort of co-operation that would have made a Christian alliance (for want of a better phrase) more initially effective. The combined Mercian–West Saxon offensive against the Host in 868, before the freshly turfed ramparts of Nottingham, may have failed in its objective but it demonstrated that a united show of strength could halt the Danish advance.

More compromising was the tradition by which the men of the mustered *fyrð*, in a world overwhelmingly dominated by the cycles of the farming season, left the field of battle and returned to their land when need arose: at harvest time, in autumn to turn their pigs into the woods and slaughter beasts; in spring to sow their corn and weed their fields. An enemy that increasingly over-wintered on British soil, that raided and fought throughout the year, posed a significant economic and military threat, to which Insular military leaders were, at first, painfully slow to respond.

The system of 'common burdens', first attested at a synod held by King Æðelbald of Mercia at Gumley in 749 and re-affirmed in Offan charters from the 790s, by which free men* were obliged

---

* It is not entirely clear just what constituted 'free men' in this period: *ceorls*, freemen and sokemen are terms that imply various levels of dependence on a lord.

to serve in the *fyrð* and assist in the repair and construction of bridges and fortifications was, in Wessex and elsewhere in Britain, in its infancy. As Bede had warned early in the eighth century, the extensive and increasingly secularist acquisition of land by minsters meant that estates once held of the king in return for military service were now largely held without such obligations and were prone to be retained by the abbot's or abbess's family: that is the overwhelming testimony of the charters. The events of the decade 870–880 show that attempts to impose the Mercian idea of the common burdens on the shires of Wessex, Sussex, Kent and Devon were by no means met with enthusiasm. It is ironic that the minsters, the most successful centres of production and consumption, should have disproportionately attracted the interest of the raiders. For a while, kings might have felt grim satisfaction that the church should be forced to give up so much of the wealth that had once belonged to them.

In 872, after the fall of Northumbria, East Anglia and parts of Mercia, the colonization of Shetland and Orkney, the Hebrides, the Western Isles and Man, the destruction of the old Gaelic overlordship of Dál Riata and of the British kingdom of Strathclyde, fortunes lay finely balanced between foes of contrasting motivations and capabilities but broadly equal in strength.

Ælfred made peace with the Host (for an undisclosed amount of silver—perhaps several thousand pounds of it) after a year in the field had exhausted both sides. In 872 the *mycel here* left London and moved north, constructing a camp on a natural rise, often cut off by flood waters, overlooking the River Trent at Torksey in Lindsey, a few miles north-west of Lincoln.* Here they overwintered. Thousands of finds, located during a collaborative

---

* Originally *Turcesige*, Turoc's island. A new article by Dawn Hadley and Julian Richards (2016) outlines the recent work there.

project between archaeologists and metal detector-users, have shown that the camp covered well over 100 acres, defended by the waters of the Trent to the west and marshes to the east. Clear evidence of trading, coin striking, smithing, textile production (and plenty of after-hours gaming) show that the Host was no mere army but a complete community on the move, numbering comfortably in the thousands. A thriving pottery industry grew up here from the period of Scandinavian occupation onwards, capitalizing on its excellent trading links and on the bounty of cash that the victorious raiders carried with them.

Torksey's brilliant strategic location shows the army to have planned their move with careful consideration: the village lies at the confluence of the Trent and the Fossdyke, the Roman canal that connected it with the former *colonia* at Lincoln. It controlled access upriver to Nottingham and the Trent headwaters,

16.
THE LOCK
AT TORKSEY,
Lincolnshire,
where the Roman
Fossdyke meets
the River Trent,
and where the *mycel
here* set up camp
in 872.

and along the main road between Lindsey and the Humber. Its pivotal role was valued and remembered for generations: at the time of the Domesday survey the inhabitants of Torksey bore special responsibility for accompanying royal messengers to York 'with their ships and their means of navigation'.[10]

Until this point the status of Northumbria is unclear. The Host seems initially to have appointed a puppet administration. But the thirteenth-century chronicler Roger of Wendover, apparently drawing on earlier sources now lost, recorded that in 872 the Northumbrians 'expelled from the kingdom their king, the Bernician Ecgberht, and Archbishop Wulfhere, who thereupon took themselves to Burghred, king of the Mercians, by whom they were honourably entertained'.[11] In his place, it seems, the Northumbrians chose one Ricsige as their king. This internal coup may have prompted the Host's move north from London; but there is no evidence that they came to York or that an engagement was fought. Roger's account suggests that the Mercians, for their part, made peace with the Host; he adds that Ecgberht died in the same year, but that Archbishop Wulfhere was restored to his see. However one tries to bring these undercurrents into focus, they remain defiantly obscure: we might surmise that Ricsige was a Deiran rival of Ecgberht; but we do not know what the Host's leaders thought of the new king or the flitting of the archbishop. The lack of recorded military campaigns in 872 suggests that all sides were considering their options. The marvellous French phrase *reculer pour mieux sauter*, 'to draw back in order to take a better jump', which has no adequate English counterpart, about sums it up.

The decisive move came late in 873 when the Host, perhaps leaving a significant section of their camp followers behind at Torksey, and for the moment ignoring events further north, took to their ships once more and sailed upriver along the Trent to Repton (*Hreopedun*) in the heart of ancient Mercia. Here they established another fortified camp and, in the bald statement of the West Saxon chroniclers, 'took winter quarters, and drove king Burghred overseas... and conquered the entire kingdom'.[12] It was a stunning military coup. All the chroniclers agree that Burghred cut his losses and travelled to Rome, where he died and was buried in St Mary's church in the *Schola Saxonum*, the English quarter. His queen, Æðelswið, King Ælfred's sister, is said to have died at Pavia in 888. In Burghred's place the Host 'gave the government of the kingdom of Mercia into the hands of Ceolwulf, a foolish king's thegn'[13]—that is to say, to a compliant native.

St Wystan's church at Repton, perched on the south side of the Trent overlooking its flood plain, and in the Viking Age directly fronting onto the river, was a royal cult centre of the so-called 'W'

17.
THE CRYPT
at St Wystan's church,
Repton: 'earthy
arboreal elegance and
candy twist columns'.

dynasty of Mercian kings from the time of Æðelbald in the eighth
century, and the crypt miraculously survives.* The site, part of
a probable royal minster complex, was excavated by pioneering
urban archaeologists Martin Biddle and the late Birthe Kjølbye-
Biddle.[14] The camp here is the only Viking fort in England to
have been systematically excavated. The *mycel here* may or may
not have destroyed the minster as a functioning religious and
economic unit; what is certain is that they did not destroy the
church, but improvised brilliantly, incorporating it into a defensive rampart of the classic Viking D-shape, so that its north and
south doors became the fort's impregnable gateway; the church
itself their military HQ.

Early antiquarian investigations in the area around the church
encountered ancient graves and recovered two swords and a
'bearded axe' of Viking type. The massive ditch dug to create
the defended enclosure was first located in 1974, much of its
course later traced by geophysical survey. When first constructed
it enclosed an area of more than 3½ acres (1.4 hectares: tiny by
comparison to the camp at Torksey); not remotely large enough
to accommodate the entire Host. Within the enclosure several
burials were recovered accompanied by weapons—including one
exhibiting unhealed battle injuries and another buried with a
Thor's hammer pendant around his neck and a boar's tusk placed
between his thighs.

In the 1980s excavation of a mound lying to the west of the
church, which had been reported and investigated on several
occasions over the centuries, dramatically revealed the remains
of another 249 bodies interred in the ruins of a stone building.
The bones seem once to have been grouped around a single individual in a stone coffin. There can be little doubt, from the coin
and weapon evidence, that several of the bodies were those of

---

* Lost but rediscovered in 1779 when the ground gave way beneath a gravedigger.
  Stroud 1999, 6.

warriors, the fallen dead of the Host's campaign—perhaps those slain in the assault on Repton itself. The identity of the individual around whom they clustered has been the subject of much speculation: was it one of the kings of the *mycel here*—perhaps the remains of Bacseg, who had died gloriously at Ashdown? The archaeologist Julian Richards has suggested that the other bodies were those of monks and nuns belonging to the minster: an example of submission to the conquerors in death?[15]

Today the scene of this extraordinary episode, through which the church survived and survives, is a quiet grassy corner of the north Midlands, graced with tombstones and immense lime trees and overlooked by the buildings of Repton's famous, very English public school. The intimate, almost claustrophobic crypt, with its narrow staircase, its quiet dank air and the earthy arboreal elegance of its candy twist columns, is perhaps the most evocative contemporary space in which one can contemplate the clash of alien worlds: sacred and profane, martial and monastic, exclusive and intrusive.

Less than 3 miles (5 km) away, in a forestry plantation from the edge of which the spire of Repton's church can clearly be seen, lies a unique monument to the Host. Heath Wood in the Viking Age was, as its name suggests, open heathland looking down across the Trent valley. At some time in the late ninth century fifty-nine mounds were thrown up over the cremated remains of warriors (some accompanied by swords and, occasionally, shields) and their wives.[16] In some cases, perhaps the founding deposits, the mound covered the site of a cremation pyre, complete with animal parts: horses, dogs (as guides to take them to Valhalla?), cows and sheep—possibly the remains of funeral feasting. In others, the cremation must have taken place elsewhere, with a portion of the remains brought to this sacred spot for burial among an élite group: those who would not assimilate with the native Christians and who wished to maintain a distinct identity in death, as in life. Heath Wood is the only Viking cremation cemetery in the British Isles: some small corner of a foreign field that is forever Scandinavia.*

The Host's relations with their new Mercian client, Ceolwulf, have excited some debate. The *Anglo-Saxon Chronicle*, with its West Saxon perspective, called him a foolish thegn, but his poor historical reputation is mitigated by several factors. The name suggests that he may have belonged to a branch of the 'C' dynasty of the ancient Hwicce and that he might, therefore, have been a descendant of Ceolwulf I (821–823), brother of Coenwulf (796–821). He managed to survive, it is thought, until 879; there is no evidence of any attempt to depose him before that.[17] The *Annales Cambriae* record that in 878 Rhodri Mawr, the powerful king of Gwynedd, was defeated in battle and killed, along with his son, by the Saxons (that is to say, the Mercians) so Ceolwulf II evidently felt sufficiently confident to take on his old enemy and win.† No mere foolish thegn, then.

More significantly, a hoard of coins and hacksilver discovered by James Mather in Watlington, Oxfordshire in 2015,‡ consisting of 186 coins, seven items of jewellery and fifteen ingots, includes silver pennies minted jointly by Ceolwulf and Ælfred during the 870s.[18] Some of these show the two kings side by side: the so-called 'Two emperors' style, in imitation of late Roman issues. The alliance forged at Nottingham and sealed by marriage had survived the fall of East Mercia and Burghred's exile; was thriving,

---

* It must be one of the most poorly curated of our national monuments: when I visited in the late winter of 2016–17 part of the site was being used for feeding pheasants; quad bike tracks wove in and out between the barely visible bracken-covered mounds; there was no signage at all.

† Rhodri, according to the *Annals of Ulster*, had briefly been in exile in Ireland during that year, 'in flight from the Dark Foreigners'—that is to say, from Ceolwulf's Viking overlords, the *mycel here*.

‡ The hoard was—admirably—reported to the authorities and subsequently block-lifted for laboratory excavation.

even. One might even go so far as to suggest that Burghred's 'retirement' and Ceolwulf's elevation were acceptable to all parties, Mercian, West Saxon and Viking, at least for the time being. On Ælfred's part, the quality of the coinage, up to more than 90 per cent pure silver from an earlier, very debased 15–20 per cent, implies that he had already begun to undertake economic reforms and understood the value (in every sense) of a trusted currency.[19] It may also be significant that many of the coins in the Watlington hoard were minted in London, that oft-disputed location on the Wessex–Mercian border.

After a year encamped at Repton the *mycel here* seems to have split into its two component parts. That under Hálfdan, which had been on the move for nearly a decade, moved to Northumbria to pick up the reins of overlordship. The so-called Summer Host, which had arrived to reinforce it at Reading in 871, went from Repton to Cambridge (*Grantebrycge*) and stayed there for a year. The *Chronicle* reports that it was led by three kings: Guðrum, Oscytel and Anund.

Hálfdan's arrival in Northumbria with the original *mycel here* was no mere overwintering. The Host 'overran that land, and made frequent raids against the Picts and against the Strathclyde Britons'.[20] The *Annals of Ulster* record that during this campaign, which may have lasted the whole year, Hálfdan killed a son of Óláfr, a Dublin Viking; that there was a great battle between the Dubhgaill* and the Picts. This may be the battle at Dollar

---

* The Dubhgaill, or 'Dark foreigners', seem to have been so labelled to distinguish them from the Finngaill, or 'Fair foreigners' by the Irish. It is dangerous to make too many assumptions about the precise connotations of the words, but the Finngaill are generally associated with the original invaders who had established Dublin in the 840s; the Dubhgaill with the Host which had crossed from the Continent to England in the 860s. This, incidentally, is the last contemporary mention of the Picts or Pictavia as a people or kingdom.

18. 'HÁLFDAN SHARED OUT the lands of the Northumbrians.'
The dales of the North York Moors abound in Scandinavian place names.

(*Dolaír*) recorded by the *Chronicle of the Kings of Alba,* in which the Pictavian army was annihilated. Constantín mac Cináeda was killed, perhaps in the same battle.[21]

The *Anglo-Saxon Chronicle* entry for 875 is just as momentous:

> *7 þy geare Healfdene Norþanhymbra lond gedælde 7 ergende wæron 7 hiera tilgende.*
>
> And in this year Hálfdan shared out the lands of the Northumbrians, and they were engaged in ploughing and making a living for themselves.

Two significant details are added to this bald account by the chronicler of St Cuthbert's community, then in exile from its island home on Lindisfarne. First, he recorded that 'Hálfdan, king of the Danes, entered the Tyne and sailed as far as *Wircesforda*, devastating and sinning cruelly against St Cuthbert'. Second, in a later chapter of the *Historia*, he recorded that one part of the Host 'rebuilt York, cultivated the surrounding land and settled there'.[22] *Wircesforda* cannot now be identified, although the topography of the Tyne suggests that Newburn, regarded as having been close to the tidal reach of the river and the site of its lowest ford, fits the bill: it may have been a royal estate from as early as the seventh century, when a famous marriage took place at a site called by Bede *Ad Muram,* 12 miles (20 km) inland from the coast.[23]

As for the sharing out of land, this episode has provoked considerable debate: did the Danish army dispossess the inhabitants of the Vale of York, driving them off their estates into exile; did they find land that had been vacated during the civil wars of the previous decade and claim it; or did they, perhaps, purchase estates from native lords with the hard cash weighing so heavily in their treasure chests?

Assumptions about the behaviour of invading armies underlie most attempts to resolve this question. The *Historia*'s 'sinning cruelly against St Cuthbert' may be taken to imply theft of property; but as we have seen there are virtually no Scandinavian names north of the Tees: northern Northumbria, ancient Bernicia, was not settled by Viking veterans. There is a certain military logic in the idea of planting one's veterans on land surrounding the military headquarters if, as it seems, York's wall were refortified at this time—the Romans provide a precise precedent with their *coloniae*. That the militarization of southern Northumbria was materially destructive, there is little doubt: virtually nothing survives of York's great Anglo-Saxon library.[24]

The intentions of the Host and its surviving king seem clear: they decided to make York their home, rather than return to their Scandinavian homeland. The best prospects for their survival and wealth lay north of the Humber and south of the Tyne, in a land where opposition was weak or non-existent. One of the principal drivers for the Scandinavian exodus in the ninth and tenth centuries seems to have been the poor economic prospects of its young male nobility, with critically limited supplies of fertile agricultural lands and few opportunities to acquire them. The lands between Tyne and Humber, long tamed by the plough or cleared of trees for pasture, and with excellent communications, would do very nicely.*

The place-name evidence, which tells of a Bernicia un-settled by Norse speakers, is just as eloquent for their arrival in substantial numbers south of the River Tees; not just as lords but as free farmers. Telltale suffixes like *–by* and *–thorpe*, and the merging of Scandinavian personal names with the Old English suffix *–tun* (the so-called 'Grimston hybrids') testify to the presence of Norse speakers whose founding of new settlements and acquisition of existing farms and estates has left a permanent mark on the

---

* The low-lying Vale of York itself remained a largely uncultivable zone, prone to frequent flooding; but the climate of the ninth century was warming and drying, opening it up to enterprising farmers.

Yorkshire landscape.* Large estates surviving north of the Tyne as 'shires' well into the medieval period show that the essential structure of land-holding evident in Bede's day was fundamentally unaffected by Scandinavian settlement, as we might expect from the absence of Norse names; the opposite argument applies in Yorkshire and the northern counties of the Midlands, where such large landholdings seem to have become fragmented during this period. Smaller estates passed into the ownership of larger numbers of farmers.

Many of the forty-two 'Grimston-type' names occurring in Yorkshire, generally on good fertile land that must already have been farmed for centuries, are probably best interpreted as new holdings carved out of originally larger estates by a first wave of settlers: the veterans themselves.[25] Perhaps not just any veterans, but the wealthier or more senior members of the *mycel here*. Place names ending in the suffix –*by*, meaning farmstead, are more numerous—more than 200 of them in Yorkshire survived to the time of the Domesday survey of the 1080s. I have already suggested elsewhere that Danby Dale, a valley which cuts deep into the north edge of the North York Moors, with its regular layout of identikit farm holdings, might represent the settling of a self-contained war band.[26]

The –*by*s tend to lie on slightly less favourable land than their Grimston counterparts (one thinks of a Viking equivalent of NCOs: tough, practical, well-organized men capable of turning their skills to hard graft and mutual co-operation; of turning mediocre land into something productive). The –*thorpe* names, of which 150 were recorded in the Domesday survey, seem to be settlements on the least fertile land; they show a high incidence of desertion and failure in the later medieval period. So it looks as though there was a stratification among the immigrant

* For a more nuanced and detailed discussion, see Townend 2014, 101ff.

population reflecting the social orders of the Host and its affiliates. We might, too, be seeing some chronological dilation, with the least attractive land being left over for the late arrivers. And it would be wrong to suppose that all the land settled by Scandinavians involved displacement. A complex pattern of fragmentation, piecemeal acquisition and gradual purchase (the spending of all that ready cash) or inheritance through marriage into local families, has the ring of truth.

That women formed, or came to form, a substantial stratum of the immigrant population is attested by finds of jewellery, especially brooches, of distinctive Scandinavian or Anglo-Scandinavian style. To date no genetic study has been able to detect a distinct Scandinavian presence in the areas settled by Vikings; but then, the genetic difference between a Jutland Viking and an Englishman or woman whose ancestors had come originally from Angeln or Saxony is not very great. Although many scholars now accept numbers for the immigrant population of the late ninth and tenth centuries in the tens or scores of thousands there are still those who argue for many fewer.

Some immigrants may have taken the opportunity afforded by the settlement of the *mycel here* in Northumbria to escape the chaos of civil war in Norway. After a great battle on Hafrsfjord, near modern Stavanger, in 872, Haraldr *Hárfagri*, Harald 'Fairhair', seems to have imposed his rule on the whole of Norway: he is regarded as its first true king. The first wave of Icelandic settlements dates from these decades and we must suppose that such large dislocations of communities, induced by the civil strife that followed Harald's battle for supremacy, propelled others to seek their fortunes further south and west.

A striking feature of the ninth-century Scandinavian settlements is the dog that did not bark in the night-time: that is, we do not hear of any form of local uprising either by or against the newcomers. There must have been local conflicts, when a farmer was ejected from his family holding or when disputes over boundaries boiled over into violence. Theft, homicide, rape and especially livestock rustling seem to have been endemic in Early Medieval society. But there is no record of concerted rebellion against Danish rule by a militia; no pitched battle between native and foreign villagers. All the evidence, documentary and archaeological, suggests that after the raiding and conquest came peace and integration, and that the integration was rapid. There is mounting evidence that native and incomer could understand one another.* This comes, partly, from cognate substitution: an Anglo-Saxon place name substituted by a Norse version which retained the original meaning; partly from words being loaned both ways between Old English and Old Norse; and partly from names that survived side by side in both languages.[27] The historian of these developments, Matthew Townend, argues that much of the North was bilingual during the late ninth and tenth centuries and that, crucially, there seems to have been no social prejudice between the two groups, as there was later between Old English and Norman French.[28] As for the veteran warlord Hálfdan, the *Historia* records enthusiastically that after his insults to St Cuthbert on the River Tyne he began to 'rave and reek so badly that his whole army drove him from its midst'.[29] More prosaically, the *Annals of Ulster* record his death in 877 in a skirmish with the Finngaill on *Loch Cuan*—Strangford Lough.

If the military and cultural fate of southern Northumbria was sealed by the events of 875, a much more fluid situation was developing in the south. The so-called Summer Host, under its three commanders, lay camped at Cambridge, presumably living off tribute exacted from East Anglian bishops, thegns and

---

* At least two Scandinavian language traditions arrived in the British Isles in the ninth century: Old West Norse (from Norway) and Old East Norse (from Denmark).

their tenants and implementing some sort of administration over that kingless realm through its own jarls or compliant indigenous ealdormen. After 870 two generations of East Anglians had no bishop: the institutional church was relieved of most of its assets and, effectively, dismantled.

The *Anglo-Saxon Chronicle* recorded under 875* that King Ælfred took to the seas and defeated seven ships' companies, capturing one and putting the others to flight. This small fleet may have been a reconnoitring party or a feint, for later in the same year the Host that had been encamped at Cambridge, or a part of it, was able to sail around the south coast and land at Wareham in what is now Dorset, building or restoring a fortification there before local militias could respond. Wareham occupied a key location at the head of Poole harbour: the site of an existing convent and royal estate naturally defended by the Rivers Frome and Piddle.

Ælfred was unable to take Wareham, just as the combined forces of Mercia and Wessex had been confounded before the ramparts of Nottingham. He must then have offered tribute in return for a promise to leave Wessex. The treaty was reinforced, if we are to believe Asser, by the swearing of oaths on Christian relics and the exchange of high-ranking hostages. But the *Chronicle* is specific in its description of the use of a sacred ring during the swearing ceremony. Ælfred, aware that Christian relics were not held in great esteem by his opponents, invited them, it seems, to swear on their own holy ring (such an object is attested in *Eyrbyggia Saga*[30] and in the *Historia* of St Cuthbert), to which they had never agreed before. The tenth-century chronicler Æðelweard specifically uses the term *armilla sacra*, a sacred arm-ring.[31]

The Host duly left Wareham in 876; but not, in the event, in great ceremony: they departed secretly, at night, under the noses of the militia, having murdered their West Saxon hostages. They

---

* Asser records the same event under 876.

split into two, a mounted party and a fleet of several hundred ships, with the aim of making a rendezvous some 70 miles (110 km) to the west at Exeter. The former Roman town had been the centre for West Saxon control of Devon for more than a century; St Boniface was educated at the abbey there. But it lay at the distant limit of Ælfred's reach and uncomfortably close to the antipathetic British kingdom of the West Wealas: Cornwall, where Danish forces might expect to recruit allies.

Fortune initially favoured the Host: their mounted force outpaced its West Saxon pursuers and, by the time Ælfred caught up with them, they had fortified themselves within the old Roman walls on the banks of the navigable River Exe. But a storm destroyed 120 of their fleet's ships and Ælfred was able to impose his terms on the remainder. More oaths were sworn; more hostages exchanged. By now the *mycel here* seems to have been under the sole command of Guðrum; the fate of the other members of the triumvirate, Anund and Oscytel, is utterly obscure.

After the stalemate of 871 and the retreat from Reading to London, the Host's ambitions for Wessex had been thwarted; now they must give up a second time in the face of unattractive odds. In 877 they moved from Exeter back into Mercia, where they called in their marker with King Ceolwulf, and 'some of it they shared out and some they gave to Ceolwulf'.[32] Ceolwulf was to rule the western half, while a Scandinavian régime which later became known as the Danelaw was established in the east, based perhaps on the old kingdom of Lindsey and the lower Trent valley. It is not clear from either Asser or the *Chronicle* where the border, if any, was drawn or where they established their base—at Nottingham, perhaps, or further east and south in Cambridge.

The desire to settle appeared, in the first instance, to have overcome the thirst for battle. But if that was the hope of the West Saxons it was illusory:

Her hiene bestæl se here on midne winter ofer tuelfan niht to Cippanhamme, 7 geridon Wesseaxna lond 7 gesæton [7] micel þæs folces [7] ofer sæ adræfdon, 7 þæs oþres þone mæstan dæl hie geridon, 7 him to gecirdon buton þam cyninge Ælfrede. 7 he lytle werede unieþelice æfter wudum for, 7 on morfæstenum.

In this year the Host went secretly in midwinter after Twelfth night to Chippenham and rode over Wessex and occupied it, and drove a great part of the inhabitants overseas, and of the rest the greater part they reduced to submission, except Ælfred the king; and he with a small company moved under difficulties through woods and into inaccessible places in marshes.[33]

In this way the *Anglo-Saxon Chronicle*, closely echoed by Asser, sets the scene for Ælfred's near-nemesis and improbable fightback. Chippenham lies on a defensible inverted U-shaped promontory on the east bank of the Somerset Avon, which issues into the Severn just west of Bristol. The Avon was probably navigable as far as Bath, and it is possible that the standard *modus operandi* of the Scandinavian armies was employed in this devastating and wholly unexpected attack on the heart of Wessex, with their fleet sailing around the south coast and disembarking at the former Roman Spa town. But it was late in the year for those dangerous winter waters. More significant, perhaps, is Chippenham's proximity to the Fosse Way, the direct cross-country Roman road linking Bath with Lincoln, which would allow a mounted force based at, say, Leicester, to achieve its object in two or three days.* Chippenham was a royal estate centre, and Ælfred's sister Æðelswið had been married to King Burghred here: its choice as a target can hardly have been fortuitous, militarily or

---

* Leicester is not mentioned in the *Anglo-Saxon Chronicle* before 914; but by then it was an established Scandinavian town and stronghold, one of the so-called Five Boroughs. Æðelweard's information was that the Host had set up camp at Gloucester in the heart of West Mercia, much closer to the borders of Wessex and more menacing. The route from Gloucester to Chippenham would involve a journey of some 40 miles (65 km) along two Roman roads: a hard day's ride. Campbell 1962, 42.

psychologically. Its capture was a decisive blow struck at a vital organ of the West Saxon state.

We have a good idea of what royal townships like Chippenham might have looked like in the ninth century from the palace and royal hunting lodge excavated at Cheddar in Somerset under Philip Rahtz's direction in the early 1960s.* Like most royal townships of the period, its great hall, 78 feet (24 m) in length, worthy of Beowulf, was undefended apart from a fence and gate, and lay at the heart of a coaxially aligned complex of prestigious wooden buildings (including a chapel and what the excavator interpreted, from its foundation, as a windmill) intended to demonstrate kingly wealth, power and influence. Built at the highest navigable point of the River Axe, Cheddar was mentioned in Ælfred's own will, and hosted a great council or *Witangemot*, three times during the tenth century.[34]

Ælfred's apparent failure to fight the invading force is, on the face of it, inexplicable. His activity in the field since the invasion of 871 shows that he could deploy substantial forces, that he was an active, enterprising commander; and there is no hint in the *Chronicle* that he had, up to that point, lost the support of his closest ealdormen. His alliance with Burghred and then Ceolwulf II had seemed secure. But he had not yet conceived of the unified defence system on which his military and administrative reputation justly rests. Such was the impact of the Host's arrival *en masse* in north-west Wessex that many of the shires seem to have immediately capitulated, submitting to Guðrum and offering him tribute; many of the nobility, we are told, sailed overseas 'through poverty and fear'.[35]

There is a hint of naïvety in Ælfred's repeated attempts to treat the Host as though it was another Anglo-Saxon army, playing by the old rules. The *mycel here* played its own game, and the Insular

---

* See below, Chapter 11.

states seem to have suffered a collective failure of imagination in countering its threat. Ælfred may simply not have anticipated this third, midwinter invasion; if so, he was also guilty of complacency. But there is another possibility: that he was himself at Chippenham, celebrating Christmas with the royal household; if so, he was the target of a bold attempt to literally decapitate the regime. In the chaos of a winter assault, with no army in the field and no means of raising one, there was nothing to be done but flee.

One small clue suggests that a key to the instant fall of Wessex lay in the disloyalty of senior figures among Ælfred's fighting élite. Those of his ealdormen who deserted the king, breaking the fundamental bond of lordship that demanded loyalty in exile, or death, were not forgotten. A charter of 901, a rare survival from the reign of Ælfred's son Eadweard, recalled the forfeiture of an estate in Wiltshire by Ealdorman Wulfhere 'when he deserted without permission both his lord King Ælfred and his country in spite of the oath which he had sworn'.[36] The land in question comprised a smallish holding of ten hides at Wylye—the site of one of the engagements of 871. Wulfhere, it seems, had been ealdorman of Wiltshire during that eventful campaigning year. Did he flee overseas after the assault on Chippenham? Were there others, as the lamenting Asser suggests, including perhaps the disempowered sons of Ælfred's older brothers?* Did one or more of them offer up the intelligence of the king's festive location?

Other events of that winter suggest that the assault on Wessex was co-ordinated, and that we are only seeing a part of the overall picture. The *Chronicle* records the arrival in Devon of a brother of Ívarr and Hálfdan with twenty-three ships and that he was killed along with 800 of his men. Several versions of the *Chronicle* add that the famous raven banner of the Norse armies was captured.

---

* For evidence that this was the case, see below, Chapter 6.

19. RECONSTRUCTION of a Viking period hall
at Fyrkat, near Hobro, Denmark.

If the kingdom of Wessex was on its knees, it was not yet dead.

Asser fills in some of the detail. The brother, whom we might suggest was Ubba, unheard of since the campaign of 871, had overwintered in Dyfed, across the estuary of the River Severn, 'slaughtering many Christians there'. Asser names the fortress which the Norse attacked as *Cynuit* (Countisbury in English), just east of the port at Lynmouth. Drawing, presumably, on knowledge from his own Welsh correspondents and from personal acquaintance with the geography, the Welsh bishop describes how the invaders besieged the naturally defensible position; how the garrison broke out of their hastily prepared defences and 'by virtue of their aggressiveness, from the very outset they overwhelmed the enemy'.[37]

Ælfred's winter in the remote fastnesses of the Somerset levels has become a legendary hero-in-exile tale, like Robert Bruce and the spider or Julius Caesar and the Cilician pirates. For Asser, it is likely to have echoed his belief that Ælfred was a latter-day

King David, the biblical exemplar for youngest sons and righteous giant-slayers. The *Chronicle* is terse in the extreme; but the drama needs no embellishment.

> *7 þæs on Eastron worhte Ælfred cyning lytle werede geweorc æt Æþelingaeigge, 7 of þam geweorce was winnende wiþ þone here, 7 Sumursætna se dæl, se þær niehst wæs.*

And the Easter* after, King Ælfred with a small company built a fortification at Athelney, and from that fortification, with the men of that part of Somerset nearest to it, he continued fighting against the Host.[38]

Athelney is a small prominence in the Somerset levels, still an island in the ninth century and periodically surrounded by floodwaters into recent times. At its highest point it rises no more than 40 feet (12 m) above sea level. It was connected westwards to the small village of Lyng by a causeway, and less than a mile away to the south, on a long spit of higher ground, perches the small village of Stoke St Gregory. It is a landscape of few trees, apart from the ubiquitous pollarded willows that line the innumerable drains and narrow, canalized rivers of the peatlands. Athelney farm, an elegant red brick structure framed by sky and Scots pines, bears a nineteenth-century monument to Ælfred's stay there. From it, on a bleak late winter's morning, the mind's eye allows the flat grassy fields around, drained by innumerable grid lines of catchwater, lode and rhyne fringed with sedge and willows, to disappear beneath dark waters reflecting only matt clouds, and a bleaker aspect for a king without a kingdom can scarcely be imagined.

Æðelweard's *Chronicle* masterfully understates the position: 'King Ælfred, indeed, was then in greater straits than was befitting.'[39] But he adds a significant detail: that the beleaguered king was accompanied by a new ealdorman of Somerset, Æðelnoth, with a 'small force'.[40] Somerset, then, remained loyal. Asser, with

---

* In 878 Easter fell on 23 March.

the benefit of more direct knowledge, describes frequent raiding parties sent out from Athelney to forage and to gather intelligence, not just from the Host but from those who had submitted to the invaders. If, as we understand it, Wiltshire and Hampshire had fallen and only Somerset, Devon and perhaps Dorset remained loyal to Ælfred, his circumstances were straitened indeed.

Remote places, like the haunts of robbers and wild beasts on the moors of Yorkshire[41] or the marshy fenlands of East Anglia, the Vale of York and the Somerset levels, were profitable sources of fear and wonder in the Early Medieval imagination, inhabited by faeries, devils and unspeakable demons. The peaty levels that drained into the Wash—'a dismal fen of immense size' with its 'black waters, overhung by fog'[42]—attracted pilgrims like St Guthlac, seekers after isolation, privation and risk. The great hall at Heorot, *villa regalis* of Beowulf's legendary king Hrothgar, was beset by the abysmal monster Grendel, 'ill-famed haunter of the marches of the land, who kept the moors, the fastness of the fens'.[43]

It is not beyond the realms of possibility, I think, that Grendel is the animal personification of that real killer of the marshes, the malarial mosquito, creeping up on unsuspecting warriors and carrying them off in their fighting prime, deprived of the glory of death in battle, to his grisly underworld. Recent research has shown a potentially very high level of mortality from malarial fever in Early Medieval fenlands.[44] In mythologizing Ælfred's sojourn in these lonely and unhealthy landscapes his hagiographers were not just preparing the ground for his miraculous survival and improbable final triumph; they were also tapping the dark recesses of the Early Medieval psyche.

Within half a day's ride (or punt) of Athelney, settlements at Taunton and Somerton, from which the county derives its name, were Ælfred's nearest sources for news and provisions. Landing stages at Stathe, below the spit on which Stoke St Gregory stands, and Langport, a little further up the River Parrett, gave navigable access to the Severn estuary from Bridgewater Bay. The king's personal retinue, his *comites*, and members of the shire thegnage, made up a meagre force. He was now forced to learn the same tactics of guerrilla warfare so adeptly practised by his enemies. Asser, recording the foundation of a monastery there in later years, describes Ælfred's construction of a fortress at the western end of the causeway at Lyng, with a smaller redoubt on Athelney itself. A natural prominence, Burrow Mump, lay just across the river, and it is often suggested that Ælfred was able to maintain a lookout here. To be sure, it offers a splendid prospect of the countryside for many miles around; the remains of a small chapel stand on its summit, looking like a miniature copy of the famous tor at Glastonbury.

The *Historia* of St Cuthbert's community, suffering its own travails hundreds of miles to the north, maintained a story that their saint appeared to Ælfred during those desperate days. The king, we are told, sent his men out fishing one day, leaving behind his wife Ælswið and a servant. A stranger appeared and asked the king for food. Being a good Christian, Ælfred shared with the man his last loaf and the little wine which he had left. The stranger subsequently disappeared; the servant came back to find the loaf whole again. Later, the king's men returned with three boats full of fish—an appropriate haul, perhaps, for an Easter miracle. That night, while the rest of the household was asleep, a great light shone like the sun on the troubled king and an old priest appeared in the apparel of a bishop. Introducing himself as Cuthbert, a soldier of Christ, the visitor confirmed that he was the stranger whom Ælfred had seen earlier. He promised to be the king's shield and sword in the fight to come; that the West Saxons would be victorious; that, in fact, Ælfred, his sons and their sons would be kings of all Britain.[45] Like King David, his throne would be established forever.

Those acquainted with Bede's eighth-century account of a visionary appearance by Bishop Paulinus before the exiled ætheling Edwin Yffing in his great hour of need at the court of King Rædwald, and with Adomnán's miracle concerning Oswald's vision the night before battle at Heavenfield in 634,[46] will recognize in the Cuthbert tale a hagiographic trope which cannot be taken at face value, evocative and appealing as it is. For the fascinating solution to the question of why Cuthbert should appear to Ælfred, one has to look at the career of his grandson, Æðelstan.*

There is another, more familiar tale relating to the Athelney exile: it involves cakes, the scolding wife of a swineherd and an admonishment by a Cornish saint, better known from the town that bears his name in Huntingdonshire and to which his relics would one day be transferred. The story is found in the late tenth- or early eleventh-century *Vita Prima Sancti Neoti* (First life of St Neot). Like Cuthbert, St Neot appears to Ælfred during his stay on Athelney and promises victory in return for his future patronage. The tale has no credence except insofar as the Æthelney episode became and remained a suitable legend for including in great stories from the past, and as a retrospective means of linking royal fortunes with saintly virtues.† Ælfred's humility when confronted with his baking *faux pas* fits nicely with his elevation, many centuries later, as England's only king worthy of the epithet 'Great'. As historian Barbara Yorke and my colleague Joy Rutter have both pointed out, Ælfred's failure to earn the status of a Christian saint (by virtue of avoiding martyrdom in battle against the heathen) allowed sixteenth- and seventeenth-century English Protestants to co-opt him as a virtuous prototype, to which they attached all sorts of libertarian and republican values

---

* See below, Chapter 10.

† The story is discussed fully in Keynes and Lapidge 1983, Appendix 1. The widespread early acceptance of the story as a 'real' event came about through its shameless copying by Matthew Parker into his original edition of Asser's *Life* in 1574.

entirely inappropriate to the ninth century. His alleged common touch, so perfectly expressed by his humility in the cake-burning episode, suited their purpose very well.[47]After Easter 878, then, Ælfred built a small fortification at Athelney, from where he seems to have sent out a stream of intelligence-gathering and ambassadorial messengers as well as raiding parties intended as much, one imagines, to raise morale among his household troops and those who had submitted to the Host, as to actually engage their forces. Abandoned by many of his ealdormen and, on the face of it, by impotent Mercian allies, cut off from eastern Wessex, from London and from the sub-kingdoms of Kent and Sussex, one imagines that Ælfred's primary concern was to find out who might rise with him against the Host. A story preserved in William of Malmesbury's *Gesta Regum Anglorum* has the king himself, disguised as a jongleur and minstrel (another biblical echo of King David), spying on the enemy in their camp at Chippenham. It is probably wishful thinking on William's part; and yet, that sort of escapade cannot be ruled out—later wars inspired many such acts of derring-do.[48]

In the second week of May 878, with spring's greenery bursting everywhere and roads and fords now passable, Ælfred made a rendezvous, with those shire forces on whose support he could still rely, at a place called Ecgberht's stone (*Ecgbryhtes stane*), in the eastern part of Selwood, a great expanse of woodland. The consensus seems to be that the stone lay (possibly lies) in the proximity of the three-shire boundary between Dorset, Somerset and Wiltshire just north of Bourton.* The name *Ecgbryhtes stane* suggests that it had been a muster site in the days

---

* By chance, I encountered the owner of the land on which a small undistinguished stone, no more than 3 feet (1 m) tall, stands by a running brook, the nascent River Stour, in the hamlet of Penselwood. Peter Fitzgerald very kindly told me what he knows of the site called Ecgberht's stone, and pointed out to me a small artificial mound close by, which might serve very well for a muster point. A more discreet location is hard to imagine.

of Ælfred's grandfather. The distance from Athelney is about 31 miles (50 km): two days' march or a day's hard ride almost dead east, using ancient roads through Selwood and perhaps passing beneath the magnificent ramparts of South Cadbury hillfort, gathering recruits and precious news of the enemy's movements along the way. Shire boundaries were very often used as meeting places; and the additional advantage of Bourton is its discreet setting in a narrow vale on the south-west corner of a broad expanse of downland. Here Ælfred must have nervously counted numbers; Asser, with the benefit of triumphalist hindsight, says that when those forces who had come to the muster saw the king, receiving him (not surprisingly) as if one restored to life after such great tribulations, they were filled with immense joy.[49]

Ælfred now moved decisively in the knowledge that his intelligence was sound; that he had sufficient forces to strike back against the Host. The day after the muster, the whole army marched north-east across country to a place that Asser identifies as Iley Oak: Eastleigh wood, just north-west of the village of Sutton Veny, overlooking the River Wylye. From Bourton to Wylye, the same river on which the engagement at Wilton had taken place in 871, is about 12 miles (20 km) over downs that rise to 800 feet (245 m) above Kingston Deverill. It is a wold landscape of plateaux dissected by mostly dry valleys and peppered with the remains of Neolithic long barrows and Bronze Age tumuli. The River Wylye runs north through those downs until, at Warminster, it executes a smart right turn, opens out into a broader flood plain, and flows south-east towards Wilton, the sometime shire town and battle site of 871. On a wooded hill overlooking the crook of the river's bend lies the site of the Iley Oak, an ancient meeting place where one can imagine the last of Ælfred's forces joining his army, and where news of the Host's position must have been obtained.*

* Now an undistinguished plantation whose northern edge is truncated by a cutting carrying the A36 trunk road.

7 þæs ymb ane to Eþandune, 7 þær gefeaht wiþ alne þone here, 7
hiene gefliemde, 7 him æfter rad oþ þæt geweorc.

And one day later [he went] to Edington and there he fought
against the entire Host and put it to flight; and pursued it up
to the fortification.[50]

Thus runs the infuriatingly brief account of Ælfred's greatest
battle in the *Anglo-Saxon Chronicle*. Edington is the generally
recognized location for *Eþandune*, 6 miles (10 km) north-east
of the site of the Iley Oak, Ælfred's pre-battle camp. It lies at
the foot of a north-facing scarp on the edge of Salisbury Plain.
Edington Hill, a plausible site for the actual battle, lies at about
650 feet (200 m) overlooking, to the north, the broad vale of
the River Avon. A long, deeply incised hollow way leads up from
the village onto the plateau, evidence of its ancient use as a cattle droveway. Chippenham, the Host's base, lay 16 miles (25 km)
further north, quite visible from the breast of the scarp across the
broad valley of the Avon. The broad, open country of the downs
was the preferred terrain of the Anglo-Saxon armies, able to survey the whole field at once and deploy the long interlocking line
of their shield wall. It is hard to say whether armies agreed the
sites for their set-piece showdowns or whether the Host, anticipating Ælfred's advance from its own intelligence, intercepted
him before he could march on Chippenham.

My sense is that the two armies agreed to meet, each willing to gamble all for the highest possible stakes as they had at
Ashdown in 871. But apart from Asser's unhelpful description of
the king 'fighting fiercely with a compact shield wall'[51] we know
nothing of the progress of the battle for Wessex, except that the
West Saxons prevailed and were able to pursue the Host back
to their fortification—either a hilltop summer camp close by, or
Chippenham itself. If the former, then Bratton camp, an impressive Iron Age enclosure with substantial ramparts, overlooking
the vale from the same escarpment a mile and a half (2 km) to the

south-west of Edington, suggests itself.*

Ælfred's advantages lay in his command of an army defending its homeland and in the tactical superiority of Anglo-Saxon open-field warfare against a marine assault force honed to perfection in the art of raiding. With them he achieved the ultimate objective of freeing Wessex from Danish domination and military peril. Such was the disarray of the Host that many of them were cut down during the retreat. Their horses and cattle were seized and West Saxon forces laid siege to their defences; the Host was unable to acquire reinforcements or escape. After fourteen days during which, Asser says, the Host was worn down by fear, cold and hunger, they capitulated. Ælfred took hostages, forced on them a promise to leave Wessex for good and imposed on their king, Guðrum, a personal commitment to submit to baptism at the king's own hand, as his sponsor and godfather.[52]

There is potentially a significant hole in the West Saxon accounts of Edington. The historian Janet Nelson has offered the intriguing possibility that those coins issued jointly by Ælfred and Ceolwulf as co-emperors might have been a special issue, struck in the aftermath of Edington's triumph. In that case, it might be necessary to allow for West Mercian participation in the battle, and a considerable adjustment of the traditional Ælfredan narrative which insists on the West Saxon king standing alone against a pagan foe.[53] Ceolwulf's death, soon after, allowed his role as the joint saviour of Wessex to be written out of history.

Everything about Asser's account suggests to me that the Host were not able to retreat as far as Chippenham. To begin with, a rout of 16 miles (25 km) after a desperate battle seems unfeasibly long. And then, the circumstances of the siege suggest that the Vikings were poorly provisioned inside their fortress: no garrison to support them and counterattack; no access to boats.

* The great white horse carved into the chalk of its steep west flank is no earlier than the seventeenth or eighteenth century.

20. ISLAND FORTRESSES in the Somerset levels:
the monument at Athelney Farm, with Burrow Mump in the distance.

Chippenham, one imagines, after a five-month occupation, would have been set up as a major fortification with stores, access routes in and out and efficient intelligence-gathering: it was, after all, a royal township designed to receive goods and people from a wide surrounding territory. And, if Ceolwulf's Mercian forces were present, they must have overrun the defences before the Host could retire there. A short siege and capitulation after two weeks suggests an ill-prepared redoubt, not the headquarters of a battle-hardened, highly experienced army. The Iron Age fortress on Bratton Hill fits Asser's account.

The defeated Host was allowed, in due course, to return to Chippenham, one imagines under a very tight escort. A month after the battle Guðrum and thirty of his retinue came to Aller, east across the Parrett from Athelney, where he was baptized and took the Christian name Æðelstan. The ceremony ended eight days later at Wedmore, no more than a few miles to the north and close to the royal palace at Cheddar, after which twelve days of feasting consolidated the outbreak of peace, and the senior commanders of the Host were given treasures. This was an education, for Scandinavian warrior raiders, of how Anglo-Saxon kingship worked: the bonds of Christendom, the giving of lavish gifts and the eternal obligation of the servant to his lord; magnanimity in victory; legitimacy. The divinity of the king's appointment and the strength of the Christian oath were messages swallowed with copious mead, celebratory songs and the mutual respect of veteran heroes of the fight.

Guðrum was now being brought into the fold of the universal church and the family of European Christian kings as one of their own. His baptismal name, too, is significant. Ælfred had an older brother of the same name, and a grandson too. If Guðrum was submitting to the West Saxon king as his overlord, then Ælfred, equally, recognized the reborn Æðelstan as a king in his own right. But king of what?

PART

II

Newton's cradle
879–918

TIMELINE 2

879 to 918

Unless otherwise stated,
narrative source entries are from
the ASC Parker 'A' text.

ABBREVIATIONS

AC – *Annales Cambriae*
ASC – *Anglo-Saxon Chronicle*
Æðelweard – *Chronicon*
Asser – *Life of King Ælfred*
AU – *Annals of Ulster*
CKA – *Chronicle of the Kings of Alba*
EHD – *English Historical Documents*
FA – *Fragmentary Annals*
HSC – *Historia de Sancto Cuthberto*
LDE – *Symeon's Libellus de Exordio*

879   Viking army relocates to East Anglia and 'occupied that land and shared it out'; probable death of Ceolwulf II, King of Mercia.

881   **Battle of Conwy**: defeat of Mercians (AC) under Ealdorman Æðelred.

883   Guðrøðr episode in the HSC; reigns in southern Northumbria to 895. Possible date for relocation of the St Cuthbert community to Chester le Street.

885   Asser comes to the court of King Ælfred in Wessex; takes up residence in 886 (Asser).

886   Ælfred takes London from Danes and gives it into the care of Ealdorman Æðelred. Possible date for marriage alliance of Æðelflæd with Æðelred.

890   King Guðrum (baptized Æðelstan) dies; succeeded in East Anglia by Eohric to 904.

    —Plegmund becomes archbishop of Canterbury (to 923).

892   Famine in north-east Francia; the Franks give Vikings 250 ships to leave the Seine; they sail to the mouth of the River Lympne in Kent; eighty more ships arrive under Hæsten from the Loire and sail up the Thames. Start of a two-year military campaign against Wessex.

893   Probable date of composition of Asser's *Life of King Ælfred*. Viking armies campaign across south Britain and are defeated in several battles and skirmishes, ending in 896 (ASC and Æðelweard). Possible date for original compilation of the *Anglo-Saxon Chronicle*.

894   The Host sails up the River Lea to Hertford. Ælfred brings the *fyrð* into the area in late summer to protect the harvesting of crops, and begins construction of a bridge and double fort across the Lea. The Host decamps and marches west as far as Bridgnorth where it overwinters.

895   Death of Guðrøðr, leader of the Northumbrian Vikings (Æðelweard). Probably succeeded by Sigfrøðr to 900.

896   The Host disperses; some stay and settle; others return overseas.

899   King Ælfred dies on 26 October; succeeded by son Eadweard 'the Elder'.

       —Possible date for the 'Arrangements for the building of fortifications at Worcester' (EHD).

900   King Eadweard inaugurated at the tide stone, Kingston on Thames.

       —Likely dendrochronology date for the construction of the Gokstad ship.

       —Death of Domnall mac Constantín (AU), killed by Vikings at Dunottar (CKA); accession of Constantín mac Áeda (to 943).

902   Overkings of Brega and Leinster attack Dublin and force its leaders out (AU).

       —Norse migration begins from Ireland to Wirral. Norse under Ingimundr invade Anglesey (AC; FA).

       —Subsequently Æðelflæd grants lands around Chester to Ingimundr's followers (FA).

903   Date after which the Cuerdale hoard of silver and coins was deposited in Ribbledale in a lead-lined chest.

904   Norse army slain at Straith Erenn [Stratheran or Strathdearn] (CKA). Ívarr, grandson of Ívarr, killed by the men of Fortriu (AU).

—Rebellion by pretender Æðelwold ends in his death at the **Battle of the Holme** (902 in Æðelweard and ASC 'C').

906 Constantín mac Áeda promulgates laws of Alba at Scone (CKA).

—Eadweard 'compelled' to make peace with the East Anglian and Northumbrian Hosts at Tiddingford (ASC 'E').

—King Oswald's Bardney remains are translated to Gloucester at the behest of Æðelflæd (ASC 'D' or 909 in ASC 'C').

907 Æðelflæd 'restores' Chester (ASC 'C'); subsequent attack on Chester by Ingimundr (FA).

908/9 Death of Bishop Asser of Sherborne.

—Probable date of death of Cadell ap Rhodri in Seisyllwg (AC); succession of Hywel ap Cadell (Dda) and his brother Cadog.

910 The army in Northumbria 'breaks the peace'; they raid Mercia. **Battle of Tettenhall** (Staffs): Mercia and Wessex defeat returning Danish force.

911 Æðelred, Ealdorman of Mercia dies; succeeded by his 'queen' Æðelflæd to 918. King Eadweard takes control of London and Oxford.

916 Æðelflæd sends force to Brycheiniog; attacks royal crannog on Llangorse lake (ASC 'C').

—Jarl Ðurcytel goes overseas with his followers under Eadweard's protection and 'with his assistance'.

912–19 Period of construction of offensive burhs by Æðelflæd and Eadweard across South and West Mercia.

914 Viking raids from Northampton and Leicester, as far as Luton and Hook Norton; they are routed, apparently by county levies (ASC 'D').

917 Æðelflæd captures Derby and its hinterland from Danes (ASC 'C'). Eadweard campaigns against Danish Mercian armies across the Midlands; he conquers East Anglia.

918 Æðelflæd receives the submission of the Men of York and gains control of Leicester (ASC 'C'). She dies at Tamworth. Eadweard occupies Tamworth and annexes Mercia.

—Rögnvaldr invades Northumbria with a Norse army: **Battle of Corbridge** against a Scottish and Northumbrian army (AU; CKA).

FORESPÆC

I SAAC NEWTON'S THIRD LAW OF MOTION SEEMS TO GOV-
ern the events of the four decades between Ælfred's victory
over the *mycel here* at Edington and the conquest of York by the
Norse warlord Rögnvaldr in 918. Each strike of foe against foe,
like the suspended steel balls of a Newton's cradle, energized the
relations between other states, conserving the political momentum of the Viking Age and producing a dizzying display of reaction and counter-reaction, opportunity and risk.

After 880 Ælfred's political capital was such that he could
forge a mutually empowering treaty with Guðrum and embark
on a programme of economic, military and educational reform
that deserves to be compared with the Frankish renaissance under
Charlemagne. Exotic visitors came to his court; the history of his
people and age was written down; churches and their saintly cults
were enthusiastically patronized. Above all, the painful lessons
Ælfred had learned from his long-time enemy were put to good
use in the series of defended garrison towns that he ordered built
across the south. Relations with Mercia were consolidated, and
flourished under his son-in-law and daughter. He put in place
provisions for his successor and when, after some years of relative
peace, a second great war of conquest broke out in 893, Wessex
and Mercia were equal to its extreme dangers. Ælfred's reign can
be said to have professionalized the Anglo-Saxon state.

Accommodations were made between native and incomer
at all social, political and economic levels. New lords, some
more benign than others, brought both threats and opportunities to disrupt the status quo in the countryside and precipitate
bold new ventures in production and trade. Archaeologists and

historians looking for clear traces of such developments, the rattling local echoes of the Newtonian cradle, have to compile their case from hoards of coins deposited in unknown circumstances, from distributions of pottery and from other artefacts recovered from excavations that have often been expedient and, more often than not, provoke questions that cannot be answered. Charters, where they survive, offer another perspective, showing how kings and bishops deployed their political capital, with increasing *savoir faire*, by acquiring and gifting land, the stage on which dynastic and petty local interests were played out in small scenes against a grander background.

Despite apparently unstoppable forces leading towards what later historians have seen as almost inevitable unification, the evidence emerging from fragments of annals, artefacts and geographies shows just how regionally diverse and conservative the Insular lands were. If one can see the founders of three great kingdoms in Ælfred, in Constantín of Alba and in the grandsons of Rhodri Mawr in Wales, there is equally a patchwork of ineradicable identities expressed in the old kingdoms of Hwicce and Lindsey, of East Anglia, Kent and Northumbria, Strathclyde, Dyfed and Gwynedd. And another set of formidable grandchildren, those of the famous Ívarr, would intervene in the decades after 900 to show just how illusory the apparent forces of centralization were.

The fallout from such tensions, when they erupted in the Viking expulsion from Dublin in 902, was felt across Britain. Alba might have fallen permanently under Norse control; Northumbria forged new and stronger links with its Irish overlords; the armies of Danish East Anglia and East Mercia retained their capacity to threaten the Wessex–Mercia alliance; and in the place names, archaeology and fragmentary annals which tell of raiding, settlement and conquest in the north and west of Britain lies a record of punch and counterpunch, shadowy undercurrents of alliance and betrayal but also of people getting by, adapting somehow to circumstances beyond their control or ken.

Part of this narrative is carried by the tenacious chroniclers of St Cuthbert's followers, as they fought to keep their estates and influence intact. They supported prospective Danish kings in their bid for power and donated lands to Christian refugees fleeing across the mountains in the west. They were able, after a period of great insecurity, to settle with their precious relics at Chester le Street on the River Wear and carve out a new *paruchia** by cannily playing one set of antagonists off against another.

Excavations across many decades have begun to sketch a pattern of settlement, acculturation and integration: on Man, where the best evidence for distinctive Norse houses and burials is wonderfully preserved beneath mound and pasture; on Anglesey, where hints of bloody regime change tell also of continuity and trading success; in the Hebrides and in Orkney, where grand sagas incant an age of derring-do, of conquest and, ultimately, organized settlement and rule.

The towns that emerge on the Danish side of England's fault line, Watling Street, from the blanket silence of the Anglo-Saxon chroniclers, do so in infuriatingly patchy detail. Four of the so-called Five Boroughs are enigmatic still, their Scandinavian phases as yet unyielding to the spade. Lincoln and York, both so distinct in their historical development, offer the best clues to the dazzling success of the Scandinavian settlers in galvanizing populations concentrated behind their formidable defensive ramparts to energize production and trade on local, regional and international scales. By the early tenth century tenements and workshops, effective coinage, wheel-thrown pottery and an exuberant love of metalwork and precious-stoned jewellery and dress

* *Paruchia*: a network of monastic foundations with their estates, functioning under the authority of a mother church.

accessories become visible. These tell of a shared self-confidence rather than triumphant exploitation of a subjected populace. In very obvious contrast, the burhs and their economies south and west of Watling Street, in the first years after Ælfred's death, show only economic stagnation and a sort of mulish reluctance to join in the new mercantile game.

By the end of the first decade of the tenth century Ælfred's son Eadweard, king of the West Saxons, and his enterprising sister Æðelflæd in Mercia were ready to restore the economic and cultural balance. Their great plan, to conquer Danish Mercia and East Anglia, was heroic in its scale and successes, even if the inevitable human cost, so sparsely attested in contemporary sources, did little to nurture a sense of Anglo-Saxon unity among the southern kingdoms. Local and regional interests fought back against national ideology.

Ancient historical and geographical realities underpinned developments on the Insular scale: ceremonies were held, treaties were signed, battles fought at locations etched into the warp and weft of hill and plain, ford and vill: tidal reaches of rivers, time-worn crossroads, royal townships, shire boundaries and the mounds where laws had been promulgated as long as people could remember. Tribal and dynastic affiliations ran deep; loyalties seemed to tilt as much against old enemies as in favour of new friends. Ælfred's Britain was a cultural and political patchwork quilt rich in the regional languages, customs and lordships of its kaleidoscope components. The Britain of his children was no different.

THE BALANCE OF POWER

5

I N 879 THE NORTHUMBRIAN MONASTIC COM-
munity of St Cuthbert had not yet adopted Ælfred and his
offspring as royal patrons. The catastrophic loss of Bernician
royal power in the ninth century, which culminated in the conquest of southern Northumbria in the 860s and 870s, precipitated a long-term crisis in their fortunes. Viking depredations
in the Western Isles and Ireland had prompted the flight of the
Iona community with the relics of their precious Colm Cille,
both to Ireland and to Dunkeld in Strathtay under the protection
of Cináed mac Ailpín. Many monasteries, the beating heart of
the northern church, had been abandoned or survived in much
reduced circumstances; others, like Portmahomack, served new,
secular masters. The economic and psychological impact of these
events on the institution of the church was extreme. It survived
by adapting.

When their patron kings failed them, royal monastic foundations had to sup with the devil in a bid to retain their power
and their estates. Without productive monastic lands and communities of priests and monks, abbots, craftsmen and farmers

21. THE VICTORIAN STATUE of Ælfred at his Berkshire birthplace of Wantage (now in Oxfordshire); unveiled in 1877, and sculpted by Victor, Count Gleichen, a captain in the Royal Navy.

protected by the king's peace, the *paruchiae*, the earthly kingdoms of Cuthbert and Bridget, David, Colm Cille and Patrick
must fall, like their temporal counterparts. And so they began to
court the enemy.

The two-centuries-long survival battle of the Northumbrian
church, beginning so inauspiciously with the notorious raid on
Lindisfarne in 793, played out like a military campaign across the
physical and political landscapes of the North. Uncanny parallels between the defensive and offensive strategies employed by
the church and those improvised by kings reinforce the idea of
policy developing on the hoof: retrenching, even fleeing when
necessary; taking opportunities when they arose to recover, reinforce and re-invent themselves, ensuring their ultimate survival.
Dynasties in Mercia, East Anglia, Ireland and Pictland had failed
to adapt; Ælfred was an apprentice learning a new set of rules.
The Insular Christian state must anticipate, comprehend and
negotiate with the Viking worldview.

We can reconstruct a surprisingly detailed account of the fortunes of St Cuthbert's community at this period. That is a testament, in the first place, to its robust survival into and beyond the
years of Norman conquest and to the assiduous, even tenacious,
records kept by its monks. These are supplemented by scattered
accounts preserved in disparate, often contradictory sources, frequently obscure and sometimes simply fabricated, which nevertheless paint a rich and complex picture of religious politics.*

By the time of the 793 Viking raid Lindisfarne's property
portfolio, assembled through the donations of Bernician kings
across 150 years, comprised large parts of the modern county

---

* In recent years they have been teased out brilliantly by a number of scholars, not
least the pre-eminent contemporary historian of the Durham church, David Rollason, the Early Medievalist Alex Woolf in Scotland and the most recent editor of
the *Historia de Sancto Cuthberto*, Ted Johnson South. Rollason 1989a; Woolf 2007;
South 2002.

of Northumberland and the Scottish Border region, from East Lothian beyond the River Tweed to the River Tyne in the south. Other lucrative and politically advantageous estates had been acquired near York and in the ancient Roman *civitas* capital at *Luguvalium* (Carlisle) on the west coast. Each of these monastic territories, like those belonging to secular lords, was made up of contiguous parcels of land centred on a *vill** and its dependencies, often in multiples of six or twelve. Farm rendered to *vill*, *vill* rendered to shire and shire to the lordship of St Cuthbert. Lindisfarne's impressive portfolio enabled its inhabitants to enjoy the fruits of a mixed agricultural economy, to specialize in the production of grain, wool and illuminated manuscripts the equal of any in Europe; to fill the shelves of their libraries with the works of ancient scholars and their churches with jewel-encrusted reliquaries and the finest stone sculpture. They sponsored missionary activities on the Continent, maintaining diplomatic relations with kings and bishops across the Atlantic region and, far beyond, with Rome. Sometimes Northumbrian kings, tired of the warrior life and seeking peace and communion outwith the war band, abdicated to retire on the Holy Island haven cut off by the tide twice a day.

Northumbria at one time encompassed no fewer than four episcopal dioceses, with seats at Lindisfarne, Abercorn on the River Forth, Hexham in the Tyne Valley and Whithorn on the Solway coast. It was an empire of élite endeavour. From Aidan, in 635, the Lindisfarne foundation was ruled under seventeen abbot-bishops up to the year 900. Its most celebrated—and reluctant—bishop, Cuthbert, died as the community's head in 687 and twelve years later his incorrupt body was translated to a special sarcophagus that became a sort of spiritual tribal totem. The stability and continuity of the community's leadership

---

* The *vills* of the *Historia* and other sources often equate in size and shape to the townships that survive in the modern landscape.

through times of internal and external strife and the ultimate threat of apostasy is a reflection, as it was with royal dynasties, of its robustness as an institution.

By the time of the Viking raids, Abercorn had already been lost to Northumbrian control. The last Bishop of Whithorn is mentioned a few years after 800, indicating the decline of that community in the face of Scandinavian expansion in the Irish Sea.* Hexham's last Anglo-Saxon bishop died in 821, its see absorbed into that of Lindisfarne to cover the whole of northern Northumbria. To the south, the ancient kingdom of Deira in southern Northumbria had been represented by a single see at York since the middle of the seventh century. After 735 it enjoyed the dignity and power of an archbishop, and has done so in an unbroken sequence since, exercising at least nominal power over the northern sees. Its survival in the crucible of Anglo-Scandinavian conflict is no less remarkable than that of St Cuthbert's community, even if it is harder to trace in detail.†

In the days of Bishop Ecgred (830–845), in response to periodic and ultimately unsustainable attacks by Viking raiders, the community on Lindisfarne decided to relocate to a place of greater safety on one of its original estates, at Norham on Tweed. Leaving behind, perhaps, an estate manager and sufficient workers to maintain the island's farms,‡ the community of St Cuthbert relocated wholesale: not just its priests and monks but its precious relics (Oswald, Aidan, Cuthbert, the bones of King Ceolwulf, and others) and its treasures; even the fabric of the wooden church. Further crises were precipitated by the civil war of the 860s between Osberht and Ælle, both of whom 'stole'

---

* The community survived, however, judging by the number of coins found at the site minted by kings up until the 860s.

† See below, Chapter 10.

‡ The site of one of these has been excavated by Deidre O'Sullivan and Rob Young at Green Shiel towards the north end of Lindisfarne. O'Sullivan and Young 1995.

lands from the saint, and by Hálfdan's second invasion of 875 when he sailed up the River Tyne, 'devastating everything and sinning cruelly' against Cuthbert.[1]

Hálfdan may shortly thereafter have been deposed by his own army, and he seems not to have been able to exercise direct royal rule over the North; he was certainly dead by 877. After that a series of client kings, the diminished successors to Osberht and Ælle, ruled in York between 867 and about 880. Ecgberht, Ricsige, and a short-lived successor, also named Ecgberht,[2] proved unsatisfactory to both the Host and the Northumbrian nobility. Weak kings were of no use to Cuthbert: without effective patrons and protectors, and in the face of heathen invaders, the power of the northern church was under the severest threat. Even the long-lived Archbishop Wulfhere endured temporary exile in Mercia, having been deposed with Ecgberht in 872.

Cuthbert himself had intervened in the Northumbrian royal succession during a crisis in the 680s;* now, his spiritual descendants must play the same hand. A single coin, very likely minted in Lincolnshire in the 880s, offers archaeological corroboration for the rule of a King Guðrøðr in southern Northumbria, otherwise known principally from a very odd entry in the *Historia de Sancto Cuthberto* describing events in the years after Hálfdan's departure.[3] It seems that St Cuthbert appeared one night in a vision to Eadred, the abbot of Carlisle. The dead saint adjured him to:

> Go over the Tyne to the army of the Danes and tell them that if they wish to be obedient to me [that is, to St Cuthbert], they should show you a certain young man named Guðrøðr son of Harthacanute, the slave of a certain widow.

Cuthbert gave detailed instructions for Eadred and the Host to offer money to the widow to redeem the boy and then to:

---

* Ælfflæd, sister of King Ecgfrith, begged Cuthbert to advise her on the succession when it looked as though the king might get himself killed in the land of the Picts; as indeed he did in 685. See Adams 2013, 374ff.

22. THE RIVER TYNE AT NEWBURN, its lowest fording point—
possibly *Oswigesdune*, the site of Guðrøð's investiture around 880.

Lead him before the whole multitude so that they may elect
him king and at the ninth hour lead him with the whole army
upon the hill which is called Oswigesdune* and there place on
his right arm a golden armlet,† and thus they shall all constitute him king.[4]

What Cuthbert had ordered was duly enacted by the abbot and
by the Host, who 'honourably received' Guðrøðr. The young
man was inaugurated as king and swore peace and fidelity over the
body of the saint in his modest wooden coffin, produced by the
abbot for the occasion. The new king, instructed by the visionary
Cuthbert through his real-life proxy, then proceeded to hand over
to the community all the lands between the Rivers Tyne and Wear.

It is one of the more extraordinary episodes in Early Medieval
British history and very difficult, if not impossible, to accept at
face value. Teasing the probable, the plausible and the realpolitik
from the miraculous, we might envisage the abbot acting as an
honest broker between the Host and the indigenous Christian
élite, identifying a candidate for the kingship who would be
acceptable to all parties and then arranging a suitable hybrid
inauguration ceremony to seal the deal. His (the dead saint's) fee
was a generous endowment of land.

On the face of it this still sounds improbable: the Scandinavian
Host, backed by military might and unopposed by credible
regional powers, ought to have been able to impose one of its
own, or a local puppet, on the natives. But Early Medieval kingship was at all times a negotiated office, dependent on customary

---

* The site has not been identified. It derives either from Oswiu or Oswine, both significant royal figures of the seventh century. The topographic suffix 'dun' suggests
a hill where royal inaugurations had taken place in the past. A small mound overlooking the Tyne from the south at Ryton, close to the tidal reach of the river at
Newburn, would suit the topography and the narrative well. See map, p. 322.

† *Armilia aurea*. The sacred arm ring had already been recognized and deployed as
a diplomatic tool by Ælfred in his dealings with the Host at Wareham, albeit with
limited success. See above, p. 137.

rules of lordship, obligation and consent. In the ranks of the Host's senior commanders, it seems, there was no suitable candidate of royal descent. The Cuthbert community, under the guidance of its abbot and bishop, was here offering up the support of the Bernician establishment to a Scandinavian-born or half-Scandinavian ex-slave of royal parentage, already assimilated into Northumbrian society, who appears to have been converted during his youth to Christianity: so long as he rewarded the saint's followers with suitably large estates.*

The inclusion of the Guðrøðr narrative in the *Historia* and in the much later *Libellus de Exordio* of Symeon is intimately connected with the fate of Cuthbert's relics, through which the spiritual and temporal power of the saint were constantly expressed. At various times between the 840s and the early 880s the community and its precious relics seem to have been on the move. We find the saint and his devoted bearers, the remnants of the Lindisfarne community, with Abbot Eadred and Bishop Eardulf in attendance, at the monastery of Whithorn; at the mouth of the River Derwent on the Cumbrian coast; at a Lindisfarne estate outside York called Crayke and, finally, at Chester le Street (*Kuncacester*), a former Roman fortress that lay at the centre of those new estates granted to Cuthbert by King Guðrøðr. There is yet more to this than meets the eye, and the internal politics, which must have swept up Cuthbert's community in a whirl of tensions and political friction, can be judged more in the imagination than in the evidence.

A so-called Seven Years' Wandering[5] (876–883), during which the treasures and body of Cuthbert are portrayed as having been

---

* The idea that members of the nobility might become slaves seems odd to modern thinking. Enslavement might come about as a result of debt or poverty, capture during battle or as a punishment. In Guðroð's case he may have been sold into slavery to reduce his chances of competing for the kingship of the Host. Now, it seems, his time had come.

constantly in motion can, in the cold light of analysis, be seen as a series of visitations, or a progress between and through the saint's extensive territorial holdings.[6] St Cuthbert, dead these 200 years, was behaving like an itinerant Early Medieval king, consuming the productive surplus of his estates, checking on their management and the rule of their minsters and generally surviving, if tenuously, the chaos of the century. In promoting a candidate for the kingship, Cuthbert's followers aimed to prevent civil war, realign their fortunes to those of the new power in the land, and consolidate their now fragile landholdings.

An episode said to have occurred at Derwentmouth (near modern Workington) is particularly significant: it relates an attempt by Abbot Eadred to take Cuthbert's relics over the sea to Ireland, an attempt confounded at the last minute by either a tempest or 'waves of blood', depending on which account one reads. It seems that there was disharmony within the community—a disagreement about whether to flee Britain or to seek some other permanent home for bishopric, relics and community, exhausted by the impermanence of its situation. Guðrøð's elevation to the kingship in about 880 or 881, sponsored by Cuthbert, killed two birds with one stone. Cuthbert, his bearers and the bishop of north Northumbria were able to settle at Chester le Street, just a few miles south of the River Tyne, surrounded by sufficient estates and with royal support ensuring their security and wealth, at the right distance to influence events further south and yet remain detached. These 'new' estates* appear to have encompassed those *vills* originally granted in the seventh century to found two great, now much reduced houses, Jarrow and Monkwearmouth, so recovering the monastic territories of Benedict Biscop and of Bede (the land of *Werhale*)[7] somehow lost during the crises of the ninth century.

* See map on p. 322.

The Lindisfarne community remained at Chester le Street for more than 100 years until its final, permanent move to Durham in 995. From Guðrøð's reign onwards new holdings were acquired overwhelmingly in what is now County Durham. For the Host this new ecclesiastical bloc was a useful buffer zone between their Deiran settlements and interests and the inconveniently independent-thinking and still-powerful Bernician lords of Bamburgh. For Cuthbert's *paruchia*, it meant survival against the odds. In exile they succeeded in forging their own kingdom within a kingdom.

The political fallout of the settlement of Yorkshire and the defeat of the Summer Host by Ælfred re-energized the Newton's cradle of southern overlordship. Ælfred's pragmatic acceptance of new realities was, for most of a decade, successful. Guðrum was true to his word. At the end of the tumultuous year of 878 the Host overwintered at Cirencester, the ancient Roman town lying some miles north of the Thames, Mercia's boundary with Wessex. Their new quarters might have seemed threatening, no more than two days' march along the Fosse Way from Chippenham; but, in retrospect, it seems that their proximity to the old border had more to do with extended negotiations with the councillors of Wessex and Mercia than to re-grouping for another attack. It was not acceptable to either party that Guðrum rule over the lands of the Mercians and settle there, as Hálfdan had done in Northumbria. A better solution presented itself: under the year 879 the *Chronicle* records that the Danish army moved to East Anglia and 'occupied that land and shared it out'.[8]

Æðelweard's tenth-century account is more nuanced than that of the *Chronicle* and, in the light of scholarly debate about the nature of Danish East Anglia, more realistic: the *mycel here* 'laid out their camp there, and brought all the inhabitants of that land under the yoke of their overlordship [*imperium*]'.[9] Having lost their last legitimate dynast with Eadmund, the East Anglians were consulted by neither the Host nor the Mercians, nor by Ælfred: Danish rule was imposed on them.

There is no surviving narrative history of the years of Guðrum's reign in East Anglia, only contradictory scraps of evidence suggesting varying degrees of Scandinavian settlement, assimilation and overlordship. The most valuable of those fragments is the unique document known as the *Treaty of Ælfred and Guðrum*, dated to some time between 880 and 890 and, reasonably, within a year or so of his arrival there.[10] We would like to know much, much more about the ceremonial aspects of such a unique testament to Anglo-Scandinavian relations. Were the bones of the treaty put in place during Guðrum's baptismal feast, man to man between the two kings; or did detailed negotiations extend over several months, involving otherwise faceless functionaries? The document's brevity suggests the former. Its nature (the boundary clause draws a line between East Anglia and Mercia, rather than with Wessex) suggests that Ceolwulf II, puppet king of Mercia and sometime Wessex ally, was by then dead, since he was not a signatory. It begins:

> This is the peace which King Ælfred and King Guðrum and the councillors of all the English race [*Angelcynn*] and all the people which is in East Anglia have all agreed on and confirmed with oaths, for themselves and for their subjects, both for the living and for those yet unborn, who care to have God's grace or ours.[11]

The first clause of the treaty, the demarcation of territory, appears straightforward: 'up the Thames, and then up the Lea, and along the Lea to its source, then in a straight line to Bedford, then up the Ouse to the Watling Street'. The Lea rises at Leagrave on the north-west outskirts of Luton at the foot of the Chiltern Hills, only a couple of miles from the Roman town of *Durocobrivis*

byrngan ne mæʒe · ⁊he ðonne ful sy · ſtonde
ondapa yldeſtana manna dome hpæðer he
hliﬆ aʒ ðe naʒ þe to ðœpe byþiʒ hy ﬄon · ⁊on
fanʒ oﬁ eal ſylht on anſepe ſy hit on ma ·
fif tyne peneʒaſ · ⁊æl con ſmalon oﬁe œﬄe
œt ſcillinʒe peni ·
Ymbe þoﬁ fanʒ pitan habbað ʒe ﬁædd þ
man oﬁep eall land ʒelíce ðo healde ·
þ iſ œt men fif tene peninʒaſ · ⁊œt horſe
heal ſpa · ſy hit oﬁep ane ſcype · ſy hit oﬁep
ma · ðe lœr ðe un mihtiʒ man peopp þoﬁ
hiſ aʒen on ſpince · ⁊eac to peola ſylle · hpi
lon ſtod þ man œt œlcon deoﬁ ﬆolenan oﬁ
ﬆe · ⁊be hiſ þoﬁ þanʒe ſylle · þ iſ œt œlcon ſcill
peniʒ · ſy ðœſ cynneſ oﬁﬁ ðe hit ſy · Gyﬁ hit
man œt deoﬁeſ handa ahﬂet · ʒyﬁ hit ðon
ne elleſ on hy ðelſe ſunden ſy ðonne mœʒ þ
þoﬁ fanʒ feoh leohﬂe beon · þoﬁ ðam bið
on lœſſe plihﬂ beʒytan · Diﬁ iſ þeo ʒe ﬁœd
nyſſ humon þ lu heo ʒeʒade pan a ymb
ʒeoﬁep pucan · ⁊þyﬁ pce œlc man oðﬁu piht ·
ʒyﬁ neod on handa ﬆande cyðe
hit man ðam hundpedeſ iﬂ · ⁊he ſyððan
ðam to ðinʒ mannu · ⁊paﬁan ealle þoﬁð
ðœﬁ him ʒod pﬁﬁʒ þ hit to cuman moton ·
do ðam deoﬁe hiſ piht ſpa hit œﬁ eadmun

(Dunstable) on Watling Street. The Ouse in question is the River Great Ouse, which crosses the Roman road again at a key point: Stony Stratford, on the north-west edge of modern Milton Keynes. From there the river flows north-east, passing through Olney (*Ollanege*—Olla's island) and then winding lazily downstream towards Bedford in a series of meanders. Between Luton, Bedford and Stony Stratford, then, is an odd triangle of territory retained to the north of Watling Street by Ælfred on Mercia's behalf, for reasons that are unclear.* The odd, straight line between the source of the Lea and the town of Bedford is today traced almost perfectly by the railway line from Luton which links the two.

Even more obscure is the question of whether the two kings intended that the boundary with Mercia was to continue north-west along Watling Street from Stony Stratford towards the Mercian heartlands around Tamworth and Lichfield, effectively leaving the Viking fortresses of Nottingham, Leicester and Repton in Guðrum's hands. Or was the Great Ouse itself effectively the western border of his new state? The latter makes more sense, even if it leaves open to question who, precisely, was ruling over north-eastern Mercia. The later history of East Anglia is distinct and separate from that of Mercia west of the fens. Huntingdon, Cambridge and Colchester seem to have been Guðrum's principal defended towns.

The four subsequent clauses of the treaty are concerned with drawing equivalent values for the lives, oaths and freedom of movement (to use a fashionable phrase) of two classes of free

---

* Roger of Wendover reports a story that King Offa (757–796) was buried in a chapel on the banks of the River Usk (Ouse) at Bedford; and a charter which may attest to his widow's possession of a monastery at *Bedeford* is sometimes cited as supporting evidence. If there was, or had been, a royal mausoleum at Bedford it might explain its otherwise odd inclusion as a border marker, with access by both sides, for the purposes of the treaty. Giles 1849, 166–7; Whitelock *EHD* 79, 508.

men,* known in some sources as *twihynde* (men worth 200 shillings—the *ceorls*) and *twelfhynde* (members of the nobility, worth
1200 shillings).[12] Overriding all other considerations is the sense
that this was intended as a permanent settlement, an acceptance
on Ælfred's side that the Danes were in Britain to stay and, on
Guðrum's, that half a loaf was better than none. The Danish king
seems to have embraced his new status as a Christian, looking
south to Wessex and east to Francia as a fully fledged member
of the Christian kings' club. He minted coins: first in imitation
of indigenous East Anglian and Frankish issues and then, using
his baptismal name Æðelstan, in imitation of Ælfred's coins,
only lighter in weight. On the reverse is a cross; and so the first
two *bona fide* Scandinavian kings of English states, Guðrøðr and
Guðrum, both seem to have adopted Insular Christian values, at
least nominally.

The treaty boundary suggests that London lay outside the
new Danish kingdom. It also suggests that by now Ælfred had
made provision for the governance of Mercia, since he was drawing up its new eastern boundary. By 881 West Mercia was ruled
by Æðelred, later Ælfred's son-in-law and always described as an
ealdorman in Wessex sources; he was not obviously connected
to any of the three main dynasties of Mercian kings but a *de
facto* king so far as Mercia was concerned. The unknown dates
of his appointment as its lord and of the creation of the treaty
pose a nice problem for historians. My guess, and it is no more
than that, is that during the discussions between Ælfred and
Guðrum, Æðelred emerged as a skilled negotiator able to carry
the weight of opinion of the Mercian nobility, that he showed
himself to be pro-Wessex and Ælfred; and that the West Saxon
king rewarded his loyalty by supporting his case to govern Mercia
after Ceolwulf's (undated) death.

---

* Ælfred's own laws contain provision also for a class of six-hundred men, the *sixhynde*.
 Keynes and Lapidge 1983, 168.

In assertion, perhaps, of his desire to show independence from direct political control, Æðelred almost immediately mounted a military campaign against Mercia's old antagonist, Gwynedd.* The campaign was disastrous: Anarawd ap Rhodri, son of the great warrior whom Ceolwulf had defeated and killed three years before, inflicted a humiliating defeat on the ealdorman, for the time being ending Mercian ambitions to overlordship in North Wales. Many historians date Æðelred's submission to Ælfred from that defeat; and yet, it is equally plausible that he had already accepted the West Saxon king as his lord and was using new-found stability deriving from the Anglo-Danish treaty to flex his military muscle. In the event the defeat, at the mouth of the River Conwy on the north-east edge of Snowdonia, allowed Anarawd to assert his supremacy over Powys in central eastern Wales and Ceredigion in the west, while curbing Mercian expansionism: the desk toy of political momentum clacked rhythmically once again.

Ælfred's later acquisition of Bishop Asser of St David's as court scholar and chronicler of his life allows the contemporary Welsh scene to be sketched, albeit in rough outline, for the first time. The invidiousness of the southern Welsh position is striking: King Haifaidd of Dyfed (roughly the territory of the Pembroke peninsula) feared the power of the sons of Rhodri Mawr: Cadell in Ceredigion bordering it to the north, Merfyn in Powys and Anarawd in Gwynedd, the latter allied with the new Northumbrian king Guðroðr. Across the Irish Sea lay the aggressive Norse kings of Dublin, Wexford and Waterford. To the immediate east of Dyfed, Ystrad Tywi is likely to have faced the same pressures.

---

* Æðelred's name only appears in connection with the battle in a thirteenth-century genealogy, as Edryd Long-Hair. The entry in the *Annales Cambriae* for 880 (corrected to 881) describes the battle as 'vengeance for Rhodri at God's hand'. Charles-Edwards 2014, 490; Morris 1980, 48.

The three south-east kingdoms of Wales—Brycheiniog under Elise ap Tewdr, Glywysing under Hywel ap Rhys and Gwent under Kings Brochfael and Ffernfael—felt additional pressure from Æðelred in Mercia, their traditional antagonist. Asser, for one (directly addressing his Welsh audience at home), regarded the Mercian ealdorman's influence over these south-east kingdoms, his immediate neighbours across the River Severn, as a predatory tyranny.[13] Beset on all sides, one by one the smaller Welsh kingdoms submitted to Ælfred, now cast in the role of the great protector, in a process which might have continued for most of the 880s and 890s as each player sought to gain maximum advantage for the least risk.

Ælfred's overlordship of the Welsh kingdoms and of Mercia was a matter of political and military expediency on both sides. Only in retrospect have over-enthusiastic commentators and nationalists encouraged the idea of an Ælfredan project to create a single kingdom of England or Britain. He might have styled himself as king of the *Angelcynn*, the English people; that is not the same as proclaiming himself king of Mercia or of the Britons or, indeed, of Kent, let alone of some notion of England which does not belong to his age. The grand unifying project of an English kingdom was not a design of the West Saxon kings; at least, not before the days of Ælfred's grandchildren.

The project may, in distant origin, have been conceived by the Venerable Bede, whose passion for the universal church had a complementary and logical secular counterpart. Ælfred, it seems to me, was content with the benefits of overlordship or *imperium*: political influence and the peace and wealth it might bring. His grand project was a Carolingian-style renaissance: spiritual, educational, philosophical, channelling political energy away from warfare towards culture and learning. Asser may have been prejudicially inclined towards his personal patron, and he may be over-egging the pudding when he describes the benefits of West

Saxon overlordship to his native Welsh constituents; but he does not overstate by much the potential advantages of submission:

> Nor did all these rulers gain the king's friendship in vain. For those who wished to increase their worldly power were able to do so; those who wished an increase of wealth obtained it; those who wished to be on more intimate terms with the king achieved such intimacy; and those who desired each and every one of these things acquired them. All of them gained support, protection and defence [*amor, tutela, defensio*].[14]

It is easy to get worked up by the idea of overlordship: it bears connotations of racial and ethnic submission that still underlie national sensitivities. But it is best seen as an extension of the rules of lordship and patronage which operated at all levels of Early Medieval society. Political submission in the age of the first Viking invasions involved a set of mutual obligations and ties concerning royal fosterage, reciprocal rights for traders, political marriages, baptism and godparenting, as well as military support, attendance at the king's councils and the rendering of tribute in various kinds, including hard cash. The record of Guðrum's submission and baptism after the battle of Edington provides the model. For a modern analogy, one thinks of Britain's post-war relationship with the United States in which Britain is expected to represent American interests in Europe and fight in its wars in order to enjoy the benefits of protection, economic favouritism and a 'special' status. Political intervention in the affairs of tributary states was and is a matter of political delicacy, and Early Medieval rulers, like their modern counterparts, were acutely aware of the importance of show and ceremony in their portrayal of such relationships.

Ælfred's establishment of a king's peace in the 880s was assisted by events on the Continent. Just as the Anglo-Saxon, Welsh and

Pictish states had been destabilized and rendered vulnerable to external attack by dynastic uncertainty, so also Francia experienced twenty years of succession disputes from the late 870s. Charles the Bald, Charlemagne's grandson and the architect of Frankish defences against Scandinavian incursions, died in 877. His eldest son Louis *le Bègue* ('the Stammerer'), survived him by just two years. Louis's successor in West Francia, his son Louis III, died in 882; his second son, Carloman II, assuming the throne in Aquitaine and Burgundy, died in 884. In East Francia Louis the German, another grandson of Charlemagne, died in 876 and was succeeded by his eldest son, another Carloman, who died in 880; his second son, another Louis, died in 882.

In that year, a sense of state impotence against the ravages of the Host in Francia was registered by Archbishop Hincmar in his final entry as the chronicler of St Bertin. Carloman, he wrote, 'lacked the resources to mount resistance to the Northmen once certain magnates of his kingdom withdrew from offering him help'.[15] Hincmar himself, aged and weak, fled in a sedan chair, barely escaping with the relics and treasures of his church.

The former Frankish empire was reunited, briefly, by Charles *le Gros* ('the Fat') until 888; but it was not until the reign of Charles *Simplex* ('the Simple' 898–929: a last, posthumous son of Louis the Stammerer) that Francia between the Jutland peninsula and the Pyrenees once more enjoyed the fruits of dynastic stability. The discreet departure of a Viking fleet from Fulham on the Thames near London in 879, heading for Ghent with unfriendly motives, shows how the runes were read by Viking chiefs in the aftermath of Guðrum's submission.[16] The Anglo-Saxon chronicler's frequent notices of these ominous events across the Channel is evidence that at Ælfred's court keen interest was taken in their movements.

Between the defeat of Guðrum in 878 and the arrival from Francia of a new Continental army on the shores of Kent in 892,

Viking interest concentrated on easy Frankish pickings: laying siege to Paris in 885–886, penetrating the rivers Scheldt, Seine and Marne with apparent impunity and attempting to wrest control of Brittany. Charles the Fat was forced to pay them off with 700 lbs (320 kg) of silver[17] and to acquiesce in their subsequent attacks on Burgundy.

That is not to say that the Anglo-Saxon kingdoms were free from external threat. In 882 Ælfred took a fleet to sea and captured two Viking ships, according to the *Chronicle*. Two years later part of the Host laid siege to Rochester in Kent; the fortress was only relieved by the king after the best part of a year. This force may have been a discontented element among Guðrum's veterans in East Anglia; in the same year Ælfred sent a fleet to the mouth of the River Stour and was able to defeat a force of sixteen ships.

These notices of engagements pepper a decade during which Ælfred began to put in place long-term plans for defence, for the revival and reform of the church and for his cultural renaissance. Asser's arrival at the court of Wessex in about 885 was complemented by the importation of several scholars from Mercia and the Continent: Bishop Wærferth of Worcester; Plegmund, whom he would elevate to the primacy of Canterbury; Grimbald and John from German Francia. Latinate scholarship, literacy and the political testimony of those who had witnessed Frankish policy towards the Scandinavian threat, armed Ælfred with weapons of intellectual and political expertise underpinned by the economic clout of the great minsters and the institutional authority of episcopal and metropolitan sees.

Ælfred's domestic battles proved just as challenging as his military campaigns but he seems, like Newton, to have grasped the underlying mechanical laws of his age better than any other. He saw that military victory must be followed by economic reform, the construction of public works and defence based on geographical realities, all underpinned by support for the church and a revival of education. But the apparent benevolence of his rule masks a hard-headed realism that required sometimes forceful impositions on the shires of Wessex and the south-east, in the face of opposition and truculence from local and regional power brokers among his ealdormen, thegns and bishops.

Ælfred had built a small fortress at Athelney at the height of the crisis in the winter of 878. He had seen the effectiveness of Viking fortresses at Reading, Wareham and Nottingham. The defences at Rochester, which held out against a Viking siege in 884 until it could be relieved, and existing Mercian fortifications at Hereford, Tamworth and Winchcombe, provided inspiration and engineering exemplars for a grand scheme later recorded in a document known as the Burghal Hidage.*

Ælfred's first concern seems to have been the defence of the south coast. Where the walls of ancient Roman towns or forts were serviceable or restorable, as at Portchester, Chichester, Exeter, Bath, *Hamtun* and Winchester, they were repaired and garrisoned. Naturally defensible sites that could be fortified by the expedient of raising a bank and palisade across a promontory, such as Halwell in Devon and *Twyneham* (Christchurch in Dorset), were enrolled in the scheme. Iron Age hillforts like *Cissanbyrig* (Chisbury) and Watchet guarded strategic routes and were refortified. Occasionally, as at Axbridge (just downstream from the township at Cheddar) and Wallingford, a new burh was constructed on or close to an existing royal estate. The smallest of the burhs, the fort at Lyng near Athelney on a low prominence in the Somerset levels, needed just 100 men for its garrison walls; the largest, at Wallingford and Winchester (the latter following the surviving

---

* Its date is much debated: the inclusion of two Mercian towns, Worcester and Warwick, has suggested to many that the unified scheme dates from the reign of Ælfred's son Eadweard. Others argue that the West Saxon king was able to influence the construction of burhs in Mercia via his son-in-law. The construction dates of the individual burhs are in most cases uncertain.

Roman wall circuit of *Venta Belgarum*), required 2,400 men.

The scale and ambition of Ælfred's scheme can, perhaps, best be seen at Wareham (see p.195), where the Host had made camp in 875 and where, between the Rivers Frome and Piddle which run eastwards into Poole's great natural harbour, a new town was constructed.* The grid layout, the still-impressive ramparts and the size of the enclosed area, requiring a garrison of 1,600 men to defend it, are impressive evidence of engineering, military and social commitment. That is not to say that the natives of south Dorset, or any other region included in the scheme, signed up with enthusiasm to burghal construction, occupation and functioning in an integrated plan of 'national' defence. Asser hints at discord, even downright obduracy among those required to enforce these burdens on the estates of Wessex:

> What of the mighty disorder and confusion of his own people—to say nothing of his own malady†—who would undertake of their own accord little or no work for the common needs of the kingdom?... By gently instructing, cajoling, urging, commanding and (in the end, when his patience was exhausted) by sharply chastising those who were disobedient and by despising popular stupidity and stubbornness in every way, he carefully and cleverly exploited and converted his bishops and ealdormen and nobles, and his thegns... and reeves.[18]

At times, Asser goes on, forts remained unbuilt or incomplete because of idleness or laxity in carrying out the king's commands. The same issues of parochialism, regional political tension and reluctance to accept the heavy burdens of Ælfred's demands fomented unease and recalcitrance which must, at times, have driven the king to distraction. These tensions reinforce a sense

---

* The possibility that a fort constructed by the Danish army there in 875, or an earlier defensive perimeter for the minster, was Ælfred's model cannot be discounted.

† Ælfred's medical history has been much discussed. Asser reflects on his bodily infirmities in several passages. Several scholars have suggested that he suffered from Crohn's disease, a painful and debilitating intestinal condition.

that even among the *Angelcynn*, regional and factional interests were more pervasive than any sense of 'Englishness'.

It is particularly significant that burhs were raised at key strategic points along the Thames: at Southwark, opposite the Roman city of London; on Sashes Island in Berkshire, at Wallingford, Oxford and Cricklade at the river's head. They might just as well have been sited to reinforce a message to Mercia as to provide a general line of defence against Scandinavian threats from the north. A thousand-odd years later in the 1940s the Thames once more became a strategic frontier, part of the General Headquarters Line—a natural defensible ditch against an invading army possessed of tanks and aircraft. Passing along the upper reaches of the river today one can still see the remains of many of the pill boxes which face the river on its north (Mercian) side. At Wallingford the Ælfredan defences are still visible, as is the classic grid pattern of the town.*

The development of many of the burhs into successful commercial trading centres in the tenth century at Oxford, Hastings, Lewes, Wareham, Chichester and elsewhere, is a reminder that one of their functions was to concentrate population, both for defence and to bolster the internal economy of Wessex. The extent to which Ælfred conceived of their economic potential is unclear. He had the defunct trading ports to hint at such potential, but he also appreciated the need to incentivize the regional populations who must garrison them. One potential solution was to give rights of freehold and trade in the burhs (the origins of medieval burghal rights) in return for co-operation, and the clearest statement of this strategy comes from a charter belonging to the last decade of his reign.

* The burghal towns were not, for the most part, designed with complete internal grids of streets. Martin Biddle has shown that centrally opposed gates linked by two roads crossing each other at the centre of the burh naturally developed into a grid of streets as the towns were populated over, perhaps, several decades. Biddle 1976.

The 'Arrangements for the building of fortifications at Worcester',[19] as this charter is known, offers a partial glimpse of some of the processes involved. The burh had been founded or refounded by Æðelred and his wife Æðelflæd, Ælfred's formidable daughter. The charter, dating between 880 and 899, records that some time after its establishment they decided to grant half of their rights 'whether in the market or in the street, both within the fortification or outside' to Bishop Wærferth. In addition, land-rents, fines for fighting or theft and dishonest trading, damages to the burh wall and other offences admitting of compensation, were to be shared between the ealdorman and the bishop. Significantly, the waggon-shilling and load-penny were to go to the king, 'as they have always done at Droitwich'. These latter were dues on cart-loads or mule-loads of salt, a traditional royal perquisite.* The document was drawn up in Mercia before its councillors and with King Ælfred as chief witness.

There is much in this document to intrigue the historian. First, the detail shows that burhs were defined as much by their regulations as by their physical form. The marketplace operated under its own rules, not defined here but perhaps similar to those later prescribed under King Æðelstan (924–939).† Here the *port-gerefa* or port-reeve administered rules and tariffs on behalf of the ealdorman and king. He may also have played an increasing judiciary role, maintaining defences and order within the ramparts. Early Medieval law had to adapt to these new judicial and economic entities. That ealdormen and bishops were to enjoy many of the fruits of these new, protected trading entrepôts shows how commercial and political capital was being deployed by the king

---

* The ancient salt route from Droitwich to Worcester is less than 5 miles (8 km) by either Roman road or along the River Salwarpe. From Worcester salt is likely to have been loaded into barges and floated down the River Severn to Gloucester, whence it could be transported overland to the head of the navigable Thames at Cricklade.
† The so-called *Grately code*, of about 930. See below, Chapter 9.

to ensure their success and his councillors' loyalty to the project; and how those powers and commercial rights were to be concentrated in the late Saxon town.

The Worcester charter also offers hints to help solve some of the difficulties caused by the uncertain chronology of the Burghal Hidage and the difficulty of dating its sequence, which are crucial to understanding Ælfred's development as a political and military thinker. The telling clue, I think, is that the burh at Worcester had been founded some time before the charter was drawn up. In that time Bishop Wærferth's status had changed. Asser tells us that in the years after Edington, when Ælfred conceived his vision for a renaissance among the *Angelcynn*, he drew to his court scholars from Kent, from Wales (Asser himself), from the Continent (Grimbald and John) and particularly from Mercia. One of these, Plegmund, would be rewarded with the spiritual throne of Canterbury in 890. Wærferth, Bishop of Worcester, whose huge diocese comprised the ancient territory of the Hwicce, was another. Asser says that he (Asser) was rewarded with many gifts for his contribution to the court, including two monasteries.* Wærferth, we know from other sources, was granted lands by Ælfred and Æðelred at *Hwaetmundes stane* in London, together with commercial privileges there.[20] A later grant, dating from Ælfred's last years, confers lands at *Æðeredes hyd* (Queenshythe, on Thames Street) on Plegmund and Wærferth. It has been suggested that both sites were part of Ælfred's plan to restore 'the city of London splendidly—after so many towns had been burned and so many people slaughtered'.[21]

We know that Asser came to the royal court in about 885, and that he believed Ælfred's London project to have been in train the following year, at the latest. It is tempting, therefore, to date the Worcester charter to the second half of the decade, and the original

---

* Congresbury and Banwell; that is to say, he was to enjoy the income from their estates and exercise a role as absentee abbot. See below, Chapter 12.

construction of the burh there to a few years before. The generous royal grants at Worcester, London and elsewhere can be seen, in this context, as Ælfred's recognition of the contribution made by key loyalists to the grand design. A more cynical view might be that he was purchasing their approbation and co-operation: Wærferth was being rewarded with lucrative protectionist trading rights.*

Like Ælfred's other bishops, Wærferth also received a personal copy of the king's own translation of Pope Gregory's *Cura Pastoralis*, or Pastoral Care. By great fortune, his is the only copy that survives—in the Bodleian library at Oxford.[22] Ælfred had chosen his trustees carefully, not least in his support for Æðelred with whom he maintained a close relationship throughout the last two decades of his rule. By the time of his death at the age of fifty Ælfred had constructed a network of more than thirty defended trading and military strongholds across the breadth of Wessex and beyond: his influence on the geography of the South is profound and enduring.

Asser dates the restoration of London to 886 and this may indeed be the year in which some formal recognition of the ancient city's new status was made. There is every reason to believe that Ælfred gave his daughter, Æðelflæd, in marriage to the Mercian lord at this time, sealing their alliance. The *Chronicle*'s version of Asser's statement is that Ælfred 'occupied London, and all the English people submitted to him, except those who were in captivity to the Danes; and then entrusted the city to Ealdorman Æðelred'.[23] It sounds as though London's and Mercia's status were consolidated in a single event; and it is not impossible that the written treaty with Guðrum dates from this period of consolidation.

Many commentators now suspect, however, that new commercial life had been growing within the old Roman walls since

---

* This is the same Bishop of Worcester who, in 872, had been forced to lease lands to raise tribute for the Host overwintering in London. See above, p. 117n.

the demise of *Lundenwic* in the 830s or 840s. The archaeologist Jeremy Haslam argues that, apart from a brief period between 877 and 878, the Host, with its Mercian appointee Ceolwulf, was in control of the port.[24] The departure of the fleet from Fulham in 880 and of Ceolwulf at about the same time, together with Ælfred's endorsement of Æðelred, allowed him to assert control over the pre-eminent site on the navigable Thames, a pivotal location in the defence of Wessex and in its trading links with Mercia and the Continent.

The occupation of the city recorded under 886 in the *Chronicle*, described later by Æðelweard as a 'citadel', may have been an additional response to the military activities at Rochester in 884 and on the coast of East Anglia in 885, as well as a core component of the burghal system rolled out during the same decade.[25] A notable coin issue, the Ælfredan 'London monogram' of the 880s, was very public confirmation that the king intended to associate his military, political and economic successes with the former Roman capital.

Mapping Ælfred's control and influence during the 880s and 890s is relatively straightforward, even if the chronology floats uncertainly. The nature and extent of Æðelred's power in Mercia is much more difficult to determine in detail. We know that London was placed under his protection after its capture (for want of a better word) by Ælfred some time between 878 and 886. We also know that the boundary of Guðrum's lands, at least nominally, followed the line of the River Lea and then the River Great Ouse as far as its conjunction with Watling Street at Stony Stratford, on what later became the Buckinghamshire border with Northamptonshire.*

---

* The Midland shires take their names from settlements which became important during the early tenth century. For earlier political divisions we have to go back to the Tribal Hidage of the seventh or eighth century, when that part belonged, perhaps, to the Chilternsæte of Middle Anglia.

To the west and north of that point the geography of power in the last decades of the ninth century becomes more obscure. Buckingham itself appears, slightly anomalously, in the Burghal Hidage, along with those Mercian outposts Worcester and Warwick, indicating that during Æðelred's rule as ealdorman he was able to extend his control to the upper reaches of the Warwickshire Avon and the Great Ouse. Bedford, we know, lay at the edge of Guðrum's East Anglian territory. The fortified towns under Scandinavian control are the next pointers, albeit negative: Derby (*Norðworðig* to the native Mercians), Leicester, Nottingham, Lincoln and Stamford, the so-called Five Boroughs,* are regarded as having been settled by veterans of the *mycel here*.

Key to the pattern of Danish control of the north Midlands is the course of the River Trent. Fortified redoubts on the river at Torksey, Nottingham, Derby (on the Derwent, a tributary) and Repton, which became the foci of more substantial settlements, provided the communications and trading network from which the settlers supported themselves after initial phases of raiding and looting. From these centres, which would become the medieval shire towns of the Midlands, existing estates were bought, stolen, fragmented and redistributed to create a patchwork of land-holding, based on ancient divisions but distinct, perhaps, in their management and composition. No historian believes that Danish veterans formed anything like a majority of the rural population; but they occupied key landholdings and, we must suppose, positions of civic and rural authority. From Lincoln the Danish settlement spread east to the coast. Additional forts, raised in later defence against aggressive West Saxon and Mercian military campaigns, were constructed at Northampton and Towcester. The River Great Ouse may have acted as the boundary between the Midlands Scandinavian settlers and those under the rule of Guðrum.

* See below, Chapter 8, p. 409.

It is striking, on a map showing Scandinavian place names in the Midlands,* that they occur almost exclusively north and east of Watling Street, often shown on maps as a continuation of the Ælfred–Guðrum treaty line.[26] Further along that line, towards the north-west, Æðelred's ability to engage with the forces of Gwynedd at Conwy shows that he was in control of the Cheshire plain and the old territories of the *Magonsæte* and *Wrocansæte*. There was, then, a congruent if sparsely detailed zone of influence which remained under West Mercian control and which does not seem to have come under concerted external attack after 878. It is striking that a large number of minster foundations survived the first Viking Age in West Mercia, just as the institutional apparatus of bishop and diocese was also sustained there long enough to re-emerge, more or less unscathed, in the reform movement of the late tenth century.

The *mycel here* and its adherents, whatever their status in Eastern Mercia, had given up their ambitions to conquer Mercia south and west of Watling Street. Æðelred's authority was that of a *de facto* king, judging by the geographical spread and une-quivocally independent nature of his charter grants.[27] But no coinage bearing his name has been found, even though there is strong evidence for minting in Mercia, possibly at Chester, Shrewsbury and Hereford, during the latter part of Æðelred's reign and that of his widow, Æðelflæd.[28] Ælfred's mints struck coins in his name as *Rex* at the Mercian burhs of Gloucester, Oxford and London. Just as Ælfred's militarized peace guaran-teed Mercian authority with its neighbours, so his coinage guar-anteed the value of the economy throughout the lands of the *Angelcynn*.

---

* The interpretation of place names as direct evidence for the distribution of settlers and especially of ethnicity is fraught with complexity. See Hadley 2006, 99, for example. I use it here in the most general way. But there is a stark geographical real-ity to this line, which I explore below in Chapter 8.

Although the documentary and literary evidence from later
centuries shows how deeply embedded Scandinavian influence
became in central Britain, archaeologists trying to detect the
invaders' settlements in the excavated buildings and landscapes
of the period have had much less luck. To begin with, large-scale
excavations of the sort needed to understand the fine detail of
settlement development, function and layout are understandably
rare in towns which have been occupied ever since. The justly
famous Viking dig on Coppergate in York in the late 1970s provides the exception rather than the rule.*

The Five Boroughs have not yet given up their secrets.[29] But it
is significant that both Derby and Leicester were important ecclesiastical centres before the middle of the ninth century, and that
both had been the sites of Roman forts. Derby's Roman name
was *Derventio*, strikingly like its Norse name but unlike the Old
English *Norðworðig*. Lincoln, a former Roman *colonia* (*Lindum*)
like York (*Eboracum*) and London (*Londinium*), had probably
been the seat of the bishops of Lindsey, the last of whom is
recorded in about 870 before a long hiatus. Nottingham is
unusual: its Brittonic name *Tig Guocobauc*, the 'city of caves', was
recorded (by Asser) alongside the Old English *Snotengaham*—
whose form suggests that it had once been the centre of a *regio* or
tribal territory: that of Snota's people.[30] Its fate at the hands of the
mycel here in 867, when they captured and fortified it, is directly
attested in the *Anglo-Saxon Chronicle*. Excavations have so far
only hinted at the nature of a D-shaped fortification enclosing a
clifftop promontory overlooking the River Leen, less than a mile
above its confluence with the Trent.[31] Stamford, the lowest crossing point of the River Welland west of the fens in Lincolnshire,

* See below, Chapters 7 and 8: p. 293 onwards.

where the Roman Ermine Street runs north-west, was a borough by 972, but its history before that is more or less obscure: it is the only one of the Five Boroughs not to have become a county town.

If nothing else, then, it seems that the leaders of the *mycel here* were careful in their choice of targets, seizing existing central places to control new territories. They took advantage of both military opportunities and the tax-raising, administrative and legal reins which made them effectively kings of East Mercia, Northumbria and East Anglia.

Perhaps the most accessible (accessible, that is, to archaeologists excavating in advance of construction) of the towns that fell under Scandinavian rule in the ninth century is Thetford on the Norfolk–Suffolk border, England's sixth largest town at the time of the Domesday survey in 1086. It suffered severe decline in subsequent centuries and the focus of settlement moved away from the late Saxon core on the south bank of the River Little Ouse; so it remained largely undeveloped until after the Second World War. Thetford obeys the first rule of Early Medieval connectivity on the Viking travel map: lying on a navigable waterway at a ford, close to an Iron Age hillfort and on the line of the ancient Icknield Way on the east edge of the fenlands. It was occupied in 870 by the *mycel here*, and by the reign of King Eadgar (959–975) at the latest it had its own mint.[32] It supported ten churches in the period before the Conquest of 1066.

Excavations in recent decades have shown that defensible earthen ramparts stood on both sides of the river.[33] By the end of the tenth century the town was a thriving trading centre, producing distinctive Thetford ware pottery and supporting a range of crafts: bone- and antler-working, silver-smithing, weaving and leather-working. The Viking Age might have left the natives with a fear of invasion; it seems also to have driven Britain towards a new urban and industrial confidence. But we would have considerable difficulty in discriminating between a 'Danish' town like

Thetford and an Ælfredan burh without supporting historical evidence—which itself has to be read with caution.

The same problems of identification and interpretation bedevil attempts to trace rural Scandinavian settlement—the dwellings of the veterans who settled as farmers and integrated with the *ceorls* and thegns of the countryside. The Norse and Old English languages were mutually intelligible, at least at a basic functional level; their cultures shared Germanic origins and interactions. But would we be able to distinguish a 'Viking' house in rural Lincolnshire from that of an indigene? Did Scandinavians build new houses in their own style, or occupy the existing dwellings of the natives? Did they rapidly copy local building traditions so as to fit in and not attract undue attention? Even outstanding examples of exotic longhouses, apparently so diagnostic a feature of Scandinavian settlement in the far north and west, are difficult to interpret. The most often cited of these is a remote upland farmstead at Gauber high pasture, Ribblehead, high in the Yorkshire Dales at over 1000 feet (300 m). Around a paved courtyard, in the ninth century, a longhouse 60 feet by 15 feet (18 × 5 m) was constructed on a thick rubble wall base with rounded corners and entrances in the ends, along with a smaller rectangular 'kitchen block' and a smithy: a self-contained steading whose economy must have been primarily pastoral. Alan King's 1970s excavations invited the question: how can we tell the difference between a new Scandinavian settlement on apparently marginal land, and an indigenous Northumbrian farm? The question remains unresolved.[34]

If we cannot yet diagnose Scandinavian rural housing there are at least hints of where we might look. James Campbell, professor of medieval history at the University of Oxford, points to the remarkable concentration of no fewer than thirteen names ending in -*by* in two Norfolk hundreds, East and West Flegg.[35] They lie on the coast just north of Great Yarmouth in an area either side of Filby Broad, confined by the rivers Bure and Thurne, which must, in the Early Medieval period, have formed a large low-lying island in the peaty coastal marshes. Large parts of the surrounding broadlands lie below sea level; a catastrophic inundation would cut them off again. Campbell believes that something like a *longphort* may have existed here; a western counterpart to the island fortress of Walcheren in the estuary of the Scheldt, a more established version of the camp at Torksey on the lower Trent. Archaeologists concentrating resources here might one day identify and excavate the houses of those enterprising pirates and their successors.

A number of sites have produced evidence that they were occupied before, during and after the Scandinavian settlement. If we cannot identify new Norse settlers in the landscape, can we tell when they took over existing settlements? The answer, frustratingly, is very rarely. The prevailing model of pre-Viking settlement is of dispersed farms and *vill* complexes with low population concentrations, often impermanently sited, unenclosed and with mixed agricultural economies: *ceorls* producing a broad range of food renders and craft products for their lords; lords consuming instead of farming. With the secularization of the minsters in the eighth century, regularly laid-out farmsteads and hall complexes enclosed by ditch or hedge, increasingly specialized in their output and tending towards nucleation,* appear *de novo* or supersede earlier, less formal, layouts. The old, bullion-fed economy of folk-land† and render was evolving towards heritable bookland and rents paid in cash, with surpluses heading for regional markets.

Excavations spanning the entire second half of the twentieth century at the deserted medieval village of Wharram Percy, where

---

* The set of attracting processes by which geographers identify the origins of villages and towns.

† Land held for a life interest, or on lease, and subject to obligations of service or produce. It might be passed to the heirs of a tenant by the king's permission.

24. THE RAMPARTS AT WAREHAM: a model Ælfredan burh,
the site of an early royal monastery and the Viking camp of 875.

generations of archaeologists have cut their teeth, have shown that, with patience, the telltale signs of Scandinavian influence can be detected. Wharram lies 20 miles (32 km) north-east of York in a dry valley on the high chalk Wolds. At the site of what became the South Manor, occupation has been proved continuously between the eighth and fourteenth centuries. In the late ninth to early tenth century the settlement was reorganized with formal boundaries and a wooden church was built whose successor still stands, roofless, in apparent isolation from modern life. At the South Manor a smithy continued to function through the turbulence of Viking occupation at York; and distinctly Scandinavian items—strap-ends, belt-sliders and sword hilts, and a Norwegian hone stone—were among its artefacts.[36] This high-status establishment was either taken over by new Scandinavian lords, or its indigenous thegns were susceptible to their material luxuries. Given the lack of apparent violence in the Wharram record, we might offer the thought that this was an instance where an élite member of the Host married into the family of a local worthy. At the time of the Domesday survey in the 1080s, Wharram belonged to a Lagmann (*Lǫgmaðr*) and a Carli—distinctively Scandinavian names.[37]

The vastly enlarged pool of evidence from excavation during the last thirty years has created a picture of regional variability, diversity of layout and complexity of interpretation: there is no model rural settlement of the ninth and tenth centuries. Increasingly, archaeologists are running shy of ethnic explanations of dramatic changes taking place in rural settlements in those centuries and concentrating instead on social and economic evolutions that may represent indigenous change but might have been triggered by the conflicts of the Viking Age.

Sometimes, settlement archaeology has to fill in for an almost complete lack of narrative history. The political fortunes of the Cornish peninsula, the lands of the West Wealas, are invisible. A fatal alliance with a Danish war band against Wessex in the days of King Ecgberht signalled the end of its independence. A last named British king, Dungarth, drowned ignominiously in 875.[38] A thriving church, with a major minster at St Germans west of Plymouth, can be inferred from the proliferation of saintly and church enclosure place names. The modern names of Cornwall's rural settlements, a mix of Brittonic and English, reflect slow and late Anglicization. Apart from Lundy ('Puffin') Island there are no accepted Scandinavian names. Ælfred built no burhs west of the River Tamar.

The distinctiveness of Cornish culture is striking. Its Christian stone sculpture has strong affinities with traditions in Ireland, Wales and Man. Its stone and turf 'rounds' remind one of Irish raths: tightly-packed complexes of circular houses inside embanked circular enclosures, dating from the late Iron Age and continuing into the post-Roman period. Cornwall may have lain outside the developing market economies of Wessex and the Danish territories, but it was by no means isolated from trade and international influence. A unique style of cooking vessel called bar-lug ware, designed for suspension over an open hearth, is found here in large quantities. It may have its origins in Frisia, and variants are found there, in Ireland and in the Baltic lands; and since it is generally regarded as dating between the eighth and eleventh centuries its presence is happily diagnostic of Early Medieval or Viking Age settlement.

Very few definitively Early Medieval settlements have yet been excavated on the peninsula; but at Mawgan Porth, a few miles north of Newquay on the Atlantic Cornish coast, three very unusual courtyard houses, prolific in their use and disposal of bar-lug pottery and preserved by the deep layers of windblown sand that sealed their fate, tell of a society that was anything but peripheral. In each case a longhouse, built on faced rubble foundations and divided in half to accommodate both cattle and people, lay at the centre of a complex of interconnected rooms clustered around a metalled courtyard.[39] Each house seems to have been dug into the middens of its predecessor—these were long-established settlements, self-contained but outward looking. A single coin of Æðelred II, although poorly provenanced, proves that the site was still occupied in the late tenth century or later. The neat, compact internal arrangements—hearths, slab-sided cupboards and stone box-beds—are reminiscent of features found in houses in Orkney and Shetland. But there is no reason to think that this was a Norse settlement: more likely it reflects a broader shared culture of Atlantic maritime peoples whose lives and material cultures reflected common concerns such as shelter, warmth and domestic tidiness; economies based on small mixed farms occupying fertile soil but exposed to severe seasonal conditions. It is not impossible that, developing out of the indigenous tradition of the 'round', the Cornish courtyard longhouse farm itself served as a model for other Atlantic communities to follow.

The eighth- and ninth-century inhabitants of Flixborough, 5 miles (8 km) south of the confluence of the Rivers Trent and Humber in Lincolnshire, must have undergone an early and prolonged experience of Scandinavian contact. Many of the surrounding place names—nearby industrial Scunthorpe, as well as Althorpe, Appleby, Brigg and Normanby—have a strong Scandinavian flavour. After periodic exposure to coastal and estuarine raids from the beginning of the ninth century the Trent valley was penetrated early in the wars of the 860s; 20 miles (32 km) upstream the *mycel here* built their stronghold at Torksey in 872; and Lincoln was a Danish burh well into the tenth century. Flixborough's location, on top of a scarp overlooking the Trent to the west from about 150 feet (45 m) above sea level, put it in the front line of Anglo-Danish relations. It shares many characteristics with that other riverine community, Brandon in the East Anglian Breckland.*

It is not the excavated agricultural buildings of Flixborough—barns and workshops—that impress the archaeologist so much as its rubbish dumps, containing hundreds of thousands of animal bones, large quantities of pottery sherds, glass and metalworking fragments from both smithing and, in later decades, smelting; loom-weights and other weaving debris, indicating the production of woollen cloth and linen; and fine metal dress accessories.†
In its ninth-century prime the presence of window lead, writing styli and window glass indicates that Flixborough supported a literate, wealthy community. A remarkable hoard of woodworking tools found contained in a lead tank suggests that the community may have enjoyed the services of its own shipwright.[40]

The exceptional preservation of the accumulated dross of three centuries of Anglo-Saxon life (material apparently dumped in barrow-loads of alkaline wood ash) can be attributed both to the behaviour of its inhabitants and to the meteorological fates: the whole site, like that at Mawgan Porth, was later buried by 3 feet (1 m) and more of windblown sand. The excavators' good fortune was boosted by the occurrence of dateable coins, personal adornments and pottery in key phases of the stratigraphic sequence, so the time-slicing archaeological exercise which allots activity and deposition to discrete phases allowed a detailed narrative of Flixborough's history to be constructed, even if some mixing and reworking of deposits made analysis a complicated process.

Well into the early ninth century Flixborough was connected widely to the outside world: to the pottery production and

* See above, Chapter 3, p. 105.

† The excavations identified the craft and agricultural components of a more substantial, as yet unlocated complex lying to the east. Three or four sturdy buildings, with collateral workshops or outhouses clustered around a shallow valley that became a refuse dump, seem to have replaced one another over a period of three centuries of continuous occupation and activity. Loveluck 2007.

trading port at Ipswich, to its own Lincolnshire hinterland and to the Continent, whence exotic pottery and glass drinking vessels were imported. There is little doubt, from the nature and quantity of the material culture here, that this was a major estate centre, although there is ongoing debate about whether it was monastic or secular. That ambivalence may well be a signature of such sites; by the ninth century the distinction may be too subtle to matter.

Like Brandon, Flixborough has also been cited as an example of a so-called 'productive site': something between a minster and a *wic*, manufacturing objects for trade and importing luxury goods in return.[41] It was well placed to exploit inland and coastal waterways and lay just 5 miles (8 km) west of the old Roman road, Ermine Street, that linked the Humber with Lincoln. A few surviving documents from the period suggest that estate surveys, of a sort common in Carolingian France, were becoming more frequent in the increasingly complex land management environment of lowland Britain.[42] So the literate owners of Flixborough might have enjoyed reading reassuring lists of their assets during cold winter days when their barns were emptying of fodder and grain.

For the purposes of detecting Scandinavian influence at Flixborough, three features of the evidence stand out. Firstly, a major redevelopment occurred during the 860s or thereabouts.[43] Secondly, that episode did not result in fundamental re-planning of the agricultural and industrial part of the site. It was cleared and rebuilt on a different pattern: under new management, perhaps, but not necessarily foreign management. There is no suggestion of the sort of wholesale destruction graphically encountered at Portmahomack and described so vividly at many other monastic sites. After the mid- to late ninth-century horizon there is less evidence of exotic material being imported to the site, and that is a general feature of the century. Craft products seem by then to have been destined for consumption on the estate. Thirdly, archaeologist Chris Loveluck suggests that what was once a single large estate, of the type recognized across Anglo-Saxon England, seems to have been subdivided, before being restored under single lordship at the time of the Domesday survey.[44] The two parts, North Conesby, the 'King's settlement', and Flixborough, 'Flikkr's fort', both bear Scandinavian names.[45]

Lowland Britain underwent profound social and economic change in the ninth century. If historians and archaeologists are still frustrated in their attempts to detect the whiff of the smoking Scandinavian gun, they can at least begin to describe the geography and economic patterns which mark this age of transition. It may not matter, in the end, whether Viking prints are found on the trigger or not: the first Viking Age turned Europe on its head. Even so, despite the apparent chaos portrayed by the chronicles, the narrative of everyday life continued, altered but dynamically adaptive. People got by.

ARRIVALS AND DEPARTURES

A STORM BREWING—TWO HOSTS—
A GREAT CAMPAIGN—A KING'S DUTY—
PEACE, PLAGUE AND FAMINE—
THE CODEX AUREUS—THE TRAVELS
OF OHTHERE—ÆLFRED'S LEGACY—
KING EADWEARD

6

GOÐRUM SE NORÞERNA CYNING FORÞ-
*ferde, þæs fulluhtnama wæs Æþelstan, se wæs Ælfredes
cyninges godsunu, 7 he bude on Eastenglum, 7 þæt lond
ærest gesæt...*[1]

890. Guðrum, the northern king whose baptismal name was
Æðelstan, passed away; he was King Ælfred's godson, and he
dwelt in East Anglia, and was the first to take possession of
that country.

891. Three Irishmen came to King Ælfred in a boat without
any oars from Ireland... The boat in which they set out was
made from two and a half hides... and after a week they came
to land in Cornwall [*Cornwalum*] and soon went to King
Ælfred.

892.* After Easter... appeared the star which in Latin is called
'cometa'. In this year the great Host about which we formerly
spoke went again from the east kingdom westward to Boulogne [*Bunáan*] and were there provided with ships so that
they crossed in one voyage, horses and all, and then came up

---

* Hidden in these portentous arrivals and departures, recorded in the *Anglo-Saxon
Chronicle* is another: this is the last entry by the original scribe of the 'A' manuscript;
a new hand took over for 893.

25. THE DANISH GAFF CUTTER *Eda Frandsen*:
Gabriel Clarke on the bowsprit.

into the mouth of the Lympne [*Limene muþan*] with two
hundred and fifty ships... Then soon after this Hæsten came
with eighty ships into the mouth of the Thames [*Temes*], and
made himself a fort at Milton Regis [*Middeltune*], and the
other host at Appledore [*Apuldre*: literally 'Apple tree'].[2]

The departure from the political stage of Guðrum, Ælfred's former antagonist, could hardly have been more ill timed for the
king of the West Saxons. A storm was brewing in the east. In 889
one of the Scandinavian armies, which had enjoyed rich pickings
among the fractured Frankish kingdoms in the previous decade,
came out of the Seine and, sailing up the River Vire to St Lô,
was heavily defeated the following year by a Breton army. The
Host now moved north and east, penetrating the River Scheldt,
and encamped at Louvain on the River Dijle, a tributary of the
Scheldt, 10 miles (16 km) or so east of what is now Brussels.
Here it was met by an army of East Franks, Saxons and Bavarians
under King Arnulf, son of the late Carloman. The Host was put
to flight, its camp overrun. The gloating annalist of the monastery at Fulda recorded that the river was blocked by the bodies of
dead pagans.[3]

That winter a severe famine struck the region, ravaging
Christian and pagan communities alike. The Scandinavian armies,
perhaps sensing that the fates were against them, now decided
that their Frankish game was no longer worth the candle. Odo,
de facto king of the West Franks since 888, saw an opportunity to
be rid of their menace, and gave them sufficient ships to leave.
The annalist of St Vaast wrote that 'seeing the whole realm worn
down by hunger they left Francia in the autumn, and crossed the
sea'.[4] En masse, and perhaps in collusion with Northumbrian and
East Anglian allies, they determined to mount a decisive assault
on the *Angelcynn*.

A highly detailed series of entries in the *Anglo-Saxon Chronicle*
for the next three years, at precisely the time when it was first

being compiled, reads like an almost continuous war narrative, fought for the highest stakes. They crossed the Channel as two fleets: warriors, dependents, animals, the lot. Two hundred and fifty ships entered the mouth of the River Lympne on the south coast of Kent. Lympne, once a Roman port, is landlocked now, its ancient hythe lying high and dry at the foot of the chalk scarp that overlooks the flat expanse of Romney marsh; the Royal Military canal, a relic of more recent invasion fears, is its only access to the sea.* During the ninth century the river was sufficiently deep to enable the Viking Host to row as far up as Appledore, now some 8 miles (13 km) from the sea and lying at the east end of the Isle of Oxney whence the River Rother once issued.

At or close by Appledore the Host captured 'a fort of primitive structure, because there was [only] a small band of rustics in it' and made of it a winter camp.[5] Thirty miles (48 km) to the north, across the Downs of Kent, a smaller but no less menacing fleet of about eighty ships sailed up the Thames to the Isle of Sheppey; from there they rowed along the muddy channel of the River Swale and a mile or so up Milton Creek to make their winter camp uncomfortably close to the fortress at Rochester.

Canterbury offered rich pickings, as did trading settlements at Sarre and Fordwich and minsters on Thanet and Sheppey.† Kent east of the Medway had not been fortified under Ælfred's burghal plans of the 880s‡ and we do not know what, if any, provision the Kentish administration had made for its defences. Ealdorman Sigehelm seems to have been a loyal ally of Wessex: his daughter

* Conceived in 1804 and completed in 1809.

† The abrupt cessation of coinage minted at Canterbury after 892 suggests that the Host, unrecorded by the *Chronicle*, attacked and razed the town that year. The mint did not resume production until after 910. Dolley 1970, 20–1.

‡ The kings of the West Saxons and Mercians had been overlords of Kent for the whole of the eighth century; but their power to coerce its inhabitants and ealdormen to contribute the common burdens of fort and bridge building seems to have been limited or non-existent. The fort near Appledore was, it seems, only half-finished when it was overrun.

26. CANTERBURY, the site of St Augustine's missionary church of 597 and perhaps the only recognizable town in ninth-century Britain.

became the third wife of Eadweard, Ælfred's son and presumptive heir. Archbishop Plegmund was a member of Ælfred's 'renaissance' court; a close political and military relationship is implied.

Without the defensive and offensive advantages of garrisoned fortifications, Ælfred could not hope to expel such large forces; nor could he concentrate his attack on one for fear of allowing the other to penetrate west into Wessex with impunity. He had not yet, it seems, installed Eadweard, who makes his first stage entrance in the year of the invasion, as sub-king in Kent.* That Eadweard was being groomed to succeed him is in no doubt. He was provided with substantial estates in his father's will, including all Ælfred's booklands in Kent and, judging by the frequency with which he witnessed royal charters, he spent much time with the king on his itineraries through the shires.[6]

Ælfred's response to the arrival of the Continental fleets, early in 893, was to bring his own army to a point more or less equidistant between the two, unsure of their ultimate intentions. He had by this time instituted radical changes in the way his forces were able to respond to external threats. His field army, the *fyrð*, was now divided into two, so that one force was always in the field, with a contingency for those permanently on standby to garrison the burhs.[7] The system was now to be tested to its limits.

According to the *Chronicle*, the Host at Appledore disdained to take the field against Ælfred's army. Instead its scouts, mounted warriors and foraging parties probed the edges of the vast dense woodland of the Weald: *Andredesweald*, the haunt of wild beasts, charcoal burners and an ancient iron-working industry stretching across the Downs as far as Hampshire. It was a form of guerrilla warfare: testing, teasing. They moved 'through the woods in gangs and bands, wherever the margin was left unguarded; and

* He was the oldest surviving son of Ælfred and Ælswið, a year or two younger than his sister Æðelflæd. Born sometime during the 870s, he witnessed his first charter in 892.

almost every day other troops, both from the levies and also from the forts, went to attack them either by day or by night'.[8]

Only after Easter did they abandon their redoubt and their fleet at Appledore and march west; they kept to 'the thickets of a huge wood called Andred by the common people, spread as far as Wessex [*Occidentales Anglos*] and gradually wasted the adjacent provinces, that is *Hamtunscire* and *Bearrucscire*'.[9] After this campaign of plundering with no attempt, it seems, at conquest, during which they were apparently shadowed but not engaged in open battle,* they 'seized much plunder, and wished to carry that north across the Thames into Essex to meet the ships'.[10]

Sometime during the early summer of 893 they were brought to battle at Farnham (*Fearnhamme*: 'River meadow where ferns grow') on the River Wey in Surrey. The *Chronicle* is silent regarding the names of the commanders, but Æðelweard, writing a hundred years later and drawing on material from a lost version of the *Chronicle*, names the West Saxon leader as Eadweard, the king's son. Eadweard's forces inflicted a heavy defeat on the Host, injuring its leader and retrieving all the booty that had been taken during the rampage across Sussex. The *mycel here* was driven north over the Thames somewhere near Staines, apparently in such disarray that they did not even manage to find a ford. One imagines the pell mell chaos of a rout: baggage, weapons, loot and even armour cast aside; panic, slaughter on the river banks and bodies floating downstream.

---

* There is some evidence that a series of signal beacons linked the Thames valley with the south coast during this period, allowing limited intelligence of enemy movements to alert the levies. Gower 2002; David Hill and Sheila Sharp, in a short essay included in Lavelle 2010, 218ff. The burhs were not generally intervisible; but there would have been considerable advantage in a system linking them by hilltop beacons. The place name element '*weard*'—lookout, watch—often with the suffix '*dune*' (hill) giving the modern Warden plus the pleonastic Hill, supplies one clue. *Weardsetl* is an alternative form. The place name element 'Tot' is also regarded as a marker for the site of a beacon.

The survivors followed the course of the River Colne as far upstream as the island called Thorney (on the north-west periphery of the Heathrow Airport complex, now swallowed by a motorway interchange) and, their commander too ill to flee further, found themselves besieged by Eadweard.

At the point of victory the momentum was lost: according to the *Chronicle* the levies, coming to the end of their deployment, ran out of provisions and left for home. Æðelweard says that the 'barbarians' asked for peace and that the West Saxons negotiated their withdrawal with an exchange of hostages; the Host retired not to Kent, but to East Anglia. But these accounts pose more questions than they answer. After Eadweard's brief appearance at Farnham and Thorney his role in the war of 893–894 is obscure.*

Was he written out of the official Ælfredan narrative to ensure that the king stood alone as hero? Or was his inability to keep his levies in the field regarded as a failure of leadership or loyalty? Who were these levies: his own retinue, certainly, and also those of the shires which had been ravaged by the Host, perhaps: Hampshire and Berkshire? But it is an intriguing possibility that, in preparation for his installation as sub-king of Kent, which may have happened in about 898, Eadweard was already in command of the Kentish levies; that they regarded themselves as having gone far beyond the traditional call of duty in chasing the Appledore Host across the southern shires and then beyond the Thames. And then, Æðelweard says that while Eadweard was still at Thorney, his brother-in-law Æðelred, ealdorman and sub-king of Mercia, came from London to his aid. If so, why lift the siege? Despite the contemporaneity of the *Chronicle* and the value of Æðelweard's insider information at court, it seems that either the complexities of the 893 campaign were such that no coherent account could be constructed; or, if one wants to detect political

* He is not mentioned at all in the *Chronicle* before Ælfred's death in 899.

undercurrents, the West Saxon spin doctors were already at work to contrive an official account that would cover unsightly stains and keep the narrative focused on Ælfred.

Ælfred's policy had always been to bargain straight and trust the enemy's sense of decency: it seems extraordinarily naïve. Time and again the Scandinavian armies accepted Ælfred's terms and defaulted, as they had so often in Francia. Given the otherwise sophisticated strategies displayed during the Viking wars, one must surmise that the underlying rationale of the *Angelcynn* leadership was always to buy time and limit its own casualties. There is a fine line between appeasement and low cunning.

The West Saxon and Mercian leadership now anticipated fighting wars on multiple fronts. Their principal fear was probably not either Host in isolation but that the two forces should combine and that the slumbering giants of East Anglia, Danish East Mercia and Northumbria might join in. While Eadweard had expelled the Appledore Host from Wessex, Ælfred seems to have concentrated diplomatic efforts on persuading the force under Hæsten, in the Thames estuary, to cross the Thames to Essex. If this war band leader is to be identified with the Viking raider whose name appears periodically like a rash in Continental sources spanning half a century, then the *Angelcynn* had good reason to fear him. He is implicated in a notorious series of raids deep into the Mediterranean in the years 859–862, with campaigns along the Loire at the end of that decade and into the 870s. Later tradition has embellished his feats and cruelties; even so, he seems to have been an unusually successful and energetic warlord over several decades. Whatever the truth, his career took him to the mouth of the Thames in 893.

In the uncertain political aftermath of Guðrum's death, Ælfred and Æðelred may have hoped that Hæsten would compete for the East Anglian kingship, killing two birds with one stone. We gather, from events later in 893, that while the Host lay at Milton Regis, Hæsten and his family received baptism. At least, the *Chronicle* records that his two sons were godchildren of, respectively, Ælfred and Æðelred. No such ceremony is likely to have been conducted without a peace deal ensuring that the *Deniscan* would leave Wessex alone; they had, it seems, been paid off. Given that Æðelred is recorded as co-sponsor, we might reasonably argue that the venue for both negotiation and ceremony was London, the timeshare capital for Mercia and Wessex and symbol of their alliance.

Hæsten's fleet duly crossed the estuary and built a fortress in Essex, at Benfleet (*Beamfleote*: 'Tree creek') overlooking the edge of the marshes to the north of Canvey Island, even as their comrades were fighting their way out of trouble across the Upper Thames. Here the remnants of the Appledore Host also arrived that summer and the two forces now combined. The *Angelcynn* had bought time in exchange for future trouble; and they are unlikely to have anticipated the grim news coming from the West Country. A Northumbrian fleet had sailed south from a port somewhere on the Irish Sea* and landed on the north Devonshire coast, while an East Anglian fleet, sailing along the south coast, now besieged Exeter.

This turn of events in the west looks like a co-ordinated plan to draw West Saxon forces away from the east and open up a second front. Hæsten, it appears, had successfully enrolled both the East Anglians (Guðrum's veterans of the campaign of 877–878, perhaps) and those of Guðroðr, the nominally Christian king of Scandinavian York, in his plan to finish what the *mycel here* had begun in the 860s. If the community of St Cuthbert recorded their reaction to their adopted king's involvement, it has not survived.

---

* A port on the River Ribble close to the later town of Preston would be consistent with the route of the traffic we know to have existed between York and Dublin in the late ninth and tenth centuries.

Ælfred's reaction was to march westwards with the bulk of the West Saxon levies, leaving Eadweard and Æðelred* behind to confront Hæsten and the, by now, combined forces from Milton and Appledore at Benfleet. They marched east through London, picking up extra forces as they went. When they arrived at Benfleet they found a part of the combined Host in residence; but Hæsten was away on a raiding expedition in Mercia. In a stunning coup, the English put the Host to flight, stormed the fort and took possession of everything inside, including Hæsten's wife and children. The ships of their considerable fleet were burned, sunk or otherwise taken to Rochester or London. For good or ill the Host could not now retire to the Continent whence they had come.

The *Chronicle* makes much of the victory at Benfleet and of Ælfred's magnanimous treatment of Hæsten's family, restoring them to the warlord in a one-sided gesture of good faith;† but Æðelweard ignores the Benfleet episode entirely and, given that the Host was able to take to the field again very shortly, and in dangerous numbers, we may judge that the bulk of its fighting force had been absent with their commander, leaving behind only a small garrison and the baggage train in his new fort. The victory at Benfleet had not, perhaps, been all that glorious.

Far to the west, the East Anglian and Northumbrian forces retired to their ships on Ælfred's arrival, precisely achieving their broader purpose to draw the main West Saxon *fyrð* from the east. Hæsten's combined army, dispossessed of its fort at Benfleet, now took up station in a new stronghold at Shoeburyness (*Sceobyrig on Eastseaxum*: 'the fort on the shoe-shaped spit') nearly 10 miles (16 km) to the east.

---

* By inference: the *Chronicle* does not name the commanders.
† A passage in Ælfred's own translation of Gregory the Great's *Pastoral Care* makes it clear that, following the example of King David, he saw restraint of royal power over enemies as a sign of virtue. Keynes and Lapidge 1983, 128.

In that whirlwind year of punch and counterpunch, a new phase now opened. With the apparent knowledge that the *fyrð* was otherwise occupied, the *Deniscan* once again left their fortress and with extraordinary boldness marched along the entire length of the Thames into Gloucestershire, making a rendezvous with forces from Northumbria and East Anglia that seeped (or swept) through the Mercian border.

Their intention must now have been to wage a final war of conquest, staking everything on a swift victory; but the geography of southern Britain had changed since the campaigns of the 870s.* The forts of the Burghal Hidage, with their well-provisioned and trained garrisons, severely compromised the Host's ability to live off the land, to steal or buy horses and force the submission of shire ealdormen. The old river route, which had enabled deep and swift penetration into the heartlands of the *Angelcynn*, was closed to them.

At Sashes, Wallingford, Oxford and Cricklade, along the full length of the Thames, they faced opposition secure behind new walls; opposition with the benefit of intelligence forewarning them of the advancing Host. The portable wealth of the countryside, its livestock, was corralled behind ramparts. The formerly overflowing cupboard of the Anglo-Saxon landscape was bare; and, for once, the Host was unsupported by its fleet, having lost the bulk of its ships at Benfleet. Moreover, the West Saxon-Mercian alliance was solid: Æðelred's loyalty, sealed by his marriage to Ælfred's daughter, Æðelflæd, was unimpeachable. There is no hint that even disaffected ealdormen would throw in their lot with the invaders.

These were epic campaigns: battle-weary veterans on forced route marches through enemy territory, denied the means to live off the land and at all times watched, pursued and hunted by an

* See Viking Age travel map, p. 281.

exhausted but determined *fyrð* under active, committed commanders. If Francia had, finally, proved too hot to handle, then
Wessex and Mercia were now also too well guarded, too deeply
defended.

Avoiding the burhs, then, and no longer tied to the river, the
most direct route for the Host would have been to take *Akemennestraete* from London, heading north-west through St Albans
and Bicester towards the Fosse Way, which would lead them
directly towards Gloucester, avoiding the Thames burhs. Here,
perhaps, a gathering of warriors and their jarls from the north
and east, even from potential allies among the Welsh and Irish,
might have been arranged. The combined army, reaching the
River Severn, now traced a route north along the ancient marcher
lands of Hwicce (surely avoiding Worcester, already fortified with
a burh; but how?), *Magonsaete* and *Wrocansaete*, beneath the
ramparts of ancient hillforts and past the ruins of Roman towns;
and then, as the river turned west and south, into Powys.

Even here the *Angelcynn* now had allies among those Welsh
kings who had submitted to Ælfred after 880. All the time the
Host was pursued by Æðelred, supported by the shire levies of Wiltshire and Somerset under Ealdormen Æðelhelm and
Æðelnoth, who had long ago stood with Ælfred at Athelney and
fought with him at Edington. The stores of the burhs, and their
knowledge of the movements of the Host, allowed the pursuing
levies to maintain pace and strength.

At Worcester, perhaps, the levies paused to regroup and resup-
ply, to gather intelligence and take counsel. At *Buttingtune on
Sæferne staðe,** a ford just north of Welshpool where the Severn
meets Offa's Dyke beneath the naturally imposing ramparts of the
Long Mountain, the Host ran out of steam and built a fortress,
as they had so often before. On their long march they had been

---

* Buttington: probably 'Bota's settlement'—an Anglian name.

unable to capture a single major settlement although they had, in all probability, wasted many smaller estates and *vills*. With Ælfred still occupied on his watching brief in Devon, the combined levies laid siege to the Host on the banks of the river and waited: waited until those inside were half-starved and had slaughtered all their horses for meat.

At last, in desperation, they broke out and, after a fierce engagement, with much slaughter on both sides, marched overland all the way back to Essex. This time, at least, they might retreat north-east into friendlier territory, through the lands of the Five Boroughs, tracking across Danish East Mercia and through East Anglia; Æðelred's forces were probably able to trace their progress but unable to engage them beyond the line of Watling Street.

It is an old axiom of military strategy that a powerful enemy should be afforded the means of escape. The destruction of the Host's ships at Benfleet closed its back door to the Continent. Another plan seems now to have occurred to Hæsten. For the third time in twelve months, and with winter's dark days approaching, he led his forces overland again and this time, according to the *Chronicle*, they marched day and night, right along the Mercian frontier. At this speed, perhaps, they might use the metalled road of Watling Street and outrun the *fyrð*. They reached a 'deserted fortress in Wirral [*Wirhealum*: 'the hollows where the bog myrtle grows'], called Chester' (*þæt hie gedydon on anre westre ceastre on Wirhealum, seo is Legaceaster gehaten*).[11]

If Hæsten hoped to buy himself time, to refortify and provision Chester, to make contact, perhaps, with friends in Gwynedd and across the Irish Sea in Dublin, he had again underestimated the capabilities of his enemy. Shortly after the Host's arrival at Chester, Æðelred's Mercian levies surrounded the old Roman fort and set about implementing an aggressive scorched-earth policy, stripping its hinterland of cattle, grain and horses and sweeping up unsuspecting foraging parties so that the Host should have no provisions for winter. By now, with corn reaped and threshed and trees losing their leaves* it must have been difficult to keep any army in the field. It seems that the *fyrð* now withdrew; Hæsten, his options diminishing, marched his army into Wales, hoping to scavenge sufficient provisions for the winter. Here again he was denied, the land having been emptied of cattle and grain; instead, he plundered booty: bullion, jewellery, coin—anything to make this disastrous campaign seem worthwhile and satisfy his veterans.

The Welsh raid, diminished by a dismissive account in the *Chronicle*, was serious: the *Annales Cambriae* record its progress all through Brycheiniog and Gwent. Hæsten led the Host on a final, dispiriting march all the way across Northumbria and East Anglia out of the reach of the levies, to Mersea on the Essex coast, and relative safety, some time in the New Year of 894. Here they were joined by the remnants of the East Anglian fleet which had invested Exeter and which, raiding along the south coast on its way home, had been put to flight by the burh garrison at Chichester.

Now, at least, the Host had ships again, perhaps even sufficient to carry its forces back to the Continent. But its commanders were not done yet. Once more probing the edges of Wessex and Mercia, testing the mettle of the alliance, the Host left its baggage and camp followers, took to its ships and, during the summer of 894, sailed up the Thames estuary to the mouth of the River Lea opposite what is now Greenwich. The fleet rowed north past Stratford and its tidal corn mills, tracing the western edge of the great forest of Epping; past King Offa's minster at Waltham (one wonders if it had been pillaged by earlier raiders) as far perhaps as Ware, whose name, literally 'Weirs', suggests the highest navigable point, close to Hertford. In 895 they built a

---

* Tree foliage is a valuable, often underestimated source of fodder: particularly elm and holly.

new fortress at an unidentified spot, this time with access to their fleet: their escape route. In the late summer of that year the *fyrð* was sent to dislodge them; it was repulsed with serious casualties including, the *Chronicle* says, the loss of four of the king's thegns. The Host's intention was evidently to threaten London's rich hinterland.

Ælfred, finally released from his long watching brief in the south-west, now brought his army across the Thames and camped somewhere on the south-west side of the Lea, 'while the corn was being reaped'. This small detail evokes a vision of labourers in the fields, harvesting wheat with their saw-edged sickles; of oxen grazing on the stubble, stooks drying in hot August sun; of weary soldiers watching, leaning on their spears under shady trees; of barns filling with winter's grain—like a bucolic passage from John Stewart Collis's wartime reminiscences of the 1940s, perhaps.[12]

Nothing more perfectly captures Ælfred's own vision of the duties owed by a king to his people: of the idea of economic security guaranteed by the king's peace in return for duty and render. Content that the harvest was protected, Ælfred set his mind to a military solution. Inspired, it seems, by the example of Charles the Bald in Francia, Ælfred now sought to block the fleet's escape. He and his engineers found a suitable spot on the Lea, downriver from the enemy's camp, and set the *fyrð* to constructing a bridge that would connect forts built on both banks.

The threat was sufficient; even before the bridge and forts were complete the Host abandoned their new fortress and once again marched west, this time as far as *æt Cwatbrycge be Sæfern*:* Bridgnorth, a key crossing of the Severn in what is now Shropshire, some 13 miles (21 km) south of Watling Street, their likely route. Here they constructed a new fort, most likely on the west

---

* It means, unhelpfully, the Bridge to Quatt, a small village 3 or 4 miles (5–6 km) south-east of the bridge. Watts 2004.

bank, and overwintered. Ælfred seems to have used the breath-
ing space to bolster diplomatic efforts to isolate the Host. He
sent Æðelnoth, his loyal Somerset ealdorman, to York to broker
a treaty with Guðroðr. A year earlier the British chronicler of the
Annales Cambriae had noted that Anarawd of Gwynedd 'came
with Englishmen to lay waste Ceredigion and Ystrad Tywi'; with
Mercia and Gwynedd in collusion against the weaker Welsh
kingdoms the Host's last hope for a northern and Welsh alliance
evaporated.

The *Anglo-Saxon Chronicle*, its scribe seemingly as exhausted
as his countrymen, has the following anticlimactic entry for the
year 896:

> on ðysum gere tofor se here, sum on Eastengle, sum on Norðhym-
> bre, 7 þa þe feohlease wæron him þær scipu begeton 7 suð ofer sæ
> foron to Sigene...

> In this year, the Host dispersed, some to East Anglia, some to
> Northumbria, and those without stock got themselves ships
> there, and sailed south oversea to the Seine. The Host, by the
> mercy of God, had not altogether utterly crushed the Eng-
> lish people, but they were much more severely crushed during
> those years by murrain* and plague, most of all by the fact that
> many of the best of the king's servants in the land passed away
> during those three years.[13]

It is a salutary lesson for the historian, whose window on the
remote past offers mostly the narrow view of great events, to
learn that more damage was wreaked by the everyday woes of
illness, poor harvests and diseased livestock—by the fates—than
by the depredations of the Host. It is little wonder that while the
Angelcynn reposed considerable and justifiable faith in their king,
they also prayed to their God; and also, perhaps, to those capricious deities who had seemed for so long to favour their enemy:
Oðin, Thor, Frey and the rest. Those same gods had run out

---

* An archaic term for a variety of cattle maladies.

of patience with the warriors whose apocalyptic thirst for battle, plunder and conquest had not, in the end, brought about Ragnarök, the last battle, and the dawning of a new world order.

The states of Wessex and Mercia, who had entered the lists against their Scandinavian antagonists so seemingly ill-prepared, had paid a heavy price for their education in modern warfare. They had been forced by extreme circumstances to adapt and to learn. Above all, perhaps, their appreciation of economic, military and political geography had undergone a decisive shift: by the end of the conflict they were more than a match for their enemies. They had mastered their own landscape. Ælfred had won his final victory at the age of forty-seven.* He had successfully exploited the rules of lordship to embark on a most ambitious programme of military reform, maintaining the support of most of his nobility and attracting the loyalty of Mercians, Welsh and many others including, according to Asser, an assortment of Vikings, Gauls, Franks and Bretons.[14] Now Ælfred was able to enjoy a few last years of peace in which to set the political and cultural seal on his brilliant military legacy.

Unimaginable treasures were looted from the minsters and palaces of the Insular kingdoms during the first Viking Age. Metalwork was cut into hacksilver, reforged as jewellery, weapons or coin; precious stones were recycled and given new life in distinctly Scandinavian ornaments like oval brooches. Much was set alight or cast into rivers and oceans; much more was buried for safekeeping, and some of those hoards turn up still. The greatest cultural destruction was wrought on the libraries of the monastic schools: York, Jarrow, Portmahomack, Iona and elsewhere. Countless manuscripts were burned or discarded, including

---

* The same age, incidentally, as Nelson when he died at Trafalgar 900 years later fending off another Continental invasion.

single copies of annals whose loss leaves immense gaps in our narrative histories. The *Historia de Sancto Cuthberto* is a lucky testament to that community's extraordinary, stoical survival.

Rarely, very rarely, items were recovered after they had been looted and, in a unique instance, we have the testimony of those who recovered them. The *Codex Aureus*, a grand illustrated eighth-century gospel book now kept in the Royal Library in Stockholm but undoubtedly Anglo-Saxon in origin, was stolen, probably from Canterbury, in a Viking raid. On its eleventh folio (see p. 219) is a remarkable inscription written in a very elegant Old English hand, which reads as follows:

> + *In nomine Domini nostri Ihesu Christi. Ic Aelfred aldormon ond Werburg min gefera begetan ðas bec æt hæðnum herge mid uncre clæne feo; ðæt ðonne wæs mid clæne golde...*

> In the name of our Lord Jesus Christ. I, Ealdorman Ælfred, and my wife Werburg procured these books from the heathen invading army with our own money; the purchase was made with pure gold. And we did that for the love of God and for the benefit of our souls, and because neither of us wanted these holy works to remain any longer in heathen hands. And now we wish to present them to Christ Church to God's praise and glory and honour, and as thanksgiving for his sufferings, and for the use of the religious community which glorifies God daily in Christ Church; in order that they should be read aloud every month for Ælfred and for Werburg and for Alhðryðe, for the eternal salvation of their souls, as long as God decrees that Christianity should survive in that place. And also I, Earl Ælfred, and Werburg beg and entreat in the name of Almighty God and of all his saints that no man should be so presumptuous as to give away or remove these holy works from Christ Church as long as Christianity survives there.[15]

It would be gratifying to know during which raid on Canterbury the *Codex* was stolen. The only *Chronicle* record of such an event is in 851. If we can date the theft that early, then the resulting campaign which led to the destruction of the Host at *Acleah* in

27. THE *CODEX AUREUS*, a magnificent bible of Anglo-Saxon origin,
acquired by Ealdorman Ælfred and his wife Werburg from the *mycel here*.
'In the name of our Lord Jesus Christ. I, Ealdorman Ælfred,
and my wife Werburg procured these books from the heathen
invading army with our own money.'

that year might well fit the bill if Ælfred, the ealdorman of Surrey, was active in the 850s.* The campaign of 892 is another obvious possibility. We cannot be sure. We can, however, say a little more about Ælfred and his wife and daughter because, by happy chance, his will also survives.[16] It must date from before 888 when one of its witnesses died. For historians it is rich in interest, not just because of its association with the *Codex Aureus*.

Ælfred lists his bookland (his heritable estates) at places like Clapham, Sanderstead and Lingfield, all within the shire of Surrey, as well as two in Kent. These are left to his wife and their daughter, together with livestock and crops including 2,000 pigs (so long as his widow does not remarry). The property is to be inherited through his daughter's children—in other words it would not pass to a new husband. Werburg, his widow, is 'to take to St Peter's' (that is, to Rome) his two wergilds† by virtue of his birth and his title 'if it be God's will that she performs that journey'.

Ælfred also had a son, Æðelwold, to whom he leaves three hides of bookland and 100 swine, a comparatively small bequest. The son is also to have his father's 'folkland', a clause that has given rise to some debate since it is explicit that the king himself must approve its transfer. There are other, minor legatees. One wonders why the wife and daughter were favoured over the son, unless he were the issue of an earlier marriage, or illegitimate.‡ The *Codex*, we know, Ælfred intended to be returned to Christ Church at Canterbury, that it might never leave there again. In that, at least, he hoped in vain. It is not known how the *Codex*

---

* See above, p. 93.

† Wergild: the value of a man for purposes of compensation; otherwise an indication of his worth and social standing. Ælfred was a *twelfhynde* man, worth 1200 shillings. See above, p. 176.

‡ Another charter survives bearing the ealdorman's name (S1202, between 870 and 899). In it, Ælfred donates an estate to the monastic community at Chartham in the Kent downs, a few miles west of Canterbury, in return for a life interest in land at Croydon.

Aureus ended up in Scandinavia, except that it had spent time in Spain. One doubts if its owner would have appreciated the irony.

During these last years other, more welcome Scandinavian visitors came to King Ælfred's court. The celebrated tales of Ohthere and Wulfstan are preserved in an unlikely source: an Old English translation of Orosius's fifth-century *Historiarum Adversum Paganos libri Septem*, 'Seven histories against the pagans'. Ælfred, advised by his two Continental scholars, Grimbald and John the Old Saxon, and by his senior clerics Plegmund, Wærferth and Asser, had compiled a list of those books 'most necessary for all men to know'.[17] Latin, he believed, was the rightful preserve of clerics and of charters; he wanted the children of his nobles and, inferentially, his administrators, to be able to read and write in their own language so that their counsel and judgement should be better informed through the wisdom and knowledge of their illustrious forbears. The evidence of the *Codex Aureus* shows that some, at least, of his ealdormen took this seriously and were capable of high standards of literacy; and a number of vernacular prayer books belonging to noblewomen survive from the period.*

To this end a new generation of literate scribes would produce Old English versions of Bede's *Ecclesiastical history of the English People* and its historical sequel, the *Anglo-Saxon Chronicle*; of Orosius's *Historiae*, Augustine's *Soliloquies* and the *Pastoral Care* of Gregory the Great.† The king's own law code, the *Domboc*, was inscribed in Old English.

Ohthere's account of travels along the Norwegian coast and among the Danish islands of the Baltic was logically appended to

---

* I think it possible that the inscription added to the *Codex Aureus* was written in the hand of Werburg on behalf of her husband.

† Gregory was Pope between 590 and his death in 604. Augustine's mission to the Anglo-Saxons in 597 was conceived by Gregory after a famous meeting with Deiran slave boys in a market in Rome.

Orosius's account, derived partly from Pliny, of the geography of Northern Europe.[18]

> *Ohthere sæde his hlaforde,** *Ælfrede cyning, þat he ealra Norð-*
> *monna norþest bude...*[19]
>
> Ohthere told his lord, King Ælfred, that he lived the furthest
> north of all Norwegians. He said that he lived in the north of
> Norway on the coast of the Atlantic [*Westsæ*]. He also said that
> the land extends very far north beyond that point, but it is all
> uninhabited, except for a few places here and there where the
> Finnas have their camps, hunting in winter, and in summer
> fishing in the sea.

That Ælfred is described as Ohthere's lord is an intriguing detail. The Norseman, outside his own land, was lordless and literally outwith the law. It was part of the duty of an Anglo-Saxon king to provide legal protection (his *mund*) and bona fides to such men and, therefore, Ælfred was his de facto lord while he dwelt in the kingdom.

The Norseman was a farmer of reindeer, wealthy in his own land, and a trader along the Norwegian coast and in the western Baltic. He must have brought some of his wares to the West Saxon court as gifts, to open access to wealthy buyers. Equally valuable were his accounts of the geography of the far north (he had sailed as far as the White Sea) and of the trading settlements at *Sciringesheal* (Kaupang, in Oslofjord) and *Hæþum* (Hedeby or Schleswig) at the base of the Jutland peninsula. The news-hungry West Saxon court must have been fascinated by his account of the tribute paid to his kind by the hunter-gatherer peoples he called *Finnas* (the nomadic Lapps). Their furs (bear, otter, marten), valuable ship-rope made from seal and whale-skin, and super-precious walrus ivory, highly prized by ornamental carvers,

---

* Originally *hlafweard*, a loaf-keeper. *Hlafdige*, 'lady', derives from words for 'loaf' and for 'kneading': in other words, the providers of a household.

were the goods that had made Ohthere so wealthy despite the surprising—to the farmers of the *Angelcynn*—poverty of his own livestock: twenty each of cattle, sheep and pigs raised on the narrow cultivable coastal lands of Norway.

More exotic still was Wulfstan's account of travels in the eastern Baltic and along the River Vistula; of a land of honey and plentiful fishing, of the habits of foreign kings and their burial rites and inheritance practices. In a time of war the *Angelcynn* were, at heart, still curious about the world beyond their shores. Modern scholars have also gleaned much from the detail of these stories, so carefully preserved by the Orosius scribe.* The Danish ship historian Ole Crumlin-Pedersen has shown that with the technology and type of ship likely used for coastal trading by the two captains entertained at Ælfred's court (something like the capacious Skuldelev I, or the Klåstad ship found near Kaupang and dating from around 800), Ohthere's testimony that he sailed from his home to Kaupang in a month equates to something like a 2-knot net progress into the south-westerly prevailing winds; given better winds, the ships would have made as much as 5 knots on average. Even a single voyage a year, carrying the most valuable freight, would have accumulated sufficient profit for such skippers to justify the expense and risk.[20]

The celebrated English historian of the Anglo-Viking period, Peter Sawyer, has studied the implications of both accounts for our understanding of Northern trade and shown how the entrepreneurs of southern Scandinavia were able successfully to exploit both the hunter-gatherers of the north and the voracious appetites of European courts for their produce—not just furs, skins and ivory, but also amber and other precious stones, jewellery

---

* The same, scribe, incidentally, who picked up his quill at the 893 entry in the Parker MS of the *Anglo-Saxon Chronicle*; but probably not the original translator of Orosius, according to the archivist at the British Library. Information accessed from: http://www.bl.uk/manuscripts/FullDisplay.aspx?ref=Add_MS_47967, July 2016.

and rare natural minerals.[21] The trading and craft centres of the western Baltic acted as gateway emporia between Atlantic and Arab markets via the great rivers of the east. If there was passion for raiding and conquest among land-hungry Scandinavians there was, equally, a brilliant aptitude for exploration, trading and manufacture; a curiosity to explore and compass the world not matched until, perhaps, the fifteenth century.

Ælfred's admiring biographer Bishop Asser saw the same curiosity and endeavour in his more homebound patron and deployed a favourite Anglo-Saxon simile to capture its essence:

> Just like the clever bee which at first light in summertime departs from its beloved honeycomb, finds its way with swift flight on its unpredictable journey through the air, lights upon the many and various flowers of grasses, plants and shrubs, discovers what pleases it most and then carries it back home, King Ælfred directed the eyes of his mind far afield and sought without what he did not possess within, that is to say, within his own kingdom.[22]

Ælfred's desire for knowledge and wisdom was as much a personal crusade, an attempt to follow the Old Testament example of King Solomon, as it was politically and economically pragmatic. His pursuit of literacy, enthusiastically recorded by Bishop Asser, has something of the convert's zeal about it. He famously, in writing of the books that he wished to be more widely read, commissioned the production of æstels, or ornamented book pointers, which he gave to his bishops to accompany the volumes of his own translations intended to be placed in their churches. One of these may survive in the beautiful crystal, cloisonné enamel and gold jewel found in 1693 a few miles from Athelney, where Ælfred established a small monastery in thanks for the victory at Edington. The Alfred jewel is now kept in the Ashmolean museum in Oxford. The tooled inscription on the jewel reads ÆLFRED MEC HEHT GEWYRCAN: Ælfred had me made.

28. THE ÆLFRED JEWEL, found near Athelney in 1693
—probably one of the æstels or book pointers given
by the king to his favoured bishops.

In his bespoke gifts, his book production, in the disposition
of estates and preferments and the material evidence of his rule,
Ælfred was exercising the political capital of hard-won patronage.
The historian James Campbell goes so far as to argue that copies
of the *Anglo-Saxon Chronicle*, and others of his works, were kept
on chains in major church buildings, to be publicly consulted by
a newly literate élite.[23]

The magnanimity of protection afforded to foreign traders and to the kings of Wales and of Danish East Anglia was an
expression of the dominance and universality of Christian kingship; of Ælfred's victories over the twin evils of heathenism and
ignorance. His coinage reflects this maturing comprehension of
the political tools available to him. Even with his extensive itineraries the king could not be everywhere; the average *ceorl*, peasant,
dreng or thegn would never have set eyes on him except through
the image (highly stylized, in profile like a Roman emperor) that

appeared on his coins with the words ÆLFRED REX or ÆLFRED REX ANGLOR(UM). Wherever those coins ended up the message was understood: the Christian English looked to one king only. Mercians, owing their loyalty to the redoubtable and highly competent Æðelred, understood very well the meaning of overlordship, its benefits and costs.

At the beginning of Ælfred's reign in 871, at a time of great crisis, his coinage was heavily debased, not above 20 per cent silver: useful for trade, but as a direct reflection of royal power the content spoke louder than words. During the 870s Ælfred undertook major reforms to bring the silver content up to Continental standards. He issued the joint 'Two emperors' series with Ceolwulf II of Mercia and then, after the victory and treaty of 879 and the West Saxon acquisition of London, increasingly confident, he issued the London monogram pennies. In the 880s and 890s the number of moneyers increased rapidly, even as trade with the Continent declined in the face of piracy and economic instability.

Whether the West Saxon administration immediately appreciated the symbiotic potential of the burhs, with their new free-holding market stall holders and customs regimes, to deploy and reinforce the political value of coinage in the economic recovery of the kingdom, is less certain. Before the Viking wars of the late ninth century central places in the British landscape, where people, services, ceremonials and production were concentrated, existed only at the sites of great minsters and royal palaces, in archaeological terms almost indistinguishable from each other, and at the few trading ports engaged in international trade. Villages and towns as we would recognize them did not exist.*

The processes of nucleation had not begun or were in their infancy. The population of the Insular lands was dispersed: ealdorman, king and bishop were lords who lived off renders and

---

* With the possible, as yet unproven, exception of the ancient Roman *civitas* capital at Canterbury.

dispensed power by virtue of their progress through estate lands. People did not congregate in large settlements either for defence or for mutual economic benefit. With the secularization of minsters in the eighth century and their increased exploitation of specialized production and trade, the first signs of nucleation are witnessed in the excavated record. Church, barn, hall, cemetery, all exercised a centripetal force on the population and resources of their neighbourhoods.

The trading ports at *Lundenwic, Hamwic, Eoforwic* and *Gipeswic* attracted merchants, potters, craftsmen and the economic interest of kings. If lords were still itinerant, their reeves were nevertheless able to exercise elements of direct control over larger numbers of productive people. The nucleating forces were weak but dynamic: as the trading ports declined with the threat of piracy and as the great minsters, also undefended, were picked off, so the burhs began to attract population: at first for mutual defence and service, then for commerce under the protection of reeve, garrison and turf ramparts 15 feet (5 m) tall. The increasingly complex machinery of West Saxon and Mercian government applied similar forces to the royal court. For the first time, under Ælfred, it is possible to argue the case for a state capital.

Winchester had been a substantial Roman town: *Venta Belgarum*, the *civitas* capital of a powerful tribe. The urbanizing project which had proven so successful in Rome's Mediterranean projects was imported almost like a flat-pack into Iron Age Britain. Winchester, like any other town, had its forum, its posh merchants' and functionaries' houses (mosaics, bath suites, underfloor heating and all), its sewage system and grid-square streets. In later centuries the towns of Roman Britain were provided with walls, to define their limits and to keep out undesirables. The name *Venta* was a native British term for a meeting or assembly place—what else could the indigenes call this new phenomenon? The urban experiment ultimately failed in Roman Britain: the toga-wearing élite retired to their country villas, then to their ancient hillforts, and left the towns to fall into ruin.

The centre of Winchester, lying on the west bank of the River Itchen,* betrays the same telltale grid pattern in its streets today. High Street leads directly away from the river, running just north of west. Set back to north and south are parallel roads, linked by cross streets at right angles. The northern limit of the old town is marked by a road called North Walls, which rather speaks for itself. Close to where the east gate would have stood stands a Victorian statue of King Ælfred.

The apparent continuity of medieval Winchester from its Roman origins is an illusion; or, at least, it is partly coincidental. Between about 400 and 600 there is no evidence that *Venta Belgarum* functioned as a settlement, let alone as a thriving town. In the seventh century a plot in the old Roman town was given by King Cenwealh to found a second episcopal see for the West Saxons.† Like York, Canterbury, Lincoln and London, the ruined Roman town was property in the gift of the king, regarded as suitable for the establishment of a church under royal patronage. At the beginning of Ælfred's reign it had a small population: the church community, a royal residence and one or two small private estate complexes belonging to an élite benefiting from the king's personal patronage.[24]

Like other Roman towns, Winchester was seen as a suitable site for rebuilding as a defended burh in Ælfred's ambitious scheme of the 880s: metalled road surfaces from an early phase of construction, excavated beneath the Norman castle, have been closely dated to the late ninth century by two coins: an Arab dirham and an Anglo-Saxon penny. The river crossing and the line of the Roman walls dictated that a similar size and grid plan were adopted for

---

* In the Early Medieval period it may have been navigable to this point from its issue on Southampton Water.

* Bede *HE* III.7 The first West Saxon see was established at Dorchester on Thames.

29. STATUE OF KING ÆLFRED at Winchester,
royal burh and sometime 'capital' of Wessex;
sculpted by Hamo Thornycroft and unveiled in 1901.

the new burh, whose massive ditch and ramparts enclosed the site of a grand basilica known as the Old Minster, burial place of the celebrated St Swiðun, a former bishop who died in 862.

Winchester superseded the coastal site at *Hamwic* as a principal, more secure trading emporium for southern Wessex. Under Ælfred it could not be described as a town in the modern sense; but urban elements were being assembled here, as in London, Oxford and elsewhere. What is now High Street, the main thoroughfare, was *Cheap straet*, the street of traders and stall holders; and a mint was established to service its market and supplement the royal coffers. With Wallingford on the Thames it was the largest of the Ælfredan burhs, requiring a nominal garrison of 2,400 men. The primary manuscript of the *Anglo-Saxon Chronicle* was compiled here and by 896 the *Chronicle* was recording the death of its *wicgerefa*, the *wic* reeve Beornulf, as a noteworthy event. When, that same year, a pirate fleet was intercepted and destroyed off the south coast, two of its crews were brought to the king at Winchester, where he had them hanged.* Here also, after his death six days before All Hallows in the year 899, Ælfred was buried in the Old Minster.

Eadweard's accession to the throne of Wessex, his overlordship of Mercia and the Welsh kingdoms loyal to Ælfred, had been anticipated by both: in 898 the heir presumptive was styled *Rex* in a Kentish charter; he was the principal legatee in his father's will and a close attendant at court.[25] His older sister Æðelflæd

---

* The 896 entry contains the well-known reference to Ælfred's construction of 'warships to be built to meet the Danish ships: they were almost twice as long as the others, some had sixty oars, some more; they were both swifter, steadier and with more freeboard than the others; they were built neither after the Frisian design nor after the Danish, but as it seemed to himself that they could be most serviceable'. Keynes and Lapidge 1983, 90. Few historians would now suggest that this constitutes evidence that Ælfred founded the Royal Navy.

was successfully married to Æðelred, the Lord of Mercia. He had been bloodied in battle against the Host. His first marriage, to Ecgwynn, had borne a daughter, possibly Eadgið, and a son, Æðelstan, who had been subject to investiture by Ælfred, legitimizing him as a future king. Eadweard's new wife Ælfflæd, daughter of the ealdorman of Wiltshire, would bear him seven children. Ælfred's line seemed secure.

There was, however, another candidate for the throne: Æðelwold, son of Ælfred's immediately older brother King Æðelred, who had died in the year of nine engagements, 871. Æðelwold may have been a prime mover in the less than fulsome support that Ælfred received from his ealdormen in 877–878, the winter of greatest crisis.* With the old king barely cold in his bed, Æðelwold, with a small force of retainers, his *comites*, seized royal townships on the River Stour in Dorset at Christchurch and at Wimborne, his own father's burial place. In response Eadweard brought a force to Badbury Rings, an abandoned but eminently defensible Iron Age hillfort some 3 miles (5 km) north-west of Wimborne.

Æðelwold must have hoped for, or been promised, substantial support from disaffected collateral members of the House of Wessex; perhaps also from Mercia. If so, he was to be disappointed: no help came; no promises were fulfilled. The *Chronicle* recorded that he stayed at Wimborne, barricaded behind the gates of the minster enclosure, and resolved to remain there 'alive or dead'. Eadweard waited with his army.

Under cover of night Æðelwold abandoned his redoubt, perhaps embarking on boats that allowed him to escape through Christchurch harbour. Alex Woolf has raised the intriguing possibility that a nun, said to have been seized by the pretender before or during his stay at Wimborne, was none other than Æðelgifu, Eadweard's second sister, and that the usurper intended her to

* See above, p. 139.

become his consort.[26] But if so, she was inadvertently left behind, and the *Chronicle* records her 'arrest'. Somehow Æðelwold was able to lead his force as far as Northumbria where, it appears, a convenient interregnum after the death of Sigfrøðr, the successor to Guðroðr in 895, offered fresh opportunities. At York Æðelwold seems to have been acclaimed as king and passed out of the *Chronicle*'s orbit for three or four years.

Eadweard 'the Elder'* was able to celebrate his coronation at Whitsun in May 900.[27] Later tradition and practice suggests that the coronation took place in the church of St Mary at Kingston upon Thames where, in 838, a symbolic conciliatory meeting had been held between Archbishop Ceolnoth and King Ecgberht.[28] The church collapsed in 1730; from the rubble a modest, rectangular block of stone was retrieved which, tradition suggests, is the coronation stone of the tenth-century Anglo-Saxon kings. Today it stands surrounded by an ornate iron railing next to the town's Guildhall.

The site suggests two key aspects of the ceremony, about which there has been much speculation: first that, instead of choosing the perhaps more natural royal burh at Winchester, a site on the Thames symbolized the continuity of the Wessex–Mercia alliance.[29] Secondly, Alex Woolf, the historian of Scotland in this period, notes the similarity in time and geography with a great meeting held by Constantín mac Áeda at Scone within five years of Eadweard's coronation.[30] Both sites lie at the natural tidal limits of great rivers: the Thames and Tay. Two other possible sites for important Insular meetings and inaugurations, Govan on the Clyde and Newburn on the Tyne, the latter also close to a tidal reach, inclines one to think that there was something uniquely symbolic about such places. Both Govan and Newburn may have had moot hills close by, the equivalents of Iceland's Things, Scotland's Dings (the place

---

* A cognomen first used in Wulfstan's late tenth-century *Life of St Æðelwold* to distinguish him from Eadweard 'the Martyr' (975–978).

30. THE TIDE STONE at Kingston upon Thames,
where Anglo-Saxon kings were anointed
on the frontier between Wessex and Mercia.

name Dingwall, for example) and Man's Tynwald.

The accession of Constantín, grandson of Cináed mac Ailpín, in Alba in about 900, marks a significant moment in the history of North Britain. So too, two years later, does the expulsion of the Norse from Dublin, driven out by the Irish overkings of Brega and Leinster.[31] Again, the clatter of great events in one part of the Atlantic world echoed across the sea, re-energizing the political dynamics of Britain's kingdoms. Newton's cradle was set in motion once more, this time responding to a new set of complex rhythms.

FRAGMENTARY ANNALS

INGIMUNDR—ÆÐELRED AND ÆÐELFLÆD—ANGLESEY
AND MAN—ORKNEYINGA SAGA—CONSTANTÍN
MAC ÁEDA—ÆÐELWOLD AND EADWEARD—
UNDERCURRENTS

7

T HE 893 ENTRY IN THE 'A' VERSION OF THE
Anglo-Saxon Chronicle, an almost continuous and breath-
less narrative of field campaigns, sieges, fleet movements
and forced marches over twelve months, runs to more than 1,000
words. From 897, the year after the Host dispersed, until 909 the
accumulated entries of more than a decade recorded in the same
Chronicle run to just over half that. If the first twelve years of
the tenth century appear from a superficial, West Saxon point of
view, to have been predominantly uneventful, the focus of historical attention is now drawn inexorably to the west and north.
Even here, that long decade can only tentatively be sketched in
outline, from annals thin on detail and obscure in their genesis.

Nevertheless, the rebounding impact of great events across
the sea at the turn of the century was to have a profound effect on
the British political landscape for a century and more. A terse but
telling entry in the *Annals of Ulster* for 902 fires the starting gun:

> The heathens were driven from Ireland... from the fortress of
> Áth Cliath, by Mael Finnia son of Flannacán with the men of
> Brega and by Cerball son of Muiricán, with the Laigin; and

236

31. NORSE RUNES ON A CROSS SHAFT
from St Andrew's church, Andreas, Isle of Man.
Settlement and conquest were swiftly followed by assimilation.

they abandoned a good number of their ships, and escaped half dead after they had been wounded and broken.[1]

Áth Cliath is Dublin, the Norse *longphort* on the River Liffey. Here the Norse Vikings made their principal stronghold in 841 and by the end of the century it supported close-packed housing, perhaps on more than one site, indicating its expansion from a mere pirate base (part dockyard, part defensive redoubt, part slave market and production centre) into something resembling its Scandinavian prototypes at Kaupang and elsewhere. The immediate, material fallout from this sudden, overwhelming attack by a combined force of Irish included a large stash of silver, buried at Drogheda in Brega shortly afterwards.* The loss of men and ships was probably of small concern compared with the loss of the Norse Irish capital, their long-held centre of power. Refugees, not just pirate captains and their crews but families, dependents and artisans, fled across the sea in panic. It is impossible to know how many drowned in the dangerous waters of the Irish Sea.

Very shortly afterwards, notices appearing in Insular sources testify to ominous repercussions in the east. The *Annales Cambriae* entry for the year 902 records that 'Ingimund came to Mona, and took Maes Osfeilion'. Another contemporary entry, in the *Brut y Tywysogion* under 903, records that 'Igmund' was defeated in a battle for Ros Meilion. The two places are likely to be the same: Llanfaes, a small settlement north of Beaumaris overlooking the Menai Straits on Anglesey.[2]

A third source, if it can be trusted, provides compelling supporting detail of a series of events played out over the following half dozen years. The same warlord, Ingimund, Old Norse Ingimundr, appears in a set of *Three Fragmentary Irish Annals* which exist only in third- or fourth-hand form, having been

---

* The hoard, containing about 5,000 coins, was found in 1846 but has since been lost. Edwards 1996, 177.

transcribed from lost copies of unidentifiable annals in the seventeenth century; that is to say, we are picking up a pretty cool trail. Even so, historians from F. W. Wainright onwards have seen in Ingimund's adventures the forging of a new career by the leader of one of the war bands expelled from Dublin.[3]

The annal describes eloquently, if all too briefly, the departure from Ireland, a defeat in battle against Cadell ap Rhodri* and an appeal to Mercia for sanctuary:

> Afterwards Hingamund with his forces came to Edlefrida, queen of the Saxons, for her husband, that is Edelfrid, was at that time in a disease... Now Hingamund was asking lands of the queen in which he would settle, and on which he would build huts and dwellings, for he was at this time weary of war. Then Edelfrida gave him lands near *Castra*, and he stayed there for a time.[4]

And so Ælfred's celebrated daughter Æðelflæd (Edelfrida) makes her belated entry on to the stage in the first years of the tenth century. She was the Wessex king's oldest child, born perhaps about 870 and married to her father's godson and ally, Ealdorman Æðelred, in the mid-880s—perhaps to seal the transfer of London to Mercian control after 886. The couple had one surviving child, a daughter called Ælfwynn. Æðelred had proven himself a stalwart ally through the travails of the 890s. Ælfred's grandson Æðelstan seems to have been fostered at his court, and Mercian and West Saxon policy against the Danish threat had been solidly aligned since the 860s.

Mercian relations with its traditional antagonists in Powys and Gwynedd were conducted independently of Wessex. Under Anarawd, son of Rhodri the Great, Gwynedd had initially been antipathetic to both Wessex and its old enemy Mercia, throwing in its lot with Guðroð's kingdom in York. But by the 890s

---

* Cadell was king of Seisyllwg; his brother, Anarawd, was king of Gwynedd, of which Anglesey was a core territory, and is regarded as the more likely antagonist.

Anarawd had abandoned his Northumbrian allies (Guðroðr died in 895, according to Æðelweard) and submitted to Ælfred's overlordship. Now, with Ælfred dead and a new dynamic force in play from across the Irish Sea, Venedotian*/Mercian relations were once more subject to ancient tensions.

It is widely accepted that after about 902 Æðelred was in some way incapacitated, as suggested by the *Fragmentary Annals*, and that his queen effectively took the reins of power in Mercia, mirroring her brother Eadweard's overlordship of Wessex and the South. That she acquiesced in Ingimund's request for land on which to settle his exhausted veterans demonstrates her independence of thought: the policy was as much anti-Venedotian as it was a defensive acceptance of the peaceful alternative to invasion. It echoes the expedient strategies of the Frankish kings, settling one band of raiders in the hope of fending off other enemies; buying them into a less aggressive means of supporting themselves. Ingimund's people are unlikely to have been the only Irish Norse war band kicking about the Irish Sea looking for fresh opportunities in the aftermath of the Dublin expulsion.

Guðroð's granting of the lands between Tyne and Wear to Cuthbert's spiritual host had been intended to serve the same purpose: to create a buffer against Bernician antagonists. The land that Æðelflæd now chose to give Ingimundr was territory lying between her heartlands and those of Anarawd: that is, the area around *Castra*, Chester on the River Dee, which had in the previous decade been the object of Hæsten's attentions. It is possible that this part of north-west Mercia, now Cheshire, had been depopulated in the past; that a settlement of veterans might in time bring economic advantages by carving productive farms out of unproductive waste and by submission to Mercian overlordship. It is hard to imagine that Æðelflæd passively acquiesced in

* The adjectival form of Gwynedd.

the displacement of a large indigenous population. Chester itself, with riverine access to the Irish Sea, was evidently a prize worth having.

Had the so-called Lady of the Mercians (*Myrcna hlæfdige* in the *Mercian Register* incorporated in several versions of the *Chronicle*) been a student of more ancient British historical tradition, she might have recalled the cautionary tale of Vortigern, the legendary fifth-century British overlord who received a similar request from Hengest and Horsa, arriving on the coast of Kent in three ships exiled from their homelands. Vortigern gave them Thanet, and they settled their Saxon comrades there before seizing the whole kingdom from its hapless incumbent. Four centuries later, Ingimundr saw the same opportunity.

> When he [Ingimundr] saw the city full of wealth and the choice land around it, he desired to possess them. Afterwards [he] came to the leaders of the Norsemen and the Danes; he made a great complaint in their presence, and he said that they were not well off without good lands, and that it was right for them all to come to seize Castra and to possess it with its wealth and its lands.[5]

Who were these other Norsemen and Danes? The fissile expulsion of the Norse from Dublin had scattered individual war bands and their dependents across the Irish Sea and beyond. Some of these, we know, went north to try their fortunes in Alba; perhaps also in *Suðreyar*, the Hebrides. Ingimundr may be only one of several Norse warlords who attempted small-scale invasion or settlement of the British mainland. That others attempted to make common cause with the Vikings of York is suggested by both place names and by the sensational discovery of an enormous silver hoard (63 lbs or 29 kg in weight) at Cuerdale on the banks of the River Ribble in 1840. The nearly 9,000 items comprised not just large quantities of hacksilver and other bullion but also coin, much of it minted at York. Encased in a lead box, it

32. The CUERDALE HOARD, deposited in about 905 on the banks of the River Ribble, Lancashire. Comprising an immense quantity of silver items, it is perhaps the war chest of a Dublin Norse army.

looks as though it had been a war chest, assembled either to support the retaking of Dublin or to found a new colony, perhaps on the western fringes of Northumbria. The Norse place name Copeland—'kaupa land', meaning 'bought land'—on the west coast of Cumbria may reflect the acquisition of estates by wealthy veterans of campaigns in the Irish Sea. The route through the Ribble Valley and up over the Pennines connected the Irish Sea directly with sympathetic allies in York.

Did Ingimundr hold his conference with former comrades and prospective York allies somewhere on the Ribble, perhaps near modern Preston? Circumstantial evidence of a displacement of indigenous landowners from Cumbria comes from an entry in St Cuthbert's *Historia*:

> In these days Elfred son of Brihtwulf, fleeing pirates, came over the mountains in the West and sought the mercy of St Cuthbert and Bishop Cuthheard so that they might present him with some lands.[6]

This Elfred does not appear in any other contemporary source; but 'mountains in the West' suggests that he had fled Cumbria or western Northumbria; and the size of the lands given or sold to him by the Cuthbert community, no less than the twelve vills of a complete Early Medieval shire around Easington in modern County Durham,* indicates that he had been a high-ranking noble, probably an ealdorman.

Whatever the context of Ingimund's confidential plan to seize Chester, its details leaked: 'the queen came to know of it [and] collected large forces around her in every direction'.[7] Confrontation was inevitable. A clue to the timing of these events is provided by a brief entry in the 'C' or *Mercian Register* version of the *Chronicle*, which records that in 907 Chester 'was rebuilt'.†
Its impressive surviving walls show that in the tenth century it must still have enjoyed substantial defences standing from its days as the headquarters of Rome's famous *Legio XX Valeria Victrix*. In 894 the Host had camped there and had to be removed by a policy of starvation.

The 907 entry suggests that Æðelflæd had been monitoring increasing tensions among Ingimund's Norse settlers over

---

* See map on p. 322.

† There seems to have been more activity in Chester than the written sources suggest. Coins were minted here, perhaps in a trading settlement by the Dee, as early as the last years of Ælfred. Lyon 2001, 75.

several years. Whether she actually got wind of a rebellion, as the *Fragmentary Annals* suggest, we might doubt. Intuition and experience inclined her to fortify and garrison Chester: to make of it a burh like that at Worcester, from which she could mount both defensive and offensive operations and develop the stagnant economy of north-west Mercia. Mention in the *Fragmentary Annals'* account of numbers of 'freemen' within the city supports the idea of a properly constituted burghal foundation. In earlier times Chester's refortification and garrisoning would have been seen by the kings of Gwynedd as a provocative, offensive gesture; now, perhaps, it was accepted as a military expedient against a common enemy. Æðelflæd had fine examples of recent burh foundations at Worcester and, perhaps, Tamworth on which to base her design; even so, neither the garrison nor the new defences* could prevent an assault by Ingimund's combined Norse and Danish forces.

The historian must, regrettably, discount the gory siege narrative contained in the *Fragmentary Annals*, despite such evocative imagery as cauldrons of boiling ale being poured onto the Norse attackers and the release of all the garrison's bees as an offensive weapon against them. We must put such colour down to over-exuberance on the part of later scribes, imagining and embellishing. The simple truth is that the Mercian fortress was more than a match for its attackers. That the siege is not even mentioned in the *Mercian Register,* let alone the main *Chronicle*, suggests that fame's trumpet did not sound very far.

Æðelflæd kept her fortress on the Dee. Even so, Ingimund's veterans had come to stay in Cheshire; and they were not alone.

---

* There is continuing debate about the location of the new defences, which seem to have abandoned or replaced the west and south walls of the Roman fortress and projected the north wall west to the river, and the east wall, likewise, to the south. This would have formed a protected riverfront and considerably enlarged the area of the future town; but excavations have not so far proved conclusive. Ward 2001.

Among the fanciful detail of the *Fragmentary Annals* is mention of those Irish, the *Gall-Ghaedhil* of other sources, who had intermarried with or become acculturated by the Dublin Norse. Their impact on the human geography and linguistic history of the Irish Sea 'province', as it is often called, was as profound in its way as that of the Norse.

The long-term impact of the Irish Norse arrival on the west coast cannot be in doubt: archaeology, legal and administrative terms, personal and place names supply ample evidence that after the expulsion from Dublin they settled here. It has long been recognized that there is an abundance of Norse-derived names on the Wirral peninsula between the estuaries of the Mersey and Dee and in coastal Lancashire; not just in settlements that survive to the present day: Irby, Kirby, Meols,* Thingwall, Croxteth, Aigburth, Tranmere and so on; but also in personal names and the names of landholdings recorded at the time of the Domesday survey. In the same document are distinct patterns of manorial valuations and fines whose numbers indicate an origin with the Scandinavian Ora, equivalent to sixteen English pennies. We find among the lawmen of Cheshire a 'sacraber', from the Norse *sakaráberi*, a prosecutor, and a concept of denial termed *thwertnic*: 'absolutely no'.[8]

Anglesey, or Môn, where Ingimundr had suffered a hot reception in 902, displays few Norse names, but there is a concentration of evidence for Scandinavian activity on its east coast, particularly around the fringes of Red Wharf Bay. Ingimund's battle with the forces of Gwynedd at *Maes Osfeilion*, Llanfaes, may well have been precipitated by a landing at this broad, sandy inlet,

---

* A particularly significant site: the location of a beach market on the north-west sands of Wirral, it has yielded an extraordinarily rich inventory of exotic artefacts from the Early Medieval and medieval periods. The names derive, respectively, as follows: Irby ('settlement of the Irish'), Kirby ('church settlement'), Meols ('sandbank'), Thingwall ('assembly field'), Croxteth ('landing place on a bend'), Aigburth ('Oakwood hill'), and Tranmere ('crane sandbank').

33. RED WHARF BAY, Anglesey,
a day's sail east of the *longphort* of Dublin: an attractive
and obvious target for Norse raiders and settlers.

north-east facing and sheltered from the prevailing winds. At Benllech, close by, there is a record of a 'Scandinavian' burial, and a sustained campaign of metal detection has produced concentrations of finds in the area around Llanbedrgoch, two thirds of a mile inland. A hoard of silver arm-rings, whose remarkably consistent weight shows them to have been a form of 'ring-money', a cross between bullion, ornament and exchangeable cash, also comes from Red Wharf Bay.*

While the focus of Early Medieval Venedotian royal power lay at Aberffraw in the south-west of the island, the contemporary archaeology of the eastern tip of Anglesey is rich in ecclesiastical settlement and sculpture, indicative of productive farmland and powerful territorial control. In the ninth century this was no empty land waiting for pioneer farmers; it was wealthy, an attractive target for the Dublin Norse whose *longphort* lay a day's sail due west. That the majority of Norse names in East Anglesey are prominent coastal navigation marks is ominous proof of mariners' interest in its coastline. The modern English 'Anglesey' (*Önguls-ey*, Öngull's island) for the Welsh 'Môn' is itself Norse in origin.

Recent excavations at Llanbedrgoch[9] have produced striking evidence for the fortunes of its native community at the turn of the tenth century, as a secular counterpart to the monastery at Portmahomack and the possible minsters at Flixborough and Brandon. Like an earlier site some miles to the north at Din Llugwy, the inhabitants of Llanbedrgoch combined a conservative, native round house tradition with rectangular halls typical of Germanic or Scandinavian architecture. A kidney-shaped ditch and bank enclosure, which had been constructed perhaps during the fifth or sixth century, contained houses and a hall, a smithy and a stone-lined spring cistern (the upper fills of the latter included a penny of King Eadmund [939–946]). To the

---

* Many of the hundreds of arm rings recovered from Viking period hoards conform to a weight standard, known as the Dublin ounce, of about 26.6g.

north of the pool lay a paved and kerbed road surface. During the ninth century the enclosure was rebuilt with a defensible stone wall and re-cut ditch. The buildings were also refurbished during the ninth or tenth century with either sill beam or stone wall foundations, sunken floors and sufficient constructional detail to demonstrate that they were substantial and well-engineered structures, with affinities to Scandinavian-style buildings elsewhere in the Atlantic west.

Llanbedrgoch seems to have enjoyed a long life, continuing into the late tenth century or later: its character fits within a context of wealthy rural agricultural élites, what in Anglo-Saxon England would be the thegnage caste and in Wales was the *maenol*. Mark Redknap, its excavator, suggests that it would have lain at the heart of an agricultural estate with outlying dependent farms and farmers; that, perhaps, it was sufficiently prestigious to have earned the title *llys*, a 'court'.* He further suggests that it was ideally placed for the collection of tolls on traffic entering or exiting the Rivers Dee and Mersey on their way to and from Dublin and Man. The inhabitants of Llanbedrgoch survived by adapting to circumstances.

Archaeologists investigating such sites spanning dynamic historical periods are sensitive to possible evidence for cultural disruption, of violence, even. At Portmahomack the presence of shattered sculpture and deposits of catastrophic burning rather speak for themselves. Equally redolent of violence is the discovery, at Llanbedrgoch, of five skeletons 'casually' interred in shallow graves in the upper fills of its enclosure ditch.[10] Burial disposition suggested to the excavators that at least two of the bodies had had their hands tied, and there was sufficiently clear pathology on one of these to suggest sharp-object trauma: evidence of murder. Naturally, the excavator has been cautiously drawn to

* Citing also the presence among the finds of a silver pendant whetstone, an almost universal symbol of warrior power and prestige in the period.

the inference that Norse raiding may have precipitated a sudden, forced change in ownership; but one must allow other, less dramatic scenarios. Execution with prejudice is not an irrefutable marker of invaders; Early Medieval justice could be brutal, and violence was not the exclusive preserve of ethnic incomers.

Like Flixborough, Brandon and Portmahomack, Llanbedrgoch seems to have become a 'productive' settlement with wide trade links. Antler, non-ferrous metals and leather-working tools came from active workshops. Glass beads, a fragment of a Kufic dirham, hacksilver, lead trial-pieces and weights tell of a site and an island fully integrated into the maritime Atlantic world, ensuring its place on the mental Tube map of Viking Age Britain. More locally, it lay at the heart of a nexus connecting Chester and the Mercian hinterland with Dublin, Man, Whithorn on the Wigtownshire coast and York via the Ribble Valley. A number of clench nails and other ship-fittings from the site suggest the recycling of materials from time-expired (or wrecked or captured) marine craft. To add to the site's period cachet, a Scandinavian-style ring-chain motif on a belt buckle, from a deposit above the floor of one of the buildings, replicates a motif on a cross at nearby Penmon Abbey.[11]

The extent to which Llanbedrgoch's enhanced economic activity was a function of Norse takeover, or merely of Norse patronage, cannot be determined. The upturn in its fortunes may, equally, have been an indirect product of the revival of Chester as a centre of trade and production under Æðelflæd. Wherever Irish, Norse, British, Pictish and Anglo-Saxon met, whatever their conflicts, their cultures hybridized; so, probably, did their people.

At the heart of the Irish Sea basin, Man (*Ellan Vannin* in Manx) was the hub around which a dynamic Atlantic Age spun. With its central peak, Snaefell, at 2,037 feet (621 m), Man is visible from

Wales, Ireland, north-west England and south-west Scotland. Mariners of all ages have traded with, sheltered in and taken pilotage from good but infrequent harbours on both east and west coasts. Important Early Christian sites at Maughold, at St Patrick's Isle and elsewhere, and annal entries recording its involvement in the dynastic rivalries of the Insular kingdoms, ensure the island's continuing interest for historians and archaeologists.* At various times it was subject to Northumbrian, Irish and British overlordship. There has often been speculation that Merfyn Frych, founder of the great Venedotian dynasty that produced Rhodri Mawr and, later, Hywel Dda, came from Man— perhaps displaced by new Norse overlords like Ingimundr.[12]

It is surprising, perhaps, that the island was not settled by an overtly Scandinavian population any earlier than the very end of the ninth century. David Wilson, the former director of the British Museum who has made a special study of the island's Viking archaeology, believes that a lack of existing commercial markets there, the fierce tides and currents of its coastal waters and ample opportunities for settlement elsewhere delayed what seems its inevitable subjugation.[13] Gradual encroachment on the Irish Sea from settlements on surrounding coasts and the expulsion from Dublin in 902 seem finally to have propelled one or more warlords to displace its indigenous kings; but it is possible that Norse were already settling there independently. The physical evidence for a Norse presence is striking; so much so that Insular scholars look to Man for archetypes in farmsteads, building styles, burials and, later, the conversion to Christianity.

Man's long north-east to south-west lozenge shape has three distinct zones. In the centre the Snaefell massif provides

---

* Man's Viking archaeology was first systematically explored not by a native archaeologist but by an interned German during the 1940s. Gerhard Bersu, a gifted and innovative excavator, was allowed more or less free run of the enigmatic mounds and half-buried enclosures that dot the Manx landscape.

an internal barrier to settlement and landward communication. To the north the mountains are bounded by the Sulby River running east into the sea at Ramsey (Old Norse: *hrams á*, 'wild garlic river'). The low-lying green coastal plains that look north towards Galloway are rich in Norse settlement and burial sites, Scandinavian place names like Jurby and Phurt jostling with Gaelic Ballaugh and Carrick. Jurby parish, on the north-west coast, boasts three 'pagan' graves of the Viking period. Gerhard Bersu's pioneering excavation of the mound at Ballateare in the 1940s revealed the complex, structured burial of a warrior male interred with the trappings of his profession. The excellence of the excavation and a burial environment favourable to preservation afford us perhaps the most detailed and intimate portrait of a Norse Viking from the British Isles, paralleled most vividly in the poetry of *Beowulf* and the accounts of Norse burials among the *Rus* encountered by the Arab diplomat Ibn Fadlán.[14]

The man interred at Ballateare was between eighteen and thirty years old. On his death a grave was dug into which his wooden coffin was placed. He was dressed in a cloak held fast at the throat by a ring pin absolutely diagnostic of Irish manufacture. With him inside the coffin were a knife, lying on his chest; a sword of Norwegian manufacture, its hilt inlaid with copper wire and silver, still sheathed in a scabbard of probable Anglo-Saxon design; and a spear. The sword and scabbard had been ritually 'killed' by breaking them into several pieces. Outside the coffin, perhaps laid on top in military fashion, were his shield and two more spears. The shield boss, like the sword, had been deliberately hacked; even so, some of the shield wood survived, with its colours remarkably intact: black and white striped bands with red dots—the insignia of his war band or family. Over the grave a mound of turfs, the earth of his new land, was constructed, still standing to more than 9 feet (3 m) high and nearly 40 feet (12 m) across when it was excavated. On top of the mound was placed the body of a female, executed by means of a single, devastating sword-blow to the back of the head, and above her lay the cremated remains of animals: ox, horse, sheep and dog. On top of the completed mound a wooden post had been erected.[15]

Scandinavian pagan burial was a highly engineered affair. The social and material effort invested in securing passage to the warrior's hall at Valhalla was considerable, its symbolism profound. The ritual 'killing' of personal possessions ensured that there was no coming back—fear of revenants was widespread and deeply felt. The ceremonial and ritual elements and the time devoted to the burial of a powerful warrior and landowner, in so many ways reminiscent of the investment afforded to the holy men and women of the Age of Saints, reinforced ties to the land: of family, honour and reverence. Conspicuous consumption of labour, material possessions and the likely sacrifice of the man's personal slave-girl reflected his wealth and prestige, and the honour due to him in death.

The apparent conservatism of this ancient suite of customs (even without the cremation rite of the legendary Beowulf) must be set against a backdrop of strong Christian affiliation on the island represented by stone sculpture and a landscape littered with churches; and, indeed, against the Insular context of prominently visible Bronze Age monumental burials that proclaimed ownership of and ties to land time out of mind. Tensions between old and new, Christian and pagan, native and incomer would be played out in the subtle (and sometimes not so subtle) imagery of a new hybrid form of memorial art across the tenth and eleventh centuries, as Norse and Manx negotiated novel cultural expressions of their increasingly shared experience.

The southern third of Man, hillier and with a more rugged coastline than the north, shows an even greater density of Scandinavian burials and settlements, from the natural stronghold and sheltered harbour of St Patrick's Isle at Peel in the west to the probable beach market site at Ronaldsway in the south-east. Hoards, graves and the likely Viking Age re-use of some of its many prehistoric promontory forts paint a picture of active settlement and a vigorous, outward-looking seagoing culture. At the Braaid, in Marown parish a little west of Douglas, the most impressive surviving remains of Scandinavian settlement south of Orkney give a strong impression of the ways in which Norse incomers carved out (or bought into) active agricultural landholdings.

Here, set among improved upland sheep pasture, the stone footings of a large native circular house, similar to those at the village of Din Llugwy on Anglesey, lie next to their replacements: a straight-sided stone byre with internal stalls and a bow-sided house, more than 60 feet (18 m) long and nearly 30 feet (9 m) wide, whose internal walls showed traces of the lateral stone benches so characteristic of Scandinavian houses further north. Timber-porched entrances at both ends must have created an impressive sense of space and grandeur for the home-cum-feasting barn of a substantial landowner: the mead hall of thegn or jarl, with an effect on the locals every bit as intimidating as the Roman legionary boot on the British mainland in previous centuries.

Whether the inhabitants of the grand circular house next door were displaced, murdered, betrothed to or sold out to the new lords can only be a matter of speculation: the Norse Sagas provide plenty of more or less likely stories to choose from. Most of what must have been hundreds of distinctive native or Scandinavian buildings on Man eventually suffered the common fate of houses that outlive their design or use: they were rebuilt, dismantled, burned down or relocated elsewhere. Only very rarely do they survive, as here, for archaeologists to investigate.

34. *Overleaf,* THE BRAAID:
Norse houses on the Isle of Man,
replacing native dwellings (foreground)
and perhaps displacing the natives.

The Braaid lies 1.5 miles (2.5 km) south of, and overlooks from a height of nearly 500 feet (150 m) above sea level, a natural pass through the hills formed by the valleys of the Rivers Neb and Dhoo, linking the ports of Peel in the west with Douglas in the east; and it is no coincidence that on this route lies the most famous of Manx institutions, the Tynwald (Manx *Tinvaal*, derived from Old Norse *Þingvollr*, an assembly place) whose origins must lie in the Norse period when Man and the Scottish islands formed the heart of a piratical thalassocracy: an empire of the Western seaways.

Appropriately, the expressive stamp of Norse warrior identity is also displayed in Manx boat burials. At the north end of the island, at Knock-e-Dooney, a burial mound excavated in 1927 revealed the remains of a vessel about 30 feet (9 m) in length dating from between 900 and 950, represented by some 300 iron rivets. The body, wrapped in a cloak, was accompanied by sword, shield and spear, and the more prosaic tools of fishing gear, hammer and tongs. At Balladoole, in Arbory parish on the south coast, the unmistakeable outline of a boat, its mound flanked with a kerb of boulders like those at Lindholm Høje on Limfjord in Jutland, was erected inside an existing Christian cemetery, itself occupying the site of a prehistoric enclosure. The burial beneath lay inside the remains of a real boat, some 36 feet (11 m) long.[16]

The exposed western shores of the Outer Hebrides, *Suðreyar* to the Norse, are slowly yielding their Viking Age settlements, on the fertile machair plains of South Uist at Bornais and Cille Pheadair, on North Uist at the fort of Udal, and elsewhere;[17] but the core of that empire lay far to the north. Orkney was, perhaps, the earliest of the Atlantic Norse settlements, an increasingly influential focus of power during a period when Norway's kings were consolidating theirs and when Iceland was first being settled.

35. THE OUTLINE OF A NORSE SHIP BURIAL
at Balladoole, Isle of Man, looking out to sea.
It overlies an earlier, Christian cemetery.

Here the archaeological evidence for Norse cultural intervention is incomparably rich: campaigns of excavation at Brough of Birsay and Skaill, among other sites, have revealed the complex detail of daily life and domestic ritual over several centuries; hoards from Skaill and Stenness indicate how some of Orkney's Viking wealth was accumulated, while Scandinavian-style interments, including a spectacular boat burial at Scar on Sanday, combine with abundant material culture to paint a picture of Norse conquest and integration much more nuanced than the sagas and annals allow.

Brough of Birsay presents the visitor with one of those dramatic arrival scenes reminiscent of Iona and Lindisfarne, as if one has come to the world's edge; more so, perhaps. It sits on a rocky island cut off from Orkney's Mainland west coast at high tide: a great smooth slab of rock tilted slightly away from the land, its bluff bows pointing directly at the surf as if to ride out the relentless Atlantic storms of autumn and winter; absolutely treeless, but capped with green bent grass. The only conceivable harbour is a modified natural rock ramp butting the narrow neck at Point of Buckquoy and hard by the causeway, up which boats might be drawn. An indigenous Pictish settlement was established here long before any Scandinavian interest in the islands. Its elaborate symbol stone and evidence for metal and glass working suggest that a monastery was established close by, well before 800, alongside more secular habitation; perhaps St Findan knew it as a haven after his adventures at the hands of pirates. Orkney's wealth of marine resources is, perhaps improbably, matched by the fertile, cultivable soils of its low plains; wind aside, very cold winters are rare, and from the Neolithic period onwards it supported a substantial population with an abundance of convenient, sheltered harbours. Orkney was anything but peripheral.

Birsay's very evident stone foundations attracted early and continuing archaeological interest; but the most substantial and important excavations (and re-excavations) took place from

1974 under the direction of Chris Morris and John Hunter, following a campaign by Anna Ritchie close by on the Mainland at Buckquoy. Among Orkney's key natural resources is easily quarried and split sandstone: tightly constructed drystone walls are the norm for domestic, agricultural, religious and memorial structures, from the stupendous chambered tombs of the Neolithic period onwards, allowing for marvellous sophistication in the architecture of every age.

The distinctive Pictish form is the figure of eight, a double circular cell arrangement looking, in plan, like a pair of handcuffs. Norse buildings, which replaced the indigenous form from the first half of the ninth century, are of familiar longhouse design in the ratio 3:1: often about 45 feet long by 15 feet wide (14 × 5 m), with various entrances designed to accommodate changing wind patterns. Stone flagged drains and side benches with carefully designed internal partitions (distinctively Orcadian ergonomics, matched only in Shetland, and at Mawgan Porth) are common.

Even without excavation reports to hand, the imagination can easily populate these substantial dwellings with the domestic fug of kitchen and hearth, straw-lined bed cubicle and wall cupboards: dwellings absolutely crammed with space-saving devices.* Timber and turf roofs insulated; peat provided the fuel. Spinning and weaving, metalworking, fishing and animal husbandry are all evidenced by the artefacts of industry: Birsay was a wealthy and busy place. This was a major power base of Pictish monastic and secular power and, later, of the Norse earls of Orkney.[18]

Those earls first come into focus in one of the most enduringly readable of Norse literary achievements: *Orkneyinga Saga*. None of the surviving written sagas are remotely contemporary with the events they describe and, in spinning the thin strands of Orkney's history, its twelfth- to thirteenth-century compiler

---

* To use the ironic phrasing of songwriter John Richards.

presents the sort of creation myth of Atlantic settlement that defies historical analysis. Even so, there are shards of reality here. Haraldr *Hárfagri*, Harald 'Finehair', whose successful rule over Norway can be placed across a swathe of decades either side of 900, and whose intemperate relations with his own people propelled many a longship across the seas, dominates the early part of a grand narrative. Much of the story is based on surviving fragments of Skaldic verse; some comes from sources now lost, or is sparsely supplemented by references in other sagas.

According to the *Saga*, Harald's councillor and military ally, the celebrated Earl Rögnvaldr Eysteinsson, had five sons, among them that Hrólfr who became Rollo of Normandy* and founded his own successful expatriate dynasty, from whom William I and subsequent English kings are descended. After a long campaign during which Haraldr raided Norse pirate bases as far as the Hebrides and Man, he gave Orkney and Shetland to his faithful commander Rögnvaldr, both as reward and to hold them against potential competitors. Rögnvaldr in turn gave these lands to his brother Sigurðr. Sigurðr, so the saga says, became so powerful that he was able in his day to subdue much of Caithness, Moray, Argyll and Ross. His campaign against Maelbrigte, 'Earl of the Scots', ended in the latter's defeat and death; but, according to the compiler, after Sigurðr strapped Maelbrigte's severed head to the saddle of his horse in victory, his calf was pierced by the dead man's tooth and the wound became infected: he died pathetically of sepsis.

One of Rögnvald's sons, Hallad, was subsequently given control of Orkney and confirmed by Haraldr in the title of earl. But

---

* Rollo was cited by the Frankish chronicler Richer de Rheims, as the leader of the Viking raiders who besieged Paris in 885–886. The tenth-century writer Dudo of St Quentin wrote an account of his acquisition of Normandy. Somerville and McDonald 2014, 252ff. By similarity of name he is associated with the Göngu-Hrólfr of *Orkneyinga Saga*: Ganger-Rolf or Rolf 'the Walker', a man so big that a horse could not carry him.

he found the onerous task of defending the islands' farmers from Viking raids too much and returned to Norway in ignominy. The islands were subsequently seized, we are told, by two Danish chiefs, Thorir 'Treebeard' and Kalf 'Scurvy', whose nicknames rather speak for themselves. Rögnvaldr now sent his youngest, 'natural' son, slave-born on his mother's side, to see what he could make of Orkney, although with little hope, it seems, of success. Torf Einar set out with Harald's blessing, the earldom and a twenty-bench ship provided by his father.[19] Tall, ugly and one-eyed, as the saga tells us, Torf Einar was nevertheless far-sighted: he killed his Danish antagonists, took control of Orkney and, in an odd aside that might account for his nickname, we are told that he was the first to dig peat, or turf, for fuel.* The very real fortunes of the communities at Portmahomack and the lands of Fortriu around the Moray Firth fit somehow into this semi-historical context. Einar's turf-cutting took place, appropriately, on 'Torfness': the Tarbat peninsula.[20]

Einar seems to have spent periods in exile in Caithness after the death of his father and a fallout with King Haraldr, which might have been precipitated by his increasingly successful rule of Orkney. In the end the two were reconciled and a deal was thrashed out, whose detail seems at least historically plausible and admirably pragmatic:

> Haraldr imposed a tax on the islands amounting to sixty gold marks. Einar offered to pay the whole sum out of his own pocket on condition that he should hold all the estates in fee [freehold], and to these terms the farmers agreed since the wealthier ones hoped to redeem their estates later, while the poorer ones were unable to pay the tribute anyway... Earl Einar ruled over Orkney for many years and died in his bed.[21]

---

* An alternative story to that told in *Orkneyinga Saga*, and preserved in the *Three Fragmentary Annals*, says that Rögnvaldr and his sons were all exiled in Orkney. *FA* 330.

These semi-mythical events are only dimly perceived in the Insular sources. Sigurð's ravages on the Scottish mainland might just be identified with an attack on Dunottar, the great rocky promontory fort just south of Stonehaven in Aberdeenshire, noted in the *Chronicle of the Kings of Alba* under the year 900.[22] In this battle Domnall son of Constantín,* king of Alba, was killed, an event of sufficient importance for it to be recorded by the *Annals of Ulster*. The Alban *Chronicle* also relates that Pictavia was wasted; and it is conceivable that Scotland might have fallen permanently under Norse rule in the aftermath, with powerful earls controlling the islands to north and west while land-hungry Irish exiles, thwarted in their attempts to wrest the southern kingdoms from the Anglo-Saxons, looked for easier conquests in northern Britain.

That Alba did not fall can be attributed in large part to the long and politically astute rule of Constantín mac Áeda, Domnall's cousin, who held the kingdom for forty years and who can properly be regarded as the founder of the medieval Scottish state. He was the first Scottish king to interact with a recognizably coherent kingdom of the *Angelcynn*; capable, too, of mounting a serious military campaign against Northumbria and the southern kingdoms. He was to abdicate in 943 and retire to a life of monastic contemplation as abbot at St Andrews, where he died nine years later.

Under Constantín, in the early years of the tenth century, a distinctive Alban state emerged in the east. If Ælfred had professionalized kingship and royal administration in the south, Constantín seems to have been able to enact parallel reforms in the north, although there is insufficient detail to be certain: no coins

---

* Constantín mac Cináeda or Constantín I; Domnall was, therefore, a grandson of Cináed mac Ailpín. Constantín mac Áed is commonly referred to as Constantin II. It is possible that both Domnall and his cousin spent some years exiled in Ireland with their aunt, which might explain the more than ordinary interest in their careers recorded in the Irish annals. Woolf 2007, 122–6.

36. DUNOTTAR CASTLE, on its rocky promontory
in Aberdeenshire—a target for both Norse raiders
and Anglo-Saxon kings.

were minted in Alba during his reign; no chronicle survives in
which a thousand words might be lavished on the events of a
single year. All that remain are hints, mere fragments.

The first significant events in Constantín's reign seem to reflect
a series of campaigns against invading Norse from Ireland in the
aftermath of their expulsion from Dublin. In 903 'Northmen
plundered Dunkeld and all Albania'. But a year later the same
Chronicle of the Kings of Alba announces that 'Northmen were
slain in Strath Erenn'* and a parallel record in the *Annals of Ulster*
gives the crucial detail: 'Ímar grandson of Ímar was slain by the
men of Fortriu, and there was a great slaughter about him.'[23]
Ímar is the Goidelic form of the Old Norse Ívarr, the outstanding
Viking dynast and scourge of the Insular kingdoms in the 860s.

* Probably Strathearn, but possibly Strath Dearn on the south side of the Moray
  Firth.

Constantín was able to draw almost immediate political capital from this victory:

> In the vi year* king Constantín and Bishop Cellach pledged to keep the laws and disciplines of the faith and the rights of the church and the gospels, *pariter cum Scottis* on the Hill of Belief next to the royal *civitas* of Scone.[24]

The wording is reminiscent, as Alex Woolf points out, of the *Anglo-Saxon Chronicle* account of the meeting between King Ecgberht and Archbishop Ceolnoth at Kingston in 838; so too is the location, on a royal estate at the tidal head of the River Tay. This was a state occasion, the promulgation of formal relations between church and king, mutually reinforcing legitimacy, rights of patronage and law-making. Each party had aligned its immense powers of patronage with the other. It must be seen, too, as an act of Christian solidarity in the face of overtly pagan military threats, backed by the authority of Colm Cille, St Columba, whose precious relics lay higher up Strathtay at Dunkeld. The future of the Scottish state lay in the south-east, not in exposed Argyll or Fortriu. The tricky phrase *pariter cum Scottis* has caused much debate among historians. Alex Woolf concludes that it should best be translated 'in the fashion of the Gaels': that is, following precedents set anciently in Argyll between the kings of Dál Riata and the abbot-bishops of Iona.[25] Alba was a Gaelic rather than a Pictish kingdom.

Even more obscure undercurrents swirling beneath the still waters of its opening decade warn us that the apparently inexorable emergence of three long-lasting polities in England, Scotland and Wales during the tenth century is a simplistic retro-fit. There is nothing inevitable about unification; Britain in the eighth and ninth centuries was intensely regional, not much less so in the tenth. Elements of the old Heptarchy,† even of smaller regional

---

* The sixth year of his rule, i.e. 906.

† Kent, Wessex, East Anglia, Northumbria, Mercia, Essex and Sussex. It is not a con-

polities and territorial rivalries, continued to surface during the period when the great dynasts of Wessex, Gwynedd and Alba were rewriting, or suppressing, alternative histories. Under scrutiny the apparently neat façade of national identity shows structural cracks.

To begin with, Constantín could not lay claim to overlordship of the whole of what we call Scotland. Cait (Caithness) seems to have lain entirely outside his control. The Northern and Western Isles belonged to a Norse thalassocracy. The ancient British kingdom of Strathclyde, which temporarily disappears from annalistic records after the sack of Dumbarton in 870, reappears as Cumbria in later centuries. In the time of Constantín its capital lay at Govan, judging by the extraordinary wealth of Brittonic–Norse sculpture at Govan Old Church on the south bank of the Clyde, and the Thing-mound that seems to have stood nearby.* Strathclyde was capable of extending its cultural and political reach as far south as the Lake District, formerly subject to Northumbrian overlordship; its armies formed an important element of the confederacy that would face Æðelstan at *Brunanburh* in 937 and it seems not to have been conquered by Scottish kings until the eleventh century.

To the south, Northumbria's always uncomfortable projection of unity, if it was ever more than a pipe dream of Bede's and the dynasty of the Idings, did not survive: the kingdom split into its ancient constituent parts. The later pre-Conquest earls of Bamburgh were the descendants of the sixth- and seventh-century kings of Bernicia. When the community of St Cuthbert threw in its lot with the Scandinavian kingdom of York in the late

---

temporary term. In the twelfth century Henry of Huntingdon introduced the idea of the division of seven Anglo-Saxon kingdoms in his *Historia Anglorum*. We might further identify sub-kingdoms in Lindsey, West Wealas, Hwicce, Deira and Bernicia.

* See below, Chapters 9 and 12. Ritchie 2011.

ninth century they were transferring their allegiance away from Bernicia, where their core territorial holdings had lain, to Deira: the kingdom of York.

Even the long-held idea of a wholly Scandinavian kingdom based on York looks a little flimsy under the microscope, at least before the third decade of the tenth century. Several of its kings might have acted as proxies for Danish war bands but the Cuthbert community's dealings with them show how much power was retained by ancient institutions; and the archbishops of York might even be said to have enhanced their position as territorial and economic power brokers under nominal Scandinavian rule. That southern Northumbria's political agenda was anti-Bernician and anti-Wessex, rather than pro-Viking, seems a reasonable conclusion to draw from both its dealings with the Host and its apparently enthusiastic adoption of Æðelwold, the ætheling of Wessex.

Æðelwold had emerged after Ælfred's death in 899 as an alternative candidate for the throne of Wessex. He attempted to attract disaffected elements among the Wessex élite to his banner just as, in 877–878, rival claimants had acquiesced in or sided with the Host's attempts to decapitate the regime. Failing to gain traction in the south he had escaped, made his way to York and there been either received as king (during what seems to have been a brief interregnum), or at least recognized as a legitimate claimant to the throne of Wessex. A number of coins bearing the name ALVALDUS have been found over the years and are generally believed to have been minted in York for the pretender.[26] In 903, according to the *Chronicle*, he sailed with his fleet to the land of the East Saxons. This ancient kingdom, once inclusive of the modern counties of Middlesex and Hertfordshire, had been claimed by Mercia and Wessex alternately in the eighth and early ninth centuries; its last native king, Sigered, had died in 825.

Ancient antagonisms between Essex, its former overlords and the kingdom of Kent across the Thames estuary seem to have rendered it fertile ground for Scandinavian armies seeking a secure base and sympathetic friends. Its muddy estuaries, numberless creeks and tidal islands were perfect hunting grounds and sanctuaries for longships ghosting in and out under sail or oar. Since the treaty between Ælfred and Guðrum it had belonged to the sphere of Danish rule, or at least lay outwith the control of Wessex or Mercia. Now, the West Saxon ætheling took advantage of its strategic position on the Thames estuary to launch a fresh attack on his cousin Eadweard.

He did not strike immediately. Instead he seized the opportunity to exploit more regional antipathy towards Wessex by moving, the following year, into East Anglia where he was able to assemble a much more serious force, capable of invasion. We know, from lists of subsequent casualties recorded in the *Chronicle*, that his army included, perhaps was jointly led by, one King Eohric (properly Old Norse Eiríkr). Eiríkr, otherwise invisible to us, seems to have been the successor to Guðrum, possibly one of the younger commanders in the wars against Wessex in the 870s or 890s or a son thereof, who had proved himself worthy of leading the East Anglian Host.

East Anglia, probably at this time comprising what is now Norfolk, Suffolk and Cambridgeshire, maintained a strong regional identity, demonstrated not just by its acceptance of Æðelwold's claims but also by the remarkable emergence of a cult of the martyred, indigenous King Eadmund. In time this cult would be recognized by Eadweard's successor, Æðelstan, as part of his unification strategy. That the Scandinavian kings of East Anglia took it seriously as an expression of regional solidarity cannot be doubted: from 895 onwards a series of coins, some of whose obverse inscriptions read SCE EADMUND REX (O St Eadmund the King) is widely evidenced. These were no mere memorial tokens: more than 1,800 of them, from more than seventy moneyers, come from the Cuerdale hoard alone.[27] They were minted up until about 915 and show the strength of a thriving coin-based market economy in the kingdom: Scandinavian settlement had been swiftly followed by booming trade. Norwich, the old trading settlement at Ipswich and the newer town at Thetford were productive and successful. King Eadmund's body was transferred from its original burial place to a new church at *Beadoriceworth*, later Bury St Edmunds, enthusiastically patronized by successive English kings. Towards the end of the tenth century a *Life* of the martyred king was commissioned.

Æðelwold's allies in his prospective campaign against Wessex included not only disaffected branches of the West Saxon ruling dynasty, Northumbrian freebooters, glory-seeking members of Essex's and East Anglia's senior families and Danish war bands; he was also able to attract to his banner Beorhtsige, son of the 'ætheling' Beornnoth. It has been suggested that the name offers an alliterative clue to identifying members of the old Mercian 'B' dynasty of kings whose heartlands lay around Breedon on the Hill in Leicestershire.[28] This, it seems, was truly an anti-Wessex alliance, which shows how simmering regional tensions might be brought to the boil by the appearance of a candidate capable of uniting them into a credible force.

Credible that army might have been; but the defences of Wessex, Mercia and Kent, thanks to the reforms undertaken by Ælfred and Æðelred and proven in the campaign of 893–896, were deep and solid; so too was the alliance that bound the southern kingdoms by mutual interest. Decades of Scandinavian predations had strengthened them against both external invasion and internal dissension. Land, its power and wealth woven tightly into the political fabric, lay in the control of the king and church, whose lines of patronage ensured its advantageous distribution.

In 904 Æðelwold led his coalition west into Mercia, raiding and testing support for his venture. Very little detail of the campaign is recorded, except that at Cricklade, the highest navigable point on the River Thames, now defended by a burh, the army crossed into Wessex and 'seized all they could' before returning home.[29] It hardly seems like a sustained attempt to engage Eadweard or his sister Æðelflæd in a do-or-die battle. Eadweard nevertheless pursued the army eastwards, ravaging the country south of the Fens in Cambridgeshire. Intending, then, to retire, Eadweard issued a general order for disengagement which seems to have been ignored by the Men of Kent.

Either caught unawares or pursuing their own ancient rivalries, they engaged Æðelwold's army in a serious and bloody battle that left many of their senior commanders dead but also accounted for King Eiríkr, the ætheling Æðelwold and countless others of his army. The remainder may have kept the field of slaughter; but the anti-Wessex coalition was finished. Looking back from the end of that century, the chronicler Æðelweard completely ignored Æðelwold's part in the campaign which he had inspired, recording only a battle at Holme* under the year 902, against 'the Eastern enemy'; the same battle is recorded in the *Mercian Register* as a conflict between Kentishmen and Danes.

The sparseness of the *Chronicle*'s entries for the opening decade of the tenth century acts as a fog blanketing other political undercurrents. Internal and external tensions and noises heard offstage from the Irish Sea, the Continent and the far north, are as the distant thrum of a bombardment beyond the horizon. The almost universal experience of Early Medieval kings was that, after their succession, they must spend several years constructing, or reconstructing, elaborate webs of lordship and patronage fractured or dissolved by the death of their predecessor. Eadweard's political capital in the aftermath of his defeat of the West Saxon

---

* The site has never been conclusively identified; Holme in Cambridgeshire seems a plausible location.

pretender, and with his redoubtable sister and brother-in-law in firm alliance, ought to have been high. He had been groomed for the kingship; his father had constructed a powerful state apparatus, revolutionizing defence and military service; West Saxon and Mercian interests were secure; the enemy was weak. And yet...

The evidence of coinage, so independent and neutral a witness in these centuries, suggests that, unlike the economies of the Danelaw, East Anglia and York, those of Wessex and Mercia were weak in the early part of Eadweard's reign.[30] Silver seems to have been in short supply, either because of the immense cost of Ælfredan military defences and tributary payments, because of economic neglect in Ælfred's last years, or perhaps as a result of three years of 'murrain and plague' in the late 890s. A lack of silver with which to secure loyalties, pay off enemies and purchase landed estates and prestige goods is a strong indicator of relative political poverty, the detail of which is now impenetrable.

London and Canterbury hardly seem to have been operative as mints in this period. Winchester, Eadweard's heartland, was his only seriously productive mint and, given that no independent Mercian coinage was produced under Æðelred or his wife, we suspect that the West Mercian economy, whose only markets before the revival of Chester were isolated inland, was suffering equal stagnation. A more concrete hint of economic woe in the first decade after Ælfred's death is contained in a charter account in which land was leased to Eadweard by Denewulf, his bishop at Winchester. The bishop recalls that when Eadweard first gave him the land 'it was quite without stock, and stripped bare by heathen men'. Now (in perhaps 907 or 908) the bishop was pleased to say that there were 9 full-grown oxen, 114 pigs and 50 wethers [castrated rams] and a surplus of corn, with 90 acres under crops.[31] It seems as if the post-war Insular southern kingdoms had been economically exhausted by thirty years of war.

We are presented with an abrupt, acontextual message from

the laconic chronicler of Wessex for the year 905:

> *Her on þys geare gefor Ælfred, wæs æt Baðum gerefa. 7 on þæm ilcan gere mon fæstnode þone frið æt Yttingaforda, swa swa Eadweard cyng gerædde, ægðer wið Eastengle ge wið Norðhymbre.*

In this year died Ælfred, who was reeve at Bath; and in the same year peace was ratified at Tiddingford,* as king Eadweard ordained, both with the Host from East Anglia and with the Northumbrians.[32]

The *Chronicle*'s 'E' version, from Peterborough, with its more distinctly northern outlook, reinforces the suspicion that Eadweard was weaker than the official account suggests: it records that Eadweard was 'compelled to make peace'.[33] One wonders, on what terms and with what money?

---

* Tiddingford, no longer in existence, is identified with Linslade just west of Leighton Buzzard next to the River Ouzel on the Bedfordshire–Buckinghamshire border. It lies a few miles south-west of the boundary described in the Treaty of Ælfred and Guðrum (pp. 173–6).

POLITICS BY OTHER MEANS

ROYAL CULTS—A BATTLE—AN ALLIANCE OF SIBLINGS—
WAR OF THE NEW BURHS—FIVE BOROUGHS—EVERYDAY
LIFE IN LINDSEY—SUBMISSION—COUP D'ÉTAT—
RÖGNVALDR AND CUTHBERT

8

ACURIOUSLY ANACHRONISTIC EVENT
stands out among the *Chronicle* entries for the
first decade of the tenth century. In 906 or 909*
the bones of a long-dead saint were 'translated' from Bardney
in Lindsey to Gloucester. On the face of it this seems improbable, for a number of reasons. Oswald was the Northumbrian
king celebrated by Bede, who, in the year 635, brought an Irish
Christian mission from Iona to mainland Britain: the mission by
which the monastery at Lindisfarne was founded. Oswald was
killed in the year 642, by the pagan Mercian warlord Penda, and
dismembered, his head impaled on a stake at a place that came
to be called, in grisly irony, Oswald's Tree, or Oswestry, on the
Mercian–Welsh border. Oswald's head and right arm were later
retrieved by his brother Oswiu and taken back to Bernicia. The
head found its way into the coffin of St Cuthbert (both now lie in
Durham Cathedral); the uncorrupted right arm was enshrined at
Bamburgh. Many miracles and healing episodes were said to have
occurred at the place of Oswald's martyrdom.

---

* The 'C' and 'D' manuscripts that record it do not agree.

37. ÆÐELFLÆD, LADY OF THE MERCIANS,
with her nephew, Æðelstan: the statue at Tamworth,
dedicated in 1913, was sculpted by Edward Bramwell.

The fate of the torso did not become apparent for some thirty-seven years until, oddly, it was presented by a Mercian king, Æðelwulf, and his Northumbrian queen, Osðryð, to their royal monastic foundation at Bardney, an event accompanied by a suitably miraculous celestial revelation and much curing of ills. In the eighth century King Offa endowed the shrine with precious gifts.[1]

Bardney lies on the western edge of the Lincolnshire Wolds, overlooking the peaty flatlands of the River Witham, some 9 miles (14 km) south-east of Lincoln. In the early tenth century Lincoln was a Scandinavian fortress town, one of the so-called Five Boroughs established after the invasion of 865. Two questions immediately present themselves: why did Æðelred and Æðelflæd so desire the relics of a Northumbrian king and saint; and how did they acquire them from within such apparently hostile territory?

Several historians have speculated that a large-scale raid in 909 might have presented an opportunity to steal the relics from under the noses of Lincoln's Danish garrison:

> *7 þy ilcan gere sende Eadweard cyng firde ægðer ge of Westseaxum ge of Mercum, 7 heo gehergade swiðe micel on þæm norðhere...*
>
> And in this year King Eadweard sent levies from both Wessex and Mercia, and severely harried the Host in the north, destroying both people and every kind of cattle: they slew many Danes and were five weeks in their territory.[2]

Well, perhaps. In that scenario the acquisition of Oswald's relics was an opportunistic find of the returning army, or a specifically targeted prize. There are other possibilities: one is that, like Ealdorman Ælfred's acquisition of the *Codex Aureus*, the relics were ransomed from the Host by the Mercian royal couple, and for similar reasons, as a devotional offering to a great ecclesiastical foundation. Another, if we accept the 'D' manuscript's date of 906, is that the return of the relics was negotiated as part of the peace treaty brokered at Tiddingford that year; and that perhaps they were re-interred at Gloucester three years later. Either way, we must explain their value to the Mercian royal house and the timing of their acquisition.

Gloucester, Roman *Glevum*, was the ruined fortress and *colonia* which controlled an important crossing of the River Severn at the core of the old kingdom of Hwicce. In its northern angle stood a minster founded in the seventh century. Half a mile further north, at Kingsholm, lay a royal *vill* complex. Æðelred and Æðelflæd are thought to have begun refortification, perhaps after the campaign of 893, as a pivotal extension of the burghal

38. A FIERCE BEAST bound by intricate interlace
from St Oswald's Priory, Gloucester. King Oswald's great reputation
was a source of inspiration to the Mercian royal house.

network. Like Chester, its riverside walls were either abandoned or used as quarries for stone to extend its other walls so that they enclosed a length of riverbank, within which lay the new burh.

At the same time, it seems, the couple conceived of a new royal minster, constructed close to the river but just outside the walls. It was a remarkable church, built in dressed stone: small by comparison to Eadweard's New Minster at Winchester and some other contemporary grandiose designs, but still magnificent. An apse was constructed, most unusually, at its western end and at its east end stood a crypt or mausoleum, apparently very like that at Repton with its candy twist columns and intimate, almost claustrophobic atmosphere.[3] The ealdorman and his spouse would be buried here in time. The relics of King Oswald were also interred at the new church, a reflection of its royal credentials and the sainted king's unearthly powers at a time of considerable political uncertainty. Part of one of its walls still stands, much altered by later works.

A similar scheme seems to have been carried out at Chester, reconstructed and fortified as a burh by Æðelflæd in 907 to counter the threat of Ingimund's settlement in north-west Cheshire. Here, too, she seems to have re-interred the translated relics of a celebrated royal saint—in this case Wærburg, a granddaughter, ironically, of Oswald's slayer, King Penda.* In later years the church was rededicated jointly to her and Oswald. The Oswald cult was in time patronized by Eadweard's son and successor King Æðelstan (924–939), who was probably fostered at the Mercian court. It seems he believed himself, mistakenly, to be descended from Oswald, who featured prominently in Bede's list of those who had held *imperium* over all Britain (one of the *Bretwaldas* listed by the *Chronicle* under the year 828).[4]

From West Saxon royal investment in the cult of another

---

* Donald Scragg argues that other relics of Oswald were acquired by Æðelflæd for her new Chester foundation at the same time. Scragg 2008.

39.
CHESTER:
the Roman fort
was rebuilt as a burh
by Æðelflæd in
the aftermath of
Ingimund's
invasion of 902.

Northumbrian hero, St Cuthbert,* and Eadweard's re-interment of King Ælfred as effectively a secular saint at his New Minster in Winchester, a picture emerges of political and physical capital being invested by the children of Ælfred in appropriating charismatic cult figures of a heroic, golden past to new political ends. It is almost like a Democratic presidential candidate claiming that his or her father had known Kennedy: the magic is supposed to rub off, as political endorsement. The Mercians were buying into Oswald's and the more credibly indigenous Wærburg's immense prestige.

* See above, p. 145 and below, p. 366ff. Under Æðelstan the Oswald cult also became firmly embedded in Continental tradition.

This investment in cult figures of the past is paralleled in Alba by the Ailpín dynasty's acquisition of Columban relics and by the royal cult of St Andrew, and in Wales by long-lasting royal patronage of St David, the least disturbed of all the Insular patron saints (until the eleventh century, at least, when a series of devastating attacks wrought destruction on cathedral, shrine and relics alike). In the British kingdom of Strathclyde or Cumbria investment in more obscure and ancient, semi-mythical saints (Constantine at Govan, Kentigern at Glasgow and Ninian at Whithorn) reinforced claims of legitimacy, sanctity and deep ancestral roots for their emerging dynasts. From a long historical perspective, this renewed interest in royal-sponsored cults can be seen as part of a confident, offensive political strategy countering arriviste Danish rule in East Mercia, Northumbria and East Anglia. In the latter kingdom, the Scandinavian rulers appropriated one of their own victims, St Eadmund, as a royal cult: a case of having one's homicidal cake and eating it. It may be significant that both Oswald and Eadmund seem to have been the focus of head cults, a deeply ancient, pre-Christian Insular phenomenon.

There is a curious footnote to Gloucester's acquisition of Oswald's relics. In 910 the *Chronicle* reported that a fleet of Continental Vikings based in Brittany sailed up the Severn estuary. Eadweard seems to have received intelligence of their imminent departure from Brittany, for he had mustered his fleet in the harbours of Kent. Perhaps informed of his absence in the far south, the Northumbrian Host 'broke the truce' and harried Mercia, seemingly taking the opportunity to retaliate for the aggression perpetrated by the armies of the *Angelcynn* the previous year.

There was evident danger in the two Scandinavian forces combining somewhere in the lands of the Hwicce; but Mercian and West Saxon levies, co-ordinated through the burhs, intercepted the Northumbrian force and, at Tettenhall, on the north-west outskirts of what is now Wolverhampton,* put it to flight. Two Danish kings,† Eowils (Old Norse Auðgísl) and Hálfdan, were slain along with several of their senior commanders. The Severn fleet seems also to have been put to flight.

Æðelweard, writing as a court insider a hundred years later, indicates that the battle was fought on 5 August; the 'D' version of the *Chronicle* sets it a day later. None of the Mercian or West Saxon participants would have been unaware of the significance of 5 August, especially given the recent translation of remains to Gloucester: this was the day on which, in 642, King Oswald was slain by Penda's forces at *Maserfeld* near Oswestry, with the famous proverb on his dying lips, 'May God have mercy on their souls.'[5] The Mercian royal project to bring Bede's great English martyr into Mercia had, it must have seemed, been given divine approval: absolute proof of the power of the dead saint's virtue.

Eadweard and his sister moved swiftly to take advantage of Northumbrian losses at Tettenhall. The *Mercian Register* noted that in the same year, 910, Æðelflæd built a new fortress at an unidentified site called *Bremesburh*.‡ The year after Tettenhall, Ealdorman Æðelred, reviver of Mercian fortunes and staunch ally of Ælfred and his children, died after his long illness and was

* Æðelweard sets the battle at Wednesbury, a few miles to the east; this may indicate that there was more than one engagement and might explain the slight disparity in dates with the *Chronicle*. Campbell 1961, 53. Tettenhall is *Teotanheale*: Teotta's nook; Wednesbury is *Wadnesberie*: Woden's fort. Watts 2004. Æðelweard adds that the Host recrossed the Severn at Bridgnorth, the closest vulnerable access across the Severn from the territories of the Five Boroughs. Tettenhall lies at the source of the River Penk, which runs north through Staffordshire before joining the River Sow and thence the Trent. Campbell 1961, 53.

† Æðelweard adds a third: Inwaer, or Ívarr.

‡ The locations of three of the burhs built in this decade have yet to be identified: *Bremesburh* might be Bromsgrove, close to the head of the River Salwarpe, which would have protected royal interests in salt production at Droitwich. *Weardburh* (915), *Scergeat* (912) and *Wigingamere* (920) are similarly obscure, although strategic gaps in both the Wessex and Mercian garrison provisions provide endless opportunities for speculation.

buried, most likely, in his new minster at Gloucester alongside Oswald's relics. In the immediate aftermath, according to the *Chronicle*, Eadweard occupied London and Oxford 'and all the lands which belonged thereto'.[6] Historians have variously seen this move as opportunism by Eadweard or as part of a long-term strategy to weaken his sister. At this remove it is hard to decide; but family sentiment is not a conspicuous feature of Early Medieval politics.

Notwithstanding Eadweard's annexation of two Mercian towns, what looks like a co-ordinated project to drive a military wedge into the heart of Danish-held territory now began. Before the second decade of the tenth century was out, new fortresses or burhs were constructed at nineteen sites strung out on a broad line between Thames and Mersey, unmistakeable in their offensive purpose. That line roughly follows Watling Street, north-east of which Scandinavian place names are common and south-west of which they are virtually unknown. It has an ancient and continuing geographic distinction, barely noticed by today's Midlanders. Broadly speaking,* to the north-east all the rivers flow into the Wash or North Sea on the east side, or the Irish Sea on the west. To the south and west every river drains into either Severn or Thames. This is England's natural fault line, its continental divide: the watershed that divided and divides north from south (epitomized by the famous Watford Gap, on the A5/M1 north-east of Daventry); and I have no doubt that Scandinavian armies and settlers knew its imperatives. Now, its status as the front line between the Anglo-Saxon and Danish kingdoms was to be marked and enhanced by military infrastructure: the new burhs were border garrisons, first for a defensive barrier protecting the headwaters of its own rivers and their road connections, then for an offensive frontier, crossing the watershed from south to north.

---

* Watling Street seems consciously to rationalize the zig-zag line of the watershed.

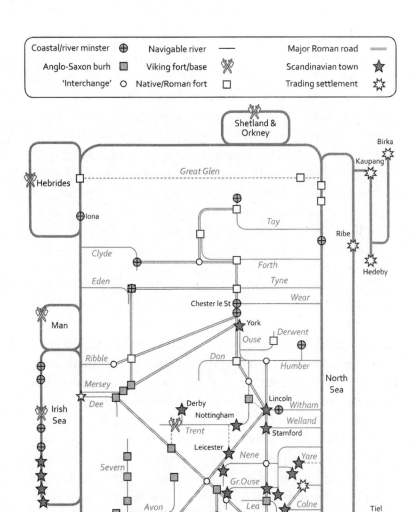

Legend

Coastal/river minster	⊕	Navigable river	—	Major Roman road	=
Anglo-Saxon burh	◾	Viking fort/base	⚔	Scandinavian town	★
'Interchange'	O	Native/Roman fort	☐	Trading settlement	✳

Viking Age travel map: British Isles c. 872–950

That military confidence was backed by a strengthening economy. The number of moneyers, mints and coins dating from the years after about 910 increased dramatically. A series of coins of distinct ornament and carrying Eadweard's name has been shown to originate in West Mercia, most significantly at Chester but also from moneyers in Shrewsbury, Hereford and Gloucester. These coins were not minted by or for him: they are Mercian, an indication that co-operation between Æðelflæd and her brother allowed for considerable independence of action on her part, but also of a revival in trade and a reinvigorated supply of silver. In the south-east, Archbishop Plegmund was responsible for a substantial new coinage minted at Canterbury, while Eadweard's Winchester mint was now supplemented by production in Oxford, London, Chichester, Wareham and Exeter. By the end of his reign the number of moneyers has been estimated at more than sixty in the south and over twenty in West Mercia.[7]

In 912 Æðelflæd had forts constructed at the lost *Scergeat*, perhaps Shrewsbury, and at Bridgnorth, to prevent further incursions across the Severn there and to provide a base for raiding into Danish territory. In the same year Eadweard raised defences at Hertford, on the traditional boundary of Danish East Anglia, and at Maldon in Essex. The latter, at the head of the broad Blackwater estuary and close to the line of the old road from London to Colchester, must have seemed particularly threatening to Danish commanders; later in the tenth century a celebrated battle would be fought close by.

In 913 Æðelflæd, with the assurance of new burhs protecting the Severn and, perhaps, the Roman road towards the valuable salt springs of Droitwich, made her aggressive intentions clear with the construction of burhs at Tamworth* and Stafford, close to the thin blue line of the River Trent and within a day's forced

---

* The ancient Mercian capital may already have been fortified under King Offa.

march of Danish defences at Derby and Leicester. Eadweard, having secured his bridgehead at Maldon the previous year, now built another fortress right on the line of the London to Colchester road at Witham, and a second across the River Lea at Hertford to create a double barrier across the river there, no doubt remembering his father's inspired *coup de main* against a Viking fleet on that very river in 894.

It is inconceivable that these projects were not co-ordinated in advance by the two siblings. Burh construction required a large commitment of labour from the levies, co-operation of ealdormen and fine-tuned planning with military support; not to mention large quantities of cash. The boldness of the programme paid almost immediate dividends. While Eadweard was stationed at Maldon, protecting the builders at Witham, 'a good number of people who had earlier been under Danish domination submitted to him'.[8] Parts, if not all, of Essex now came under his control.

The pace and scope of Eadweard's and Æðelflæd's offensive showed dazzling ambition; and it could not be allowed to continue unopposed. In 914, as Æðelflæd implemented the next phase of the scheme with new forts at Eddisbury* and Warwick, Danish forces came out from Northampton and Leicester and raided southwards. They advanced as far as Hook Norton, southwest of Banbury, and Luton. Both were repulsed by 'the people of the country', who 'fought against them and routed them completely, recovering all that they had taken and also a great part of their horses and their weapons'.[9]

In 915, pressing the advantage, Æðelflæd's levies constructed three new fortresses: at Runcorn, on the peninsula between the Rivers Mersey and Weaver; at Chirbury, close to the Severn and the line of Offa's Dyke at Montgomery (which shows that her

---

* A few miles south-east of Chester, protecting its approach through the Beeston gap and providing a forward base to penetrate further east.

offensive ambitions extended to the Welsh kingdoms); and at the unidentified *Weardburh*.*

The Severn estuary had always been vulnerable to seaborne attack: the same year saw another marine assault, again from Brittany, under two jarls, Ohtor and Harold.† They harried inland and seized Cyfeiliog, the Bishop of Archenfield.‡ Levies from the burhs at Hereford and Gloucester were mobilized and routed them, besieging them in 'an enclosure' until they could extract from them hostages and promises to leave. Retreating to their boats, the Vikings raided coastal sites in Cornwall, at Porlock and at a site east of Watchet in Somerset; again they were driven off, forced to shelter on one of the small islands in the Bristol Channel, before departing.

Late in the same year Eadweard supervised the construction of two fortresses at Buckingham, one on each side of the River Great Ouse. Danish Jarls from Bedford and Northampton and many of the chiefs who owed allegiance to those two towns submitted to him, according to the Chronicle. Eadweard then took the fortress at Bedford and built another on the opposite bank of the Great Ouse. In the aftermath, according to a laconic note in the 'A' version of the Chronicle, Jarl Đurcytel 'went oversea to Froncland with men who wished to follow him, under the protection of King Eadweard and with his assistance': paid off, one supposes; or given ships.[10]

In 916, taking advantage of a distracted Wessex–Mercian

---

* I would place my chips, for what they are worth, somewhere along a line between Whitchurch and Newcastle-under-Lyme.

† The *Annals of Ulster* note a 'great new fleet of the heathens' basing itself on *Loch dá Caech*, that is Waterford harbour, in the previous and following years; it was probably the same fleet.

‡ Edward later ransomed him for 40 lbs (18 kg) of silver, according to the detailed account of this campaign in the 'D' manuscript of the *Chronicle*. Archenfield, the earlier Welsh kingdom of Ergyng, seems to be the subject of the *Dunsæte Ordinance*; see Chapter 9.

leadership to pursue more local interests, the king of Brycheiniog in southern Wales killed an abbot, called Ecgberht, with his companions, provoking the vengeful wrath of the *Myrcna hlæfdige*. She sent a force to his *llys* at *Brecenanmere*, the crannog on Llangorse lake, stormed it and captured his queen with more than thirty others.* Æðelflæd at this time appears to be all-seeing, in absolute command of political developments in her increasing orbit and capable of immediate, effective military response.

Frustratingly, there are dislocations between the several versions of the *Chronicle* in the middle years of the decade which are hard to reconcile. The result is an unsatisfactory scrapbook of events that makes a straightforward linear narrative almost impossible to construct. One is in danger of reversing the order of raid and counter-raid, fort construction and submission; the rhythmic click-clack of Newton's cradle becomes a chaotic racket. With that proviso, one can pick out a new pattern from the year 917: the tattoo of invasion.

Before Easter, Eadweard refortified the old Roman fort at Towcester, not far from Northampton, right on the line of Watling Street and lying close to the head of the north-east flowing Great Ouse. He constructed another at the unidentified *Wigingamere*.† A co-ordinated Danish leadership sent forces from Leicester and Northampton and 'north from there' to lay siege to Towcester. Its defences were too strong, however, and a relief force arrived to disperse the Danish army. In response they took to raiding at night, 'taking considerable spoil both in captives and cattle between Aylesbury and Bernwood'.[11] Another Host now came into the field from Huntingdon, joining forces with an army

---

* The name of the king is unknown, as is the identity of the monastery which he raided. Llangorse is the only crannog, or lake dwelling, so far identified in Wales or England; they were widespread in Scotland and Ireland.

† Jeremy Haslam (1997) identifies it as Old Linslade, a probable location for the signing of the Peace of Tiddingford, close to Leighton Buzzard. If so, it protected the line of Watling Street some 15 miles (24 km) to the south-east towards London.

from East Anglia and constructing a fortress of their own at Tempsford, a few miles north-east of Bedford at the confluence of the Rivers Great Ouse and Izel. The *Chronicle* tells us that the fort at Huntingdon was now abandoned and that the Host came to focus its forces on this crucial front line close to Bedford and Watling Street. Their first new venture was to attack Bedford itself; but the garrison there sallied and put them to flight.

Now, at the height of summer of 917, a second Host came out of East Anglia and East Mercia. They laid siege to the new fort at *Wigingamere*, attempting to storm it; again they were repelled. Eadweard's response was to gather a strong army from the surrounding garrisons.

> *7 foron to Tæmeseforda 7 besæton ða burg 7 fuhton ðæron oð hi hie abræcon 7 ofslogon þone cyning, 7 Toglos eorl, 7 Mannan eorl his sunu...*

> And they marched to Tempsford and besieged the burh and attacked it until they took it by storm, and slew the king, and Jarl Toglos and his son Jarl Manna and his brother and all the garrison who put up a resistance, making prisoners of the rest and seizing everything inside the fortress.[12]

Seizing the initiative, Eadweard now assembled a force from Kent, Surrey and Essex and sent them to attack Colchester, ransacking it and killing all its inhabitants 'except those who escaped over the wall'. Again the Host fought back, bringing their forces, and those of 'pirates whom they had enticed to their aid' against Eadweard's new burh at Maldon. Once more a relieving army saw them off.

As autumn wore on the pace of events did not slacken. Eadweard brought the levies of Wessex to protect the garrison at Towcester while they reinforced its walls with stone (the first mention of such construction at a new burh). The Scandinavian commanders in the area around Northampton submitted to him. Part of the Wessex levy was now relieved and a new force came into the field to take and repair the abandoned fort at Huntingdon, deep inside Danish territory. They moved on to Colchester and occupied it too; and as autumn turned to winter the Host at Cambridge and the people of East Anglia came to Eadweard and submitted to him.

The king could not have left his Mercian flanks unprotected during this furiously hectic campaigning year; but nor did his sister sit idly by in support. Before Lammas 917 (i.e. between 1 August and 1 September, the month of harvest) the *Mercian Register* records that Æðelflæd:

> Won the borough called Derby with God's help, together with all the region which it controlled: four of her thegns, who were dear to her, were slain there within the gates.

And in 918:

> In the early part of this year, with God's help, she secured the possession of the borough of Leicester by peaceful means; and the majority of the Mercian forces that owed allegiance to it became subject to her.[13]

The first two towns of the Five Boroughs of Danish Mercia had fallen, not to Eadweard but to the forces of the *Myrcna hlæf-dige*, Ælfred's daughter. The fighting at Derby was bloody even if, as some historians have suggested, the town's main force was absent, occupied in fighting against Eadweard's levies;[14] Leicester was won by negotiation, either through the acclamation of its inhabitants or by bare-faced bribery.

Since the burhs of East Mercia were invisible to the chroniclers during a period of more than forty years, their history under Danish rule is obscure: it is not at all clear from the historical sources what had been going on beyond the frontiers of West Mercia and Wessex. We can, I think, say that any idea of a model

Anglo-Scandinavian burh is a non-starter. The excavated evidence is patchy or non-existent in many towns; and those where archaeology has produced detailed evidence of ninth- and tenth-century life through its version of keyhole surgery may well be atypical of the wider settlement, let alone other towns. Even attempts at basic classification will defeat the unwary. To take the so-called Five Boroughs as a starting point, we might read too much into their debut in the *Anglo-Saxon Chronicle* entry for 942, in a poetic list of territories conquered by King Eadmund (939–946) which included:

> *Burga fife, Ligoraceaster 7 Lindcylene 7 Snotingaham, swylce Stanford eac Deoraby.*[15]

The names are immediately recognizable as Leicester, Lincoln, Nottingham, Stamford and Derby. Four of these would become the shire towns of counties; and historians naturally see these as the five principal strongholds and trading centres of the Danish-controlled Midlands. But what of those other places that seem to have enjoyed similar status under Danish rule? Northampton was fortified and became a shire town; the same goes for Bedford. Torksey, the Viking camp and production site on the Trent, appears to have manifested some urban characteristics; Repton, too, boasted defences. In Essex, Benfleet might qualify. In East Anglia, Norwich, Thetford, Ipswich, Huntingdon and Cambridge were all towns before the Norman Conquest; and of these Ipswich, at least, shows continuity of urban function, including pottery production, from the early eighth century onwards. Coins were minted in this period in at least four of the Anglo-Scandinavian towns: York, Norwich, Lincoln and Stamford.

Can we characterize these places by the nature of their supposed pre-Scandinavian status? Yes... and no. Leicester had been a Roman town; Lincoln no less than a *colonia*, a regional provincial centre supporting a settlement of retired legionary veterans.

A Roman fort stood close to Derby; but not at Nottingham, Bedford, Northampton or Cambridge. Leicester, Lincoln, probably Northampton and Derby and possibly Stamford were the sites of important minsters before the middle of the ninth century. Leicester was, and Lincoln may have been, the seats of the bishops of Middle Anglia and Lindsey respectively. There is no single suite of characteristics that allows us to either create a hierarchy of Anglo-Scandinavian towns, or differentiate them by earlier or later status.

The Five Boroughs were all, to be sure, geographically well connected. Leicester was the focus of a major Roman road network and lay on the River Soar, a possibly navigable tributary of the Trent. Lincoln was perhaps even better positioned: astride the Roman Ermine Street, one of the key north–south roads in eastern Britain with riverine links to the Humber via the Fossdyke and Trent, and to the Wash via the River Witham. Nottingham sat on the navigable Trent, Derby on a tributary of it. Stamford lies on both Ermine Street and the River Welland, which empties into the Wash. Northampton, Ipswich, Thetford and Norwich also enjoy the advantages of navigable rivers well connected to the existing Roman road system. The Danes, as I have suggested before, knew their geography and chose their sites well; and in various of these places existing defences or enclosures may have been adapted or enlarged by their armies. Not one of the putative towns or burhs of Danish East Mercia or East Anglia lay on a river that drained southwards into West Saxon or Mercian territory: they looked north and east for markets, for retreat and for alliances.

Places that worked as strongholds, with excellent communications by road and water, naturally enough made good trading sites; and if we look at the growth of manufacturing, a key feature of the late pre-Conquest town, their character comes into sharper focus. By the middle of the tenth century wheel-thrown pottery was being produced on an industrial scale at most of the sites I have mentioned, and there is a very clear distinction between these industries, with their restricted but consistent range of bowls and jars, their sophisticated kilns and their zones of regional distribution, and the relatively shabby products of the contemporary West Saxon burhs.[16] The pottery offers us both a discrete set of Anglo-Scandinavian traits and a sense of distinct regional identity. Not only did West Saxons and Danish Mercians employ their own pottery styles; they also rejected the use of pottery made by their counterparts. Late 'Saxon' pottery was a two-fingered gesture, as well as a functional domestic artefact. On display at the heart of the domestic milieu, it transmitted social and ideological messages on a quite different, perhaps equally significant scale to the coins that carried, or did not carry, the king's head.

Even the pottery picture suffers from fuzzy edges and a partially torn canvas. For one thing, excavated evidence shows that in Ipswich, Stamford, Thetford, Lincoln and Leicester kilns were already productive when the Host decided to set up camp and overwinter as the first stage of its grand conquests. And the ceramicist Paul Blinkhorn has shown that at least four of the pottery traditions present at other urban sites by the end of the tenth century were probably only founded around the middle of that century—that is to say, after those regions had been subsumed by the West Saxon and Mercian campaign of expansion that began in the late 910s with the conquest of Derby and Leicester.

There is more than one way of looking at the evidence. One is to argue that central places with important minsters, increasingly secularized and specializing in a variety of products for regional markets, were attractive targets for the jarls of the Host; that they were hijacked, their mercantile development accelerated by a sudden influx of entrepreneurial foreigners, slaves and shed-loads of hard cash. One might picture, as a comparison, the arrival of thousands of American GIs in Britain in the mid-1940s, and its effect on the economy (and birth rate).

We might offer a little more nuance than that, however. It is well understood that the potteries of Danish Mercia and East Anglia owe much of their character to those of Francia. A post-865 model of urban expansion and production would comfortably see Frankish potters being brought over by persuasion or coercion and set to work to produce kitchenware for Vikings who couldn't get it locally. That argument fails to convince those who point out that there was no great pottery tradition in Scandinavia—the Vikings were not simply missing their homely porridge bowls.

One model, which would allow for Frankish potters to arrive in Mercia and East Anglia *before* the Host, would take its example from waves of exiled artisans in a more recent period: the Huguenot weavers and metalworkers who fled France and the Low Countries after the revocation in 1685 of the tolerant Edict of Nantes. Might our Frankish potters have crossed the Channel in the 840s and 850s as refugees from Continental Viking raids, with skilled labour on offer, to be enthusiastically patronized by the local élite just in time for them to be dispossessed by new landlords with bulging pockets and a taste for Continental goods? We cannot say; at least, not yet.

Nor can we say much about what daily life was like in those towns, so familiar in their busy modern high streets and dense housing, their industrial quarters and their fine medieval churches, where excavation has yet to produce the workshops and house plots of their Viking Age inhabitants. For that sort of detail we have to look elsewhere, in some respects uncomfortably far to make credible parallels. Outside of the Scandinavian homelands the largest number, by far, of Viking period urban houses to have been uncovered is in Ireland, where they are counted comfortably in the hundreds.[17] The domestic form there is distinct and homogenous, conservative even. Houses were rectangular with straight walls and sometimes rounded corners, constructed of upright posts infilled with wattle panelling, later upgraded to plank walls. Two lines of internal posts supported a pitched roof of thatch, giving an internal space divided longitudinally into thirds. Raised bedding platforms were set against the side walls. There was a hearth at the centre and doors stood at both ends; smoke and the fug of cooking escaped through turfed or thatched eaves where, one suspects, meat and fish hung for curing.

These houses were built on long narrow plots fronting on to streets, much like their earlier prototypes in the *wics* or riverside trading settlements. The overriding impression is of a hugger-mugger existence, of constant tension between the values of space and privacy, industry and domesticity. Although rebuilt, sometimes several times over the generations, the form and size, at their largest 7 yards by 5 yards but often as little as 4 yards by 3 yards, was replicated again and again; these are family houses the size of modern living rooms. Some of the plots boasted ancillary buildings, with or without hearths, along with cesspits, wells, pathways and kitchen gardens.

These are such distinctly urban dwellings and so striking in their uniformity that it is hard to shake off the impression of planning, of organization and a shared sense of identity, even of urbanity. We might well expect to see such structures emerging from future excavations in cities like Nottingham or Derby, especially given the apparent constraints of crowded urban space and competition for street and river frontage, apparently immutable urban truths. Winchester's Ælfredan re-planning has shown something of the same street-frontage arrangement in several excavations.

Whether all town-dwellers were occupied in trade, craft and industry is more difficult to assess. Perhaps the greatest distinction between urban and rural populations was in food production and consumption. Town-dwellers did, and do, keep chickens and other poultry; perhaps also pigs to recycle food waste and as a winter protein source; but there is no grazing land in their plots. Sheep seem mostly to have been consumed at estate centres in the countryside; they hardly figure on the urban menu. Cattle, the most important source of animal protein, seem, by dint of the skeletal information gained from rubbish deposits, to have been brought from countryside to town on the hoof, as they were right up until the railway age; and here they were slaughtered and sold on streets that would, in later centuries, be called Shambles. Fish and shellfish were a popular and valuable source of protein; grain, butter and cheese, it almost goes without saying, must have come from towns' hinterlands: from farms specializing in dairy, cereals or livestock whence they were transported by boat, cart or packhorse to central markets in a more or less formal series of arrangements whose detail is opaque.

The urban diet, when it can be reconstructed from food remains preserved in rubbish and cesspits,* relied for its staples on bread and cereals, honey, lentils, leeks, peas and beans, fruits, nuts and fungi, washed down with weak beer whose alcohol effectively purified dodgy water.[18] Food seems to have been stored and processed domestically in small quantities. The evident widespread consumption of sloes, hawthorn and rowan berries reflects the need for antiscorbutics† during late winter when fresh fruit and vegetables were in short supply.

If every urban home wove its own cloth from wool and flax, other buildings show that craft specialization was an increasingly important function of towns as productive and trading sites. At York, the famous Viking dig at Coppergate, and excavations in many other sites across the city, produced very substantial

---

* The analysts of York's Coppergate environmental remains, Allan Hall and Harry Kenward, estimate that a staggering 45 cubic metres of human faecal waste was deposited in Anglo-Scandinavian Coppergate, much of it preserved in anoxic 'composting' conditions. Hall and Kenward 2005.

† That is, foods rich in vitamin C, to prevent scurvy.

evidence for trade and industrial production from the end of the ninth century onwards. The trading settlement of pre-Viking York, evidenced by artisan production and finds of exotic imports, was dispersed along its riversides and around the fringes of the Roman citadel; but it was hardly a populous place.[19] The interior of the former Roman fortress was dominated by ecclesiastical precincts and, perhaps, a royal estate, probably appropriated by its new Scandinavian leaders after 875.

Coppergate's four excavated tenements belong to the first decades of the tenth century and indicate a new, dynamic phase in that city's history, when the population grew to perhaps 10,000. The long, narrow plots seen in other Viking Age towns are present here for the first time. Coppergate was the street of the wood-turners (coopers) and archaeology shows that specialized crafts occupied distinct urban niches—the origins, perhaps, of the medieval guild system. But it is not clear whether the people of Coppergate were full-time, seasonal or merely domestic producers of bowls, tools, handles and so on; even, in fact, whether they were dwellers, rather than commuters. Coppergate also housed metal, leather and textile craftsmen and women—dyers, weavers, spinners and finishers.

Elsewhere, on other streets so far only partially excavated or inferred from stray finds, comb-makers, potters, jewellers and glass-makers plied their trades, satisfying local, regional, élite and foreign markets. Coppergate was well placed: it lay 100 yards (90 m) south of the corner of the old fortress and the same distance from a new crossing of the River Ouse, whose approach road, Micklegate (the 'Great Street'), turns away from the site of the former Roman bridge towards the new bridge and skews the neat grid street pattern around it.

South of the River Humber, Lincoln, which seems to have remained under Scandinavian control until the 930s, was closely integrated into the Danish Mercian borough network. There are

40. LINCOLN: the Viking town was superbly sited to exploit the economic potential of Roman road, canal and river connections.

good reasons for thinking that the ancient kingdom of Lindsey maintained a stronger regional identity than any of the new shires forged from East Mercia in the tenth century, and that it remained the most Scandinavian of all the towns south of the Humber. It had never comfortably been part of either Mercia or Northumbria; had never been tributary to the West Saxon kings.

Lincolnshire is much larger than any of those other Anglo-Scandinavian shires centred on towns; and the city's geography is striking: highly visible in its landscape, sitting on a bluff overlooking a gap in the long straight limestone ridge along which the dead-straight Ermine Street runs north towards the Roman crossing of the Humber. It looks down on a semi-natural pool at the confluence of two rivers, the Witham and Till. The Witham flows into the Wash near Boston; but Lincoln is also connected to the great watery highway of the Trent by the Roman canal called the Fossdyke, which terminates at the site of the Danish camp and productive site at Torksey. It was a superbly well-connected place.

Lincoln's medieval cathedral, its castle and bailey occupy the northern core of what had been the Roman city, with its *colonia* projecting south to the edge of the high ground. Bishop Paulinus founded a church here in the seventh century and at least one of Lincoln's churches, St Paul in-the-Bail, shows evidence of Christian continuity from the fourth century onwards.* As at York, the interior of the Roman city seems to have remained the preserve of élite landowners, among them bishops and petty kings, while its Early Medieval population clustered south along the river in a small suburb called Wigford, and outside the east gate in a settlement called Butwerk, dominated by potters. By the time of the Domesday survey, Lincoln could boast more than thirty churches, and analysis of their histories, archaeology and geography has yielded significant insights into the city's development.[20]

---

* Whether it is the church founded or refounded by Bishop Paulinus is the subject of ongoing debate.

Some churches were founded there by wealthy rural patrons owning lucrative urban estates. Others seem to have been established on small burghal plots in response to pressure from town-dwellers needing a place to worship and be buried. Another group of churches served more specific interests, set up in or next to markets where potters, salters and other artisans had their quarters and traded their wares. Some churches seem to have catered for the needs of travellers, or were sited to collect lucrative tolls on entry and/or exit.

There is no hint that Lincoln offered any provision for the veneration of the pagan idols of its conquerors: far from it. A rare coinage series minted here in the 920s bears the name of St Martin,* derivative of the York St Peter money and an echo of the St Eadmund coinage of East Anglia, indicating ecclesiastical patronage of and close involvement in trade. There is some speculation that this dedication, to a legendary saint and bishop of fourth-century Tours in Gaul, might in some way reflect a special trading relationship between Lincoln and the Loire, possibly under the ultimate patronage of the kings or archbishops of York. The single church in Lincoln dedicated to St Martin lies at the dead centre of what had been the Roman *colonia*.

Characteristic of all those towns and productive sites founded in or flourishing from the early tenth century is the manufacture of metalwork. A detailed study of decorated metal dress accessories (brooches, tags and fittings) by Early Medievalist Letty Ten Harkel has yielded valuable insights into the ways in which Scandinavian and indigene interacted and expressed their hybrid identities† in Lincoln, and also into the development of a substantial industry whose output was dispersed widely across the

---

* Bearing the inscription LINCOLIA CIVITAS on the reverse; Stewart 1967. For more on the context, see Hadley 2007, 165 and Stocker 2013, 135.

† See below, Chapter 9, for more on the interaction of native and incomer in the tenth century.

region.[21] In turn, their motifs, style and production techniques demonstrate a subtle set of interactions with and influences from Scandinavia and Francia, set within a strong indigenous tradition. Brooches, strap-ends and harness fittings in myriad varieties were made in shapes and styles either distinctly Scandinavian (such as convex brooches) or as local variants (flat brooches with Scandinavian-style motifs). Some designs were inspired by Scandinavian motifs but deployed in novel media, or using base metal rather than silver.[22] The firm impression is of incomers adapting to local ways, with little evidence of a defensive or self-conscious need to express their Scandinavian identity overtly through material culture.

An equally fascinating study integrating finds of Lincoln-made pottery with a digital view of Lincolnshire's hinterland (a Geographical Information System, or GIS) opens a window onto what might be called the cognitive landscape of Anglo-Scandinavian Lincolnshire.[23] Researchers Leigh Symonds and R. J. Ling created a map of sites that have yielded pottery made in Lincoln, Stamford and Torksey—about 1,000 sherds in all. It shows that the distribution of pottery declines with distance from the production site, as one might expect. The further away from the potter's workshop, the less of his or her product is found. But the picture is messy: behind this apparently simple observation lies some complexity. As the Tube map concept of Viking Age Britain demonstrates, linear distance 'as crows fly' is a poor indicator of the way in which travellers (armies or traders) experience their landscape;[24] and traders move in ways dictated by the bulk, fragility, value and perishability of their goods. For relatively low-value, bulky, heavy and fragile goods like pottery, water transport by barge or punt, or road transport by pack horse were competing delivery systems. We might ask, does the distribution of pottery across Lincoln's hinterland tell us anything about the Viking Age delivery system?

In a digital model of the landscape, estimates of average speed by known Roman road and navigable waterway reflect not linear distance from production centres, but the time taken to deliver goods. The results are striking: when measured by road-time, there is a very clear cluster of pottery consumption at sites at the limit of a day's travel from Lincoln, with smaller clusters at two and three days' distance. When measured by river routes the clusters lie at about a day and a third. My reading of the latter figure is that the model underestimates the speed of water transport.

In a ring around Lincoln, at the distance of a day's travel by road or water, wealthy thegns lived in large timber halls whence they could easily travel into town and from which they could be supplied with an attractive range of goods. Another day's travel out from town, thegns and jarls had less access to consumer goods, and must have paid more for them; they would have heard town gossip less often; been less connected with the movers and shakers of Lincoln's busy markets.

Symonds and Ling suggest, in a highly appealing insight, that those high-status rural sites (what would later become Domesday survey manors), where pottery was consumed en masse, belonged to proprietors owning lucrative urban estates in Lincoln, with access to the new products of its growing mercantile and industrial population; and perhaps these are the same patrons who founded the burghal churches there. It is too early to suggest that the same economic and social rules applied in the other towns of Danish Mercia, let alone the new burhs of Wessex; even so, it provides an attractive and plausible model of distribution and consumption, integrating town and countryside.

The lords of Lincolnshire's more remote farms and estates may have been among the last to hear of Æðelflæd's violent occupation of Derby in the late summer of 917; to hear of the surrender of Leicester, Northampton and Bedford and the assaults on Danish burhs at Colchester, Tempsford and Huntingdon. These events marked hugely significant territorial gains for the Mercian–West Saxon alliance. Their effects on the populations of those burhs and the territories they controlled (effectively, the later shires of Essex, Bedford, Northampton, Cambridge, Huntingdon, Leicester and Derby) can only be imagined. Potters' kilns and smiths' forges may have lain cold for days, if not weeks. Only the most intrepid trader would take to his punt with a full cargo, not knowing whom or what he might meet on the river.

Wise old heads among the townspeople would have cheered the conquering heroes, offering them meat and ale and metaphorically sticking flowers in the muzzles of their guns. The alternative, to judge from hundreds of earlier and later examples of towns being sacked by victorious troops, is an unattractive but real possibility: theft, despoliation, rape, massacre and arson. The truth probably lies on a spectrum between the two; Derby's population suffered more than that of Leicester, perhaps, if we accept the *Chronicle*'s account that the former was stormed by Æðelflæd with great loss of life while the latter was taken 'by peaceful means'.* Merchants and artisans might well have wondered how long it would take to revive their trade, having lost loyal customers and fearful of the instability that new regimes bring. One ought, certainly, to be wary of over-egging an image of crumbling battlements, crowd-filled streets, burning tenements and the chaos of surrender or flight. Huntingdon, for example, was perhaps only partially occupied; most, if not all, the burh walls (Towcester a recent exception) were no more than wooden palisades crowning earth ramparts. Their streets may have numbered half a dozen or fewer: their traders and merchants departed to their country piles leaving the fighters to it, their stalls taken down, their tenements boarded up and empty of goods.

* See above, p. 287.

That native Mercian and East Anglian burghers saw the West Saxon and West Mercian levies as liberators is very doubtful. Antipathy towards the house of Ælfred Æðulfing* may have overridden any anti-Danish sentiment, especially since the Host and its active merchants and artisans seem to have successfully revived a flagging economy and integrated successfully with the native population.

In the immediate aftermath of this reversal in the fortunes of Danish Mercia and East Anglia, there must have been a real possibility of insurgency from scattered elements of the Host— some of them naturalized Mercians and East Anglians, or of mixed ancestry. If so, the *Chronicle* is silent. On the other hand, ecclesiastical institutions, mindful of the extensive patronage that Ælfred's children were beginning to lavish on the churches of West Mercia and Wessex, might have seen nothing less than salvation in the arrival of the levies. There is evidence, too, that Eadweard had prepared the ground for military conquest with more subtle means at his disposal. Two charters from the reign of Æðelstan confirm grants of lands in Derbyshire and Bedfordshire which had, in the time of King Eadweard, been bought 'from the Pagans' with 10 lbs (4.5 kg) of gold and silver.[25] By encouraging, perhaps funding, the purchase of estates by West Saxon thegns in Danish Mercia, Eadweard could begin to establish secure lines of patronage in his and his sister's new conquests.

By the time of the conquests of 917, then, ownership of land and its concomitant rights of patronage, its trading and production networks, may already have looked more like a patchwork, especially in the border zone. Formerly great estates, once the sole perquisite of a king to dispose of as he saw fit, had been subject to fragmentation and the possibility of purchase for cash. Their tenants would have had no choice in the matter.

* From Æðelwulf, Ælfred's father.

In the early part of 918, according to the *Mercian Register*, the people of York, that is to say the nobility of southern Northumbria, negotiated a peace with Æðelflæd. At the very least this suggests that Danish control of the North, so apparently effective during the previous half century, had suffered some reverse and that York's thegns, jarls and burghers now actively sought the Mercian leader's protection, preferring her overlordship to that of her brother, perhaps. We might go further and suggest that the Danish king slaughtered with so many of his senior commanders at Tempsford the previous summer had been the king of Anglo-Scandinavian York, and that no suitable candidate had emerged to succeed him. Other northern events at this time, unrecorded by the West Saxon scribes of the *Anglo-Saxon Chronicle*, tell of the revived fortunes of the kings of Bernicia and of a perhaps even greater threat, from Constantín in Alba.

That hazy picture would come into sharp focus after midsummer when Æðelflæd, seemingly at the peak of her military powers and on the brink of achieving greatness for Mercia, died at the royal burh in Tamworth. She was probably in her late forties. Eadweard received this momentous intelligence at Stamford, where he had just built a fortress on the south bank of the River Welland and where the Danish fortress now surrendered. He went immediately with his forces to Tamworth, 60 miles (95 km) due west, and occupied it. The seamless account preserved in the *Chronicle* masks any suspicion of opposition or discontent:

> *7 him cierde to eall se þeodscype on Myrcna lande þe Æðelflæde ær underþeoded wæs...*

And all the people of Mercia who had been under allegiance to Æðelflæd turned in submission to him. The kings of North Wales, Hywel, Cladog and Idwal, and all the North Welsh

[*Norðweallcyn*] gave him their allegiance. Then, he went thence to Nottingham and occupied the borough: he had it repaired and garrisoned by both Danish and English and all the people settled in Mercia, both Danish and English, submitted to him.[26]

Eadweard's triumphant coup in Mercia, Wales and Danish Mercia was completed when he removed Æðelflæd's presumptive successor, her daughter Ælfwynn, to Wessex. She seems to have been 'retired' to a secure life of monastic contemplation, and lived out her days.[27] Eadweard's intention, now that his celebrated sister was dead and Mercian independence neutralized, was to rule Wessex and Mercia together under his own formidable leadership. He might have capitalized on the earlier submission of the Men of York, too, but for the unanticipated emergence of a new power in the North.

The *Chronicle* has nothing to say of these events. The most compelling Insular account is that of the faithful chronicler of St Cuthbert, continuing the story of that Elfred who had been driven across the mountains by Norse pirates harrying or settling in Cumbria after the expulsion from Dublin in 902.* He, we are told, faithfully held the lands given him by the community, rendered services to them (military protection, in other words) until King Rægnald came with a great multitude of ships and occupied the territory of Ældred son of Eadwulf.

Ældred, who has been identified with the Bernician dynasty at Bamburgh,[28] sought aid not from Eadweard but from King Constantín of Alba. It was too good an opportunity for the Scot to pass up. The Men of Alba rode south along the ancient Roman Dere Street to join their Bernician allies and, at the point where it crosses the River Tyne at Corbridge, engaged the Irish Norse forces of Rægnald (entering stage left from a beach head at Carlisle,

* See above, pp. 236 and 238; *HSC* 22.

surely) in a fierce battle. The date of the conflict is securely fixed in the year of Æðelflæd's death, 918, by a notice in the *Chronicle of the Kings of Alba* and by a fuller account in the *Annals of Ulster*.

So far as the Alban chronicler was concerned, the Scotti 'had the victory'. The Ulster annalist saw it rather differently, offering convincing detail of Constantín's initial success, killing two Norse commanders, before a late rally by Rægnald slaughtered many of his opponents. The *Historia* of St Cuthbert agrees that the Norse won the victory; it also records that the faithful Elfred was put to flight; that all the English magnates were killed except Ældred and his brother Uhtred. The following passage in the *Historia* explains the devastating effect of this new invasion on the community:

> When they had fled and the whole land was conquered, he [Rægnald] divided the estates of Cuthbert... And this son of the devil was the enemy, in whatever ways he was able, of God and St Cuthbert.[29]

Who was this Rægnald, more properly Rögnvaldr in Old Norse? He first appears in the *Annals of Ulster* under the year 914, fighting and winning a naval battle off the Isle of Man against Barðr Óttarsson, who might be identified as the son of that jarl Ohtor whose ships harried the Severn estuary the following year. That great fleet had sailed from Brittany and in 914, apparently after the fight off Man and its disastrous expedition up the Severn, it arrived somewhat battered in Waterford harbour, the *Loch dá Caech* of the Irish Annals. They were joined the following year by more ships and enjoyed several seasons of plundering.

The year 916 drew to a close, we are told, with a terrible winter of snow, extreme cold and unnatural ice, during which many Irish rivers froze, cattle and fish died and comets in the night sky foretold evil times.[30] In the following year Sigtryggr, grandson of Ívarr, and his senior cousin Rögnvaldr, made separate but co-ordinated attacks on southern Ireland, on the coast of Laigin and against the fleet from Brittany which had set up in Waterford harbour.

Niall Glúndub mac Áedo, king of the Cenél nEógain (centred on the Inishowen peninsula north of Derry/Londonderry) and high king of Ireland, marched south with a large army to make war against the combined Norse forces. In August they fought a battle at Mag Femen in Leinster, in which they inflicted heavy casualties on the Norse. A second battle was more decisively won by Sigtryggr, whose men slaughtered more than 500 of the Irish. In the aftermath, Sigtryggr entered Dublin, re-establishing Norse rule over the city for the first time in fifteen years.

The following year, 918, his cousin invaded North Britain. I am inclined to suggest that Rögnvaldr must, by this time, have imposed himself as king of Man, giving him a base from which to plan and implement raids on both sides of the Irish Sea. That he was able to successfully impose his rule on the old Danish kingdom of York after the battle at Corbridge is attested by coins bearing his name. But his rule was cut short,* and when 'this same accursed king perished with his sons and friends... of the things that he had stolen from St Cuthbert he took away nothing except [his] sin'.[31]

One of the recipients of these stolen lands was a jarl called Onlafbald, the 'son of a devil':

> One day, while filled with an unclean spirit, he entered the church of the holy confessor in a rage... and with the whole congregation standing there he said, 'What can this dead man Cuthbert, whose threats are mentioned everywhere, do to me? I swear by my powerful gods Thor and Odin that from this hour I will be the bitterest enemy to you all'... [then] turned away with great arrogance and disdain, intending to leave. But just when he had placed one foot over the threshold, he felt as if an iron bar was fixed deeply into the other foot. With the pain trans-fixing his diabolical heart, he fell, and the devil thrust his sinful soul into Hell. St Cuthbert, as was just, regained his land.[32]

* The *Annals of Ulster* record his passing in 921.

PART

III

Going native
919–955

TIMELINE 3

919 to 955

Unless otherwise stated,
narrative source entries are from
the ASC Parker 'A' text.

ABBREVIATIONS
AC – *Annales Cambriae*
AClon – *Annals of Clonmacnoise*
AFM – *Annals of the Four Masters*
ASC – *Anglo-Saxon Chronicle*
AU – *Annals of Ulster*
CKA – *Chronicle of the Kings of Alba*
EHD – *English Historical Documents*
GRA – *Gesta Regum Anglorum*
HR – *Historia Regum*
HSC – *Historia de Sancto Cuthberto*
RoW – *Roger of Wendover*

919 Rögnvaldr captures York (HR).
— Eadweard gives his daughter Eadgifu in marriage to Charles the Simple, nephew of Ælfred's stepmother Judith (GRA).

920 Eadweard recognized as overking of Anglo-Saxon and Welsh kingdoms and Northumbria: the so-called 'Submission to Eadweard'.
— Sigtryggr moves to York and extends his control as far south as Lincoln (HR).

924 Chester rebels against Eadweard in alliance with 'Britons' (GRA); defeated.
— Eadweard dies at Farndon, on the east bank of the Dee; succeeded by his second son Ælfweard (in Wessex) for sixteen days; he dies at Oxford and is succeeded by Eadweard's oldest son Æðelstan.

925   Æðelstan crowned King of Wessex and Mercia at Kingston in September; meets Sigtryggr at Tamworth (ASC 'D'); gives him his half-sister in marriage.

927   Æðelstan expels the kings of York (ASC 'D'). The **Peace of Eamont** is signed. Æðelstan's overlordship is established over Hywel, Constantín mac Áeda and Owain of Gwent.

930   Possible date for composition of II Æðelstan: the *Grately Code*.

933   Possible date for death of Harald Fairhair (Haraldr *Hárfagri*) of Norway.

— Death of Eadwine atheling, half-brother of Aðelstan, by drowning at sea (ASC 'E', HR and EHD).

934   Death of Guðrøðr, king in Dublin (AU).

— Death of Adulf mcEtulf (AClon)—possibly Ældred son of Eadwulf of Bernicia.

— Amounderness land grant to the church of York (EHD).

— Æðelstan visits the shrine of St Cuthbert at Chester le Street (HSC).

— Æðelstan invades Alba in a raid as far as Dunottar; the fleet ravages as far as Caithness (HR; EHD).

937   Óláfr Guðrøðsson wins major victory on Lough Re and captures the king of Limerick (AFM); sails to England.

— **Battle of Brunanburh**: coalition under Óláfr Guðrøðsson including Owain of Strathclyde and Constantín mac Áeda of Alba fights against Æðelstan and allies at unidentified site, probably in the Wirral (ASC; GRA).

— Possible date of composition of the *Armes Prydein Fawr*.

939   Æðelstan sends fleet to support Louis IV in Francia (EHD).

— Death of Æðelstan at Gloucester; succeeded by his half-brother Eadmund.

940   Óláfr Guðrøðsson re-invades; Northumbrians choose him as their king (ASC 'D'). He besieges Northampton; ravages *regio* of Tamworth (HR); meets the king's army at Leicester and archbishops broker peace; Óláfr becomes king of England north of Watling Street.

— Óláfr Guðrøðsson's York coins inscribed in Old Norse: ANLAF CVNVNC.

941   Destruction of Tyninghame and Lindisfarne by the army of Óláfr (HR).

—Death of Óláfr Guðrøðsson (RoW); succeeded by Óláfr *Kváran* in York.

942 Death of Idwal Foel and his son Elise at English hands (AC); Hywel expels his sons from Gwynedd and annexes it and Powys.

—King Eadmund reclaims the Five Boroughs (ASC: first documentary reference).

943 End of reign of Constantín mac Áeda (CKA). He abdicates in favour of Mael Coluim mac Domnall and retires to the Culdee monastery at St Andrews.

—Northumbrians 'drive out their king' Óláfr (HR).

944 King Eadmund ravages Northumbria and brings it under his sway: expels *Kváran*, who returns to Ireland, and Rögnvaldr Guðrøðsson, who is killed.

945 King Eadmund ravages Cumbria/Strathclyde (AC) and 'gives' it to Mael Coluim mac Domnall of Alba on condition of an alliance.

946 Louis IV d'Outremer is restored to the West Frankish throne.

—King Eadmund is assassinated by Liofa (ASC 'D'). Succeeded by his brother, Eadred (to 955). Eadred subdues Northumbria and the Scots give him submission oaths.

947 Convention at Tanshelf (ASC 'D'). Wulfstan and the Northumbrians submit to Eadred.

948 Eadred ravages Northumbria; Ripon church is burned (ASC 'D'). After the campaign the Northumbrians destroy the rear of his army; the Northumbrians repudiate Eiríkr and submit to Eadred (HR).

949 Return of Óláfr *Kváran* as king at York.

950 Death of Hywel Dda (AU); succeeded by Owain ap Hywel (dies 988); Gwynedd is reclaimed by the sons of Idwal Foel.

952 The sons of Idwal ravage Gwent (AC).

—Eadred has Wulfstan imprisoned in the unidentified *Iudanburh* for alleged plotting (ASC 'D').

—Death of Constantín mac Áeda (CKA).

—Battle between 'the Men of Alba and the Britons and the English' against the foreigners (AU).

—Óláfr is driven out of York by the Northumbrians. Return of Eiríkr to York (ASC 'E').

954   The North submits to King Eadred; Eiríkr is expelled from York. Oswulf, reeve of Bamburgh, is given control of York by Eadred.
— Death of Mael Coluim mac Domnall, King of Alba (CKA); succeeded by Indulf (to 962).

955   Death of King Eadred; succeeded by Eadmund's son Eadwig (to 959).

FORESPÆC

KING ÆLFRED'S LEGACY WAS CEMENTED BY THE OUT-
standing achievements of his son Eadweard, his daughter Æðelflæd and grandson Æðelstan; but they are much more
obscure figures, lacking contemporary champions like Asser and
also, perhaps, lacking Ælfred's philosophical and moral sense
of his own place in history. Eadweard and his sister were canny
and aggressive, seemingly unburdened by their father's reflective
spirit. They inherited a highly organized and professionalized
state machinery from their father (and his godson, Æðelflæd's
husband) and with it they constructed a military and economic
powerhouse. The once formidable Scandinavian armies were no
match for the juggernaut of the *Angelcynn*.*

By the time of his death in 924 Eadweard would largely complete the task of bringing the Danish territories under his control,
extending the burghal system to north and west and apparently
effecting the unification of Wessex with West Mercia. The reign
of his eldest son Æðelstan at first appears to seamlessly continue
the process of West Saxon expansion in the direction of a unified
Anglo-Saxon state in which the kingdoms of the *Angelcynn* and
of the *Deniscan* became England. But in an age of consummate
propagandists one must tread carefully. Æðelstan's succession
was not straightforward and, in the swirling currents of dynastic
rivalry another, less comfortable narrative can be traced.

Increasingly, historians look to the dispassionate evidence
of coinage to test their models of kingship and emergent statehood, while a superabundance of archaeological excavation and

---

* Compare the Viking Age travel map of the ninth century (p. 50) to that of the early
tenth, (p. 281), which shows the defence in depth of the burghal system.

geographical analysis keeps a stage-full of social and economic plates spinning. It is a time of dizzying complexity from which, nevertheless, King Æðelstan emerges in recognizable human form, solidifying from the background action. Vulnerabilities can be sensed in his choice of assembly venues and courtiers; in the defensiveness of his self-aggrandizing titles; in the need to have poets offer up verses of sycophantic praise. He surrounded himself with foster sons from across the political spectrum and from over the seas; he actively sought good matches for his many half-sisters, yet he did not marry himself, and produced no heirs. He was remembered by later generations as a warlike king; but he seems to have devoted much of his time to the pursuit of holy relics and to defining punishments for sometimes trivial offences. He seems to have avoided his own capital, Winchester, for nearly a decade after his succession.

The ambitions of Ælfred's heirs to imitate the *Bretwaldas* of the seventh century in exerting *imperium*, or overlordship, over all the other kingdoms of the island were largely frustrated. The Irish Norse grandsons of the famous Ívarr continued to pursue their interests in the kingdom of Northumbria, sometimes successfully, sometimes less so, mostly at the expense of West Saxon strategies to render the lands north of the Humber tributary. And then, West Saxon lines of patronage did not extend to the lands held for so long by Danish kings and jarls. Attempts were made to purchase estates off Scandinavian lords, but they appear to have been small in scale. The historic bonds of loyalty and kinship which, for the most part, united the ealdormen and thegns of Wessex with their king did not stretch to the Five Boroughs or East Anglia, let alone Northumbria.

Æðelstan deployed a full range of political, legal and economic means to gain influence in those newly won territories. The community of St Cuthbert proved itself amenable to his approaches, backed as they were with land and a large quantity of cash and gifts. Together with the distinctly more ambivalent archbishop of York, they supported and legitimized his northern campaigns. Even so, Æðelstan must contend with more deep-seated ambiguities of identity in both native and incomer populations whose sense of regional affinity was far stronger than any wish to be subject to West Saxon rule. Those ambiguities were felt even more sharply in the Welsh kingdoms, despite the increasingly compliant and favourable behaviour of the grandsons of Rhodri Mawr. A remarkable nationalist tract called *Armes Prydein Fawr** survives to show that one man's realpolitik is another's base appeasement.

For all of the first four decades of the tenth century a single king sat on the throne of Alba: Constantín mac Áeda, who first promulgated the laws of the Scots at Scone in 906. At the time of his succession there was a real chance that all Alba would fall under Scandinavian rule from ambitious Norwegian exiles or the Norse rulers of Dublin. But, increasingly self-confident and effective, Constantín intervened in the political and military evolution of North Britain; and if he was forced by circumstances to submit to Æðelstan, he ensured an enduring Scots identity from which the distinct medieval nation would emerge. Even so, the Northern and Western Isles became, and remained, thoroughly Norse.

When Scot, Anglo-Saxon, Briton and Irish Norse met in a great battle at *Brunanburh* in 937, Æðelstan claimed victory; but he achieved no more than a defence of the status quo. In the half century after Ælfred's death Dane integrated with Anglo-Saxon, and there remains a distinctly regional flavour to the legal and territorial identities of pre-Conquest East Mercia and East Anglia; likewise in Lancashire and north Cheshire. The Midland shires evolved directly out of territories based on the Five Danish boroughs of Derby, Nottingham, Leicester, Lincoln and Stamford,

* See below, p. 373.

and from other towns that they had fortified, settled and transformed into commercially successful central places. When archaeologists excavate the imposing defended settlements of the East Mercian élite at sites like Goltho in Lincolnshire, they cannot tell if the lords of the estate were Danish or English; and it may not matter. The mutual intelligibility of Old English and Old Norse and the sharing of many cultural and artistic expressions of identity, fostered integration. Anglo-Saxon, Welsh or Dane, the late tenth-century inhabitants of Britain south of the Humber were nearly all Christian.

Towns and mercantile economies flourished under Scandinavian influence, and their example was taken up by their would-be overlords. The same cannot be said of the ancient minsters, many of them absorbed into the secular property portfolios of kings and lay lords, abandoned or shrunk to the point of invisibility. Ælfred had attempted a form of ecclesiastic reform while systematically treating the minsters as a currency of royal patronage. Eadweard had much else on his mind. Æðelstan spent money on churches and, especially, on endowing them with costly relics and treasures. But only under his half brothers Eadmund and Eadred did the Anglo-Saxon state once more put its weight behind a monastic movement, of Continental inspiration but distinctly indigenous form.

The final expulsion of the last Norse king of York in 954 coincided with increasing economic and spiritual self-confidence, and with a stable environment in which agriculture and local communities flourished, so that by the end of the tenth century a landscape of nucleated villages, with small churches and graveyards, looking to their nearest town for markets and for justice, begins to look like the medieval world in embryonic form. For a generation the Insular kingdoms enjoyed relative peace without fear of invasion.

A traveller passing through Britain in the 960s would find much that had changed from the days when Ælfred's father brought a Frankish bride home. But the British Isles were probably still as regionally distinct as they ever had been; certainly as wealthy, certainly as attractive, if a little less vulnerable to conquest by jealous kings watching from overseas.

INNATE AFFINITIES WITH AMBIGUITY

AMBITION AND REALITY—NORTHUMBRIA—GOOD FENCES
—THE STATUS QUO—GOVAN—FAMILY WEDDINGS—
DEATH OF EADWEARD—DIPLOMACY AND PATRONAGE
—ÆÐELSTAN, OVERLORD

9

I N THE NORTHERN POLITICS OF THE VIKING period nothing is quite so simple as it seems. Land surely changed hands by fair means and foul; but the bald account of theft and insult, of good lords and perfidious heathens in the piously partisan *Historia de Sancto Cuthberto* masks a more subtle navigation through these difficult waters.

The lands which the community of St Cuthbert had given to the faithful Elfred before his flight from Corbridge comprised three large estates in a contiguous strip along the north Durham coast, between the rivers Wear and Tees.* North of these lay territories that the community had acquired (or reacquired) by dint of its support for King Guðroðr in the 880s, during which time it settled on generous estates in and around Chester le Street, the old Roman fort straddling the Great North Road on the banks of the Wear. Another set of lands which came into the possession of the community of St Cuthbert during that period consisted of

---

* See map, p. 322

41. THE STORY OF THE FISHERS OF MEN—
or Thor's fishing expedition: a cross fragment from
St Andrew's church, Andreas, Isle of Man.

a large triangular tract in the north-west of what is now County Durham, circumscribed by the rivers Derwent and Wear and Roman Dere Street.[1]

In the aftermath of his famous victory at Corbridge in 918, Rögnvaldr gave Elfred's coastal estates to two of his senior jarls, Scula and Onlafbald (the latter supposedly struck down by Cuthbert's wrath in the church at Chester le Street). The *Historia* records that in this same time one Eadred, son of Ricsige, 'rode westwards across the mountains and slew Prince Eardwulf, seized his wife' and then fled to the protection of St Cuthbert at Chester le Street.[2] Like Elfred, Eadred was given lands by the community—the very triangular parcel, in fact, that lay in the north-west of the county. Like Elfred, he held his lands faithfully until the arrival of Rögnvaldr, who slew him at the Battle of Corbridge in 918. This huge estate was now given by the Norse conqueror not to one of his own followers, as one might expect, but to Eadred's sons.

How to unpick this? To start with the realpolitik of the Early Medieval North, we can say that there was historical antipathy between the kings of southern Northumbria—that is, ancient Deira—and the lords of Bamburgh, formerly the seat of the kings of Bernicia. St Cuthbert had been a protégé of the Bernician dynasty of Oswald (now a posthumous cult figure in Mercia); but since the infamous raid on Lindisfarne in 793 the weakness of Bernician royal authority had driven Cuthbert's community west and south on an epic seven-year tour around their lands, until they settled on their estate at Chester le Street. These territories were the ancient marcher lands between Deira and Bernicia; and it seems that by cleverly sponsoring the half-Scandinavian Guðroðr in the early 880s the community had taken up a buffer position between the two rival kingdoms. A buffer, certainly, but very much as the ally of the Men of York. It was Guðroðr who donated the estates between Tyne and Wear to Cuthbert's community. The saint had abandoned his former patrons in Bernicia; or they had abandoned him.

His community (in the guise of its bishop) generously allowed two successive exiles, Elfred and Eadred, to enjoy the fruits of these lands in return, we suppose, for military service: for protection. But for protection against whom? First, it seems, against the revived lordship of Bamburgh, whose alliance in 918 with Constantín in Scotland must have seemed threatening to them. Second, against the new and even more unappealing threat (unappealing because the grandsons of Ívarr were, and always would be, unrepentant heathens) represented by Rögnvaldr. Elfred's background is obscure, although it is quite possible that he was a brother of Eadred. The latter, we are told, was the son of Ricsige—a rare name. A Ricsige was king in York in the 870s, in the days of Rögnvald's infamous grandfather and of Hálfdan and, therefore, a Deiran client (or puppet) of the Great Host.*

Now, perhaps, we can put the pieces together. Suppose that the 'prince' Eardwulf slain by Eadred somewhere in the west was a member of the Bernician royal household, a brother of Ældred son of Eadwulf.† It would follow that the community at Chester le Street had employed these senior Deiran warriors as military proxies against their enemies in the north and west, in return for the renders of several large estates. They rewarded Eadred with the lands that protected their north-west flank, and Elfred with the vulnerable coastal strip. But their protectors were driven off or killed during the invasion by Rögnvaldr which the combined armies of Alba and Bernicia could not halt on the battlefield. The community of St Cuthbert now lay dramatically exposed and vulnerable, its lands a prey to faithless incomers and historic rivals.

---

* See above, p. 124.

† It is just possible that Eardwulf and Eadwulf are the same person, i.e. the father of Ældred.

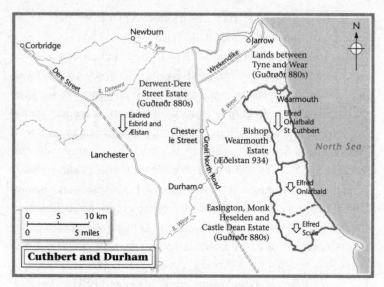

THE ESTATES of the community of St Cuthbert
in the ninth and tenth centuries

Rögnvaldr assumed the reins of power at York where there had
been, as we suspect from its submission to Æðelflæd earlier that
year, an interregnum—a vacuum in military and regal authority.
In doing so he might, without too much perfidy, have regained
control of lands which his predecessor Guðroðr had 'given', or
leased, to St Cuthbert. One bloc of that land he divided and gave
to two of his jarls as a reward for their part in his victory; the
other he allowed to be kept by Esbrid and Ælstan, the sons of the
slain Eadred who were, as members of the Deiran royal house,
entitled to such magnanimity as the price of their loyalty to the
new power in the land. And Rögnvald's interests in protecting
his marcher lands against threats from the north were shared by
the community at Chester le Street. Their interests were, at least
partially, aligned.

Eventually, as the wheels of dynastic fortune turned during
the later tenth century, and as the *Historia* laconically puts it,

St Cuthbert 'regained his land'.* The psychological power of the long-dead saint, and the political power of the militarily vulnerable community at Chester le Street, allowed them to maintain their lands and status through thick and thin, aligning their interests with those who would support them, or leave them alone. They played for high stakes and, by and large, were successful. Sometimes they got through by the skin of their teeth.

In the search for evidence of such expressions of tension and accommodation, the excavated remains of urban and rural settlement are of limited help. The cultures of north-west Europe built houses much like each other. They raised cattle and sheep in the same ways; they ate pretty much the same diet. Their choices in dress and accessories, as much matters of personal concern then as now, were dictated by fashion, price and availability so that in early tenth-century York, for example, native and Scandinavian alike seem to have made, traded, bought and worn a mix of local, regional and foreign ornaments, trims and fabrics. Cultural imperialism seems not to have been expressed in the domination of foreign tastes over native. The patterns of people's lives were dictated, for the most part, by local custom and by their distant lords, their humdrum lives played out well below the radar of kingly warfare, treaty and submission.

Richard Hall, the excavator of Coppergate, in reviewing the mass of evidence for Viking Age York or *Jorvík*, concluded that instead of aligning themselves overtly either with native Northumbrian cultural values, or with those of incoming Scandinavian warlords, its citizens may have consciously adopted both, occupying a cultural centre ground: what Dawn Hadley, the Viking Age scholar, has paraphrased as 'innate affinities with

* I am particularly grateful to fellow members of the Bernician Studies Group for a discussion of the three relevant passages in the HSC: 22–24.

42. NORSE RUNES ON A CROSS SHAFT
from Kirk Braddan Old Church, Isle of Man.

ambiguity'.[3] It is a striking thought: an exercise in delicate cultural fence-sitting, constantly negotiating identity in ways familiar to expatriate communities everywhere. How conscious people
were of the significance of their behaviour is another matter.*

Only occasionally are we afforded glimpses of the mechanisms by which royal authorities tried to balance such cultural
tensions. The *Ordinance concerning the Dunsæte* survives as
copies in two medieval law texts, but most scholars place it in a
tenth-century milieu.[4] Written in Old English and from a West
Saxon perspective, it nevertheless details matters of mutual interest to English and Welsh populations dwelling on either side of a
river. The *Dunsæte* are identified with an area called Archenfield

---

* As an aside, I am drawn to the 'Mercian' response to large-scale twentieth-century
immigration from Asia, one of the many fruits of which was the invention of the
Balti dish whose popularity expresses an affinity with ambiguity every bit as ironic as
those of the Coppergate artisans of tenth-century York.

in English and Ercyng in Welsh, which flanked the River Wye between Monmouth and Hereford and which is now part of Herefordshire. The nine brief clauses of the ordinance are a reminder that the paramount interests of the Insular population were vested in livestock:

> Ðæt is gif man trode bedrifð forstolenes yrfes of stæde on oðer...
>
> That is: if anyone follow the track of stolen cattle from one river bank to the other, then he must hand over the tracking to the men of that land, or show by some mark that the track is rightfully pursued.[5]

Other clauses deal with the resolution of disputes, distraint,* the nature of oaths and so on. Such are the means by which cross-border relations are managed, ensuring that good fences (or rivers) make good neighbours, diffusing cultural tensions that seem so easy to inflame. More significant, perhaps, is the fact that in the *Dunsæte Ordinance* Welsh and English were treated equally: six men from each side were to sit in judgement on disputes; penalties for crimes committed by either side were the same, and English and Welsh livestock had the same values: 30 shillings for a horse (equal to that of a man) or 20 for a mare; 12 shillings for wild cattle; 30 pence for a sow; a shilling for a sheep; 8 pence for a pig; and twopence for the lowly goat. Here, largely isolated from the grand narrative of invasion and counterattack being played out hundreds of miles away, local issues were met with local solutions.

More than thirty years previously Ælfred and Guðrum had negotiated a similar set of ordinances, albeit on a larger territorial scale, to manage rights and obligations between their two jurisdictions where West Saxon and Mercian came into contact with the new Anglo-Danish entity in East Anglia. That treaty concerned itself with the legitimate movement of people from one

---

* The seizure of the property of a debtor.

side to the other; with trade relations and the pursuit of fugitives, the bona fides of traders and the warranties required for purchasing horses, oxen and slaves.

Eadweard's policies, in the confused second decade of his reign when he was, so to speak, fighting fires along a broad front and had little time for formal law-giving, were part expedient and part local accommodation. His so-called *Exeter law code*, dating to between 906 and 917,* refers once to 'the whole nation', then to 'the eastern and northern kingdoms' in contrast to 'our own kingdom'.[6]

In 916, after a successful campaign against Bedford, Eadweard persuaded the defeated Jarl Đurcytel to depart with his men for Francia, under his protection and 'with his assistance'.[7] However long the Danish warlord had been in the English Midlands, it had not been long enough for him to call it home and, equally, the locals may have been glad to see the back of him; maybe they helped raise the fare. Bedford was its own borderland; its tensions perhaps more overt and problematic than those further north in Northumbria and the Five Boroughs. Early tenth-century statehood was a molten fluid being forged with old tools, but from unfamiliar materials.

Elsewhere, the king's new peace in the conquered towns of Danish Mercia was more considered and subtle, as Rögnvald's disposition of his new conquests in the north had been. Eadweard was able to reward his own followers with lands forfeited from jarls like Đurcytel and in some cases he seems to have allowed Scandinavian lords to retain estates that they had acquired.[8] In either case, as the final clause in the *Dunsæte Ordinance* makes clear, submission to the king, whether by Scandinavian jarls or indigenes, involved handing over tribute and hostages as sureties.

---

* *II Eadweard*; the date range is suggested by Simon Keynes. Keynes 2001, 58. The code contains just eight clauses; an adjunct to the codes promulgated by earlier West Saxon kings rather than a replacement.

Eadweard came to East Mercia not as liberator, but as expansionist overlord.

A corollary to large numbers of hostages and subject jarls arriving at the West Saxon and Mercian courts was that young nobles of Scandinavian or half-Scandinavian blood came to learn the ways of a new milieu; to mix with others of their own status and with the native élite. One imagines lively cultural interaction in both directions. On their ultimate return to whichever Midland territory they belonged, they must bring something of West Saxon or Mercian culture, laws and education with them, not to mention brides; and the same processes probably happened in reverse.

After the large-scale submissions at the end of a tumultuous year in 918, Eadweard sustained the hectic pace of offensive action and construction, apparently undaunted by the death of his sister and ally. The following year he secured the submission of Nottingham, which he occupied and garrisoned, diplomatically, with both Englishmen and Danes, according to the *Chronicle*. This was the cue for all the people of Mercia, of both races, to submit and accept him as their overlord.

Turning his attention now to the northern frontier, he had a fortress built at Thelwall on the River Mersey, the westernmost point of the boundary between Mercia and Rögnvald's Northumbria.* A few miles upstream, on the north side of the river, he ordered that the ancient Roman fort at Manchester (*Mamucium*) be rebuilt and garrisoned.

In 920 Eadweard again went to Nottingham, that key site on the River Trent controlling trade and military access between Mercia's heart and the North Sea. Now his levies constructed a fortress on the south side of the river, opposite the existing

---

* Mersey is 'boundary river' in Old English.

defences, and built a bridge to connect the two sides in the fashion employed by his father on the River Lea and following the precedent set so long ago in Francia.* In the same year the king advanced further north and constructed a new burh at Bakewell in the land of the *Pecsætan*, the dwellers among the Peaks. Then, the *Chronicle* records:

> The king of the Scots and the whole Scottish nation accepted him as 'father and lord'; so also did Rægnald and the sons of Eadwulf and all the inhabitants of Northumbria, both English and Danish, Norwegians and others, together with the king of the Strathclyde Welsh and all his subjects.[9]

This passage has stirred the blood of many a patriot historian over the centuries. Some have seen it as the founding charter of an English subjection of North Britain. Most modern commentators treat it with caution: first, because it is the propagandist account of the West Saxon court; and second, because submission to a temporarily superior overlord was an expedient fact of Early Medieval kingship. It is even possible that no such submission occurred at all outside Eadweard's imagination. More likely, I think, he was able to agree with counterparts beyond the Humber that the status quo of 920 should be maintained, that hostages be exchanged and oaths sworn by all parties to uphold the peace within current territorial bounds. That is to say, Eadweard wished that the northern kingdoms should recognize his recent gains in the Midlands. He was in a strong position to make such a demand; they had little to lose by agreeing.

What, then, was the status quo in 920? In Alba, Constantín had proved himself able and willing to engage in great events beyond the southern edge of his kingdom. If we do not know

---

* Traditionally the burh and bridge have been placed at the well-known Trent Bridge crossing. Archaeologist Jeremy Haslam has proposed a site further to the west at Wilford, partly protected by a broad meander of the river and close to a settlement focused on St Wilfred's church; Haslam 1987.

the detail of his now twenty-year-long reign, we can say that his ambition and capabilities reflect dynastic stability, economic affluence and military competence, even if he had not been victorious at Corbridge. He could, in modern terms, mix it with Dublin Norse and with the kingdom of York; he established and maintained diplomatic relations with the southern English, as well as with the Bernician lords of Bamburgh. Some of his political capital was spent on endowing and patronizing the reformist Irish Céli Dé monastic movement:* he would be buried in their great foundation at St Andrews.

Something is also known of the geography of Scottish royal power in this period. The old core of northern Pictavia in Fortriu, around the Moray Firth, must now have been vulnerable to Norse predation and the threat of invasion. If Scone, in the old territory of Atholl, was a ceremonial and symbolic centre of royal and ecclesiastical power, and St Andrews a royal monastic foundation, then the focus of Constantín's kingdom must now be placed in Strathtay and Strathearn. A royal palace and chapel stood at Forteviot, in a fertile alluvial landscape graced with grand high crosses (at Dupplin, for example) and craggy fortresses dominating the northern edge of the Ochils, the Gask ridge and Sidlaw hills and looking always towards the broad River Tay. Dunkeld, whose monastery had housed the relics of St Colm Cille, lay higher up Strathtay. Along with apparent political reform came a cultural Gaelicization which displaced the Pictish language, a process shrouded in deep and frustrating obscurity.

Constantín's political control did not extend to the Western or Northern Isles; nor, probably, to Caithness, Sutherland and Ross. His rule seems also to have coincided with the revival of the ancient British kingdom whose kings had once been based at *Alclud*, Dumbarton rock. Strathclyde, or Cumbria, survived

---

* Also known as the church of the Culdees, possibly 'Companions of God', an extreme ascetic, communal movement seeming to originate in Ireland. Woolf 2007, 314.

the destruction of its great fortress in a Norse attack of 870; its kings re-emerged as leaders of a cultural and military revival. If Constantín had invested his political capital along the upper reaches of the Tay basin, the kings of Strathclyde seem to have chosen a site further up the Clyde from Dumbarton on the south side of the river, at Govan. The Old Church here (an uncompromising late Victorian pile overlooking the post-industrial remnants of its once-great shipbuilding yards) contains a collection of Early Medieval sculpture whose only rival, in numbers and quality, is on Iona. The graveyard is huge and roughly circular, perhaps indicating an early foundation. In the Middle Ages this was the site of an important ferry crossing.

Thanks to recent investment the crosses, grave slabs, hogback tomb covers and a remarkable sarcophagus are beautifully displayed, with careful lighting that reveals the subtlety and creative achievement of an energetic, confident royal church. Like York, Govan displays ambiguities of identity: the hogback tombs are a distinct hybrid of native and Norse, pagan and Christian, embracing the tensions between a warrior caste and its pious responsibilities to the church, the playing out of old rules of patronage on a new psychological canvas. A possible Thing-mound called Doomster Hill once stood nearby, before its sacrifice to Glasgow's nineteenth-century expansion.

43. THE MAGNIFICENT SARCOPHAGUS
at Govan Old Church near Glasgow: a royal hunting scene.

The impressive lidless sandstone sarcophagus now housed inside the church, retrieved from the graveyard in 1855 and restored to a place of honour close to the altar, seems to have once housed the body or relics of a king.[10] Its relief-carved decorative interlace encloses panels portraying a mounted warrior hunting deer with hounds; an unidentifiable animal trampling another underfoot; a serpent and various four-footed beasts. The dedication of the church is to St Constantine, perhaps reflecting the community's original, or acquired, affiliation with a cult of the Roman emperor;[11] but the style of the carving belongs to the ninth or tenth centuries, expressive of a revival of Strathclyde's fortunes and of their historical pretensions. By the time that the British kingdom comes once more on to the radar of the *Anglo-Saxon Chronicle* in the 'submission' of 920 its king, Owain, seems to have extended his overlordship as far south as Galloway and possibly into the lands that later became English Cumbria.

The kings of the Welsh, the *Norðweallcyn* (that is, by contrast to West Wealas, or Cornwall) had submitted to Eadweard at Tamworth in 918, not as conqueror but as the regal power inheriting an *imperium* exerted over them by Æðelflæd. That, at least, is the implication of the account in the *Chronicle*. But Thomas Charles-Edwards, the distinguished historian of Early Medieval Wales, offers another possibility. After an apparent Norse attack on Anglesey in 918 and a raid on Davenport, deep inside Cheshire, by Sigtryggr, the brother of Rögnvaldr, in 920, Eadweard moved decisively to reinforce north-west Mercia. In 921 he had a fortress constructed at *Cledamupa*, which most scholars accept must mean Rhuddlan at the mouth of the River Clwyd.

In the same year the *Annales Cambriae* record a battle at *Dinas Newydd*—the 'New Fortress', which Charles-Edwards suggests may also be identified with *Cledamupa*. In that context, of an unprecedented West Saxon move into Venedotian territory, rebellion by Idwal, the king of Gwynedd, followed by defeat and the joint submission of the grandsons of Rhodri Mawr is plausible. It is equally possible, as Charles-Edwards allows, that the battle was fought against forces from Dublin, Man and/or York, or against those Norse who had settled around Chester and the Ribble Valley; that Idwal and his cousins allied themselves with Eadweard against a common enemy, having sought his protection.

Rhodri Mawr, like Ælfred, Cináed mac Ailpín and Ívarr, is seen retrospectively as the progenitor of a great dynasty. His oldest son, Anarawd, inherited Gwynedd, with its principal royal *llys* at Aberffraw in south-west Anglesey. On his death in 916 Anarawd was succeeded in Gwynedd by his son Idwal Foel. Rhodri's son Merfyn inherited the rule of Powys and was succeeded by his son Llewellyn in 900. Cadell, a third son, who had inherited the south-west kingdom of Seisyllwg by virtue of Rhodri's marriage to a princess of that kingdom named Angharad, must, it seems, have acquired Dyfed too before his death in 909, wresting control from the native kings of Ceredigion. His sons Hywel (who appears to have married the last princess of Ceredigion) and Clydog seem to have jointly inherited control of Seisyllwg and Dyfed and, therefore, of the major Welsh cult centre at St David's. The three cousins jointly submitted to Eadweard in 918 or 921, continuing their alignment with the dynasty of Ælfred.

There is no further record of Norse military activity against the Welsh kingdoms before 954; now a long period of consolidation in the hands of a single dynasty and active co-operation with the kings of Wessex and Mercia allowed the grandsons of Rhodri to play their own parts in the grand political circus of tenth-century Britain.

The grandsons of Ívarr had reconquered Dublin and wrested control of its sister city, York, after 918. Dublin now underwent rapid urban expansion under one Guðrøðr, either a cousin or brother of Rögnvaldr and Sigtryggr. In 919 the latter departed from Dublin 'through the power of God', according to an unhelpful entry in the *Annals of Ulster*. The next we hear of him, he had joined the impious Rögnvaldr in York. In 919, according to a retrospective entry in the Northumbrian annal known as the *Historia Regum*,* Rögnvaldr 'broke into York'. The arrival of his cousin the following year might be seen either as a request for support or a sibling coup; the same annal is the only source to mention Sigtrygg's raid on Cheshire. The treaty with Eadweard, of the same year, reinforces the idea that these ambitious Norse kings were content, for the moment, to consolidate their position.

Rögnvaldr died, according to the *Annals of Ulster*, in 921, succeeded immediately by Sigtryggr. Rögnvald's short reign is evidenced in a series of coins: just twenty-three examples have survived, minted at York in those two years; but the numismatist Mark Blackburn estimated from these few survivals that more than fifty dies had been produced for the Norse king, from which many hundreds, if not thousands, of coins must have been struck.[12] One set carries a rare bust on the reverse, with an odd *Karolus* monogram deriving from originals of Charles the Simple (897–922) in Francia; another carries an image of a drawn bow and arrow on the obverse, with either Thor's hammer or a Tau cross on the reverse: an idolater he may have been, but Rögnvald's sensitivities to the propaganda potential of ambiguous military/Christian and imperial iconography on his coins suggests a man

---

* A long-awaited modern edition with an English translation, by the eminent Durham historian David Rollason, is to be published shortly. The *Historia Regum* was compiled at Durham in the twelfth century but contains a miscellany of earlier material, including otherwise unknown regional annals.

of greater subtlety and creative energy than his enemies would wish us to know.

Both before and after Rögnvaldr the coinage produced by Northumbrian kings is dominated by so-called St Peter issues, first appearing in about 905 and then continuing under Sigtryggr. A total of nearly 300 coins has been retrieved so far from hoards and single finds, representing more than 100 dies. These carry the name not of the king but of the city, as EBRAICE or EBORACE CIVITAS, together with the inscription SCI PETRI MO (*Sancti Petri moneta*) on the reverse. In form they are derivative of coins produced by Ælfred and Eadweard.[13] The earlier issues carry a cross on one side; after Rögnvaldr they tend to be accompanied by a sword or hammer. Stylistically and ideologically they have affinities with the St Eadmund and St Martin coin series of East Anglia and Lincoln, and there is a strong temptation to suggest, as David Rollason argues, that these are ecclesiastical issues of the archbishops of York in their roles as economic tsars.[14]

A counter-argument is proposed by the numismatist Mark Blackburn, who believes that there is no evidence of large-scale coin production in Europe in this period outwith the fiscal control of kings.[15] It is clear that, either way, York was an active and productive economic hub from which the twin faces of the state, secular and spiritual, were apparently doing rather well in the first quarter of the tenth century. But numismatists also detect, in a lack of innovation in the St Peter series and in their continuing decline in weight and literacy, an economy that was beginning to stagnate, either because of instability in the ruling establishment or because of Eadweard's success in reviving the southern economy, drawing trade and production towards Wessex and Mercia— where Æðelflæd's revival of Chester led to the establishment of a flourishing mint, pottery production and vigorous trade.

Eadweard seems to have made no further attempt, after 921, to penetrate deeper into the Anglo-Scandinavian North. A complete absence of entries in the Wessex *Chronicle* for three years has suggested to some historians that the king's health, or at least his martial energy, was in decline. There is no evidence that Lincoln or the old kingdom of Lindsey had fallen to Eadweard's armies by the end of his reign; Northumbria lay outside his control and, perhaps, beyond his ambitions.

In his last years, as befitted a king in his late forties, dynastic concerns needed to be addressed. Eadweard had married three times. With his first wife, Ecgwynn, he had a son, Æðelstan, and a daughter, perhaps called Ealdgith.* William of Malmesbury maintained a tradition that Æðelstan was raised in fosterage at the royal court in Mercia;[16] if so, the implication, against William's own partisan testimony, is that he was meant to succeed there as his father's regent, in preference to Æðelred's and Æðelflæd's daughter Ælfwynn. A Frankish and possibly Insular tradition, that only sons born to a king after his succession were regarded as eligible for the kingship, may have precipitated Eadweard's desire to remarry after Ælfred's death in 899 and produce an heir more acceptable to West Saxon propriety.

Ecgwynn was either dead or had been repudiated by 901, by which time the new king had married Ælfflæd, probably a daughter of Æðelhelm, the ealdorman of Wiltshire.† She bore eight children. Her eldest son, Ælfweard, seems to have been intended as Eadweard's heir in Wessex. By 920 she had apparently 'retired' to the monastic life in a foundation at Wilton[17] and Eadweard married for a third time. His new bride, Eadgifu, was the politically expedient daughter of Sigehelm, ealdorman of Kent, a key ally in the south-east. She bore at least two sons, both of whom would ultimately succeed to the kingship, and two daughters. At

* Sometimes associated with St Edith of Polesworth.

† She witnessed a charter of that year (S363) as *coniunx regis*.

Eadweard's death neither of those sons, Eadmund or Eadred, was old enough to be seriously considered for the West Saxon throne.

A large family presented challenges and opportunities. Royal princesses, potentially wielding considerable personal power and wealth (the examples of Cwenðryð, at the turn of the ninth century, Ælfred's daughter Æðelflæd and Eadweard's third wife Eadgifu are prominent) were also political commodities to be deployed as capital by their fathers, brothers and sons. From the seventh century it had been the practice of the earliest Christian kings of Northumbria to gift daughters (and sisters) to the church and to endow them with large estates from which they could implement dynastic policy via extensive networks of patronage. Princesses were often married to dynasts from other kingdoms and, in the diplomatic pecking order established time out of mind among the European Christian states, the gift of a royal princess as a bride generally indicated submission to the prospective father-in-law. King Offa of Mercia had managed to outrage Charlemagne by offering his son Ecgberht as a spouse to the Frankish king's daughter, Bertha, and suffered a trade embargo as a result. However, when Ælfred married his daughter Æðelflæd to his 'godson' Æðelred, ealdorman of Mercia, it was evidently seen as an act of political superiority; while another daughter, Ælfðryð, dispatched to become the bride of Baldwin II, count of Flanders, may have been a diplomatically neutral bride.

In that light, the Wessex regime's disposition of Eadweard's daughters is significant. By the end of his reign he had made substantial diplomatic progress on the Continent. His grandfather and uncle had notoriously both been married to Judith, the daughter of Charles II the Bald. By about 919 Eadweard had sent Eadgifu, the second of his daughters by Ælfflæd, to the court of Charles III the Simple, the forty-five-year-old posthumous son of Louis the Stammerer. Two others, Eadflæd and Æðelhild, 'renounced the pleasure of earthly nuptials', according to William of Malmesbury's account: the former to take holy orders and the latter in a lay habit.[18] Eadweard's third wife, Eadgifu, saw one of her daughters married off to a more or less eligible Continental, Louis of Aquitaine, while the other was 'dedicated to Christ'. So high was the current stock of the West Saxon dynasty that Eadweard's ultimate successor, the perhaps unlikely Æðelstan, was able to distribute the royal gift of his other half-sisters, Eadhild and Eadgyð, respectively to Hugh the Great, count of Paris and duke of the Franks, and Otto I, duke of Saxony and future Holy Roman Emperor.

William of Malmesbury elaborates on the splendour of the embassy through which Hugh, hearing of Eadhild's incomparable beauty, sought her hand in 926:

> The leader of this embassy was Adelolf, son of Baldwin, count of Flanders, by Ælfðryð, [sister of] King Edward. When he had set forth the wooer's requests in an assembly of nobles at Abingdon, he offered indeed most ample gifts, which might instantly satisfy the cupidity of the most avaricious: perfumes such as never before had been seen in England; jewellery, especially of emeralds, in whose greenness the reflected sun lit up the eyes of the bystanders with a pleasing light; many fleet horses, with trappings.[19]

The list goes on to include the sword of Constantine the Great, on whose pommel an iron nail from the True Cross was fixed. How could the princess's brother refuse?*

Historians are rightly sceptical of this account, which aims to exalt William's biographical subject, Æðelstan. But such magnificent objects were to be found at the West Saxon court. One of them survives, improbably. A very rare and splendidly embroidered stole and maniple, recovered from St Cuthbert's coffin in 1827 and now conserved at Durham Cathedral, carry inscriptions which indicate that they were commissioned by Eadweard's

---

* The embassy is dated to 926, the second year of Æðelstan's reign, by Flodoard of Rheims. Foot 2011, 47.

second wife, Ælfflæd, and intended for her 'pious bishop Friðestan', bishop of Winchester between 909 and 931. Narrow vertical bands contain figures of the Old Testament prophets, of St James and St Thomas the Apostles, of Gregory the Great and the Lamb of God, among sprays of acanthus leaves and pairs of beasts. Analysis by Elizabeth Plenderleith in the 1950s showed that the designs were stitched on to fine tabby weave silk, using varieties of coloured silk stitching including gold thread.[20] If such wonders were intended to grace the shoulders of favoured bishops, it cannot be doubted that the West Saxon court enjoyed access to very high levels of technology and craftsmanship (and craftswomanship), not to mention exotic raw materials from the East. How they came into the possession of the Cuthbert community at Chester le Street is another matter.*

Such interactions at the highest level allow us to picture frequent contact between courts as envoys passed to and fro with news, offers, gifts and intelligence of mutual benefit. Kings took a keen interest in trade, as evinced by Offa's sometimes fraught relations with Charlemagne and by the arrival of notable travellers to the court of Ælfred. Frankish influences on Insular pottery and coinage (Rögnvald's *Karolus* monogram, for example) and possibly on ecclesiastical architecture, as well as dress style and more intellectual pursuits, along with periodic pressure for ecclesiastical reform from Rome, were in cultural competition with closer and more obvious influences travelling west, east and south from areas under Scandinavian control.

Eadweard may not have been as sensitive as his father to the values of literature, philosophy and education; but he knew political advantage when he saw it and proved himself capable of exploiting opportunities as they arose. The Æðulfings of the tenth century were nothing if not well connected and, increasingly, they

* See below, Chapter 10.

were drawn into the complex, not to say Byzantine, affairs of the fragmenting Frankish kingdoms.

The silence of the *Anglo-Saxon Chronicle* during Eadweard's last years can be read in a number of ways, the least probable of which is that there were no significant events to record. Impending regime change may have induced caution in the chronicler of Winchester; the court's intellectual energy might have turned to lassitude with the decline in the king's health and vitality after his twenty-five years' rule. The only hint of political trouble that shows on the surface is a note in the often unreliable account provided by William of Malmesbury, drawing on sources now lost, indicating that Eadweard, 'a few days before his death, subdued the contumacy of the city of Chester, which was rebelling in confederacy with the Britons'.[21]

All versions of the *Chronicle* for the year 924 agree that Eadweard died at Farndon-on-Dee, 8 or so miles (13 km) south of Chester, on the Mercian–Welsh border. The location suggests that William's account has merit. Whatever tensions were now emerging at the West Saxon court may have been transmitted to vulnerable borderlands where British, Scandinavian and native interests were held in fragile balance by the perceived strength of Eadweard's formidable, but now ageing, military machine.

The Winchester *Chronicle* is terse: 'In this year passed away Eadweard, and Æðelstan, his son, came to the throne.'[22] As it stands, that will not do, because the 'D' and 'C' (*Mercian Register*) variants offer significant additional detail:

> King Eadweard died at Farndon-on-Dee in Mercia; and very soon, sixteen days after, his son Ælfweard died at Oxford; they were buried at Winchester. Æðelstan was accepted as king by the Mercians.[23]

The *Historia de Sancto Cuthberto*, with finely tuned hindsight, continued its running commentary on the fortunes of the Chester le Street community's future sponsors:

> At that time King Eadweard, full of days, and worn down by ripe old age, summoned his son Æðelstan, handed his kingdom over to him, and diligently instructed [him] to love St Cuthbert and honour him above all saints, revealing to him how he had mercifully succoured his father King Elfred [Ælfred] in poverty and exile.[24]

Æðelstan's supposed fostering at the Mercian court* gave him solid support among his aunt's ealdormen. Winchester and the West Saxon court were, it may be inferred, more or less solidly behind Eadweard's chosen heir Ælfweard. Had he not died so soon after his father, there must have been a very real possibility of Eadweard's recently consolidated kingdom dividing on historical and regional lines; even of a civil war. That Æðelstan was not immediately accepted by the West Saxons seems likely from the delay in his inauguration, which took place at Kingston upon Thames a year later, and from the exclusively Mercian witnesses to his first charter issued in 925.[25] Kingston looks like a suitably diplomatic site, on the Wessex–Mercian border at the headway of the Thames and the place where his father had been inaugurated. It was a very obvious statement of legitimacy.

If William of Malmesbury is to be believed, an objection had been raised that Æðelstan was 'born of a concubine'—in other words, that since his mother had been married to Eadweard before his assumption of the throne, he was ineligible because she was not then the wife of a king. One detects factionalism beneath the smoothly flowing narrative of the *Chronicle*: indeed, that smooth flow was substantially choked off between 924,

---

* William of Malmesbury's testimony is supported by a grant of privileges from the new king to Æðelred's and Æðelflæd's minster, St Oswald's in Gloucester, in the year of his succession. Foot 2011, 34.

the year of Eadweard's death, and 931, when the Winchester *Chronicle* sees its first entry for seven years. On his own death in 939 Æðelstan was not buried with his father and half-brother at Winchester but at Malmesbury Abbey (hence, perhaps, William's partisan treatment of him). In any event, a potential West Saxon rebellion failed to materialize* and Æðelstan succeeded to Wessex, West Mercia, and those lands which had been won from Danish Mercia and East Anglia.

Æðelstan's inauguration ceremony at Kingston affords a rare glimpse of contemporary conceptions of kingship at first hand. He styled himself *rex Saxonum et Anglorum*, according to a charter issued on that same day, 4 September 925.[26] The formal benediction ceremony has been preserved in a text known as the *Second Coronation Ordo*.† He seems also to have been presented with crown (a Frankish-influenced departure from earlier Insular use of the more martial helmet), ring, rod and sceptre by the new archbishop of Canterbury, Æðelhelm. The king's responsibilities towards Christianity (represented by the ring), towards widows, orphans and the destitute (the sword) and to 'soothe the righteous and terrify the reprobate' (the rod) were given material form. There are references to the two united peoples (West Saxons and Mercian Angles) whom he had been 'elected' to rule, and a solemn prayer that the king would 'hold fast the state'.[27]

Æðelstan's sensitivity to his split loyalties, which would extend to the inclusion of Danish nobles among his household and to active diplomatic engagement with Anglo-Scandinavian York, may find remarkable expression in the greatest Anglo-Saxon poem.

---

* William of Malmesbury relates the story of an attempted coup by the otherwise unknown Ælfred, who tried to blind the new king at Winchester and who subsequently fled to Rome, where he died. *EHD* Secular narrative sources 8. Whitelock 1979, 303.

† Debate continues about whether its first use was Eadweard's, Æðelstan's or, indeed, Edgar's inauguration. Foot 2011, 75ff. Janet Nelson's convincing arguments in a recent paper carry the day, so far. Nelson 2008.

The single surviving manuscript of *Beowulf*, that Dark Age epic of monster and exiled prince, of loyalty, brotherhood and much more besides, dates to around the year 1000. The combined research of hundreds of scholars and poets has reached no firm conclusion about its origins, transmission, date or provenance. In current thought the first transcription of a legendary poetic form, whose origins lie somewhere in the era of pagan Anglo-Saxon, Scandinavian, Germanic and early Irish Christian myth, must have taken place some time in the eighth century. It survived by oral or written transmission, or both, until the two scribes whose work survives fossilized it in a single monumental form.

Æðelstan's biographer Sarah Foot makes a case that at least one transcription and evolution of the poem occurred during the reign of Æðelstan, when it would have provided a unique multi-cultural expression of common origins.[28] One might add to her argument that the martyred seventh-century Northumbrian King Oswald, a recent favourite at Gloucester and at the Mercian court, has been proposed as the epitome for righteous exiled princes—not least by J. R. R. Tolkien, who deployed Oswald as a prototype for his fictional returning king in the *Lord of the Rings*.[29] As a king with his own split loyalties, an Oswald obsession and a demonstrable love of poetry, Æðelstan is a good candidate for propagating *Beowulf* among an increasingly literate audience trying to make sense of its own innate affinities with ambiguity.

The new king lost little time in entering the diplomatic and political fray, deploying the immense political and military capital accumulated by his father, aunt and grandfather. More than thirty years old and schooled in the politics of Anglo-Scandinavian relations by the expert dynasts of the West Saxon ruling house, Æðelstan's political maturity is evident from the start. By the end of 926 he had received the Continental embassy which resulted in the dispatch of his half-sister Eadhild to the marriage bed of Hugh, count of Paris and duke of the Franks.

Æðelstan had already, earlier that same year, contracted a union of potentially greater significance: the 'D' Worcester version of the *Chronicle* records that 'King Æðelstan and Sigtryggr, king of Northumbria, met at Tamworth on 30 January and Æðelstan gave him his sister in marriage.'[30] Tamworth was the Mercian royal burh where Æðelflæd had died and where a 1913 statue of her* stands close by the walls of the later medieval castle. Tamworth (*Tomworðig*: 'enclosure by the River Tame') lay on a tributary of the upper Trent river system and was the caput of an early *regio* or petty kingdom. Its natives, the *Tomsæte* of the Tribal Hidage, had been absorbed into the Mercian overstate by the eighth century, from which time it became a favourite royal residence and possible minster foundation, close to the principal Mercian see at Lichfield and to Watling Street, less than 2 miles (3 km) to the south. During the annexation of much of Mercia by Scandinavian armies in the 870s, Tamworth may have fallen under Danish authority; but it acted as a sort of offensive border garrison for West Mercian forces after Æðelflæd constructed a new fortress here in 913.

Tamworth is celebrated among archaeologists for its Anglo-Saxon water mill complex, excavated by Philip Rahtz and Roger Meeson in two campaigns in the 1970s. It stood on the north bank of the River Anker, close to its confluence with the Tame and to the south-east corner of the later burh defences.[31] The second of two successive horizontal paddle mills on the site, providing a rich and invaluable insight into the sophistication of Early Medieval civil engineering (including, for example, the survival of a high-quality steel bearing from the wheelhouse), has been dated by its well-preserved timbers to about 855. Its late ninth-century destruction by fire might plausibly, but with

---

* Commissioned to mark the millennium of her construction of the burh here. She is depicted in modest robes with her arm around a youthful nephew, Æðelstan (see p. 271).

caution, be laid at the door of the *mycel here*. Eadweard's immediate occupation of the burh on his sister's death indicates its continuing symbolic and strategic importance. Æðelstan established
a mint here, and his choice of Tamworth as a venue for a royal
wedding and diplomatic alliance echoes his own political affinities as much as it does the convenience of a border town for
inter-kingdom negotiations.

The grandson of Ívarr who married the king's sister in 925
may or may not have been aware that for the *Angelcynn* such a
marriage transaction implied political submission. He may have
seen it as an alliance of equals, and the *Chronicle* affords him the
title of king. Whatever the case, his apparent enthusiasm for a
rapprochement with the southern English kingdoms, and the
implication that he must have been baptized in order for his marriage to be consecrated, indicates a greater willingness to make
accommodations with native culture than his cousin Rögnvaldr
had shown. So too does his readoption of the St Peter coinage
in York and, perhaps, Lincoln. His wife's fate is not known; nor,
oddly, is her name.

How Sigtrygg's reign might have played out over the next decade cannot now be established: he was dead within a year.[32] He
was immediately succeeded by the most aggressive of the grandsons of Ívarr, that Guðrøðr who had imposed his military rule on
Dublin so effectively after 921, who had plundered the Patrician
cult centre at Armagh and more recently attacked Limerick,
according to the *Annals of Ulster*. But his attempted coup at
York was swiftly countered by Æðelstan and by the end of 927 he
had returned to Dublin.* The Worcester version of the *Chronicle*
records Æðelstan's 'annexation' of Northumbria in the aftermath
of Guðrøð's expulsion. In this fortuitous and expedient series

---

* He may not even have got so far as York. Symeon, *Historia Regum*, reports his
  expulsion from the kingdom of the Britons, i.e. Cumbria. Charles-Edwards 2013,
  521.

44. PLACE NAMES on a signpost in the East Riding of Yorkshire: 'telltale suffixes like *–by* and *–Thorpe* testify to the presence of Norse speakers'.

of events one can, perhaps, detect a step-change in Æðelstan's thinking about Northumbria: from dangerous enemy to dynastically entwined ally, to its potential absorption into his kingdom. Now he marshalled military, political and cultural forces behind the project; but, despite later historians' wishful thinking, the fall of York did not fire the starting gun on a race towards the unification of England; and it could not.

Early Medieval kingship relied on the preservation and expansion of networks of patronage constructed across generations. The kings of Wessex owned large estates spread across the southern shires, from Kent to Devon, accumulated by their forbears. Æðelstan was able to expand his portfolio by right of succession to Æðelred and his aunt Æðelflæd—although those estates seem to have been confined to lands in Gloucestershire and Worcestershire, the ancient territories of the Hwicce where Æðelred's line had once probably been kings in their own right.* There is almost nothing from further north; nothing in the Mercian heartlands around Tamworth and Lichfield—we do not know in whose portfolio they lay.

Some of the kings' wealth in the south had been alienated by grants, as bookland, to the great minsters and to ealdormen and thegns, ensuring their support and spiritual protection and spreading the munificence of the king. Some of that land had returned to the king's portfolio through lapses in ownership, legal forfeit and the fallout from the heyday of the Viking armies. The remainder was often distributed by Æðelstan in rebuilding the fortunes of those southern churches that he so conspicuously favoured. But he was not the only great landowner, and even with sceptre and rod in hand and a crown on his head, he must negotiate power with others who held it. As the machinations of the community of St Cuthbert show, the manipulation of grants was a subtle, complex affair. Tenth-century politics rarely consisted of the simple military arrogation of rights to land: it required the conversion of capital into power by exploiting webs of obligation and gift which, like the root systems of trees, lie substantially obscured and hidden from us. Even when they are exposed to our limited view, we never get to see the whole picture.

The fragmentation and theft of estates that had occurred in areas of Scandinavian control, the collapse of episcopal and minster administration and the inability of the southern kings to access those lines of patronage meant that in East Mercia and Lindsey, in East Anglia and Northumbria, even if the king's writ ran, his ability to manipulate landholdings to buy favour and support was limited in the extreme. Those networks would have to be built from scratch, accumulated through military victory or

---

* Many of the south Mercian charters which attest such estates are, in any case, under a cloud of doubt regarding their authenticity. Foot 2011, 135.

bought with hard cash.* Two grants of Eadweard, confirmed by Æðelstan, show that the West Saxon kings were active in the business of acquiring and strategically deploying estates in key areas along and across the border with Danish Mercia.† Now, those techniques needed to be implemented on a vastly grander scale, over a much longer period.

How, then, was Æðelstan to bring the North into the orbit of an expanded Wessex? The Worcester version of the *Chronicle* offers one clue in its extended entry for 926, properly 927:

> He brought into submission all the kings in this island: first Hywel, king of the West Welsh, and Constantín, king of Scots, and Owain, king of Gwent‡ and Ealdred Eadulfing from Bamburgh. They established a covenant of peace with pledges and oaths at a place called Eamont Bridge on 12 July: they forbade all idolatrous practices, and then separated in accord.[33]

The historian is wisely sceptical of such one-sided accounts, especially when there is no surviving record from any of the other participants. But the Worcester *Chronicle* embeds a more northern perspective than the Winchester prototype, which is absolutely silent in these years; and in any case the location and form of these ceremonial 'submissions' is telling.§ Eamont Bridge can be identified: just south of Penrith on a narrow spur of land between two rivers, the Eamont and Lowther. Roman roads run north to south and east from here (including the A66 trans-Pennine route towards Stainmore). The Roman fortress and later medieval cas-

---

* See below, Chapter 11: the Amounderness purchase. The matter of Æðelstan's cash wealth and estates is treated fully in Foot 2011, 148ff.

† See above Chapter 8, p. 301.

‡ Most historians think that this is an error for Owain of Strathclyde; but there was a possibly contemporary king of Gwent named Owain, and it is possible that both kings were originally meant. Charles-Edwards 2013, 512.

§ I am inclined to discount William of Malmesbury's lurid, expanded version in which Guðroðr flees to Scotland and Æðelstan slights the defences of York and loots the city. But it is worth reading for the possible insider information on which William may be elaborating. *EHD*: Whitelock 1979, 307.

tle of *Brocavum*, or Brougham, occupies a strategically important site close by at the rivers' confluence and, just to the west,
an impressive henge monument speaks of a landscape steeped
in symbols of earthly and unearthly power. More importantly,
Eamont Bridge lay in an area that had once formed part of the
British kingdom of Rheged and had fallen under Northumbrian
control by the end of the sixth century. That control had lasted
perhaps 100 years; in Æðelstan's time it seems as though the
region was disputed between the kings of York and Strathclyde,
with the possible territories of Dublin Norse abutting it to the
south. Æðelstan's confidence and military capability was such
that he was able to conduct peace negotiations on his antagonists' patch or, at least, on their borders.

This was a landscape of pastoralists living in widely dispersed
settlements with nothing like a burh for several days' travel in any
direction. Carlisle may have retained some minster functions and
perhaps a harbour; a monastery existed just to the west of Penrith
at Dacre, where four enigmatic, distinctly Anglo-Scandinavian
stone bears guard the compass points of the church; and contemporary sculpture has been retrieved from Penrith itself. This was
by no means an empty landscape; but so far as royal power was
concerned it may have constituted neutral territory: a debatable
land. This was a meeting of wary neighbours, not a surrender,
and it follows an established pattern of siting what, these days,
would be called political summits on frontiers.[34]

The oaths and pledges recorded in the *Chronicle* must have
been supplemented by the exchange of royal, or at least noble,
hostages as guarantors of that peace. Æðelstan will have swelled
the coffers of his treasure chests with tribute; and with fresh
cash assets he was in a better position to purchase rights to land
beyond his homeland. The treaty signed at Eamont looks like a
repeat of the 'status quo' agreement which had pertained under
Eadweard from 920, reinforced by the dynastic marriage between

Æðelstan's only full sister and Sigtryggr. But Æðelstan's hand had been considerably strengthened by Sigtrygg's death and by the timely departure of Guðroðr to Dublin.

The significance of the renunciation by all participants of idolatrous practices, apparently aimed at those with Norse affiliations, is unclear. No Scandinavian king was present, so far as the *Chronicle* was concerned, so one suspects the presence of a number of jarls with authority over parts of the kingdom of York or of East Mercia, acting as local regents to Æðelstan's undeniable overlordship.

A poet, seemingly present at the event and acting in semi-official capacity as a correspondent embedded within the king's entourage, has left some lines of verse for historians to chew on. The *Carta dirige gressus*, as it is known from its first line, survives in two manuscripts. One, curiously, is an eighth-century gospel book, probably produced at Lindisfarne, which was in the possession of the St Cuthbert community at Chester le Street in the tenth century.[35] The poem was copied on to the lower margin of a page some time in the late tenth or early eleventh century. That a scribe at Chester le Street was interested in composing or copying a laudatory poem concerning Æðelstan is not surprising.* The verses, in six stanzas, have been convincingly dated to the immediate aftermath of the Eamont peace treaty by Michael Lapidge, the scholar of medieval Latin literature who has made a special study of poetry in the reign of Æðelstan.

> *Carta, dirige gressus*
> *per maria navigans*
> *tellurisque spacium*
> *ad regis palacium.*

> Letter, direct your steps
> Sailing across the seas
> And an expanse of land
> To the king's burh.[36]

---

* See below, Chapter 10.

The poem directs itself to the queen, the prince, distinguished ealdormen and arms-bearing thegns 'whom he now rules with this *Saxonia** [now] made whole† [*perfecta*]: King Æðelstan lives glorious through his deeds'. The poet, who helpfully records his own name, Peter, in the last stanza, goes on to versify the death of Sigtryggr and the arrival of Constantín, eager to display his loyalty to the king, securely placing the poem in the context of the events of 927. He ends with a prayer that the king might live well and long through the Saviour's grace. Michael Lapidge argues that the poem acted as a sort of headline dispatch to the court at home, a Neville Chamberlain-like brandishing of a treaty. He also argues that the court in question must be Winchester; but, given the hostility of that burh and its minster to Æðelstan's regime, I wonder if Gloucester was its intended destination: a royal possession very much more closely affiliated to the king and his interests.

One minor problem concerns the identity of the queen, one of the poet's addressees. Æðelstan, conspicuously, had not married and would not marry or produce any children, legitimate or otherwise.‡ The queen concerned must, I think, be the mother of the prince addressed in the same line: that is to say, Eadweard's third wife Eadgifu, whose sons Eadmund and Eadred would succeed their half-brother, Æðelstan, in due course and who herself died after 966.§ The shadowy influence of that interesting woman surfaces from time to time in the middle of the tenth century, a reminder that political power could be exercised by means more

---

* Lapidge, I think significantly, translates Saxonia as 'England'. The poet is implying a united kingdom, 'made whole', of the Saxons. The lands of the Angles – that is, in the east and north, are seemingly excluded.

† Perhaps more correctly 'complete'.

‡ The Æðida cited in *Liber Eliensis* III.50 as a daughter of Æðelstan looks suspiciously like an error for a sister, perhaps that otherwise unnamed sister given in marriage to Sigtryggr. Fairweather 2005, 356.

§ The last date on which she appears as a charter witness.

subtle than the king's army or even that of the poet's hand.

If Æðelstan could not yet unify all the peoples of the island under his governance he could at least use the time-worn tools of the propagandist's quill to spread the message that all was well in *Saxonia* under his God-given rule. By 930 the king's moneyers, whose message penetrated deeper and more widely than those of the versifier, were portraying him wearing a crown and styled REX TOTIUS BRITANNIÆ.

Æðelstan's pretensions to supremacy over the whole island of Britain, and apparent desire to take his place on the list of *Bretwaldas*, those who had anciently wielded *imperium* over the whole island of Britain, feed into a well-rehearsed narrative of English unification and supremacy, etched onto the dies of his coinage and inscribed in the lists of those who witnessed his laws and gifts. It is superbly ironic that of all the sources available to us for his reign, the coins and charters should also most convincingly undermine those claims.

LAWYERS, GUNS AND MONEY

LAW CODES—COINS—EADWINE ÆTHELING
—ÆÐELSTAN'S NORTHERN ADVENTURE—
CUTHBERT'S WISH-LIST—ARMES PRYDEIN
FAWR—EMBASSIES AND REGENTS—
ART AND IDENTITY

10

WITHIN A YEAR OR SO OF THE PEACE
of Eamont Bridge, Æðelstan and his councillors
promulgated a law code at Grately in north-west
Hampshire, during a great assembly designed also to consult and
to display. Grately was not the site of a royal estate (the nearest,
Andover, lay a few short miles to the north-east along a Roman
road known as the Portway) but of an Iron Age hillfort, Quarley
Hill, whose powerful atavistic symbolism, and good local hunting, may have dictated the location.[1] Equally significant, perhaps,
is that Grately lay a day's ride from Winchester: close, but not
too close. Some of Æðelstan's assemblies were attended by up to
forty sub-kings, prelates, ealdormen and thegns, not to mention
his stepmother Eadgifu, each with an entourage of their own.

At Grately, one imagines a magnificent temporary township
encampment of hundreds of leather tents, awnings and lean-to
shelters, ensuring a sense of occasion both portentous and festive.
Farriers, smiths, falconers, masters of hounds, clerics, the royal
entourage, hostages and ministers congregated in their hundreds.

45. YORK: the centre of a Scandinavian kingdom
and a powerhouse of the northern church.

As the Anglo-Saxon state grew in size and administrative complexity, so its assemblies became greater but less agile occasions, taking longer to plan and deliver. For visitors (embassies, fostered exiles, élite merchants, *subreguli*, churchmen and scholars) they must have succeeded in creating an atmosphere of sublime intimidation. For artisans, traders, local worthies and thieves the meetings of the *Witan*, the wise councillors of the state, were ripe with opportunity.

II *Æðelstan*, or the *Grately Code* as it is known, sets out ordinances for the treatment of crimes petty and capital;* punishments for sorcery; rules for the exchange and recovery of livestock, for trial by the ordeals of water and iron and for the treatment of fugitives. The *Witan's* concerns extended to the collection of tithes, and to the charitable treatment of the poor, while the king was also interested in making broad provisions for the economic management of his enlarged kingdom.

Seemingly inserted from earlier or separate *coda*, otherwise novel clauses from 12 to 18 deal specifically with the administration of burhs and trade. Burh defences were to be repaired by a fortnight after Rogation days.† Goods over the value of 20 pence were only to be bought and sold inside a town, in the witness of the town-reeve at a public meeting (*gerefena gewitnesse on folcgemote*).[2] Then:

> Be myneterum... Ðridda: þæt an mynet sy ofer eall ðæs cynges onweald: 7 nan mon ne mynetige buton on port.

> Concerning moneyers: thirdly, that there is to be one coinage over all the king's dominion, and no-one is to mint money except in a town.[3]

A single coinage for a single kingdom: the intent could not be

---

* Among the more extreme punishments are stoning, burning, throwing off a cliff, drowning and the cutting off of hands. A later ordinance of Æðelstan declared a general amnesty. *III Æðelstan and IV Æðelstan*. Attenborough 1922, 143–51.

† Days of prayer and fasting to celebrate the Ascension in the Christian calendar.

clearer. Another clause deals with the penalties to be meted out to fraudulent moneyers: the severing of the offending hand, or trial by the ordeal of hot iron. And the following clause provides an invaluable list of the mints that Æðelstan has established, or intends to establish, in his towns: seven at Canterbury, three at Rochester, eight in London, six in Winchester, two in Lewes, two each in Southampton, Wareham, Exeter and Shaftesbury and one each at the other burhs.

The simplest observation to make of this list is that all the named mints lie in Wessex or Kent: so much for a national coinage. London, Canterbury and Winchester are to provide the bulk of the king's currency. What of York, Chester and the Five Boroughs; what of East Anglia? Historians must turn to the independent witness of the coins themselves. A brilliant analysis by numismatist Christopher Blunt in the 1970s demonstrated just how far the complex reality of managing coin production and trade over such a heterogeneous geographical and political landscape diverged from intention, ambition and law code.[4] The regular use of inscriptions on Æðelstan's coins, recording both the name of the moneyer and that of the mint during the 930s, allows numismatists, almost for the first time, to create a geography of currency for an Insular king.

Oddly enough, the largest single collection of coins, more than 400, from Æðelstan's reign comes from a hoard excavated in the ancient Forum at Rome in the nineteenth century, deposited between 942 and 946, while the most diverse belongs to a hoard found on Skye, buried in about 935. The coins from the Roman Forum hoard have been convincingly identified as a consignment of Peter's pence,* sent to Pope Marinus II in the mid-

---

* An annual cash render owed to the Holy See; King Offa seems to have initiated the practice. King Æðelwulf willed 300 mancuses (each worth 30 shillings) to be sent to Rome annually after his death. Observance of the practice seems to have been intermittent.

940s. Along with many other individual finds and smaller hoards widely scattered across Britain, Ireland and Scandinavia, these paint a rich and telling picture of political and economic tensions at variance with the unification narrative. Blunt's stark conclusion was that in the 'second quarter of the tenth century the coinage of England was still being organised on a regional basis'.[5]

By 928, a year after Eamont, a series of coins was issued bearing the abbreviated style REX TOT. BRIT., or a variation thereof. But these coins, portraying a crowned bust on the obverse and a cross on the reverse, were not produced uniformly in all the king's mints and their chronological span is only about half of a decade. The single East Anglian mint, at Norwich, omitted the regal style entirely; in West Mercia the same series carries the title REX SAXORUM (a mistake for REX SAXONUM). Three unprovenanced series, which seem to have been minted at Lincoln, also omit the REX. TOT. BRIT. style. Mercian mints seem to have avoided use of the bust motif altogether. In York, a single moneyer produced all the coins issued there during the later part of Æðelstan's reign, displacing a mint which seems to have been under the influence of York's archbishops. Here, too, portraits of the king occur rarely on coins.

Detailed analysis shows that distinct expressions of regionality were displayed by moneyers in the Western marches, in the area of the Five Boroughs, in East Anglia, Northumbria and north-west Mercia. Outside Wessex the most active mints, those where the level of economic activity required the greatest output of currency, were at Chester (probably second only to London), Shrewsbury, Derby, Oxford and Norwich—judging, at least, by the numbers of identifiable moneyers at each. By numbers of coins, York may have been the second most productive mint. None of these is mentioned in the *Grately Code*. Blunt also regarded some of the more irregular groups of coins as Scandinavian copies of the official series.

46. ÆÐELSTAN PRESENTS A BOOK to St Cuthbert:
'If Æðelstan was, indeed, a *Rex Totius Britanniae*, he was careful
not to proclaim it too loudly outside Wessex.'

The king was, it seems, successful in keeping foreign coinage out of circulation, even if he could not prevent fraud altogether. And his extension of *imperium* is impressive: he could impose a single currency over the nations of the old Anglo-Saxon kingdoms so that all trade was, effectively, carried out in his name and for his partial profit. That is not, however, the same thing as unification. If Æðelstan was, indeed, *Rex Totius Britanniae*, he was careful not to proclaim it too loudly outside Wessex.

The coin evidence prompts a more sceptical view of Æðelstan's unifying message, that in fact it was by no means welcome in all quarters; that old, and possibly new, regional affinities prevailed. The evidence of the king's own travels accentuates that view. Just as the moneyers of the central part of his reign were assiduous in recording their names and locations, so a single, meticulous scribe (historians unimaginatively call him 'Æðelstan A') recorded assemblies and land grants with impeccable lists of attendees and witnesses, dated and located: we can often pin down the movements of the king and his itinerant court; sometimes minutely so. Between 927, the year of the Eamont convention, and 934 the king could be found at royal estates in Exeter (at least twice), in Sussex, Gloucestershire, Hampshire, Wiltshire and once, on a single, exceptional occasion, in Colchester. There is otherwise no evidence of Æðelstan visiting or campaigning north of the Thames or holding assemblies in any of the Mercian burhs, where he might be expected to have had political and economic interests. He does not seem to have ventured into the territories of the Five Boroughs in those seven years. Nor do the charters suggest that he had property transactions to conduct outside the West Saxon heartlands or the south-west corner of Mercia.

To see Æðelstan's grand project as unification is to impose much more recent ideas of conquest and dominion on an age in which *imperium*, the right to boss subject kings and extract tribute from them, to enforce their attendance at court and marry one's daughters off to them, to be seen to have won gloriously in battle, mattered more than any sense of unifying peoples whose Mercian, Deiran, Danish or East Anglian affinities over-rode the notion that they belonged to an idea of England.

For a stay-at-home king the alternative means of governing disparate and distant parts of this enlarged *imperium* was to have his ealdormen and earls come to him. In November 931, at the royal estate of Lifton on the River Tamar, bordering the lands of the Britons of West Wealas, the king's *Witan* or council was attended by the Welsh kings Hywel and Idwal, by both archbishops and, among many others, no fewer than seven Danish *duces* or jarls: Urm, Guðrum, Haward, Gunner, Ðurferð, Hadd and Scule.* The ancient truism of keeping one's enemies close at hand was well understood by the heirs of Ælfred.

If Æðelstan was reluctant to travel far from Wessex, apparently for the most part even avoiding his old Mercian constituents, an entry in the 'E' version of the *Anglo-Saxon Chronicle* for 933 may offer a partial explanation. In this year, we are told, Æðelstan's half-brother Prince Eadwine was drowned at sea. Eadwine was the younger brother of Ælfweard, who had so briefly succeeded his father Eadweard in 924; his mother was Eadweard's second wife, Ælfflæd. He was, therefore, the king's half-brother. Eadwine, too young to challenge for power in 924 but now of an age to command an army, might legitimately have harboured a superior claim to his father's kingdom, having been born after his father became king. In view of Æðelstan's Mercian loyalties, one suspects that Winchester's apparent antipathy towards him was a function of Eadwine's claim.

---

* In Old Norse: Urm, Guðþormr, Hávarðr, Gunnarr, Ðorrøðr, Haddr and Skúli. S416: Stenton 1971, 351. Of these, Gunnarr, Urm and Skúli were still attesting charters in 949, under King Eadred: S 552a. Urm (see below, p. 404). Jarl Urm's last charter attestation took place as late as 958/9: S679 during the reign of Eadgar.

Accidents happen at sea; we can read no more than that into the brief entry in the *Chronicle*. But a Frankish source, the *Acts of the abbots of St Bertin*, offers more suggestive detail:

> King Edwin, the brother of this same famous king [Æðelstan, was] buried in the monastery of St Bertin. For in the year of the Incarnate Word 933, when the same King Edwin, driven by some disturbance in his kingdom, embarked on a ship, wishing to cross to this side of the sea, a storm arose and the ship was wrecked and he was overwhelmed in the midst of the waves. And when his body was washed ashore, Count Adelolf, since he was his kinsman,* received it with honour and bore it to the monastery of St Bertin for burial.[6]

The much later *Historia Regum* is even more explicit: 'King Æðelstan ordered his brother Eadwine to be drowned at sea.'[7] Eadwine might not have been pushed; but he does at least seem to have been pushed out, and a plausible motive for his expulsion is that he had failed in an attempted coup against his older half-brother. That the Frankish chronicler afforded him a regal title may be significant in that context. His death, convenient or otherwise, removed the threat of usurpation which seems to have kept Æðelstan in such close attendance on, but not in, Winchester.

Finally secure in his West Saxon heartlands, the king might now flex his muscles. Three other deaths, in close succession, allowed or propelled the king to contemplate actions that would justify his pretensions to be styled *Rex Totius Britanniae*. In 933, or thereabouts, King Haraldr *Hárfagri* of Norway, Harald Fairhair, died in what must have been something like his eightieth year, leaving a large number of sons to potentially compete for his kingdom and overseas interests.† The loss of such a large personality lent new impulse to the Newton's cradle of the Atlantic kingdoms. Then, the *Annals of Ulster* report that in 934

---

* King Ælfred's daughter Ælfthryth was Adelof's mother; his father was Baldwin II of Flanders.

† One of these sons may have been fostered at Æðelstan's court. See below p. 377.

Guðroðr, grandson of Ívarr and recent contender for the throne of York, died of sickness. His dominance over Dublin and the Irish Sea, including the kingdom of Man, ensured that his death injected yet more instability into the multiplicities of Insular politics.

Another Irish chronicle, that of the monastic community at Clonmacnoise, records a third significant death in the same year: 'Adulf mcEtulf, king of the North Saxons'.[8] Alex Woolf argues that this is a garbled reference to a king of Northumbria, probably an heir to the Bernician lords of Bamburgh who had already intervened in the fortunes of Rögnvaldr and St Cuthbert in 918. Alternatively, it is not impossible that Adulf, or Eadwulf, might have been a native Deiran, holding York for its absentee overlord Æðelstan. One way or the other, his death demanded personal intervention in a year whose fortunes might swing in any number of ways. How might the Irish Sea Norse seek to take advantage; how might Constantín react in Alba? What of the apparently compliant jarls of Danish Mercia?

We can track the progress of Æðelstan's second northern adventure, seven years after the Peace of Eamont Bridge, thanks to the meticulous records of his court scribe, 'Æðelstan A'. In May 934 the king held court at Winchester for the first time, basking in the novelty of domestic security. The land grant whose text survives in the archives of Christ Church, Canterbury to attest this council, seems insignificant in itself: a 12-hide estate at an unidentified place called *Derantune*, to be transferred to one of his ministers.[9] But the list of witnesses present tells us that the grant was only a minor element in a much grander occasion. Both archbishops attended; so too did Hywel Dda, his cousin Idwal Foel (son of Anarawd), Morgan of Gwent and Tewdr of Brycheiniog (all listed as *subreguli*—tributary kings), no fewer than seventeen bishops and many dozens of *ministri* and *duces*. Five of the *duces*, or earls, present bore Danish names: Ragnald,

Ivar, Hadder, Scule* and Hálfdan in the English tongue; and it is reasonable to suggest that they held, if not conveniently the Five Boroughs themselves, then significant territories in Danish Mercia.

The court now passed into and through those territories. By 7 June, just ten days after the date of the Winchester grant, the whole court had travelled 170 miles (275 km) northwards to reassemble at Nottingham on the River Trent, presumably at one of the two burhs flanking the river. The most obvious road route would have taken them through the fortified towns at Reading, Wallingford and Oxford via the old West Saxon episcopal centre of Dorchester on Thames; thence to Buckingham, Towcester, Northampton and Leicester. It is a substantial logistical feat, which shows that considerable planning underlay the entire campaign. The court must either have been sure of its reception in the towns of the Five Boroughs, or it was accompanied by a military force sufficient to ensure its security in a land where royal patronage did not extend its centripetal web of loyalties.

The grant that survives from this assembly, with a closely similar witness list to that issued at Winchester, is of great significance in its own right.[10] It begins with a pompous preamble, which the king's scribe seems to have delighted in copying out but which must have been torturous to attend to:†

> The wanton fortune of this deceiving world, not lovely with the milk-white radiance of unfading lilies, but odious with the gall-steeped bitterness of lamentable corruption, raging with venomous wide-stretched jaws, bitingly rends the sons of stinking flesh in this vale of tears; and although by its smiles it may be able to draw unfortunates to the bottom of Acherontic Cocytus, unless the Creator of the roaring deep lend his

---

* Hadder and Scule had previously witnessed the 931 charter at Lifton (S416).

† The scribe 'Æðelstan A' must, it seems, represent the flowering of Ælfred's programme to revive literacy and improve the quality of ecclesiastical Latinity. If so, its success is self-evident.

aid, it is shamelessly fickle; and, therefore, because this ruinous fortune falls and mortally decays, one should chiefly hasten to the pleasant fields of indescribable joy, where are the angelic instruments of hymn-singing jubilation and the mellifluous scents of blooming roses perceived with inconceivable sweetness by the nostrils of the good and blessed and harmonies are heard by their ears forever. Allured by love of that felicity— when now depths disgust, heights grow sweet—and in order to perceive and enjoy them always in unfailing beauty, I, Athelstan, king of the English...[11]

It is as if the king had swallowed the Book of Revelation whole and hybridized the Christian apocalypse with the Ragnarök of the *Edda*; that may, indeed, have been his intention. Its relevance to a grant of land might seem tangential. The main body of the text confirms that Æðelstan had purchased 'with no little money of my own'* the substantial territory of Amounderness, 'without the hateful yoke of servitude [i.e. it was freehold, or 'booked' land], with meadows, pastures, woods, streams and all conveniences', and gifted it in perpetuity to Almighty God and the Apostle Peter: in other words, to the minster church at York under its archbishop, Wulfstan (931–954/6). The preamble, I think, enshrines Æðelstan's desire, as a Christian king, to impose order and rightfulness onto the actual fabric of his dominions, ensuring that their landed wealth be devoted to God, not to the impious and undeserving secular lords who had formerly possessed it.

Dire imprecations were aimed at anyone who would dare to challenge the king's will or 'infringe this little document'. Before the signatures of the fifty-eight witnesses, there is a description of the bounds of the Amounderness estate. Its northern edge was defined by the channel of the tiny River Cocker, rising a few miles south-east of Lancaster and falling into the River Lune close to the sea. From the source of the Cocker the boundary ran more

---

* A version of the grant held at York includes the telling phrase 'from the pagans'. *EHD* 104: Whitelock 1979, 549n.

or less straight to the east as far as 'another spring which is called in Saxon *Dunshop*'. From this riverlet, now Dunsop, whose twin sources lie high up on the moors of the Forest of Bowland east of Lancaster, the boundary ran due south to the River Hodder at Dunsop Bridge, then downstream to its confluence with the River Ribble and thence to the sea. From the small town of Whalley, north-east of Blackburn, river and boundary alike follow the line of the Roman road as far as Preston, and the sea route to Ireland and Man. Along the way it passes the spot where the celebrated Cuerdale hoard was hidden in about 905.

The Amounderness of the tenth century was a large tract of land incorporating substantial parts of modern Lancashire. Its name probably derives from the Old Norse personal name Agmundr.[12] Matthew Townend, a historian of Viking Age York, notes the presence of a *hold* bearing the name Agmundr at the Battle of Tettenhall in 910.[13] He also makes a connection with Holderness, a similar-sized territory on the east coast whose name means 'headland of the *hold*'. In northern Northumbria such territorial units were known as shires, the large territories centred on a royal *vill* and traditionally comprising twelve townships from which renders of goods and services, later rents, were gathered centrally for consumption by its lord. Townend suggests that these shire-sized territories were the sorts of lands that might be given by the kings of the Host to his *holds* or *hölðar*, senior military followers one rank below the jarls or *duces* of the charters; and this agrees with the size and strategic nature of the Cuthbert lands given by Rögnvaldr to his powerful warrior, the *potens miles* Onlafbald, after 918.* It is possible that in the early tenth century, before Æðelstan purchased it, Amounderness

---

* In *Norðleoda laga*, The law of the North People, a tract from the beginning of the following century, the wergild, or head-price, of the *hold* equates to that of the king's high-reeve, half that of a bishop or ealdorman and twice that of a thegn. EHD 51: Whitelock 1979, 469.

owed its renders not to any political centre on the Insular mainland, but to a lord on Man, or in Dublin.

In the late seventh century the ultra-orthodox Bishop Wilfrid had acquired for his monastery at Ripon the lands of former British churches west of the Pennines whose clergy had supposedly deserted or fled them. Of these estates, Dent in Cumbria and land 'around Ribble' belong in the area bounded by the Amounderness grant.[14] What we might be seeing in Æðelstan's purchase and gift is evidence of a long-standing claim to this territory by the church establishment at York; of its being bought out of Norse lordship and 'returned' to its rightful owner. Implicitly, Æðelstan was purchasing the loyalty of Northumbria's institutional church and seeking its approval for his planned campaign in the North.

Whether Amounderness was actually worth very much in cash terms is quite another matter. Academic opinion is in any case divided on just how 'Scandinavian' the region was in the tenth century. There are, it is true, substantial numbers of Norse place names in western Lancashire and coastal Cumbria, which have often been associated with Ingimundr's invasion and settlement following the expulsion from Dublin in 902. Most recently, though, archaeologist and Early Medieval historian Nick Higham has sought to cast doubt on the idea of a mass migration[15] and paints instead a portrait of mixed or patchwork communities with distinct and complex regional affinities, rather than a single people identifying themselves as either 'English' or 'Norse'. It must be significant that Amounderness lay some 50 miles (80 km) south of Eamont, the location of Æðelstan's treaty of submission in 927, and that its southern boundary formed a principal route between Dublin, Man and York. The transfer to the Northumbrian church of such an important estate, fringing the Irish Sea and within the borders of the king's extended dominion, looks like an astute political move.

The link with Ripon might be reinforced by a charter of
Æðelstan purporting to confirm the liberties and customs of that
foundation;[16] but most commentators regard it as a later forgery. It is entirely possible that the court did visit Ripon on its
way north: the minster with its famous crypt was certainly standing in the 930s.* That Æðelstan had further business with the
Northumbrian church cannot be doubted, however:

> While king Æðelstan was leading a great army from the south
> to the northern region, taking it to Scotland, he made a diver-
> sion to the church of St Cuthbert and gave royal gifts to him,
> and then composed this signed testament and placed it at
> Cuthbert's head.[17]

The charter recording gifts of land and fabulous treasures to the
community at Chester le Street is preserved in the *Historia de
Sancto Cuthberto*. It lists, among sundry other items, a chasuble
and alb (both priestly vestments), a thurible or censer, three gospel books, a *Life of St Cuthbert*, a stole with maniple, chalice and
paten, a 'royal headdress woven with gold', a cross and two silver
candelabra, cups, tapestries, horns of gold and silver, bells, banners, a lance† and two golden armlets. The king 'also filled the
aforementioned cups with best coin, and at his order his whole
army offered Cuthbert 1200 shillings'.[18] In addition, he gave to
St Cuthbert an estate of twelve vills (an entire coastal shire in
Early Medieval terms) at Bishop Wearmouth, on the south side
of the Wear in what is now Sunderland.

The remarkable survival of the *Historia* is matched by the

---

* It was destroyed twelve years later. See below, Chapter 12.
† It is possible that this was the lance with which Æðelstan had been presented by
   Adelolf, on behalf of Hugh the Great, in the great embassy of 926 at which Hugh
   had acquired Eadweard's daughter and Æðelstan's sister, Eadhild. It was said to be
   the lance with which a Roman soldier (St Longinus) had pierced the side of Christ:
   one of the most precious relics in Christendom. No historian takes seriously the idea
   that this was actually a first-century lance; but the significance of the gift would not
   have been lost on any of the participants.

preservation of some of these splendid gifts. One of the gospel books, which contained an inscription matching the text of the charter, survived until its virtually complete destruction in the disastrous Cotton Library fire of 1731. It bore a portrait of both king and saint before a church, the king with an open book in his hand, perhaps in an act of presentation. Its loss would be all the more lamentable were it not for the fact that the *Life of St Cuthbert* recorded in the list of Æðelstan's gifts seems still to exist. It belongs in the Parker Library, the rare books and manuscripts collection of Corpus Christi College Cambridge, listed as MS 183 (see p. 355). Folio 1, verso, shows a slightly different version of this same image: the king, three-point crown on his bowed head, presents the tonsured saint with a gospel book on the steps of his church at Chester le Street. A thick border is richly decorated with plant scrolls in a style linked to the court at Winchester. That same style is evident on the stole and maniple which also survive, almost miraculously, in the collections at Durham Cathedral, having spent most of the last thousand years with the saint's relics.* Those unique examples of Anglo-Saxon embroidery are the same items made by or under the supervision of Ælfflæd (mother of the unfortunate æthelings Ælfweard and Eadwine) during the reign of Eadweard.†

The meeting between King Æðelstan and St Cuthbert (in the terrestrial guise of Bishop Wigred, incumbent of the Lindisfarne see) at Chester le Street during the high summer of 934 enacted a ceremony of mutual legitimization. The king gave the saint the promise of his protection, wonderful treasures, cash and lands

---

* David Rollason shows that the manuscript cannot have been written as early as 934 and might, therefore, have been given to the community at Chester le Street in 937 on Æðelstan's subsequent northern campaign (see below, Chapter 11); equally, he might have brought it north in 936 if, as seems likely, he was at York in that year. But he also allows the possibility that the manuscript was no gift to Cuthbert, but a possession of the king's. Rollason 1989b.

† See above, Chapter 9.

suitable to the needs of a great monastic house. St Cuthbert, in return, gave his blessing and backing to the king's military campaign and to his claim to wield *imperium* over all Britain (like the first royal patron of Lindisfarne, and Mercian cult hero, King Oswald). By the well-understood rules of such transactions the relationship between the Chester le Street community and the royal house of the West Saxons was also back-dated.

Æðelstan's magnificent patronage of the Bernician saint during the 930s surely lies behind 'earlier' entries in the *Historia* in which St Cuthbert appeared to the isolated and desperate Ælfred in the dismal marshes of Athelney at a time of extreme distress.* Æðelstan's visit was not, then, meant to be seen as opportunistic but as the fulfilment of a visionary meeting between his grandfather and the saint. Whether the fond remembrance of that episode would have survived military defeat at the hands of Constantín of Alba is another matter.

The king's Mercian progress, his grant to the archbishop, his visit to Chester le Street and the nature of the gifts themselves require some explanation. Why choose Nottingham as the venue for a grant of Cumbrian land to York? Why ply St Cuthbert's church with what looks like the contents of a clearance sale, albeit an extravagant one? And how did the king acquire a coastal estate on the banks of the River Wear in the first place? One detects the operation of careful diplomacy.

We know, from the witness list appended to the Nottingham charter of 7 June 934, that both Archbishop Wulfstan of York and Bishop Wigred of Chester le Street were present.[19] Here was the perfect opportunity to negotiate terms in advance of the visit: to ensure a peaceful reception, to sound out the archbishop's position regarding the proposed campaign; to seek his advice on the niceties of the Northern political situation. The

* See above, Chapter 4, pp. 145–6.

Amounderness grant might be seen as his brokerage fee. Instead of seeing the Cuthbert gifts as a random collection of baubles and the odd patch of land, we might better regard them as a sort of wish-list, provided by the community to indicate the sorts of gifts that would be acceptable to the saint in return for endorsing the king's Alban expedition. The very specific nature of some of the gifts is telling: at the end of MS 183 is a list of kitchen utensils and what looks like part of a dinner service.

Æðelstan must either have purchased the estate of Bishop Wearmouth from its current Norse lord (it had been given by Rögnvaldr to Onlafbald after 918), or was merely confirming rights to the estate that had lapsed with time. These were his means of extending those thin northern lines of patronage.* His army's donation to Cuthbert of 60 pounds of silver (1200 shillings) was, significantly, matched by an identical later gift from King Eadmund's army: evidently 60 pounds was the going rate for blessing an entire host on its way to do battle. It is tempting to think of it as a shilling per warrior—if so, it would be useful evidence for the size of a tenth-century army.

The campaign was duly successful, reinforcing the pact between the Æðulfings and St Cuthbert. The *Chronicle* (all versions are identical here) records merely that Æðelstan invaded Alba with a land and naval force and that he harried much of the country. There is additional detail in the pages of the *Historia Regum*, drawing on a more regional tradition. Here we are told that Æðelstan's land army laid Alba waste as far as Dunottar (the great coastal fortress just south of Stonehaven, which had been attacked by Norse raiders in 900 and where Constantín's immediate predecessor had been killed) and the mountains of Fortriu; and that his fleet raided as far as Caithness in the extreme north-east.[20]

---

* I am, once again, grateful to the members of the Bernician Studies Group for insightful discussions on the Æðelstan–Cuthbert charter.

Much has been written about the implications of this campaign for understanding Æðelstan's military capabilities. So little is known of late Anglo-Saxon fleets that it is difficult to draw very much from the notice of a raid along the east coast of Scotland, except that these would appear to be hostile and dangerous waters, requiring skilled pilotage and knowledge of safe anchorages (such as Portmahomack). It is pointless to speculate where the fleet was based. It is equally difficult to know how often, if at all, the land army was forced to fight in the open against a significant military force, or whether Constantín was content to stand off and limit the damage to raiding. Æðelstan, for his part, may have been satisfied to demonstrate that, like his illustrious seventh century Northumbrian predecessors Æðelfrið, Oswald and Oswiu (and, for that matter, the Roman emperors), he could claim *imperium* over all the lands of Britain. There can be no doubt that the king of Alba submitted to him, despite the shortness of the campaign. The whole enterprise cannot have lasted much more than a month: on 13 September the king, on his way south again, issued a charter at Buckingham; this time Constantín *subregulus* headed the list of witnesses, while the Welsh kings' names were not recorded.[21] Constantín was still in attendance at the king's assemblies in the first part of 935, unrecorded by the diplomatically silent *Chronicle of the Kings of Alba*. An abridged copy of a lost charter records his presence at what must have been a grand occasion '*in civitate a Romanis olim constructa quæ Cirnecester dicitur*':

> In the city at one time built by the Romans that is called Cirencester has been recorded by the whole class of nobles rejoicing under the arms of royal generosity—I, Æthelstan, endowed with the rank of extraordinary prerogative, king, etc.—I, Constantine, sub-king. I, Eogan mac Domnaill, sub-king. I, Hywel Dda ap Cadell, sub-king. I, Idwal Foel ab Anarawd, sub-king. I, Morgan ab Owain, sub-king. I, Ælfwine, bishop.[22]

47. THE ROMAN AMPHITHEATRE
at Cirencester: an imperial venue to impress
Æðelstan's royal guests.

Cirencester is a throwback to the geography of Ælfred's campaigns against the *mycel here* in the 870s, when Guðrum's beaten army retired there before embarking on its final journey into East Anglia. Lying a few miles north-west of Cricklade, the burh sited at the highest navigable point on the Thames and the historic boundary between Mercia and Wessex, the Roman town of Cirencester (*Corinium Dobunnorum, civitas* capital of the *Dobunni*) was a key royal estate in the lands of the Hwicce, enjoying the fruits of a productive landscape and well connected to all parts.* Its grand amphitheatre, which still stands on the outskirts of the town, may still have been thought of as a suitable venue for a royal council, endowed with imperial associations that could hardly have been lost on a king bearing such an illustrious name as Constantín. The magnificent minster church here, rebuilt in the early ninth century, is known primarily from excavation; it seems to have matched basilicas at Brixworth and Wareham for grandeur and what John Blair calls Roman monumentality.[23] All three would have made suitable settings for royal or ecclesiastical councils.

The apparent harmony of these occasions masks serious tensions. The sub-kings required to attend Æðelstan were isolated from whatever political developments their absence was fomenting back home. Worse, perhaps, was the large quantity of tribute that they had to raise annually for their overlord. William of Malmesbury seems to have had access to a now-lost source when he records that, in the aftermath of the Peace of Eamont in 927, Æðelstan forced the Welsh kings to meet him at the burh of Hereford, at the northern edge of the region inhabited by the Dunsæte. Here, he imposed on them an annual tribute of 20 lbs of gold (9 kg), 300 lbs (136 kg) of silver, 25,000 oxen, 'besides as many dogs as he should choose'.[24]

---

* Cirencester is the meeting point of the Fosse Way, *Akemennestraete* and Ermine Street.

Some of those kings' constituents might have wondered if they would have been better off suffering the periodic depredations of Norse raiders. To some, the relationship of their kings with Æðelstan went beyond expedient tribute; amounted, in fact, to supine capitulation to the old enemy. An extraordinary, bitter expression of Welsh resentment survives in a 199-line poem called *Armes Prydein Fawr:* the *Prophecy of Britain.* The dating of the poem is not certain, but some time in the second quarter of the tenth century during the reign of Æðelstan would suit its themes and message very well.[25]

> The muse foretells that the day will come
> When the men of Wessex meet for counsel
> In one chorus, with one counsel, and England will burn.[26]

The targets of the prophecy's ire are the 'high king' and his officers, particularly those at Cirencester (*meiryon Kaer Geri*): 'the taxes that they try to raise are a great source of trouble'.[27] The high king is likely to be the man whose coins proclaimed him *Rex Totius Britanniae;* but the title also invokes the cursed memory of a more ancient figure, Vortigern (the name carries the same meaning in Brittonic) the British tyrant who rashly lost Thanet in the middle of the fifth century when Hengest and Horsa, legendary Saxon warlords, acquired it 'by mendacious guile'.[28] Since then, the ignoble, arrogant progress of the English, the *Lloegr,** has been inexorable: the 'slaves from Thanet are our rulers',[29] and the present *subreguli* of the Welsh are castigated for their timidity.

The poet predicts a war in which the free Welsh, 'excellent men in the tumult of battle, wild and steadfast, quick under pressure, stubborn in defence... will drive the foreigners as far as *Caer Wair'.*[30] The war will be won when the Welsh forge an alliance with the Men of Dublin, the Irish of Ireland, Anglesey and

---

* *Lloegr* is a term of unknown derivation, but seems always to have been the name applied, perhaps pejoratively, to the English by the Cymri. Elsewhere in the poem, the West Saxons (*Iwys* or *Gewisse*) are more specifically identified as the enemy.

Pictland, the Men of Cornwall and Strathclyde. In the vision of the poet, English and Welsh meet on the banks of the River Wye with enormous armies. There will be 'cry after cry on the shining water', with banners discarded and the English falling like 'wild cat's fodder'.[31] The high king's treacherous tax gatherers will wallow in their own blood, fleeing through the forest before they are banished forever from the island of Britain. The Cymri will have their Day of Judgement. In modern terms, the *Armes Prydein Fawr* is a patriotic call to arms, or the nationalist manifesto of a liberation movement. Just how much traction it achieved cannot now be measured.

Just as the West Saxons and Mercians had appropriated the battle-saints of the Northumbrians, Cuthbert and Oswald, to drive forward their political and military ambitions, so the Welsh invoked St David and his martial lieutenants Cynan and Cadwaladr to carry them to victory. St David's relics lay in the tiny city that bears his name in the extreme west of Wales in Dyfed, on the Pembrokeshire coast north of St Bride's bay. In the early tenth century these were the lands ruled by Hywel ap Cadell, the king later blessed with the nickname Dda, 'the Good'. Hywel was a grandson of Rhodri Mawr, the king of Gwynedd (reigned *c.*844–878) whose dynasty had probably crossed from Man earlier in the ninth century. Famous for notable battles against Viking war bands and for having been slain by King Ceolwulf II of Mercia, Rhodri consolidated Venedotian power over much of north and central Wales. On his death he left the rule of Gwynedd to his son Anarawd, who was succeeded by Idwal Foel ('the bald'). Rhodri's son Cadell inherited Seisyllwg, anciently Ceredigion, and divided it between his sons Hywel and Clydog. On Clydog's death in about 920[32] Hywel became sole ruler of both Seisyllwg and Dyfed, the latter acquired by marriage, and this new polity became known as Deheubarth: the 'Right-hand part' (that is, the south, looking from an Irish Sea perspective).

By 930 Hywel seems to have extended his control to include Brycheiniog; he and Idwal had submitted to Eadweard and he had made an unlikely pilgrimage to Rome in 928.

That the policy of aligning the Welsh kingdoms with the West Saxons (a continuation of the strategy encouraged by Bishop Asser during his time at the court of King Ælfred) was unpopular among some of Hywel's constituents is evident from the *Armes Prydein Fawr.* That Hywel was regarded by the poet as the principal Welsh appeaser is suggested by the invocation of St David (*Dewi Sant*) himself, and the same evidence may point to Dyfed as the origin and affiliation of the poet. The prayers of David and the other saints of Britain would ensure that the foreigners were put to flight.

More practical assistance was to be found in two legendary resistance leaders. Cadwaladr was a Venedotian king of the late seventh century, the son of the Cadwallon slain by King Oswald in 634 in a battle, described by Bede, near Corbridge on the banks of the River Tyne. He could be relied on to avenge the enemies of his father. Cynan was, in legend, associated with the founding of the Breton kingdom, an event lost deep in the mists of the fifth century before even St David had taken up episcopal residence in Dyfed:

> A candle in the darkness walks with us.
> Cynan is at the head of the troop in every attack,
> The English sing a song of woe before the Britons.
> Cadwaladr is a spear at the side of his men.[33]

Hywel, his cousin Idwal and the other native kings in attendance on Æðelstan in the mid-930s must balance domestic pressures with realpolitik. The high king, too, must be careful not to overplay his hand.

If Æðelstan was nervous at the prospect of a great alliance against him in 935–936, his response was to look to the North and to reinforce alliances overseas. At some point in 935 Constantín was allowed to return home: a charter issued close to Christmas at Dorchester in Dorset records the names of only four *subreguli*, and the king of Alba is not among them.[34] Æðelstan's own whereabouts during the following year cannot be tracked by his charters: only one survives from 936 and it was not drawn up by the informative scribe 'Æðelstan A'. The *Anglo-Saxon Chronicle* is silent, too. Only one source, and that a Frankish *Historia* compiled at the end of the century, offers a clue.

Flodoard of Rheims records an embassy sent in 936 by Hugh, duke of Francia, requesting the return from exile at Æðelstan's court of Louis *d'Outremer* ('from over the sea'). Louis was the son of Charles the Simple and Æðelstan's sister Eadgifu, whose marriage had been engineered by Eadweard in 919. Charles was deposed in 923 and Louis, with his mother, spent the next thirteen years among the *Angelcynn* with his uncle; he was one of a number of exotic foster sons at the West Saxon court. Later in the same century the annalist Richer of Rheims elaborated on Flodoard's brief narrative, describing the embassy's departure from Boulogne and arrival at the city of York, where it was known that Æðelstan's household, including Louis, was resident.[35]

If Æðelstan can be placed at York in 936, one might reasonably ask whether it was his only visit and if it may have a greater significance than mere progress through his expanded kingdom. Before the drowning of the pretender Eadwine in 933 and the northern campaign of 934 the king seems to have confined the bulk of his annual itinerary to Wessex. But William of Malmesbury suggested that after the death of Sigtryggr in 927 and the expulsion of Guðrøðr, Æðelstan razed the city's Danish defences. He can reasonably be supposed to have visited the city in 934 on his way north to Chester le Street and beyond; and his gift to Archbishop Wulfstan of the Amounderness estate suggests that he sought closer co-operation with the Northumbrian élite. He cannot have been unaware of the city's Roman past, as the site of Constantine's acclamation as emperor in 306. Parts of the ancient fortress must still have been visible and contemporary York was, as its archaeology has shown, a thriving production centre with a well-established mint. The River Great Ouse connected the city directly with the Humber and North Sea, and its Continental and Scandinavian connections are proven by the raw materials and artefacts that filled the rubbish pits and workshops of its crowded tenements.

If Hugh's embassy of 936 can credibly be placed at York, it may not have been the only grand arrival. William of Malmesbury, in accounting for the enthusiasm with which foreign rulers tried to 'purchase his friendship either by affinity or by presents', records a gift sent to Æðelstan by Haraldr *Hárfagri*, king of Norway:

> A ship with a golden beak and a purple sail, furnished within with a compacted fence of gilded shields. The names of the persons sent with it were Helgrim and Offird: who, being received with princely magnificence in the city of York, were amply compensated by rich presents, for the labour of their journey.[36]

Haraldr was certainly dead before 936, but these two independent traditions linking embassies with York suggest the court's presence there on more than one occasion spanning, perhaps, a decade. Much later Norse sagas, recounting these legendary times, accorded to Harald's son Hákon *góði* ('the Good'), the epithet *Aðalsteins fóstri*: Æðelstan's foster-son.[37] Like Louis, he was said to have been raised as a Christian at the West Saxon court and later returned to Norway to claim the kingship. His arrival at court might be linked with the gift of the gold-prowed ship. A third exile, Alain *Barbetorte* ('Crooked beard') of Brittany, had been brought up at the West Saxon court from infancy, according to the *Chronicle of Nantes*. Now, in 936, perhaps timed to coincide with the return of Louis, Alain crossed from Britain to Brittany with a few ships full of fellow Breton exiles and with Æðelstan's support, to 'cast out the Norsemen'.[38] If foreign embassies could be confident of his presence there it seems reasonable to suggest that Æðelstan's visit to York in 936 was planned and prolonged. A sustained residency would allow for administrative and legal business to be conducted; for incipient West Saxon networks of Northern patronage to be extended; for a review of coinage and trading regulations and to hear petitions from both Danish and native interests concerning land disputes, marriage negotiations, the granting of small estates and visits to appropriate shrines and churches. It was an opportunity, too, to collect tribute—not, perhaps, the immense booty rendered by the kings of the Welsh, but a substantial quantity, sufficient to keep the court in splendid luxury for a few months.

Some members of the Scandinavian élite, perhaps descendants of the warlords of the *mycel here*, might have resented the imposition enough to want keep their portable wealth discreetly out of sight. Three hoards dating from the years immediately after the death of Sigtryggr in 927 have been recovered from York's hinterland. The traditional interpretation of such caches of wealth is that they belonged to those fleeing pursuit, or to victims of battle. In recent years it has been argued that some might have constituted the equivalent of savings accounts. It is also worth contemplating the idea that some were hidden to avoid the Early Medieval tax man, the king's treasurer—with a modest remnant, displayed at home, given up to ensure compliance with the gross impositions of annual tribute. In 1807 a hoard of at least 270 coins, arm rings and silver ingots was found encased in a leaden box, turned up by the plough.* Its location, at Lobster House close to what is now the A64 road between York and Malton, some 8 miles (13 km) north-east of York, and

---

* Known as the Bossall/Flaxton hoard. The numismatist Michael Dolley believed that some elements of this hoard were dispersed, so it may originally have been even more substantial. He describes a silver armlet, weighing 2.15 oz (61 g), as of 'Viking type'. It carries a distinct stamped trefoil decoration. Dolley 1955.

the presence of freshly minted coins of Rögnvaldr and Sigtryggr but nothing later, suggests a date not long after the latter's death, during Æðelstan's supremacy; and a context of discontent with, or apprehension about, the new régime.

In 2007 two metal detectorists located a hoard, also contained in a lead chest, near Harrogate, 20 miles (32 km) west of York. A stunning silver cup decorated with vine motifs and running beasts, of ninth-century Continental manufacture, contained more than 600 coins, silver and gold arm rings, silver ingots and hacksilver. The coin collection includes parcels* from the reigns of Ælfred (51) and Eadweard (402): booty from an old raid, perhaps; a substantial group minted under Sigtryggr in the so-called Sword St Peter series; one of St Martin type minted at Lincoln, five Danelaw imitations, a score of Arab dirhams, four Frankish coins and more than 100 of Æðelstan, mostly minted at York. One of these carried the distinctive REX TOTIUS BRITANNIAE inscription.[39] Two more recent coin finds known demurely as the 'near York' hoards and retrieved during 2012, have yielded compatible, if more modest, collections dated to the late 920s or early 930s.[40]

Either substantial numbers of Scandinavian lords were on the run during Æðelstan's reign or, more likely, economic uncertainty was prompting wealthy men to exercise discretion over their wealth. We might, equally, argue that the *ancien régime* of the Scandinavian lords of York had operated a laissez-faire policy with regard to taxation from their former comrades.

If Æðelstan was now recognized as overlord in Northumbria, who governed the old kingdom day to day? The native dynasty of Bernicia survived the upheavals of the second quarter of the tenth century to emerge as the high reeves, later earls, of Bamburgh. The Deiran dynasty of York, whose scions had become puppet rulers, it seems, of successive Scandinavian kings, cannot be

---

* A numismatic term denoting all the coins in a particular find spot.

traced after their shadowy appearance in the pages of the *Historia de Sancto Cuthberto*. There has been considerable speculation that several successive archbishops either held the reins of power or governed southern Northumbria on behalf of Scandinavian lords. One of these, Wulfhere, had been expelled briefly for some act of complicity or betrayal in 872, but his longevity (he died in office in 896) suggests canny political instincts. Of the two subsequent archbishops, Æðelbald, whose archiepiscopal reign is dated tentatively 896–916, witnessed a single charter of King Ælfred, but is not recorded at Eadweard's court; and Hroðweard (*c.*916–931) appears as a witness on several of Æðelstan's charters between 928 and 931. The latter must have been a relatively familiar member of the royal court.

Wulfstan (931–956) is a much more rounded historical figure. He was prominently present at the king's assemblies and councils, witnessing all known royal charters between 931 and 935, and was the beneficiary of the Amounderness grant of 934. Like his predecessors, his chief motivation seems to have lain in maintaining the interests of the cathedral church at York. Scholars do not entirely agree whether he or any of his predecessors minted their own coins there, but the suspicion is that Wulfstan was closely involved with both coinage and trade in the city. David Rollason allows that he may have played some sort of gubernatorial role in southern Northumbria during the second part of Æðelstan's reign. Like most members of the Northumbrian élite, Wulfstan showed no signs of any special loyalty to the West Saxon dynasty; nor did he or his predecessors show any obvious antipathy to Scandinavian rule, pagan or otherwise: political pragmatism seems to have been the prevailing philosophy. That York retained its archbishops through two centuries of upheaval speaks for itself.

Æðelstan may have employed a form of direct rule, bringing an army north every year or every other year, but otherwise allowing existing institutions to exercise their customary powers. It seems likely that the Scandinavian regimes had exercised a lighter, less interventionist hand than the highly developed state institutions of the South. The arrival of Æðelstan and his centralizing legal and fiscal policies must have come as a profound shock to the locals, native and incomer alike.

David Rollason argues that some sort of royal palace existed in York; and the presence of an archiepiscopal residence close to or within the city is highly probable.[41] It is perfectly likely, though, that like their contemporaries to the north, south and west, the kings and regents of southern Northumbria progressed through royal estates in the traditional heartlands of East and West Yorkshire, and as far north as the lands of the Cuthbert community. Archaeology has yet to pin them down: Yorkshire's Yeaverings and Cheddars* have not revealed themselves. In the absence of better evidence, we must suppose that Æðelstan's rule over Northumbria was quite different from that in Wessex and Mercia. Authority seems likely to have devolved, when there was no direct Scandinavian rule, onto more local lords, with the archbishop pre-eminent. West Saxon kings' access to local and regional patronage, such an important tool of governance, was as yet limited. One is reminded forcibly of the problems which occupying powers have had in more recent centuries, lacking local intelligence and unaware of subtle, deadly undercurrents that constantly threaten to undermine the bare stick of martial law.†

Northumbria's distinctive political history is matched by a cultural diversity unfamiliar in Wessex and West Mercia. Elmet, a Brittonic-speaking kingdom with its own independent dynasty, existed in what is now West Yorkshire into the seventh century, and the names of settlements on its eastern edge survive,

---

* Royal townships revealed by excavation. Adams 2013, 221–5; Adams 2016, 226ff. And for Cheddar see above, p. 140, and below, p. 405.

† Compare the Viking Age travel map of the ninth century (p. 50) to that of the early tenth (p. 281), which shows the defence in depth of the burghal system.

improbably, into the present day with Barwick-in-Elmet and Sherburn-in-Elmet. A hybrid Anglo-British culture in Bernicia was heavily influenced at the same period by an influx of Irish intellectual and artistic talent, so that even before the arrival of the Scandinavian armies of the 860s the north-east was a melting pot. Frisian merchants are attested in York in the eighth century; one of York's own, the scholar Alcuin, was an intimate of Charlemagne and it would be surprising if merchants from the Baltic lands were not also familiar with the famous trading settlement.

In the 870s, according to the *Chronicle*, the lands of the Northumbrians were parcelled out among the followers of the Host, and the place names of Yorkshire and Durham reflect the widespread presence of Danish individuals in positions of ownership. That there are Normanbys as well as Danbys suggests that the Northumbrian connection with Norse Dublin fostered landowners from across the Irish Sea during the tenth century. Other, more obscure immigrations are suggested by settlements associated with people from the Færoes (Ferrensby). Native Irish, too, lent their ethnic badges to villages (two Yorkshire Irtons and one Irby) as did men, perhaps moneyers or specialist craftsmen, with Germanic-sounding names like Arnold and Fulcard (*Arnodestorp*, Foggathorpe).[42]

The patchwork cultural map of Northumbria south of the Tyne allows us to reconstruct a landscape of linguistic and ethnic diversity against a backdrop of mutual comprehensibility in language and many customs. To what extent that diversity led to integration, ethnic tension and spiritual conflict, or whether Northumbrian society maintained a perpetually evolving set of affinities with ambiguity, is hard to tell. We cannot say, for example, if the small silver crucifix buried with the Bossall/Flaxton hoard identifies its owner as a Christian, a pagan with a taste for apocalyptic imagery, or merely a collector of scrap metal.

A large body of evidence, in the form of stone sculpture that seems to flirt with both Christian and pagan imagery, takes the acculturation debate on to a more complex and subtle level. In the parish church of St Nicholas at North Grimston (a hybrid Scandinavian/Anglian name if ever there was one) on the western edge of the Yorkshire Wolds, a marvellous font, perhaps of the eleventh century, is carved with a continuous frieze depicting a very graphic crucifixion, the last supper and a bishop or saint. On one of the walls outside is carved the distinctly vernacular, ambivalent figure of a *sheela na gig*.* In the parish church at Middleton, on the north edge of the Vale of Pickering, a wheel-headed relief-carved cross also bears the image of a warrior with spear, axe, shield, sword and fighting knife. Similar figures appear on crosses, or fragments thereof, at Sockburn in County Durham and in St Cuthbert's at Chester le Street (see p. 419).

There is nothing inherently jarring in the portrayal of a warrior on a cross: church patronage by retired or veteran soldiers is a common enough trope in medieval and later iconography. The appearance of strange beasts on the same monuments, and of many others (both crosses and the distinctly Anglo-Scandinavian memorial known as the hogback tomb) on which more equivocal messages seem to be displayed, offers a complex set of messages to decode.

In the parish church of Gosforth, on the Cumbrian coast, where a celebrated high cross of the Viking Age still stands in the churchyard, lie several hogback tombs. One carries a frieze of warriors along its side. Set into a corner in the wall of the north aisle is a relief carving that has been widely interpreted as a story from the Norse sagas (see p. 393). Thor, in one of his many trials of strength, disguises himself as a young boy and is taken fishing by the sceptical giant Hymir. The giant will not share his bait, so Thor slaughters one of the giant's own oxen, cuts off its head and

---

* A depiction of a naked female with legs apart, the hands emphasizing the genitals. Examples are found in medieval churches in Britain and Ireland.

lashes it to a strong line. Such is their mutual determination to show prowess at the oars that they end up far out at sea, beyond the giant's fishing grounds and in the perilous waters where Jörmungandr, the Midgard serpent, lurks. Undaunted, Thor casts his monstrous line and, sure enough, hooks the infernal beast. Faced with such a foe, Thor raises his hammer, Mjolnir, to strike the beast down but the giant cuts the line and the monster returns to the deep.[43] The Gosforth carving captures the moment of greatest drama, like a cartoon panel from a storyboard.

Thor, like the other gods of the Northern pantheon, was familiar to both native and incomer; his deeds were part of the repertoire of stories told to young children and against which warriors of the Viking Age pitted their own reputations. Might one put a Christian spin on the Thor sculpture: a portrayal of hubris, perhaps, or the evangelical tale of the fishers of men? Do we need to? The sponsor of a programme of church building might decorate his or her monument how he or she pleased, challenging the priest to perform the theological feat that would convert a pagan tale to something more palatable and instructive. Other Anglo-Norse narratives, of the thumb-sucking Sigurd, of Wayland the Smith and of bloody sacrifices that might be crucifixion scenes or Oðin hanging from Yggdrasil, the world tree, offered similar opportunities for contemporaries, and for the historian, to chew on. That these stories and symbols were carved in stone and meant to last tells us that the incomers had decided to stay, and to throw in their lot with the curious theologies of the Christian natives.

Unlike coins and pottery, large stone sculpture tends to remain in the place where it was first installed: the survival of many hundreds of crosses, hogbacks, memorials and other fragments allows us to map the presence, if not the motives, of those who commissioned them. Across what are now the counties of Durham, Yorkshire and Lancashire wealthy tenth-century patrons (of whatever ethnic background) chose to invest in an art form that committed them to a Christian future, to a sense of belonging and community. But their ideologies and cultural sensitivities were neither conservative nor isolated from the wider Atlantic world; their imaginative repertoire was eclectic.

From the simple plaiting of the Borre tradition,* through the intertwined beasts of the Jellinge style, all rotating hips and elongated, writhing limbs; through its evolution towards the Mammen style and then to its ultimate expression in the floral exuberance of Ringerike ornament, Christian and non-Christian Anglo-Scandinavian art is a fluid correspondent between peoples, ideologies and cultural expressions.

A sense of unresolved spiritual tension is nevertheless played out in the wider landscape. Some place names seem to reflect a revival of paganism in the North. Roseberry Topping, the striking eminence that overlooks the Tees Valley from the edge of the North York Moors, was once *Othenesberg*—Oðin's hill; places incorporating the element *haugr*—Old Norse 'mound', as in pagan burial mound, are relatively common in Yorkshire, as at Kilgram Grange (*Kelgrimhou*: Kelfgrím's mound) and Ulshaw Bridge (*Ulveshowe*: Úlf's mound).[44] It is also true that many pre-conquest churches did not survive the Viking Age. Some of them, like Lindisfarne, Jarrow and Monkwearmouth, were refounded in the tenth or eleventh centuries while others, like Ripon, Beverley and York itself, show evidence of continuity despite records of attack and pillage or the dumb witness of neglect. Ironically, the presence of tenth-century sculpture at church sites where seventh- to eighth-century carving is also present is considered one of the most secure markers for continuity of worship and institution through the first Viking Age.

---

* These styles, named after sites in Denmark where examples were first identified, appear on both stone sculpture and metalwork, an evolving set of artistic and cultural fashions that took on a new life in the British Isles as they hybridized with indigenous styles.

Æðelstan's motives for visiting York, and his experience there, must be set against a fluid and responsive background, full of cultural and political risks and opportunities. If, in that Northern summer of 936, his intelligence sources were alert to noises off-stage in Ireland and the Irish Sea, he might also have sensed a new or perhaps recycled threat to his northern *imperium*.

By 935 Óláfr Guðrøðsson, son of the would-be conqueror of York in 927 who had died the previous year, was attracting the notice of the Ulster annalist, who recorded that he plundered the royal crannog on Lough Gabhair in Meath. In 936 the same *Annal* records the shocking news that the monastic church at Clonmacnoise had been plundered by 'the foreigners of Áth Cliath'—that is, the Dublin Vikings, probably under Óláf's leadership.

Æðelstan had few friends in the North. Kings in Cumbria and Alba might sense, in the bellicose Óláfr's ambitions, a chance to throw off the yoke of his overlordship. If Æðelstan contemplated the possibility that Óláfr might compete for the throne of Northumbria, and that a number of his tributary kings might be tempted to join a new anti-West Saxon alliance, he was being no more than prescient.

A HOUSE OF CARDS

BATTLE OF BRUNANBURH—
EGIL SKALLAGRÍMSSON—COPS AND ROBBERS
—MIRACLE AT CHEDDAR—ÓLÁFR GUÐRØÐSSON
—DANISH MERCIA—THE LORD OF GOLTHO
—HYWEL DDA—EADMUND

11

IN THE LITANY OF GREAT EARLY MEDIEVAL battles several stand out: Hastings in 1066, Edington in 878 and Heavenfield in 634, each irrevocably altering the course of British history. Stamford Bridge in 1066, Maldon in 991 and Catraeth in about 590 are conspicuous for the magnificence of their poetic or annalistic narratives of martial glory and tragic mortality. *Brunanburh*, in 937, has its poets too. It was remembered long after the event for a great slaughter of its antagonists and for the glorious victory won there by King Æðelstan. Historians have variously argued that it cemented a process of English unification or that its significance is overstated; but much more ink has been spilled in the cause of elucidating its geography. More than thirty possible sites have been suggested, ranging from Dumfriesshire to Devon.

There can be no doubt that a major battle was fought on the British mainland in 937 and that its combatants included the West Saxon king, his sixteen-year-old half-brother Eadmund, King Constantín of Alba, King Owain of Cumbria/Strathclyde

48. A CARVING from All Saints' church,
Brixworth, Northamptonshire: Christian eagle
or Norse raven?

and Óláfr Guðrøðsson, the Dublin Norse warlord. One minor combatant, possibly apocryphal, whose contribution has been preserved in a much later Icelandic saga, can be named as the Norwegian poet-adventurer Egil Skallagrímsson.

The closest contemporary records provide only very brief, if convincing details. The *Annals of Ulster* recorded that:

> A great, lamentable and horrible battle was cruelly fought between the Saxons and the Norsemen, in which several thousands of Norsemen, who are uncounted, fell, but their king, Amlaíb, [Óláfr] escaped with a few followers. A large number of Saxons fell on the other side, but Athelstan, king of the Saxons, enjoyed a great victory.[1]

The *Historia Regum*, a set of Northern annals embedded in a work attributed to Symeon of Durham, records under the same year that 'King Athelstan fought at *Wendun* and put to flight King Olaf with 615 ships, and also Constantine, king of the Scots, and the king of the Cumbrians, with all their host'.[2]

The *Anglo-Saxon Chronicle* entry for 937 for once provides fulsome detail, in a poetic interpolation of seventy-three split lines which begins:

> Her Æðelstan cyning,   eorla dryhten,
> beorna beahgifa,   7 his broþor eac,
> Eadmund æðeling,   ealdorlangne tir
> geslogon æt sæcce   sweorda ecgum
> ymbe Brunnanburh...
>
> In this year King Æðelstan, lord of nobles, dispenser of treasure to men, and his brother also, Eadmund atheling, won by the sword's edge undying glory in battle around Brunnanburh.[3]

The account of the fighting is mostly conventional. The armies of Wessex and Mercia, of Eadweard's sons, 'clove the shield-wall, hewed the linden-wood shields with hammered swords'. Rout followed battle; five young kings lay dead on the field, along with seven of Óláf's jarls. The Norse chief was put to flight, 'driven perforce to the prow of his ship with a small company'.

The king of Alba fled north, shorn of his kinsmen; his son and friends dead. The remnants of the Norse fleet, seemingly isolated from their leader:

> Put out in their studded ships onto *Dinges* mere to make for Dublin across the deep water, back to Ireland humbled at heart... They left behind them the dusky-coated one, the black raven with its horned beak, to share the corpses, and the dun-coated, white-tailed eagle, the greedy war-hawk, to enjoy the carrion, and that grey beast, the wolf of the forest.[4]

This is a grand tale of ambition, ignominy, death and glory. But what can we credibly say about *Brunanburh* as an engagement? The number of ships in the Norse fleet, recorded in the *Historia Regum* as 615, is not conventional* and might represent a contemporary, if exaggerated, estimate. Such numbers are hard to interpret; they would have been hard to count even for an eye-witness. Supposing the figure to be based in reality, but exaggerated, and the fleet to have included a wide range of seagoing vessels of various sizes, some carrying baggage, an average of twenty warriors per vessel in 400 ships might be reasonable. That constitutes a fighting force of some 8,000 men, a very large army by Early Medieval standards. Add those of Óláf's northern allies and it is possible that 10–12,000 men were able to take the field against the southern king. They still lost. Size isn't everything, even in warfare. The command structures and communications required to mobilize what were, essentially, independent war bands and levies, are unlikely to have been very sophisticated, even supposing that all the allied forces succeeded in meeting at the right time and place.

---

* Poetic conventions tend to follow simple multipliers like three hundred and three score. The *Brunanburh* figure might still be an exaggeration. Even so, fleet estimates in the annals on both sides of the English Channel seem to be quite consistent. The fleets of 893 numbered in the low hundreds of ships. Nicholas Brooks offers a very useful summary of the arguments for Early Medieval fleet and army sizes in a famous essay; Brooks 1979, 5–9.

Infuriatingly, Æðelweard, the late tenth-century court historian, who probably had better access than most to eye-witness accounts and who tells us that the battle's fame was great even in his own day, gives no details of its progress. And in the *Chronicle of the Kings of Alba* it is recorded tersely as a battle at *Dún Brunde*, in which the son of Constantín was killed.[5]

One other possible early account seems to have been preserved in another poem, which William of Malmesbury claimed to have found in a 'very old book' from which he took several excerpts for his life of Æðelstan in the *Gesta Regum Anglorum*.[6] William adds significant information: that the battle was preceded by 'continuous ravages, driving out the people, setting fire to the fields'. Only 'at length [did] the complaining rumour [rouse] the king, not to let himself be thus branded that his arms gave way before the barbarian axe'.

The last secular narrative source to add anything useful to these accounts is that commonly attributed to Florence of Worcester,* writing in the twelfth century but possibly with access to material now lost, who says that the Norse fleet arrived in Britain by way of the River Humber.[7]

Debate over the background to the battle has understandably become intertwined with speculation over its location, but there is little doubt that its inspiration lay across the Irish Sea. None of the evidence suggests that Æðelstan initiated the conflict. Despite his later martial reputation, and his two expeditions to the northern parts of Britain in 927 and 934, he was the least warlike of his recent predecessors as kings of Wessex. His interests lay elsewhere: in law-making, in his collections of precious relics and in political intervention in Francia. *Brunanburh* is the only

---

* It was originally thought that the earlier part of this chronicle was written by Florence of Worcester and the later part by his fellow monk John of Worcester; John is now recognized as the author of both, basing his writings on notes compiled by Florence.

recorded set-piece battlefield conflict in his fifteen-year reign.

Óláfr Guðrøðsson was, it seems, spoiling for a fight; in the same summer he had already captured the Norse king of Limerick, his namesake Óláfr *Cenncairech*, 'Scabby-head', during a fleet action on Lough Ree.[8] He may now have entered into alliance with Constantín and seems to have nursed designs on his father's kingdom in Northumbria: his objective must have been the recapture of York. The historian of Viking kingship, Clare Downham, notes a story later recorded by John of Worcester, that Óláfr married a daughter of Constantín who, tellingly, had a grandson of the same name.[9]

The king of Alba, the 'hoary-haired'* and now quite elderly Constantín, may have harboured bitter resentment over his humiliating treatment at Æðelstan's hands; the same might apply to Owain of Cumbria/Strathclyde. A northern and Norse alliance is highly plausible.

Notably absent from any of the sources is any mention of the kings of Wales: Hywel, Idwal and the rest. Despite the evident opportunity to raise the banner waved so enthusiastically by the poet of *Armes Prydein Fawr*, they seem to have kept diplomatically at a distance. They may have been tasked by Eadmund with defending north-west Mercia against invasion; they may also have waited to see who would win.

Four names comprise the material from which all speculation on the site of the battle has been derived: *Brunanburh*, and variants thereof; *Wendun*, or *Weondun*; *Dinges mere* (where the Norse fleet lay); and Humber. Only the last of these is obviously identifiable. None of the suggested sites for the battle has been able to accommodate all four names. The historian Michael Wood, trusting to John of Worcester's testimony that Óláf's huge fleet sailed up the Humber, has made a case for a battle along a

---

* From the poem in the *Anglo-Saxon Chronicle*.

traditional and well-attested line between York and the Mercian–
Northumbrian border, the setting for many other Early Medieval
military encounters. He offers two solutions: Brinsworth near
Sheffield, and Went Hill just south of Pontefract.[10] The Roman
road crossing of the River Went seems to have been the site of
a great battle called *Winwæd* in 655 between the armies of King
Oswiu of Northumbria and King Penda of Mercia.[11] For a conflict between kings of the North and South it is an entirely acceptable location, but no more than that, and Wood's argument is
dependent on John of Worcester's late and isolated testimony of
a landing from the Humber.

The bulk of historical opinion currently favours Bromborough
on the Wirral peninsula. It is the only known place name definitively derived from Old English *Brunanburh*.[12] It is, to be sure, a
fine destination for an Irish assault: a short crossing from Dublin
and, probably, a sympathetic local population of at least partial
Norse affiliations. Ingimund's invasion of about 902 had paved
the way. Nearby Chester, if it could be taken, would make a perfect bridgehead for raiding and preparing a northern campaign
linked as it was through the Roman road system to York.

Recent analysis by Paul Cavill and others[13] has opened up
the possibility that another key name in the sources, *Dinges
mere*, may derive from 'the marsh by the Thing'; and a convenient 'Thing' name survives in Thingwall just a few miles west
of Bromborough, close to the Dee estuary. The Wirral, then,
has odds in its favour; even so, the niggling worry over a possible River Humber landing, and the lack of a sound candidate
for the northern *Wendun* variant of the battle site, incline one
to caution. A third suggested location, the hillfort of Burnswark
near Ecclefechan on the north side of the Solway Firth, has not
received widespread support; nor has the vote cast by philologist
Andrew Breeze for Lanchester in County Durham, the site of a
Roman fort lying by Dere Street close to the River Browney.[14]

In the light of what we know about other Viking Age conflicts in Britain, and of the evidence in William of Malmesbury's poem for an extensive period of raiding, it is possible that the surviving accounts are a conflation of a running campaign beginning in the east and ending in a rout in the west, with a designated fleet rendezvous on the Wirral. So *Wendun* (on the Went) and *Brunanburh* (on the Wirral) might not be mutually exclusive sites. Military historian Ryan Lavelle has pointed out that the apparent loss of the battle site to cultural memory is significant and may be a function of the physical loss of the battlefield to Norse rule within a very few years.[15]

What of the warrior-poet Egil Skallagrímsson? In *Egil's Saga* he was the Icelandic-born son of Skalla Grímr, a refugee from a feud with the great Norwegian king Haraldr *Hárfagri*. Egil was famously ugly,* but a brilliant and precocious poet and notoriously eager to engage in combat on the slightest provocation: a perfect Norse anti-hero. He had an older brother, Ðórólfr:† handsome, brave and adventurous, and a friend of Eiríkr *blóðøx*, 'Blood-axe', King Harald's son, having given him a fine, beautifully painted longship. He enjoyed a career of raiding and trading in the old Viking tradition and when Eiríkr became king of Hordaland and Fjordane, on Norway's island-rich and fjord-riven west coast, Ðórólfr joined his retinue as a loyal follower. One summer Egil asked if he could join Ðórólfr on one of his ventures, but his brother declined: the young man was too hot-headed, too prone to causing trouble. That night, during a storm, Egil boarded his brother's ship at its moorings and cut it loose so that it drifted away and was lost. After a frank exchange of views Ðórólfr gave in and took Egil with him.

---

* There has been speculation that the historical Egil suffered from Paget's disease. See a 1995 article by Jesse L Byock: http://www.viking.ucla.edu/Scientific_American/ Egils_Bones.htm, retrieved November 2016.

† Pronounced 'Thorolf'.

That winter Egil fell ill and found himself stranded on an island called Atloy, the guest of a wealthy *hold* named Bárðr. Bárðr's lord, none other than Eiríkr, arrived for a midwinter feast with his queen, Gunnhildr. Egil took great offence at a perceived insult by his host, drank himself into a furious rage and murdered Bárðr, precipitating his desperate flight and exile and a long-running blood feud with Eiríkr, which sets the scene for a series of epic and bloodthirsty adventures in the Baltic and in Britain. In one set-piece yarn, Egil's bragging chat-up line to the eligible daughter of a Danish jarl, is suitably masculine, if poetic:

> I have wielded a blood-stained sword
> And howling spear; the bird
> Of carrion followed me
> When the Vikings pressed forth;
> In fury we fought battles
> Fire swept through men's homes,
> We made bloody bodies
> Slump by the city gates.[16]

In the year of *Brunanburh* the two brothers found themselves in Britain and volunteered, as mercenaries of great renown, to fight for Æðelstan. The *Saga's* historicity is not to be trusted: the author's knowledge of the British politics (let alone the geography) of a long-gone age, outlined in chapters 50 to 52 of the Saga, is ill-informed and not generally credible.

The *Saga* now introduces us to a number of quasi-historical characters. It tells how Æðelstan, in the face of possible Norse aggression, had appointed two jarls, Álfgeirr and Goðrekr, as regents in Northumbria. This is not inherently implausible, but the story is uncorroborated in any Insular source and no coins bear these names. The Hringr and Aðils who 'ruled Britain' at the time and who, in the *Saga* account, fight against Aðelstan, might be the Welsh kings Hywel and Idwal.

The detail of *Egil's Saga* that deals with Æðelstan cannot be

taken at face value; but the idea that Icelandic warriors in permanent exile should seek mercenary employment with a foreign king, bringing with them a substantial war band of hardened veterans, is perfectly realistic. So, too, is the *Saga*'s aside
that, because of the king's well-known piety, Þórólfr, Egil and
their war band must agree to make the sign of the cross at their
oath-swearing: a spiritual compromise well suited to the age.

In the defence of the North against Óláfr, Goðrekr was supposedly killed and Álfgeirr fled. Now Æðelstan sent an embassy
to Óláfr proposing battle at a place called *Vínheiðr*, a name which
has struck a chord with historians for its apparent similarity to the
Wendun of the *Historia Regum*, although others have seen it as a
misplaced reference to an earlier battle in which the two brothers

49.
THOR AND HYMIR
fish for the
Midgard serpent:
a relief carving in
the church of
St Mary, Gosforth,
Cumbria.

fought, at Dvina in Russia.[17] We cannot know; but the idea that battles should be fought on agreed territory on an appointed day has much to recommend it: if nothing else, it solves the problem of how opposing armies encountered one another with such regularity.

The colourful account of the battle in *Egil's Saga*, lasting several chapters, involves much preliminary bartering, accusations of deceit and false witness, surprise assaults and fluctuating fortunes over successive days. Egil and his brother, appointed leaders of the Northumbrian army in place of the disgraced Álfgeirr, distinguished themselves, but Þórólfr fell during an onslaught by the Welsh king Aðils.

At a great victory feast Æðelstan honoured Egil with a fine arm-ring, which drew from the grieving poet a line:

> The god of the armour hangs
> A jangling snare upon my clutch,
> The gibbet of hunting birds, the stamping ground of hawks.
> I raise the ring, the clasp that is worn
> On the shield-splitting arm,
> Onto my rod of the battle-storm,
> In praise of the feeder of ravens.[18]

The historical and political significance of the battle has often been exaggerated. Its immediate outcome, the expulsion of the beaten Óláfr, gave only temporary relief from the ambitions of the grandsons of Ívarr. The status quo of Æðelstan's *imperium* was maintained. Constantín had repudiated his tributary status and now stood in direct opposition to Wessex, but was in no position to mount another military campaign. Northumbria and Danish Mercia remained, for the time being, within the king's tributary portfolio. Even if Æðelstan had been defeated, it is unlikely that the Wessex–Mercia alliance would have collapsed. The participation in battle of the king's young half-brother Eadmund is a sure sign of his status as heir presumptive.

The *Brunanburh/Wendun* campaign nevertheless offers some useful insights for understanding Æðelstan's military position. Overlordship and military command, the loyalty of subject kings and allies, were matters of expediency. If we are to believe the silence of the *Chronicle* the Welsh kings, obliged by their status as *subreguli* to fight in the wars of their overlord, instead failed to heed his call. We might just allow that they were deployed defensively at Rhuddlan and on Anglesey. But, whenever kings were challenged, uncertainty offered opportunities to throw off the yoke of submission. If they joined the other side they must expect swift retribution.

If we believe the much later evidence of *Egil's Saga*, Æðelstan treated his Northumbrian military commanders (Álfgeirr and Goðrekr) likewise as *subreguli*: that is, they fought on his behalf in command of their own forces. The same applied to the jarls of Danish Mercia who would have been obliged to fight alongside the king as their personal lord at the head of their war bands; but the warriors of those war bands fought for the jarls as *their* personal lords.

The king of Wessex did not possess a national militia or *fyrð*, nor the means to raise one. The obligation to fight in his army under the reforms initiated by Ælfred was tied directly to the 'common burdens' imposed on booked land and on burhs in Wessex and West Mercia. By the early tenth century forces were raised under shire levy systems by ealdormen tied to the king and their shires by bonds of mutual obligation and kin affiliation. Outside those core kingdoms he must rely on more independent-minded subject commanders. A key theme of the later tenth century is the attempt by successive rulers to extend formal military service to the towns and shires of the East Midlands and East Anglia.

The tenth-century Anglo-Saxon state, professionalized by Ælfred and buttressed by the military and administrative vision of his heirs, was sufficiently robust to be able to survive the death of the king. Æðelstan died, aged forty-three, at Gloucester in 939, two years after *Brunanburh*, and was buried in his favoured monastery, Malmesbury, in the Wiltshire Cotswolds: in Wessex, but close to the Mercian border. He was immediately succeeded by his half-brother and protégé Eadmund, aged eighteen, who had fought by his side. Æðelstan's disinclination to marry and produce his own heir obviated the risk of rival claimants. Eadmund's accession seems to have been unopposed.

In his last two years Æðelstan's only recorded political intervention was the dispatch of a fleet in aid of his nephew, King Louis of West Francia, whose installation he had helped engineer in 936 but whose uneasy relationship with Hugh, count of Paris and duke of the Franks, had turned to open conflict. The overseas foray did not go according to plan: Flodoard of Rheims recorded in his *Annal* of that year that Æðelstan's fleet 'plundered the coast of Flanders... without accomplishing anything of their original mission'.[19]

Less securely dated, but more significant, is a series of reforms reflecting Æðelstan's ongoing concern with law and order in his expanded kingdom. In the *Grately Code* of about 930, in among provisions for theft (a seeming preoccupation of the king) and coinage, is notice of a new approach to what one might call collective judicial responsibility and executive action. In response to those who would 'not do justice nor pay the fine for disobedience', the leading men were to 'ride thither, all who belong to the borough, and take all that he owns, and put him under surety'.[20]

50.
ANLAF CVNVNC
(Anlaf, King):
the raven penny of
Óláfr Guðrøðsson,
king of York.

Those who embarked on such expeditions, the *posse comitatus* of later English law, were to split the proceeds equally with the king.

Later in his reign Æðelstan enacted, or supported the enactment of, a remarkable institution called the *Friðgegyldum*—literally 'peace-guild', recorded in *The ordinance of the bishops and reeves of the* civitas *of London*.[21] The context is an existing provision that thieves under twelve years of age (amended later in the same code, under the merciful advice of Bishop Theodred, to fifteen) and those who steal property worth less than 12 pence, were to be spared death. Guilty felons killed by 'the Fellowship' were to have their property divided into three, with the felon's wife (if innocent) receiving a third share with the king (or bishop or lord, in the case of bookland) and the guild. The subscription fee for members was to be 4 pence every year. The executive arm of the Fellowship was to consist of ten men together under a chief. Ten of these chief men were to act under the authority of a hundred-man; between them the eleven must keep accounts of moneys collected and disbursed on behalf of the guild, and enforce attendance and subscription. And:

> Each man of those that heard the summons was to be helpful to the rest both in following the trail and riding with them, as long as the trail could be seen; and after the trail had been lost, a man was to be procured [from two tithings] where the population was large, from one tithing where it was more sparse.[22]

The guild was not merely a primitive institution for policing. The hundred-men were to assemble once a month and 'have leisure... and take note how our agreement is being observed, and then 12 men shall dine together and shall supply themselves as they think fitting, and distribute all the leavings for God's sake'.[23] This was a club, joined by an urban élite drawn from a cross-section of noble and probably mercantile interests and used to ensure that those interests were protected for mutual benefit.

It is not clear whether the *Friðgegyldum* ordinance applied only to the shires of Middlesex, Hertfordshire and Surrey and to the burh of London, or was intended to act as a model for the whole of the kingdom. The impetus for the formation of the guild was burghal and its composition allowed for membership among both nobles and *ceorls*: the rhyming pun *ge eorlisce ge ceorlisce* ('both nobles and *ceorls*') in the prologue strikes a poetic and ceremonial tone confirmed by a reference to *XII hynde* and *twyhynde* men.*

Given the unresolved question of when and how the Mercian and northern shires were created, it is not yet possible to integrate the London *Ordinance* with wider 'national' provisions for law and order; but it seems likely that shire towns, such as the Five Boroughs, Gloucester, Worcester, Northampton and Cambridge, may have adopted a similar *Friðgegyldum* system. The frequent mention of reeves in the *Ordinance* anticipates the key judicial and executive roles that they would later play in devolving the king's law to the regions. The office of the *portgerefa* had increased significantly in importance since the original development of the trading settlements of the eighth century and their successors, the burhs.

There is an underlying tension here between the king's law and powerful local interests, hinted at in clause 8.2 of the London *Ordinance*:

> If it happens that any group of kinsmen—whether nobles or commoner within or beyond the borders of our district—become so strong and powerful as to prevent us from exercising our legal rights, and stand up in defence of a thief, we shall ride out against them in full force.[24]

Were these the same extended families who had stood in Ælfred's way, who had been so obstructive during the defensive

---

* 1200 shilling men and 200 shilling men. See above, Chapter 5, p. 176.

programmes of the 880s and 890s? And if such powerful kindreds existed in Wessex and Mercia, how much more troublesome might they be in East Anglia, in Danish Mercia and beyond? How far were they able to resist the ever-widening powers of the Anglo-Saxon state?

The *Chronicle* is coy about the events of the year after Æðelstan's death. Even so, it is absolutely clear that his *imperium* died with him. Later chroniclers' works preserving lost material with a more northern perspective (albeit much embellished and usable only with caution) show that the political vacuum was filled quickly. The *Historia Regum*, compiled in Durham in the twelfth century, and the *Flores Historiarum* compiled by Roger of Wendover in the thirteenth century, both record that in 940 Óláfr Guðrøðsson, miraculously recovered from the apparent disaster of 937, 'came to York'. His invasion fleet must, as in 937, have navigated the waters of the Irish Sea and Solway Firth or Mersey, or taken the much longer route via the east coast and along the Humber: we cannot say.

Either in the same year or, more likely, in 941 when the *Chronicle* records that 'the Northumbrians were false to their pledges and chose Anlaf (Óláfr) as their king',[25] a Norse army came south and besieged the burh at Northampton. Failing to take it, they swept north-west and ravaged the area around Tamworth, on the border of West Mercia, with 'great slaughter on both sides'.[26] Óláfr then turned his attention to Leicester, but by the time his army arrived there Eadmund had responded, and met him with a force sufficiently threatening that there was a stand-off.

Both Roger of Wendover and the *Historia Regum* record that a peace treaty was signed under the advice and auspices of the two archbishops, acting presumably as proxies or brokers on behalf of the Northern and Southern kingdoms. Under the terms of the agreement, Óláfr was to rule all the lands north and east of Watling Street while Eadmund retained all those to the south and west. The ancient division along the watershed line of central England, defined in the Treaty of Ælfred and Guðrum of about 879, was re-invented for a new generation of antagonists. The treaty was sealed, if we accept the testimony of Roger of Wendover, by Óláf's marriage: not to a daughter of the king, who was only twenty, but to Aldgyð, daughter of a *dux* with the distinctly Danish name of Orm, or Urm.* The same chronicler adds that Urm had given the Norse invader aid and counsel, with which he had obtained his victory.

There is much food for thought here. The *Chronicle*'s misplaced entry (under 943) for the events at Leicester tells us that Archbishop Wulfstan was among those besieged there with Óláfr, and that the pair escaped by night. If that was the case, then it was a smart piece of diplomacy for the two archbishops to broker a peaceful end to the conflict and seal it with a Christian marriage and royal baptism.† The northern primate seems, then, to have thrown in his lot with the Norse leader, although it is also possible that the archbishop, who had so recently received Amounderness in anticipation of his loyalty to Wessex, might have been held as a hostage. These are murky waters.

Perhaps the most remarkable aspect of this series of events is the identity of the new archbishop of Canterbury, enthroned in that same year. Oda (died 958) was the son of Danish parents; his father was said to have arrived with the *mycel here* in 865 and his family's estates were located in East Anglia.[27]

---

* If this is true, it implies that either Óláfr had repudiated the daughter of Constantín, whom he is recorded as having married by John of Worcester, or that the earlier marriage is a fiction.

† According to the *Chronicle* account Óláfr obtained Eadmund's friendship and the latter stood sponsor at his baptism, just as Ælfred had at Guðrum's, two generations before.

No less intriguing is the *dux* or jarl called Urm. One might speculate that he was the Danish leader who ruled the burh of Leicester and its *regio*—what would become the shire of the same name. His daughter Aldgyð's English-sounding name suggests that he had married a native. He appears several times as a witness to royal charters: first at Lifton in Devon in 931* and then periodically all the way through to 958/9 under a succession of West Saxon kings: a career of more than twenty years at court. If he is the embodiment of Richard Hall's 'innate affinities with ambiguity', it seems to have done him no harm. One can easily imagine Urm as the head of the sort of powerful local kindred about whom Æðelstan's lawyers were so wary and against whom the *Friðgegyldum* was designed to be able to act. His military muscle and key position in Danish Mercian society ensured that all parties must court his goodwill.

Óláf's brief, triumphant entry onto the lists of Insular kings has left an indelible mark in the archaeological record. Immediately replacing the stock of Æðelstan's silver penny coinage in York, more than 100 dies covering just two years' minting there (and, perhaps, further south) testify to a large series proclaiming ANLAF CVNVNC (Anlaf, King)—the first recorded appearance of Old Norse in the Roman alphabet.[28] The name surrounds a stylish and distinctly Norse-looking depiction of a raven (see p. 396). If his new wife Aldgyð disapproved, the fact is unrecorded.

Under Eadmund's new West Saxon regime the normal business of royal administration resumed on a less imperial scale than in his predecessor's day. In 941 he held a royal council *in villam qui cælebri æt Ceodre*: at the palace of 'famous' Cheddar.[29] The grant that survives to confirm the visit is insignificant: a small estate in

---

* See above, p. 359. The full list of charters attested by Urm comprises: S416; S520; S544; S522a; S550; S633; S659; S674; S679.

Hampshire, given to one of the new king's ministers. The West Saxon kings were generous with their property portfolios, buying the support and loyalty of key men in their shires both new, as in Danish Mercia, and old. In the early years of their reigns such grants were numerous, and carefully chosen.

Cheddar is the only West Saxon royal residence to have been excavated so far.[30] It stood at the navigable head of the River Axe (which empties to the north-west into the Bristol Channel), squeezed between the foot of the Mendip hills and the Somerset levels. Like several similar sites, it probably began as a small minster founded close to an earlier Roman site at the centre of a *villa regalis*, to which a royal hunting lodge was attached. During the secularization process of the ninth century the fortunes of the

51.
'THROUGH DIFFICULT PATHS unto the edge of a precipice.' A hollow way leading from Cheddar up onto the Mendip hills.'

minster declined and the lodge became a royal township like that at Yeavering in north Northumbria.

A major construction phase seems to have been undertaken in the reign of Æðelstan, providing the site with halls, a chapel, a fowl-house and a wind-powered corn mill, all protected from periodic flooding by an elaborate drainage scheme. The carefully laid-out entrance was graced by a flagpole, whose setting included a plinth made from recycled Roman brick. The palace was still being expanded and refurbished in the thirteenth and fourteenth centuries.[31] Each successive incarnation of Cheddar's great hall shows engineering taken to new levels of sophistication. The only material traces left for the archaeologist are foundations, but its architecture must have impressed and awed its visitors: the royal court, *subreguli*, archbishops, *duces*, bishops, envoys, petitioners and *ministri*.

The bland record of Eadmund's Cheddar council of 941 is enlivened by a series of events later thought to portend the future glory of a major celebrity. The greatest of the late Saxon archbishops of Canterbury, Dunstan (who held the see between 960 and 978) was born near Glastonbury in about 910 at a time when few, if any, functioning monastic houses survived. In the case of Glastonbury its community consisted of no more than a clerical school; but such were its ancient reputation and the virtues of its relics that it was much visited. Dunstan attended the school there before being introduced into Æðelstan's court by the then archbishop of Canterbury, Æðelhelm, and taking vows to become a monk.[32] Dunstan was a gifted silversmith and illustrator;* he also managed to attract the jealousy of his peers. He fell foul of court rivalries and gossip and the new king, Eadmund, threatened him with disgrace and exile.

---

* A remarkable self-portrait may survive in the *Glastonbury Classbook* attributed to Dunstan and held in the Bodleian Library at Oxford. Bodleian Library, Auct. F. 4. 32 (2176).

Both Roger of Wendover and Dunstan's anonymous biographer record the story that at Cheddar events came to a head when the king went out hunting on the wooded hills above the palace:

> A multitude of deer took to flight, one of which, of extraordinary size, the king singled out for the chase, and followed with his dogs alone driving him through difficult paths unto the edge of a precipice, over which the stag and dogs fell headlong and were dashed to pieces.[33]

The king, fearing that he must follow the beasts into the infamous depths of the gorge and unable to rein in his mount in time, is supposed to have uttered a prayer and at that instant, realizing that he must have offended Christ by his unjust treatment of the monk, was saved by the miraculous intervention of Dunstan's prayers.

The king, it was said, promptly rode with Dunstan to Glastonbury and installed him as its abbot. As it happens, a charter of 940 records King Eadmund granting Abbot Dunstan twenty hides of land at a place called *Cristemalforde* ('the ford with a crucifix') in Wiltshire.[34] If the Cheddar story is true, the event must have taken place a year earlier than the council recorded in 941. More likely, the recorded sequence is accurate, but the two events have been conflated by the wishful thinking of later biographers. Either way, Dunstan's political survival allowed him to establish, under successive kings, an organized community of monks following a form of Benedictine rule from which a great monastic reform movement was born in the 970s.[35]

The treaty signed at Leicester, meanwhile, did not prevent King Óláfr from extending his influence northwards from York, into the lands of the Bernician lords. In 941 his forces ravaged the church of St Bealdhere at Tyninghame in East Lothian; and the Men of York were said to have laid waste the Holy Island of Lindisfarne.[36] But Óláfr seems to have died during this northern campaign, 'smitten by the justice of God' according to Roger of

Wendover. In his stead, from across the Irish Sea, came a name-sake, Óláfr Sigtryggsson, nicknamed *Kváran* or 'Sandal', son of the Norse Dublin king who had married Æðelstan's sister and ruled Northumbria for six years after 921. *Kváran* may already have been in York from 940; he had by then bequeathed the kingship of Dublin to another scion of the dynasty of Ívarr, Blákári Guðrøðsson, brother of the deceased Óláfr.

When the *Chronicle* picks up the narrative again, in 942, it is in the form of thirteen split lines of alliterative poetry, one of its most celebrated entries:

> *Her Eadmund cyning   Engla þeoden,*
> *maga mundbora   Myrce geeode,*
> *dyre dædfruma...*

> Here King Edmund, lord of the English
> Men's protector, overran Mercia
> (Dear deed-doer) As bounded by Dore,
> Whitwell Gate and Humber river,
> The broad brimming stream; and Five Boroughs:
> Leicester and Lincoln,
> Nottingham, and also Stamford and
> Derby. Danes were before,
> Under the Northmen, forced into submission,
> In heathen bondage,
> A long time, until he afterwards freed them,
> For his honour, defender of warriors,
> Edward's offspring, king Eadmund.[37]

This is the first documentary source to name the Five Boroughs, and such an enigmatic entry raises more questions than it answers. It is generally understood, in the first place, that it represents a record of the military conquest of Danish Mercia by Eadmund in 942. Then, there is the clear statement in the poem of a new boundary line between the lands of the Norse kings of Northumbria and those of Eadmund, redrawn somewhat to the north of Watling Street and on a very ancient line dividing the historical Mercia from Deira: Dore (meaning literally a door, or narrow pass), half a dozen miles south-west of Sheffield, and the Whitwell Gap to the south-east. Linking this line, between the eastern Peak District (lands of the *Pecsætan*), the western fringes of Sherwood and the River Humber, the border would follow the line of either the River Idle, to its junction with the Trent in Lincolnshire or, similarly, the River Don whose course runs a little to the north.

This had been a much fought-over zone in earlier centuries and if, as Michael Wood suggests, we can place *Brunanburh* in these debatable lands, it would reinforce the sense of a dynamic landscape of fluctuating, competing fortunes. Significantly, perhaps, place names indicative of Scandinavian settlement occur much more frequently east and south of the Trent, in the heartlands of the Five Boroughs, than they do to its north and west.

The 942 poem is followed in the Winchester version of the *Chronicle* by a prose statement: that Eadmund stood sponsor for *Kváran* and a second Norse king, an otherwise obscure Rögnvaldr, at their baptisms, a sure sign of their submission. But perhaps the most intriguing element of the entry is its suggestion that Danes had been subjected to bondage by the heathen Norse. The implication is that assimilated Danes, settled north and east of Watling Street since the days of the *mycel here*, now Christianized and perhaps, like Urm, married into native families, resented the overt heathenism of the two Irish Norse kings, with their aggressively apocalyptic iconography. Danish Mercia had, finally, sided with Wessex.

It is very difficult, perhaps futile, to attempt an analysis of such niceties of identity. Overlordship was a distant influence on ordinary lives. Coinage was one thing; few inhabitants of Danish Mercia would ever have seen a king. More likely, I think, loyalties and identities were subtly complex and local, looking to the burghal towns and their governors, of whatever persuasion, for markets, opportunities for patronage and cultural influences while they guarded their own backs. Domestically, identities would have been displayed in a variety of media, from dress fashion to tableware to language and the naming of children; to the stories they were told and the games they played. One suspects that women played a far greater role in managing such subtle processes than the historical record, or even the archaeology, allows.

The lord and lady of Goltho, an abandoned medieval settlement lying close to a Roman road some 14 miles (23 km) northeast of Lincoln,* experienced these tensions at first hand. Dane or native, their family had seen the turmoil of the ninth century come and go and had prospered, although not without dramatic adaptations to events within and beyond the old territorial limits of Lindsey. Archaeologist Guy Beresford's excavations of the early 1970s, during which he pioneered the strategic use of machinery to strip and expose complex horizontal and vertical stratigraphic relationships in large, open-area excavations, revealed a settlement history spanning more than a millennium.[38]

What had appeared, from surface earthworks, to be the grassed-over remains of a Norman motte and bailey castle, in fact started life as a Romano-British farmstead. For 400 years after the end of the Roman occupation of Britain the site was abandoned, or shifted elsewhere in the vicinity, before a new farmstead, the substantial home of a senior thegn or *dux*, was refounded here in about 800. Guy Beresford believed that a complete lack of evidence for destruction deposits at the site and the paucity of Scandinavian artefacts argued for a native incumbent and that its re-establishment may have been the result of a minor land grant by a ninth-century overlord, one of the still-independent kings of Mercia.

---

* And 5 miles (8 km) north of the monastic site at Bardney, from where Oswald's relics were retrieved in about 906/9. The name only survives from the thirteenth century, when it was recorded as *Golthawe*, perhaps 'the enclosure of the (marsh) marigold'. Beresford 1987.

In about 850 Goltho's two or three moderately substantial longhouses, of a type familiar across contemporary Britain, set in a rectangular fenced enclosure, were replaced by something much more impressive. A prestigious new hall, comparable in size with the earliest hall at Cheddar and capable of hosting large public assemblies, was constructed on the same site.* It formed part of a complex, aligned squarely around a courtyard, with a large barn or weaving shed, byre and kitchen block.

After perhaps a generation (which would coincide neatly with the annexation of East Mercia by the *mycel here* and the expulsion of King Burghred) the whole was enclosed by a very substantial defensive earthwork, reconstructed analytically by Beresford even after its virtual obliteration by later ditches and ramparts. That it was genuinely defensive rather than merely pretentious is evident from its dimensions: the ditch was 8 feet (2.5 m) deep and nearly 20 feet (6 m) across, with the rampart probably topped by a palisade. Whether it was designed to prevent raids by Vikings, West Saxons, Danish war bands or fellow members of Lindsey's élite is frustratingly impossible to say but, again, one is reminded of the provisions of Æðelstan's *Friðgegyldum Ordinance*, which hint at tensions among powerful local kindreds. The lord of Goltho had enemies.

For most of the period between 865 and 950 Goltho lay outside the area subject to the kings of Wessex. Lincoln was its closest and most important central place. If one supposes that the *regio* of Lindsey, the north part of Lincolnshire, was ruled by a jarl of the stamp of Urm, then it must have been his patronage to which the thegn or *hold* of Goltho owed his status and, one presumes, the permission to construct such a powerful personal statement of his wealth and status.

---

* Two other long halls of almost identical dimensions have been excavated at Sulgrave in Northamptonshire and at Bicester in Oxfordshire. See Hamerow 2012, 47, for the striking graphic evidence of their plans.

The defended enclosure at Goltho was remodelled several times over the next two centuries, always within the same enclosure and on the same co-axial alignment. In time a regularly laid-out village of tofts* and cottages grew up close by, its earthworks partially excavated before being razed by the plough in the 1970s. The remarkable preservation of what has been called a 'private burh' owes much to the construction, in the Norman period, of a motte whose earthworks covered and sealed the earlier phases.

Large quantities of domestic refuse were recovered from the excavation, showing that Goltho was well within the distribution compass of Lincolnshire potteries, the subject of the intriguing analysis described in Chapter 8. At about a day's travel from Lincoln, Goltho is a prime candidate for the putative burghal estate proposed by Symonds and Ling, its lord perhaps owning a small estate plot and chapel in the city and fitting neatly into the élite club of its Anglo-Scandinavian heyday. If that were the case, though, we might expect more material finds reflecting contact with the highly networked metalworkers and artisans of Lincoln; and Goltho retained its Old English name while, nearby, the village of Wragby, possibly 'Vragi's settlement', underwent a period of extended Norse ownership. Goltho seems resolutely native.

Goltho must have lain at the heart of a land-holding sufficiently large to support its needs and the grandeur of its buildings. Like Flixborough and Cheddar, its management required a complex machinery of customary obligations and services in which each individual was bound by duty and privilege to all other parties.

A compilation dating from about the early eleventh century†

---

* Toft: a narrow strip of land, fronting on a lane or road, on which a cottage was built, associated with a croft – a parcel of arable or pasture land close by.

† And therefore to be treated with caution for its applicability to the conditions pertaining a hundred and more years earlier. It is contained in a collection of texts in an Old English manuscript: *Cambridge, Corpus Christi College 383*.

and known as *Gerefa*, 'the Reeve', sets out an idealized relationship between an estate and those who owed service to it under
the watchful eye of its reeve, or steward.[39]

> ÐEGEN LAGV IS *þæt he sy his boc rihtes wyrðe*
> *7 þæt he ðreo ðinc of his lande do fyrd*
> *7 burhbote 7 brycgeweorc.*

> The law of the thegn is that he be worthy of his book-right and
> that from his land he must do three things: *fyrð*-duty, *burhbote*
> and bridgework.

These 'common burdens' are first recorded under King Offa
of Mercia in the eighth century. All those of thegnly rank must
raise a company of armed and trained men when called upon by
their lord (*fyrð*-duty); must contribute to building and repairing
the walls of the burh (*burhbote*) and repair bridges (*brycgeweorc*)
when required. The use of the Old Norse term *lagu* ('law') is significant: its adoption must derive from usage in Danish Mercia.

Below the thegn comes the *geneat*: the dependent tenant or,
in earlier times, the *ceorl*. In Danish Mercia and parts of East
Anglia, but especially in Lincolnshire in the late Anglo-Saxon
period, classes of tenant called sokemen and *liberi homines*, or
freemen, are widely attested. They were able to pass their holdings onto their heirs, like booked land. Historians used to equate
their distribution with the Danelaw and drew the quite reasonable inference that here was evidence for independent, free veterans of the *mycel here* settling the land and sharing it out, just as
the *Chronicle* recorded. For many reasons the argument has not
stood the test of time.[40] Now, the survival of such distinct classes,
or more properly castes, also found in Wales and Kent, for example, is seen as another facet of regional diversity, reflecting earlier
customary territorial relations between lords and those who rendered services and goods to them.

The estate demanded duties from its free tenants in the form
of a *gafol*, or tax on the land that they held; in the provision of

horses for team work and load carrying; by providing food; in the maintenance of hedges and fencing, as well as supporting the church. In a fascinating aside, we learn that it was the duty of the *geneat* to 'lead newcomers to the enclosure': that is, to ensure that traders or free men entering on the estate lands should be supervised, given hospitality and brought to the lord to see what they were about.

The duties of the *kotesetlan*, or cottar, were defined by local custom, so conspicuous a feature of Early Medieval cultures everywhere. He had his own land and must render services to the lord and 'always be available to work'. The poor, unfree *gebur* carried the heavy burden of unremitting labour and render, working two or three days per week for his lord, paying taxes such as *heorðpænig* (hearth-penny) and ploughing and sowing the lord's fields; he must give up part of his barley harvest, two of his hens and a young sheep; he must provide half of the feed for a hunting dog and pay six loaves to the lord's swineherd when he drove his pigs to wood pasture in autumn. In return, the *gebur* was provided with tools and with 7 acres of land to plough and sow, two oxen, a cow and six sheep.

Additional clauses in the *Gerefa* address provisions for bee-keepers, bound and free swineherds, male and female slaves, oxherds, shepherds, cheesewrights and plough-followers, for the beadle and the forester. It is an idealized portrait of a well-mannered and structured hierarchical society whose wealth was produced for the benefit of men like the lord of Goltho: those worthy to ride with and attend upon the king.

The Midlands campaign of 942 may have involved military engagement; the poem preserved in the *Chronicle* entry for that year is not explicit. Some scholars have noted the granting of estates in 941 by Eadmund in the central Trent valley and suggested that, following the earlier precedents of his father and half-brother, the young king was purchasing territories from Danish or Norse control and assigning them to more Wessex-friendly lords.[41] This deployment of West Saxon patronage (and cash) which had already reached as far as Amounderness in the north-west and the community of St Cuthbert in the north-east, was an essential tool in the extension of royal authority outside the West Saxon and Mercian heartlands. But Eadmund must have been schooled, and early, in other means of showing political clout. In the same year, the *Annales Cambriae* record that Idwal Foel, grandson of Rhodri Mawr and king of Gwynedd, was killed along with his son Elisedd by the 'Saxons';* whether by military expedition or assassination is uncertain. Idwal, and Gwynedd, had maintained an uneasy relationship with the West Saxon project—regional Venedotian policy traditionally looked to Man and the Irish Sea for allies; and Norse place names suggest that, like the Wirral, there was a significant Norse/Irish constituency in the north Welsh kingdom.

In killing Idwal, Eadmund may have been exacting revenge for his possible defection at *Brunanburh*, or for his failure to submit on the new king's coronation. Idwal does not appear on the witness lists for Eadmund's charters, whose attendance was dominated by his brother Eadred, by Archbishop Oda of Canterbury (but not Wulfstan of York) and by Theodred, bishop of London. Eadgifu, the king's mother, was an occasional witness; but there are no *subreguli*, not even the generally pro-Wessex Hywel Dda. The new king's council was, it seems, a smaller, more businesslike affair, with less of the imperial pomp of the father and less overtly political, but keeping a tight circle of loyalists on hand. Urm and his fellow Danish jarls did not appear again at the king's councils until much later in the decade, after Eadmund was dead.

---

* Under the entry for 943, corrected to 942.

Hywel Dda may not have been an Eadmund insider, but he took the opportunity afforded by his brother's death to expel his two surviving nephews, Iago and Ieuaf, annexe Gwynedd and Powys and effectively, for the first time, create a kingship comprising the bulk of Wales outside Morgannwg (formerly Glywysing) and Gwent in the south-east (the latter apparently directly subject to West Saxon lordship).[42] Hywel was the most outstandingly successful of the Early Medieval Welsh kings, ranking alongside Constantín of Alba and three generations of Æðulfings in playing a key role in the founding of a medieval kingdom. Like them, he understood the rules of patronage, opportunity and alliance; and if, in the *Armes Prydein Fawr*, he was cast as a traitorous appeaser by some contemporaries, his canny adaptation to the realities of Norse invasion and West Saxon *imperium* ensured that he survived long enough for his name to be remembered as both Dda ('the Good') and as the promulgator of the impressive Welsh Law code of the Middle Ages.

He may have been influenced, in his youth, by Bishop Asser, Ælfred's most favoured Welsh intellectual. His pilgrimage to Rome in 928 (in imitation, perhaps, of the youthful Ælfred) and his attendance at successive councils convened by Æðelstan exposed him, uniquely, to a wider European milieu. A single silver penny with the inscription HOWAEL REX survives; probably minted in Chester and following a contemporary West Saxon style. It may commemorate his annexation of Gwynedd in 942.[43] The law books called *Cyfraith Hywel* (the Laws of Hywel) exist in manuscripts that date from no earlier than the thirteenth century. Several generations of scholarship have been devoted to determining key questions surrounding these books: are they the result of royal edicts identifiable with pre-Norman Welsh Law; can they be attributed to a single reign; and, if so, can their inspiration be laid at the door of Hywel Dda, as their medieval compilers wished them to be? The answers to all these questions are complicated, but some basic conclusions can be drawn from the modern edition in English by Dafydd Jenkins and a recent analysis and summary in Thomas Charles-Edwards's magnificent *Wales and the Britons*.[44]

Despite some clear but isolated instances in which Welsh Law borrowed from pre-Conquest English Law, the underlying legal philosophy is much more closely linked with Irish Law texts, which survive in voluminous and early manuscripts. The flavour is less retributive than in English legal codes but, as Jenkins points out, there is a striking internal tension between the crude and the sophisticated.[45] Homicide is treated largely as a matter for compensation: in common with most Early Medieval societies, Welsh lawmakers were keen to limit the disastrous effects of blood feud. In contrast and influenced, perhaps, by the widespread tenth-century obsession with the social consequences of property crime, theft is more a matter for punishment. Surprisingly, perhaps, robbery with violence attracts lesser penalties than common theft, being regarded as less stealthy. Truth, in the modern legal sense applied in Scottish and French law, for example, would not be recognized as relevant in the Early Medieval legal process. Proof was demonstrated by oath and by the status of the oath-taker.

The laws relating to women, especially with regard to property and divorce, seem strikingly progressive. After puberty a woman 'is entitled to control what is hers'; after seven years of marriage, separating couples split their property in shares:

> It belongs to the woman to divide and to the man to choose. The pigs for the man and the sheep for the woman... Of the sons, two thirds to the father and one to the mother... The man is entitled to the upper stone of the quern, the woman to the lower... To the woman belong the pan and the trivet and the broad axe and the hedging bill and the ploughshare, and all the flax and the linseed, and the wool.[46]

Land was partible among sons and brothers, so that holdings must inevitably become smaller over time; but mill, weir and orchard might not be alienated from a kindred, nor divided. Appropriately, for a largely pastoral and overwhelmingly agricultural economy, detailed consideration is given to the values of all the beasts of field and waste: poultry, bees, hunting dogs, birds of prey and even cats. Hazelnut, oak, yew, beech and apple trees had specific values; similarly a lengthy list of household equipment and clothes. Even the various parts of the human body were defined and valued, not as items of trade but in case of claims for compensation, theft and damage. These were laws written by and for lawyers; they were not the edicts of a king; how far they reflect actual practice and behaviour is difficult to say. Collectively, they demonstrate an outstanding vigour in Welsh intellectual thought, drawing on very ancient custom: ideologically driven but fully self-conscious and responsive to a real, living world.

After the death of Óláfr and the arrival of *Kváran* in 941, and following the recapture of Danish Mercia in 942, Eadmund pressed his advantage. In the following year Constantín mac Áeda abdicated his throne after more than forty years, retiring to the monastic community at St Andrews in Fife, perhaps as its abbot. His eldest son and presumed heir, Cellach, had been killed at *Brunanburh*. Another son, Ildulb, seems to have been too young to succeed and one might surmise that Constantín's retirement was, therefore, forced by his successor, Mael Coluim mac Domnall. Mael Coluim's father had been Constantín's predecessor, so he may have been heir presumptive by customary arrangement, but his rise to power might also have been an opportunistic response to Constantín's failure at *Brunanburh*. It is impossible to say, but it is difficult to see this middle-aged man emerging from, as it were, nowhere. He would rule Alba for eleven years.

Between the new king of Alba and the twenty-three-year-old king of Wessex lay the territories of Cumbria/Strathclyde under Dyfnwal (the Brittonic equivalent of Gaelic 'Domnall'), Bernicia under an unknown *dux*; and two kings of Northumbria: *Kváran* and Rögnvaldr. Every version of the *Chronicle* records that in 944 Eadmund 'brought all of Northumbria under his sway, and drove out two kings Anlaf Sihtricson (that is, *Kváran*) and Raegnald Guthfrithson (Rögnvaldr)'. Once again, it is unclear from this account if King Eadmund himself mounted a military campaign; but the later tenth-century chronicler Æðelweard offers intriguing extra detail:

> After the passage of the seventh year [of Eadmund's reign] [Arch]bishop Wulfstan and the ealdorman (*dux*) of Mercia expelled certain traitors, that is to say Raegnald and Anlaf [*Kváran*], from the city of York, and reduced them to submission to the king.[47]

Archbishop Wulfstan had been an ally of Óláfr. If Æðelweard's testimony is to be trusted, that alliance did not extend to his two successors, whom he was prepared to sacrifice for his own political ends. As for the Mercian ealdorman, Alex Woolf suggests that he may be identified as Æðelstan the so-called 'half-king', variously *comes* or *dux* in charter attestations between 938 and 956, who seems to have been appointed as regent in East Anglia from about 932.[48] Eadmund's judgement of character and his intuitive sense of when to deploy military force and political pressure are impressive testimony to his education in statesmanship. The Anglo-Saxon chronicler made sure that he got the credit.

A year later, we know, the king himself travelled north on campaign, apparently safe in the knowledge that Northumbria and York, with its power-broking archbishop, were once again securely part of the West Saxon *imperium*. He visited the community at Chester le Street, where he conferred more gifts on St Cuthbert and repeated the promises of allegiance which his father had given with such effective results in 934. His army, too, contributed 60 pounds of silver coin to Cuthbert, while:

> He himself with his own hand placed two golden armlets and two Greek palls upon the holy body, granted peace and law better than any it had ever had to the whole territory of St Cuthbert, [and] confirmed the grant [of his father's charter].[49]

The relationship between saint and royal house cemented, Eadmund ravaged Strathclyde/Cumbria, according to the *Annales Cambriae* and the *Chronicle*. Roger of Wendover offers the name of Leolin, king of Dyfed, as a key ally in the campaign and Alex Woolf argues that this must be a mistake for Hywel: so it seems that the old West Saxon ally had been restored to favour.[50] Roger also records the grisly fate of the two sons of King Dyfnwal: blinded, so that they could not succeed their father (they may already have been hostages at the West Saxon court). After this brief campaign the Western British kingdom that stretched between Clyde and Eamont was ceded, or let, to Mael Coluim of Alba.

At the end of 945 King Eadmund, at twenty-four years old, could boast that he was, like his distinguished half-brother Æðelstan, overlord of all Britain south of the Forth–Clyde line. Less than six months later, on 26 May 946, he was stabbed to death at Pucklechurch, in Gloucestershire, by a man called Liofa, said to be a thief.[51]

THE ILLUSORY PRIZE

CHESTER LE STREET—FALLEN MINSTERS—
NEW TOWNS—SHIRES AND HUNDREDS—
EADRED, EIRÍKR, WULFSTAN—
EGIL SKALLAGRÍMSSON AGAIN—
BRITAIN IN THE 960S

12

ON THE WHOLE, THE COMMUNITY OF St Cuthbert survived the first Viking Age in good shape. Fleeing its original island home of Lindisfarne in the ninth century with the relics of its precious saint, its leaders supped with the devil in the shape of the Scandinavian Host and forged a new geography and identity south of the River Tyne.

Its bishops played a clever hand as brokers between the native Christian élite and the kings of York and were rewarded with royal protection and valuable estates which secured its economic future. In time, they won the favour of a great southern king, Æðelstan, who lavished gifts on them and promised the loyalty of his successors. The survival of the community's unique relics and of the famous Lindisfarne Gospels is surpassed in historical value only by the *Historia de Sancto Cuthberto*, a key text in tracing the fortunes of the Insular church from its seventh-century beginnings up until the Norman Conquest.

The small town of Chester le Street, where the community made its home for more than a century after 883 and where, some

52. SUPPING WITH THE DEVIL: mounted warrior on a cross fragment from St Cuthbert's church, Chester le Street.

time in the middle of the tenth century, the *Historia* was first compiled, might seem an unlikely setting for such a momentous narrative to be written. A Roman fort, *Concangis*, was constructed here in the first century AD on a rise above the confluence of the navigable River Wear* and the Cong burn which rises in the Pennines some miles to the west. Once a staging post on the Great North Road and a busy coal transhipment port, its industries have moved elsewhere.

Chester le Street, *Kuncacester*, obeys the fundamental rules of Early Medieval connectivity, forming a node, or interchange on the Insular travel network: a day's journey upstream from the sea at Wearmouth, the centre of an important early monastic estate. The road that crossed the burn, now buried beneath the town's Front Street, directly linked the River Tyne and its Hadrianic bridge, the *Pons Aelius,* to York, Lincoln and London. A few miles to the north another Roman road, known as the Wrekendike, branched off to the north-east towards the old Roman fort at *Arbeia*, Bede's monastery at Jarrow and a seventh-century royal harbour close to the mouth of the River Tyne. Not far to the west, running parallel with the Great North Road, is the line of Dere Street which, at Corbridge, meets the Tyne and its own metalled trans-Pennine route, Stanegate, thus linking the Cuthbert community with its important holdings in Cumbria.†

By the time that the *Historia* was written the Cuthbert community had lost or shed many of their lands in north Northumbria but sat at the centre of a large *territorium* in what is now County Durham. The *Kuncacester* establishment was more than just a squatter's camp: an impressive array of carved crosses (including one depicting a mounted warrior à la mode) survives in fragments to show that the community supported a sculpture workshop; and competent scribes (whatever King Ælfred might have

---

* A Brittonic name, from *Uisura*, meaning 'flowing water'. Watts 2004.
† See map, p. 322.

believed about the decline of Latinity) plied their trade here.

At about the time when the *Historia* was being compiled from records assiduously curated and embellished by St Cuthbert's clerics, one of them, Aldred, embarked on a project to translate the Lindisfarne Gospels into Old English and, since he did so by interpolating between the elegant lines of the original, the physical record of that achievement endures, as do his invaluable notes on the history of Anglo-Saxon England's most famous book and the first lengthy samples of written Northumbrian dialect.

Symeon, writing his *Libellus de Exordio* much later, after the community had moved to its permanent Durham home on a dramatic riverine peninsula five miles upstream, records that in the eleventh century the original 'wooden church' at *Kuncacester* was taken down and replaced in stone.[1] Within the walls of the

53.
ST CUTHBERT'S
CHURCH,
Chester le Street,
County Durham.
The Lindisfarne
community made
its home here
for a century after
about 883.

old Roman fort, then, lay an establishment capable of hosting the visits of kings and other dignitaries, of producing sculpture, with its own library and scriptorium. The mother church of north Northumbria lay at the heart of its estates, its bishops acting like secular lords receiving and consuming the renders of its tenants, tenaciously defending its ancient rights against all comers. Despite the neglect of its former patron kings at Bamburgh, the theft of its lands by native and foreign warlords and the loss of core territories, the institution founded by King Oswald and Bishop Aidan in 635 rode the tides of fate, adapting to reality and opportunity and expertly navigating the labyrinth of Early Medieval politics.

Since their heyday in the early eighth century hundreds of Insular minsters, originally élite communities of high-born monks and nuns following the rule of St Benedict and often playing a pastoral role among the believers on their estates, had exploited their status as central places dominating equally pivotal landscapes: on estuaries; where important roads crossed rivers; at natural harbours; not always on the most fertile land but with access to a range of resources on which their wealth and influence depended. Their entrepreneurial talents led to concentrations of labour and skills: to the founding and maintenance of *scriptoria* and vellum workshops, schools of sculpture and glazing, specialization in arable and stock-rearing; to mill engineering; to intellectual endeavour and the production, consumption and trading of marketable surplus. When they are excavated, some of these minster establishments look for all the world like small towns.

The histories of those minsters during the first Viking Age reflect regional fortunes. Some, especially vulnerable coastal communities like Lindisfarne, Jarrow and Iona, succumbed to the accumulated pressures of theft, violence and enslavement and declined terminally or were partially abandoned in the eighth and ninth centuries, only to be reborn in the later tenth or eleventh century.

Portmahomack, the most northerly of the coastal minsters, was put to sword and fire around the turn of the ninth century, its monks likely enslaved and taken off to markets in the Baltic for resale. Its skilled craftsmen and farmers were set to new endeavours, converting looted scrap metal into objects of more immediate secular value for international trade and producing grain and beef for its new lords, rather than calves for vellum. At various periods of the ninth century Fortriu was under the control of Picts, then Gaels, then the kings of Alba and perhaps, at times, under the direct control of the Norse earls of Orkney. One, and one only, of its bishops is known: Tuathal mac Artgusso, who died in 865, the year in which the *mycel here* arrived in East Anglia.[2] If Portmahomack were no longer a suitable site for his see, then Rosemarkie, at the mouth of the Moray Firth, where ecclesiastical sculpture was still being produced, might have retained its institutional functions into the reign of Constantín after 900. The Tarbat peninsula was, much later, the scene of a great clash between Thorfinnr Sigurðsson 'the Mighty', the eleventh-century Earl of Orkney and a king of Scotland, Karl 'Hundason', better known as Macbeth.[3]

Far to the south-west on the tidal River Clyde and at the head of an important east–west route through the lowlands to the River Forth, the community at Govan on the River Clyde survived and thrived because of its status as a royal cult site that continued to be patronized and endowed by the native élite. Their trading connections, to judge by its collection of hogback tomb covers, also enabled them to acquire the products of Norse workshops. A royal estate lying on the opposite bank at Partick may also have been a centre for the consumption and display of sculpture during the tenth century.[4]

The survival into the tenth century of a working minster at the British royal cult site of St David's, on the extreme western tip of Dyfed, is most convincingly demonstrated by the career of its one-time bishop, Asser, the scholar recruited by Ælfred to bolster his programme of literary and intellectual revival in the 880s. But his loyalties were divided as he was increasingly drawn into the West Saxon king's orbit. Asser records that Ælfred presented him with two Somerset minsters, at Congresbury and Banwell, together with a lengthy list of all their possessions. Later, the king:

> Unexpectedly granted me Exeter with all the jurisdiction
> pertaining to it in Saxon territory and in Cornwall... He then
> immediately gave me permission to ride out to those two
> minsters so well provided with goods of all sorts.[5]

Asser's enjoyment of the fruits of those minsters may have ensured their wealth and future prospects, but evidence that secular lords in the West Saxon heartlands were trading minsters as gifts reflects an inexorable process of secularization that increasingly turned former monastic communities into clerical churches, the fruits of whose wealth might be consumed by visiting lords or disposed of like cash assets. In an extreme case like Cheddar, Ælfred and his descendants were able gradually to convert a minster and nearby hunting lodge into a royal palace and estate centre whose minster was subsumed into the royal portfolio.

A minster had stood in the ruins of the former Roman *civitas* capital of the *Dumnonii* at Exeter since at least the seventh century, when its thriving school produced the indefatigable missionary Boniface. After the Host's withdrawal from Wareham in 876 and forced westward march they occupied the remains of the fortress at Exeter, defying Ælfred's attempts to dislodge them. It must have suggested itself early on in his defensive plans as the perfect physical and strategic site for a burh (of relatively modest size, assessed at 734 hides) and in the epic campaigns of 893 its garrison was able to resist one of the Channel fleets of the combined Scandinavian forces until a relieving force arrived under Ælfred's command.

It is not clear into whose hands the Exeter minster fell after Asser's death in 908 or 909; twenty years later it became a favourite recipient of King Æðelstan's favours during his period of alienation from the West Saxon royal minster at Winchester. He held councils here at Easter 928 (bringing his new Welsh *sub-reguli* with him) and again in 932; and William of Malmesbury offers a dubious story that in 927 he drove the Western Britons (i.e. the Cornish population) out of the city and refortified it with towers and stone walls, setting a new boundary on Wessex's frontier with the British at the River Tamar.[6] Æðelstan's fifth law code was issued here in about 931 and he was a substantial donor of a collection of important relics to the minster.[7] Exeter's minster survived, but not as its founders knew it.

In two thirds of the forts listed in the Burghal Hidage minsters like Exeter lay inside the walls or were situated close by them. The defences offered physical protection from raiders; and it is possible that some of the earliest burhs where ancient minsters stood, like Wareham, had already been protected by earthen ramparts constructed at the behest and expense of the church. Wareham, after all, had been taken and defended against West Saxon assault in 875, before the burghal system was conceived. It may even have provided one of the models, alongside original Mercian exemplars. If the benefit to minsters of protection was one edge of the sword, the other was the inevitable militarization of their immediate environs and the diversion of ecclesiastical resources to fending off, or paying off, raiders.

Those minsters that lay in lands ruled and settled by Scandinavian pirate-farmers generally saw their estates broken up, the land redistributed among the Host in reward for loyalty and service. In East Anglia no bishops are known from the period between the 860s and the 940s and, along with its organizational framework, the church lost many communities and large swathes of land. Even here, though, minsters survived. The community at the seventh-century foundation of Ely, an island on the River Great Ouse deep in the Cambridgeshire fenlands, compiling their history half a millennium later, remembered how, in the aftermath of the Host's arrival in the 860s, the monastery had been burned down, the precious sarcophagus of the founding saint Æðelðryth defiled, their monks and nuns massacred or enslaved:

> And thus the place lay in a miserable state, totally deprived of the observance of the divine office... No one remained to carry out ministry. In the end, there returned after some years eight of the very clerics who were despoiled, and some of them remained, after the lapse of many years, in decrepit old age until the time of King Eadred. Patching up the aisles of the church as best they could at a time of such calamity, they carried out due observance of the divine office.[8]

We should swallow the detail of this story with a spoonful of scepticism, if for no other reason than that any monks surviving from the 860s would have been more than a hundred years old by the beginning of the reign of King Eadred, Eadmund's brother and successor in 946. In reality it serves as mere prologue to the more historical record of the minster's refounding in the time of Eadmund's second son, King Eadgar (959–975). Nevertheless, the process of restoration of at least some of its former lands reflects, if nothing else, the tenacious memory and record-keeping of those who regarded themselves as its spiritual keepers, able to testify to what had formerly belonged to St Æðelðryth, like their counterparts in Chester le Street.

More convincing, and not much less dramatic, is evidence from the same source for a royal minster at Horningsea, a few miles upstream from Ely, close to the Danish stronghold at Cambridge. The record in the *Liber Eliensis* of a dispute over the minster's legitimate holdings, a marvellous tale of stolen daggers, complicit priests and red-handed apprehension by lawmen, seems to refer to a genuine charter of King Eadweard (900–924) of a gift of five hides in Horningsea and two at Eye to the priest, one Cenwold, who ministered to the clerical community there.[9] If nothing else it militates against the idea of the wholesale destruction of the East Anglian church at the hands of the Host. And it is salutary to remember that the cult of the Host's most celebrated victim, the martyred King Eadmund, was fostered by and thrived under East Anglia's Danish rulers.

If minsters looked increasingly like secular economic institutions, often incorporated into the military and institutional framework of the West Saxon state, from the early tenth century onwards they were also key components in urbanization and the rapid expansion of the Insular economies. The minsters had long enjoyed the fruits of trade; the archbishops of York and Canterbury minted their own coins and claimed rights similar to those of kings over tolls and the perquisites of élite international trade. The document confirming Worcester's new status under Æðelred and Æðelflæd* shows how closely linked were the interests of church, market, ealdorman and king.

In Wessex the new burhs were slow to develop as towns and it was not until the middle of the tenth century that many of them emerged as fully urban markets. By then there is a compelling alignment of burhs and minsters with the mints that allow us to track the development of economic prosperity. David Hill, compiler of the indispensable *Atlas of Anglo-Saxon England*, is at pains to show how, from the earliest inception of the burghal system, there was a distinction between fort and town.[10] Smaller burhs enclosing less than 16 acres did not develop into urban centres, while the early southern burhs that became towns— London, Winchester, Canterbury, York, Rochester, Shaftesbury, Gloucester, Bath and Christchurch—all had existing minsters; and all but the last of these was also the site of a mint. The

* See above, p. 185.

relationship between early church foundations and productive sites is evident, too. Minster communities concentrated large labour forces and enjoyed wide-ranging portfolios of agricultural and woodland resources. They innovated, specialized, invested, produced and traded at local, regional and international scales. They often occupied key locations on navigable rivers and Roman roads. Not for nothing were their patrons and lords interested (in both senses) in minsters' economic potential. In the middle of the ninth century, after the demise of the coastal trading settlements, minsters were the largest and most developed of Insular settlements.

The relationship between the church and urban development has another intriguing strand. The centres of early saints' cults attracted pilgrims in large numbers. Those churches that successfully nurtured their cults might expect to enjoy the donations of grateful, or hopeful, petitioners to their saint. And, where large numbers of people congregated, fairs and markets developed to relieve them of their surplus wealth. Churches with important cults often developed urban characteristics alongside productivity in agriculture and trade in goods. They 'exported' the fame and virtues of their saints. Markets and/or fairs and churches occur in very close proximity in a number of towns: at St Albans, Darlington, Southwark, Oundle, Beverley and elsewhere.[11]

Tenth-century Lincoln may have supported thirty churches.[12] Up to a dozen of these seem to have stood close to market places associated with saints such as the ever-popular Cuthbert, Botolph and Martin of Tours, whose name appears on that intriguing series of Lincoln-minted coins. Whether any relics (bona fide or not) of the great saints were held by the churches bearing their names is a moot point. But there are established links between what one might call special interest groups and their holy patrons. Martin looked after beggars; Botolph after travellers.

In Ælfred's Britain moneyers operated from London, Canterbury, Winchester, Exeter, Gloucester, Leicester, Lincoln and York, the latter three under the entrepreneurial influence of Danish kings or jarls. In the time of his grandson, Æðelstan, more than thirty mints existed, of which London and Chester were the most prolific by far.[13] By the time of the Domesday survey of 1086 more than fifty towns had produced coins. London alone had more than ten moneyers at any one time. If one wants to rank the Insular towns by their coinage production (as good a measure as any), London is followed distantly by Lincoln, then York, Winchester, Chester, Thetford, Exeter, Stamford, Canterbury, Norwich, Southwark and Oxford, in that order. Four of these towns (Lincoln, Thetford, Norwich and Stamford) were substantially created under Danish lordship. The impressive self-confidence of Ælfred's heirs in Wessex and the south was matched by that of the much more obscure but no less influential jarls and *duces* of East Anglia and East Mercia, whose promotion of production and trade, unfettered perhaps by the conservative institutions and entrenched interests of southern lordship, provided much of the inspiration for West Saxon success and fuelled a new age of economic expansion through its towns and trading links.

The burhs founded as towns in the late ninth and early tenth centuries by Ælfred and his children did not, at first, succeed as urban centres. International and internal trade was stagnant. The supply of bullion accumulated by invading and defending armies seems to have been hoarded: to avoid theft and taxes and because, perhaps, there was nothing material to spend it on. The evidence from wills suggests that only after the middle of the tenth century did those who had accumulated significant quantities of loot in the campaigns of the 910s and later begin to bequeath it to a generation willing to open their lead chests and spend.[14]

The release of large amounts of cash coincided with the discovery of significant new silver deposits in Germany, with a revival of cross-Channel trade* and with the monastic reform movement under King Eadgar. Churches were newly built or rebuilt. In the burhs, tenements and cross streets began to fill in and new workshops for pottery, metal- and leather-working were established. The Danelaw territories of Lincolnshire, Norfolk and Suffolk were the most prosperous in lowland Britain, a function not just of entrepreneurial savvy and proximity to Continental markets but also, perhaps, because of the earlier fragmentation of great estates which allowed smaller, more enterprising landowners to exploit rural resources and adopt new technologies like the mouldboard plough.†

Once again lowland Britain's accessibility, its abundant natural resources and excellent farmland fostered prosperity, and its kings sought with varying degrees of success to impose consistent rules for the conduct of trade, the resolution of disputes and the stability and quality of coinage. Their own wealth and power increased with the sophistication of state institutions and with the surplus of the land.

The concern of Æðelstan and his successors to legislate for the control of regional and local institutions is preserved in a document dating from the middle decades of the tenth century called the *Hundred Ordinance*. The need for such regulation arose from the process by which Mercian territories, both west and east, of *Deniscan* and *Angelcynn* alike, were divided into shires, each based on a burh. Wessex had long since been 'shired', but its old shire centres, the royal *vills* at Dorchester, Somerton, Wilton and *Hamtun*, largely lost their relevance in Ælfred's defensive scheme, while the south-eastern counties retained older tribal and

---

* Dorestad, for example, suffered terminal decline in the late ninth century, only to be replaced in the tenth century by a site close by at Tiel at the confluence of the Rivers Waal and Linge.

† The mouldboard is a curved plate that turns the sod over after it has been cut and split by the share and coulter.

traditional centres. In the lands of the Danelaw fortified towns became the centres of fiscal administration and of the delivery of renders and justice.

With the exception of Stamford, which did not become a shire centre, the logic is impeccable: Leicestershire, Lincolnshire, Nottinghamshire and Derbyshire were the lands controlled by such *duces* or jarls as Urm, the man who helped Óláfr on his Midland campaign of 941 and whose English-named daughter married the Norse king. The jarls were equated with ealdormen by Æðelstan, if we accept the persuasive testimony of his charter witness lists, and the size of their territories gave the new shires a natural congruence with those of Wessex and the south. Cambridgeshire, Bedfordshire, Huntingdonshire, Oxfordshire and Warwickshire all, similarly, emerged as the territories at whose centres lay fortified towns. West Mercia is a more complex case and an argument has been made by David Hill and others that ancient polities, the folk territories of Hwicce, *Magonsæte*, *Wrocansæte* and *Arosætna*, were overridden by deliberate policy; and Eadweard is the favoured culprit.[15] Thus, the ancient Mercian capital at Tamworth did not become a shire town but was left stranded on the margins of Staffordshire and Warwickshire.

Æðelstan's *London Ordinance*, the *Friðgegyldum*,* apparently set up for the benefit of its bishops and reeves, introduces hundred-men and the idea of collective responsibility for the execution of justice in London's hinterland. The natural extension of this scheme to the hundredal divisions from which levies were raised to garrison the shire burhs and render burghal dues to them may have been conceived at the same time. There is no doubting its centralizing motivation, its design to overcome and overwhelm the inherent regionality of the lands south of the Humber.

---

* *VI Æðelstan*: see above, Chapter 11.

The hundred itself was nominally an area assessed at 100 hides for rendering purposes, with a meeting place and *vill* at its centre, a minster, a market place and a cemetery for judicial executions.[16] In practice, no such uniformity existed. At the time of the Domesday survey, Leicestershire comprised six hundreds, Devonshire thirty-two. Lincolnshire and Yorkshire were so large that they required an additional tier of administration, the third part, or Thrithing (Old Norse *þriðjungr*), which became the familiar Ridings. Neither they, nor the shires of the Danelaw, conformed to the hundredal ideal—instead, they were administered in equivalents called Wapentakes, from Old Norse *vápn-atak*, a 'taking of weapons'. The distinctness of the language is also reflected in separate legal customs in those areas long subject to Scandinavian influence, not least of which is the recognition by contemporaries and later Anglo-Norman legislators of 'the Danelaw' itself.[17]

In the Danelaw, compensation paid to a lord for the murder of one of his men varied with the dead man's rank, not that of his lord. Another regional peculiarity was the fine called *lahslit*, a cover-all penalty applied to a variety of offences. I have already made mention of a Norse flavour to legal and fiscal provisions in Cheshire and Lancashire.*

Between Northumbria, the lands of the Five Boroughs and East Anglia considerable internal variation reflected the historical evolutions of those regions and their fortunes under Danish and Norse rule. Since their legislators did not leave written *coda*, much of the evidence for direct Scandinavian influence comes from Southern kings' attempts to rationalize and streamline law across the geographical divide. King Æðelred II acknowledged the problem in his so-called *Wantage Code* of about 997, written when England was under sustained attack from a new wave

---

* See above, Chapter 7, in relation to Ingimund's invasion of Cheshire.

of Scandinavian armies.* That rationalization did not preclude borrowing from Scandinavian prototypes. In among the punitive fines for various crimes is a bold precedent:

> A meeting is to be held in each wapentake, and the twelve leading thegns, and with them the reeve, are to come forward and swear on the relics that are put into their hands that they will accuse no innocent man nor conceal any guilty one.

This is generally held to enshrine the concept of a jury system, unknown in English law before this date but secure in its Scandinavian origins.[18] A subsequent clause outlines, also for the first time, the principle that when the twelve thegns of the jury cannot agree, a majority verdict of eight to four is sufficient to secure a conviction. More than a century of Danish and Norse rule and settlement had left an indelible stamp on Insular law and customs.

Regional variations in customary law and administration were not confined to areas of mixed population. In Kent and Sussex much more ancient territorial units survived, of lathes and rapes, six in each county. And across the territories of the *Angelcynn* the concentration of hundredal courts at meeting places of evident antiquity, such as the Ecgberht's Stone and Iley Oak mentioned in the account of Ælfred's Edington campaign of 878, suggests that such institutions emerged from an earlier customary system of local and regional meeting places and folk-courts, perhaps convened on the quarter days to signal an inalienable bond between the invariable turn of the season's wheel and the lives of thegn, *ceorl* and slave.

In the British kingdoms of the west, *cantrefi* (a *cantref* is literally 'a hundred townships'), rough equivalents of the shires, with *commotes* ('neighbourhoods') beneath them, are suggestive of similarities in administration; but exact equivalence is not possible

---

* *III Æðelred.* The text of the code is translated in *EHD* Charters and laws 43. Whitelock 1979, 439.

or appropriate. In Scotland, the administrative system is frustratingly obscure, although the *davach*, perhaps Pictish in origin, seems to have been a measure of land that could support so many oxen. In what became Northumberland a different sort of shire administration persisted, uniquely tied to the rule of its lords at Bamburgh. South of the Tyne, the County Palatine of Durham was formed out of the buffer state created by the community of St Cuthbert.

In the *Hundred Ordinance* Eadmund, or one of his close successors, legislated for the meeting of a hundred court (*hundred-gemot*) every four weeks at which 'each man is to do justice to the other'.* Its clauses, like those of the *Dunsæte ordinance* and the *Friðgegyldum*, are concerned with the apprehension of thieves, especially of cattle, with compensation for victims and fines for contempt of the court. In all aspects of Early Medieval law-giving there is a strong sense of ideology expressed: kings envisaged a model state, with themselves at the law-giving apex of a social pyramid. The ideal may have differed greatly from reality. Rarely, if ever, were kings' laws and ordinances cited in the judicial cases for which we have evidence.

The kings of the tenth century conceived of a set of unifying, centralizing ideals, if not a single indivisible kingdom, expressed in the confident imagery and inscriptions on their coins, and in their law codes and land grants. But it was an illusory prize, offered anciently by the Venerable Bede to the virtuous, martial king who could map the universality of the Christian kingdom onto the *terra firma* of political reality. At each throw of the dice the southern overlords of the tenth century believed themselves to have *imperium* over the *Angelcynn* in their grasp, only to suffer the frustrations of their forbears. Britain remained resolutely regional in identity and affinities.

---

* Shire courts met twice a year under the auspices of, at first, the ealdorman and bishop and, later, the shire-reeve.

❀

In the aftermath of King Eadmund's murder in 946, his brother
Eadred succeeded to the throne. His first grant, a so-called 'cor-
onation-gift' of land in Northamptonshire, made at Kingston
upon Thames to a thegn called Wulfric, describes him as 'king
and ruler to the sovereignty of the quadripartite rule'. As the rest
of the text makes clear, the four kingdoms and peoples in question were the Anglo-Saxons, the Northumbrians, the pagans
(meaning the Norse of Cheshire and Lancashire rather than the
Christian Danes of East Mercia and East Anglia) and the Britons
of Wales and Cornwall.[19] The list of witnesses at this inaugural
council shows a continuity of policy: the two archbishops, Oda
(the naturalized Dane) and Wulfstan; Ðeodred, the bishop of
London; various other bishops and abbots; then Hywel Dda and
Morgan, son of King Owain of Gwent (the latter a royal hostage,
perhaps), four ealdormen and four Danish jarls, including Urm.

The new king's attentions were immediately drawn to events
in the North. Later in the same year, 946, he was able, in the
words of the *Chronicle*, to 'reduce all Northumbria to subjection',
after which the Scots 'gave him oaths and promised to do his will
in all things'.[20] His *imperium* was sealed by treaty the following
year at Tanshelf, near Castleford (*Ceaster forda*), an old crossing point of the River Aire some 15 miles (24 km) north of the
Don on the traditional border line between Mercia and southern
Northumbria. Here Archbishop Wulfstan and all the councillors
of the Northumbrians submitted to him. That, at least, is the official version contained in the *Chronicle*, whose editorial aim was
to establish that Northumbria naturally belonged under West
Saxon rule and that deviation from that narrative constituted
either rebellion or base ingratitude. The truth may be a little
more obscure; the politics are not.

Kváran's expulsion from York in 944 had left southern

Northumbria without a ruler. Eiríkr, son of Haraldr, is first mentioned in two versions of the *Chronicle* four years later; the Worcester manuscript says that by this year the Men of York had accepted him as their king and that Eadred mounted a punitive campaign against the Northumbrians in response. Eiríkr also appears, more allusively, in the life of a Scottish saint, Cathróe (of Metz) who, in the middle years of that decade, happened to be making his way south with the intention of embarking on a pilgrimage to Rome. The account of that journey places the saint at the court of both Constantín (who had abdicated in 943) and Eadmund; so his supposed visit to York, at which he was introduced to Eiríkr by virtue of Eirík's marriage to one of Cathróe's kinswomen, must have taken place before 943.[21]

Placing Eiríkr in York as early as 943 is not in itself problematic—he may have been a protégé of *Kváran*'s. Archbishop Wulfstan then plays the part of his ambassador at Tanshelf, continuing his own career of professionally ambiguous affinities. Fusing the account in the saint's *Vita* with the *Chronicle* does, however, create two problems for historians. Firstly, there is the identity of Eiríkr, often and conveniently associated with the Eiríkr *blóðøx* familiar from the sagas, whose running feud with Egil makes for such good reading. York's Eiríkr is the son of a Haraldr, just as Eiríkr *blóðøx* was the son of Haraldr *Hárfagri*. But that anti-hero's wife was called Gunnhildr, and she is not likely to have been a Gaelic kinswoman of Cathróe. Historians Clare Downham and Alex Woolf suspect a conflation of two historical figures, of whom the York variant was another grandson of Ívarr and, therefore, Irish Norse rather than Norwegian.[22] The confusion is not helped by the fact that the Egil of the eponymous *Saga* turns up at York and reignites the feud with his nemesis.

Whatever complexities underlie the events of 946–947, we know that Eadred took an army north in the year after the convention at Tanshelf and destroyed one of Archbishop Wulfstan's prize assets, the ancient and wealthy minster complex at Ripon, by fire in a punitive raid.* He did not get away scot-free; the Men of York caught up with his returning army as it recrossed the Aire at Castleford, and destroyed its rear. Even so, Eadred was able to force submission and reparations from the Northumbrians and a promise that they would expel Eiríkr.†

That departure did not signal the end of Northumbria's long-standing relationship with Irish Norse kings, the dynasty of the great Ívarr. The *Chronicle* entry for 949 blandly records the return of Óláfr *Kváran* from Dublin, where he had spent the previous few years in competition for the kingship with his cousin, Blákári Guðrøðsson. With the latter's death in 948 and the convenient expulsion of Eiríkr the same year, *Kváran* was received in York once more. The arch-operator, Wulfstan, transferred his allegiance accordingly; but he was still attending Eadred's councils in 949, possibly by this time acting formally as ambassador on *Kváran*'s behalf.

There is little doubt that kingship in York, or Lincoln, or the Five Boroughs, meant something rather different from its Mercian or West Saxon counterpart. Germanic kingship had emerged from the custom of appointing a leader 'in time of war'. The development of state institutions giving the king law-making, fiscal and administrative rights was a seventh-century phenomenon that went hand in hand with the emergence of the church as a legitimizing, powerful institution in its own right. The eternal triangle of bookland, church and kingship through which the Insular states functioned depended on that enduring relationship, steeped in rationality and mutual dependence.

In York, it seems, the church survived in robust good health;

---

* The minster survived as an institution; so, miraculously, does the crypt built by another troublesome priest, St Wilfrid, in the late seventh century. *ASC* 'D' Worcester MS.

† The expulsion is recorded in the northern annal *Historia Regum* under 950.

but its relationship with Norse warlords was ambivalent. The Cuthbert community had persuaded successive kings of York (if that is what they were) of the value of mutual support. The archbishops seem to have been able to effect a similar arrangement for themselves; but it is hard to accept the idea that Rögnvaldr, Óláfr and their like ruled over the lands north of the Humber in the way that their southern counterparts did. They do not appear to have been enthusiastic legislators. They must have overseen or allowed the fragmentation of many very large ecclesiastical estates and, although they often issued coinage from their mints, one doubts whether they possessed the administrative equivalent of the civil service professionalized by the West Saxon kings, with hierarchies of *portgerefa*, shire reeve, ealdorman and, particularly, of bishop. There is no northern equivalent of a royal secretary like Æðelstan 'A'. That is not to say that their rule was ineffective, or that they did not see the virtues of the model Christian state. But they left no enduring ruling dynasty; no stable succession holding office by divine right; no written record of their functions or achievements.

In East Mercia and East Anglia it seems as though the hierarchy of lordship followed a model comprising the dependent unfree, free farmers or sokemen, thegns, *holds* and jarls. The latter, of whom we know more than half a dozen names, appear to have controlled the *territoria* based on their towns (including the Five Boroughs) as more or less independent fiefdoms, each capable of autonomous military action and economic policy but evidently very often working co-operatively and in mutual support. The distinctiveness of legal and administrative institutions in the Midlands shows not that the jarls sought cultural conquest but that they were capable, effective rulers, economically successful and able to impose a king's peace on those regions that would become the shires of Midland England. They adapted to and modified indigenous customs and became, in time, patrons of a revived church as well as promulgators of innovative law. We have no record at all of civil war or rebellion during the nearly hundred years of their effective rule. The lords of Goltho and Flixborough were left alone, for the most part, to get on with it.

The greatest of the early Welsh kings, Hywel Dda, died in 950. He was succeeded in Deheubarth, the south and west of Wales, by his son Owain, who was able to retain control of Powys on the Mercian border; but Gwynedd was won back by the sons of Idwal Foel who, two years later, ravaged Gwent: Welsh unification was just as illusory for the dynasty of Rhodri Mawr as a kingdom of England was for that of Ælfred.

In the north, Mael Coluim mac Domnall felt sufficiently confident of his military power to raid as far south as the River Tees, according to a not altogether straightforward entry in the *Chronicle of the Kings of Alba* for 950.[23] The raid, in which the Men of Alba 'carried off many people and many droves of cattle', does not feature in the *Historia de Sancto Cuthberto*, whose annalist recorded no entries between the reign of Eadmund and his grandson Æðelred II. The raid was, perhaps, designed to test the military strength of Northumbria. The brevity of the contemporary record may well mask complex internal politics. Two years later the *Annals of Ulster* record a battle between 'the Men of Alba and the Britons [of Strathclyde] and the English [the lords of Bamburgh, perhaps]' against the foreigners (that is, the Irish Norse). If dependable, this is the faint echo of a layer of alliances that historians might otherwise not suspect. If the Irish Norse of this conflict were, in fact, the forces of *Kváran* and the Men of York, the fallout seems to have been his repudiation by the Northumbrians. *Kváran* returned once more to Dublin and, after a long martial career, retired improbably to Iona, where he died in 980.

Kváran's second expulsion from York was followed by Eirík's return. Whatever complex politics lie behind these events, Archbishop Wulfstan now found himself, for once, the victim.

According to the Worcester version of the *Anglo-Saxon Chronicle* he was imprisoned by King Eadred in an unidentified stronghold called *Iudanburh* 'because he had been frequently accused to the king.'[24] Eadred's impatience at his double-dealing, or the factional gossip of his court, had rendered to Wulfstan the same fate as Ripon's founder, St Wilfrid, under an equally exasperated king in the seventh century. Unlike St Dunstan, he was not able to produce a timely miracle to win back the king's favour at the last minute.

Eirík's return to York brought about his re-acquaintance with the colourful career of the warrior-poet and troublemaker Egil Skallagrímsson. In *Egil's Saga*, Eiríkr (*blóðøx*) is exiled from Norway by his brother Hákon, Æðelstan's foster-son, and makes his way south through Scotland, arriving in York while Æðelstan is

54.
IN YORK,
the warrior-poet
Egil Skallagrímsson
and his antagonist
Eiríkr were
re-acquainted.
Mounted warrior
from St Andrew's
church, Andreas,
Isle of Man.

still king. Egil, meanwhile, is conveniently placed by the composer of the saga on a ship, also heading for England and intent on renewing his relationship with his former patron Æðelstan.* Instead, his ship founders at the mouth of the River Humber where the crew, alive but battered, manage to get ashore. Now Egil finds that he has landed not in the kingdom of his former patron, who is in any case long dead, but in that of his enemy, for Eiríkr rules in York with his wife Gunnhildr. But he also hears that his brother-in-law Arinbjorn, an intimate of Eirík's, is with the Norse king in York.

Without the means to sail home Egil determines to go there and have it out with Eiríkr. He makes his way to Arinbjorn's house and pleads his case to be reconciled with the king. Arinbjorn agrees to petition on his behalf and, together with ten armed men, they go to the king's hall. Egil humbles himself before the great warrior, taking Eirík's foot in his hand and offering up an impromptu verse:

> I have travelled on the sea-god's steed
> A long and turbulent wave-path
> To visit the one who sits
> In command of the English land.
> In great boldness the shaker
> Of the wound-flaming sword
> Has met the mainstay of King Harald's line.[25]

Eiríkr is unimpressed; and, moreover, his implacable wife Gunnhildr demands that Egil be executed immediately. Arinbjorn pleads Egil's case to be heard again the following morning, and Eiríkr acquiesces. Arinbjorn's advice to Egil is to compose a great

---

* Scholars have long recognized that the prose narrative of the saga is largely a contrivance to link verses of skaldic poetry and create a coherent story of them. The historicity and plausibility of the saga is heavily compromised, but seems to retain substantial elements of folk-history which often form our only potential sources for these events. Readers must judge their value for themselves.

verse of praise to the king before morning: it is his only chance for mercy. In the night Egil's poetic musings are interrupted by a shape-shifter in the form of a swallow, chirping at his window; but at length he composes and then memorizes the praise poem, which he duly delivers the following morning. One imagines a hall bristling with tension and anticipation, crowded and hushed as the two antagonists settle their famous and long-standing feud not with swords and axes but with fine words and reasoning.

Nothing more perfectly captures the essence of the Scandinavian world, poised between violent destruction and the creative arts, between blood-rush, love of poetry and cool judgement:

> West over water I fared
> Bearing poetry's praise to the shore
> Of the war-god's heart.[26]

Egil employs the full palette of poetic battle-metaphor and simile in praising the king's great and bloody deeds. Eirík's sword is the 'battle-sun' or 'wound-digger'; dead men are Oðin's forest of oaks, felled by warrior's axe; corpses are eagles' food:

> Like bees, arrows flew
> From his drawn bow of yew.
> Eric fed flesh
> To the wolf afresh.

Like all great kings in Germanic and Atlantic cultures, Eirík's bellicosity is matched by magnanimity and the generosity of the ring-giver. He hands out gold by the fistful, like sand; distributes shields and brooches far and wide.

The praise of great poets was prized by warlords across the ethnic and linguistic spectra of the Atlantic west: a universal language of approbation, respect and loyalty. Likewise, the generosity of the poet must be rewarded, if not in treasure then in the gift of clemency. Eiríkr grudgingly accepts Egil's skilled verses: he may leave with his head still attached. The gift of life, in return, requires more praise from the reprieved warrior-poet:

> Ugly as my head may be
> The cliff my helmet rests upon,
> I am not loath
> To accept it from the king.
> Where is the man who ever
> Received a finer gift
> From a noble-minded
> Son of a great ruler?[27]

The aftermath of this legendary encounter speaks, if possible, even more eloquent testimony to the social mechanisms by which native and incomer were able to co-exist and integrate. Egil, leaving Eirík's kingdom under his grudging protection, exchanges gifts with his saviour, Arinbjorn, whose own reputation must have been enhanced by such skilful diplomacy. They part as good friends. The *Saga* tells us, then, that Egil's crew stayed behind, to trade the goods that they had brought with them in Jorvík's markets under Arinbjorn's watchful eye. No doubt the artisans and traders of that city were eager to see what exotic goods they had to offer.

In the event, Eirík's end came sooner than that of the erstwhile poetic troublemaker. In 954 the Northumbrians drove him from their kingdom; Northumbria submitted to Eadred and Archbishop Wulfstan was restored to episcopal dignity—this time of a less contentious, southern bishopric at Dorchester on Thames. Oswulf, the Lord of Bamburgh, was given the power of a *subregulus* over the lands north of the Humber. Only Roger of Wendover offers the detail of Eirík's fate, telling of a Bernician coup sponsored by the king of the West Saxons:

> King Eric was treacherously killed by Earl Maccus in a certain lonely place which is called Stainmore, with his son Haeric and his brother Ragnald, betrayed by Earl Oswulf; and then afterwards King Eadred ruled in these districts.[28]

Stainmore is the east–west pass on the old Roman route across the Pennines between Cumbria and Yorkshire, now the A66: a grim, bleak place to end a life. Eiríkr had no successor in York or the lands north of the Humber.

The end of the Scandinavian kingdom of York and the final unification of a kingdom that might be called England seems a reasonable place to draw a line under a narrative of the Viking Age. But the truth is, that narrative does not end in 954. On Eadred's death a year later* the kingdom was disputed between his sons Eadwig and Eadgar, with the Watling Street line once again conceived as a possible frontier. Only after 959 can Eadgar be said to have ruled over something resembling a kingdom of England. Twenty years later Scandinavian raids resumed. From 991 English kings once again paid tribute to Viking warlords; burhs were refortified or constructed *de novo*. Two kings of England in the early eleventh century were Danish. In 1066 further invasion attempts were launched. The first, led by the legendary Norwegian warrior King Haraldr *harðráði*, failed to overcome a desperate English defence in the North, at Stamford Bridge. The other, led by William of Normandy, descendant of the Viking chief Hrólfr, was conspicuously successful at Hastings.

In the 960s a trader crossing the Channel from Rouen to Britain in a smallish seagoing vessel, a *faering*, might carry a cargo of lava quern stones, as we know the Graveney boat did when it sank sometime in the tenth century.† The craft would accommodate one or two passengers, perhaps clerics bringing news of the

---

* Among many generous bequests he left 'his people 1600 pounds to the end that they may redeem themselves from a famine and from a heathen army if they need'. *EHD* 107. Whitelock 1979, 555.

† See Chapter 2, p. 74.

55. 'OHTHERE TOLD HIS LORD, King Ælfred, that he lived the furthest north of all Norwegians...' The contents of a reconstructed cargo vessel at Roskilde Ship Museum, Denmark.

monastic reform movement in Francia to sympathetic clerics like Dunstan, recently bishop of London and about to be elevated to the archiepiscopal see at Canterbury.

The *færing* passing up the broad, silty estuary of the Thames would land not at the deserted strand of *Lundenwic*, the defunct and largely empty trading settlement of the eighth century, but at wharves a mile or so downstream at *Lundenburg*. There may by now have been a wooden bridge spanning the river here, joining the defended burhs on either side at Southwark and in the old Roman city. Boats might moor at one of the stathes constructed in the late ninth century—at *Æðeredes hyd*, perhaps, on what is now Thames Street, before their skippers presented themselves to the *portgerefa* to state their business and pay their tolls.

Ælfred's refounding of the city after 886, with military, political and economic motives in mind, had borne fruit. Markets now existed along Cheapside* and, perhaps, at Aldgate. The church built long ago by the first Roman missionaries of the English church at *Paulesbyrig* was now sufficiently large and important that King Æðelred II would be buried there in 1016. As we know from Æðelstan's *London Ordinance*, the reeves and bishop of the burh were sufficiently jealous of their rights and attuned to the benefits of peaceful trade that they had organized themselves into a guild to protect their interests.

More trading potential lay upriver. Exchanging quern stones and Rhineland silver for King Eadgar's pennies whose portrait bore the imprimatur of the late Anglo-Saxon state, the merchant would now find himself within a single economic entity, with a single coinage and, in theory at least, a single set of rules governing his opportunities and responsibilities. He could not trade on a Sunday, for example—at least, not without a sweetener to the reeve.

A hundred and fifty years previously, at the beginning of the Viking Age, a *færing* continuing upriver would have passed minsters at Kingston, Chertsey and Dorchester. Kingston was now a favoured site for the inauguration of kings; Chertsey lay, if not abandoned and ruined, then dormant, awaiting its refounding in 964. The trader's passengers might have taken more than passing interest in its potential.

The Viking stronghold at Reading, now four generations old, must have been no more than a grassy embankment by the river, a curiosity. Further along the Thames, past fish traps, flash weirs and increasing numbers of water mills, lay the indomitable and enduring strongholds of the Ælfredan project: Sashes Island (*Sceaftessige*: Sceaf's Isle), Wallingford and Oxford, controlling

---

* The Old English word *ceap*, like the surname Chapman and the Norse variant Kaup, as in Kaupang and Kopeland, identifies the site or profession of trading, markets and purchase.

passage along the great trading corridor and taking tolls off merchants. By the 960s these burhs were truly towns, their road frontages so desirable that cross streets were now filling the spaces inside the walls, giving them their characteristic gridiron plans. The trader must make himself known to the *portgerefa* and, probably, distribute a few choice gifts and the soft currency of news and downriver gossip, to oil the wheels of commerce.

At the farthest navigable reach of the river stood its last burh, Cricklade, one of those which never developed into a town despite its proximity to a network of roads leading in all directions. Now, the traveller wishing to head north and east into less familiar territory must journey overland: no navigable river crosses England's timeless internal boundary. A day's walk from Cricklade would bring the traveller to Cirencester, to where Guðrum's defeated Viking army retreated in 878 after Edington; where the Roman amphitheatre must still have been visible and where royal councils (and the tax gatherers so hated by the poet of the *Armes Prydein Fawr*) met in the tenth century. From here roads led along the Fosse Way south-west to Exeter or north-east towards Leicester and Lincoln. Another ancient road led to the burh at Gloucester, where the Mercian royal mausoleum stood in its minster and whence vessels might ply up and down the River Severn, with ferrymen taking passengers over into the British kingdoms of Gwent and Morgannwg.

I will suppose that my hypothetical trader chooses a route just north of east, along *Akemennestraete* and at Bicester, where an ancient minster may have survived into the tenth century, then turns north to see what opportunities await in the so-called Danelaw. Towcester (Roman *Lactodorum*), like Tamworth, was a burh built directly on Watling Street: an offensive frontier garrison whose value, evident in the Roman period and, perhaps, long before, was its control of the river heads of the Great Ouse and the Nene, as well as the road route between London and Chester.

Who can say if entry to the Danelaw at this point was controlled, or if the traveller experienced the feeling of coming into a different land: new dialects; new customs to learn; different dress and ways of counting; more risks and opportunities?

The dispersed Midland farms and hamlets of the tenth century had begun a slow, complex process of nucleation into what would become the open-field villages so recognizable in the medieval and later countryside. Fortified towns, orderly and regulated, were replacing minsters as central places, although often at the same sites. A warming climate, the king's peace and raised productivity breathed new life into the rural economy; markets drew produce, crafts and trade, concentrating labour and profit. The entrepreneurial talents of Danish jarls, *holds* and traders, amplified by their material wealth and by the fragmentation of very large estates, energized a farming landscape now open to technical and social innovation.

Any traveller arriving at the Anglo-Danish town of Northampton, set in a typically-Scandinavian D-shaped earthwork enclosing a 60-acre site north of the Nene and east of its tributary, the Brampton Nene, must have been impressed by its busy-ness. Up until the reign of Æðelred and Æðelflæd *Hamtun*, as it was then, could boast of one of the largest and most impressive buildings in Britain, a unique stone hall, more than 100 feet (30 m) long and constructed using mortar from rotary mixers excavated close by during the 1970s.[29] Whether it lay at the heart of a minster or palace complex, or both, is unclear. It was demolished at the end of the ninth century or the beginning of the tenth; by what agency we also cannot say, even if there is a temptation to blame the *mycel here*.

Like the thriving ecclesiastical production settlements at Portmahomack and Brandon, the site of the great hall was turned over to industrial use, from whose hearths and rubbish pits pennies of the East Anglian St Eadmund coinage have been retrieved.

Now Northampton began to produce wheel-thrown pottery, unknown in contemporary Wessex. Iron, copper, silver and bone were worked here, providing any number of commercial opportunities for traders passing through or deliberately courting its craftsmen and markets. Norwegian hone-stones have been found here as well as the bones of saltwater fish. By the 960s Northampton supported a mint.

If, as seems likely, the Nene was navigable as far upstream as the town, it enjoyed excellent access to the Wash and the North Sea. Embarking there and coasting downriver on the streamway, the traveller would pass a magnificent new church at Earls Barton, under construction some time in the late tenth century, and an important estate centre and incipient manor, with its own church and cemetery, at Raunds, subject of extensive excavations in the 1970s and 1980s. Further downstream lay Oundle, a foundation (and the burial place) of St Wilfrid in the seventh century.

As the Nene valley opens out on to the Fens at Peterborough, the river passes beneath the magnificent walls of Peterborough Cathedral and its bishops' palace. *Medehamstede*, as the seventh-century minster foundation was called, is supposed to have been destroyed by Ívarr's *mycel here* in 869 and not refounded until the late 960s. The site might have been deserted in mid-century; but the survival of elements of its pre-Viking archives and of the remarkable Hedda stone bearing portraits of robed figures, which is displayed in the present cathedral, are hints that some form of community may have been sustained through the decades of uncertainty.

In the tenth century Wisbech must have lain on or close to the shores of the Wash; perhaps there was a beach market or harbour here. For those sailing north out of those shallow, sheltered but fickle waters, the east-facing North Sea coast, where so many of Britain's celebrated early church foundations had flourished under royal patronage, was no longer a focus of ecclesiastical politics or trade. Humber, Trent and Great Ouse all gave access to inland towns and trade. Minster sites at Whitby, Jarrow, Lindisfarne and beyond retained some human presence, but none of the splendour with which they had been endowed in the seventh century; none of the power. Perhaps a week's sail to the north, a royal cult centre survived and thrived at *Rígmonaid*, St Andrews in Fife, where King Constantín had retired in 943 and where he died in 952.

Whether the kings of Alba or the Norse lords of the Orkneys ruled Moray and Fortriu at this time is not clear; but their dominance of the Northern Isles was permanent, at least into the fifteenth century when Orkney and Shetland were finally ceded by the kings of Norway to Scotland. The intrepid traveller crossing the Pentland Firth (*Petlandsfjörð*: the fjord of Pictland) to Orkney and then Shetland would have encountered islands now thoroughly Norse in language and material culture. Early native settlements seem often to have been directly overlain by characteristically Norse houses. Whether that cultural colonization was aggressive and involved displacing or rendering the native population servile, or whether it was gradual, peaceful and co-operative, through marriage and purchase, is rarely evident from the archaeology. Current academic opinion inclines to the former. The Pictish variety of the British languages was not intelligible to the Norse speaker; nor was the Goidelic of the Irish. Bilingualism must have been common; but place names tell overwhelmingly a story of Norsification; and no Pictish settlement form overlies an obviously Norse structure.

The more intrepid sailors, pulling their boat up onto the sandy beaches of an inlet at the southern tip of Shetland close to Sumburgh Head, must have been impressed by the thriving farm complex whose early twentieth-century excavators knew it as Jarlshof. The quality of life, the domestic sophistication and solidity of the drystone and turf-built houses, byres, smithies and ancillary structures must have matched anything on the British mainland outside the royal palaces. The late ninth- or early tenth-century longhouse of the second building phase bears comparison in size with the great stone hall at Northampton. Kitchen blocks, paving, internal ovens and sweat-lodges would all, further south, be regarded as markers of high status, like the courtyard complex of the 'private burh' at Goltho. Each generation made its own improvements, and there is a strong sense that in Norse hands the settlement here, founded in the Bronze Age and occupied more or less continuously ever since, was the stable familial homestead of a wealthy, powerful clan, perhaps of a trader like the Norwegian Ohthere (who had given an account of his travels to King Ælfred) or a *hold* like Ingimundr.[30]

A ship's crew landing at any one of dozens of sheltered harbours and beaches in the Orkney archipelago, a day's sail to the south-west, must have been equally impressed, not just by the technical achievement of the settlements but by their numbers and by the wealth and fertility of the land, which supported large herds of cattle and prosperous arable farms. If we are to believe the evidence of *Orkneyinga Saga* the islands were subject to some form of devolved Norwegian royal authority. In its early Norse phase Orkney came under the direct rule of Norwegian kings, especially the famous Haraldr *Hárfagri*; and, subsequently, to those wishing to demonstrate their independence from him. By the middle of the tenth century Orkney may have come under the sway of Haraldr *blátǫnn* Gormsson, Haraldr 'Bluetooth' (ruled *c.*958–986), often regarded as the founder of the Danish medieval state, whose conversion to Christianity is so convincingly monumentalized at Jelling.[31]

At the north-westernmost point of Orkney's mainland the aspiring trader or warrior must surely have presented himself at the splendid court of the jarl who ruled from the massive natural fortress on Brough of Birsay and at nearby Buckquoy, later seat of

56. VIEW ACROSS THE TIDAL CAUSEWAY
from Brough of Birsay to Buckquoy, Mainland, Orkney.

the earls of Orkney.* But other impressive settlement complexes also existed by the tenth century to complement the wealth of Norse-style burials, hoards and place names that give the islands their uniquely Scandinavian flavour: at Pool, on Sanday, at Skaill near Deerness and at Saevar Howe.

Orkney was not peripheral to the Atlantic Norse world, but central: its colonizers did not just pillage and displace its indigenes; they exploited the archipelago's riches as fully as its famous Neolithic and Bronze Age inhabitants, whose rich cultural and spiritual lives they matched fully. The great twelfth-century cathedral of St Magnus in Kirkwall is an enduring monument to Norse wealth, ambition and success, just as it is to the endurance, through these troubled times, of the institutional church. One could hardly blame our hypothetical trader if, on acquaintance with the opportunities presented by Orkney, he decided not to move on, but to stay.

---

* See above, p. 258.

APPENDIX

—

Regnal tables

RULERS OF WESSEX

802–955

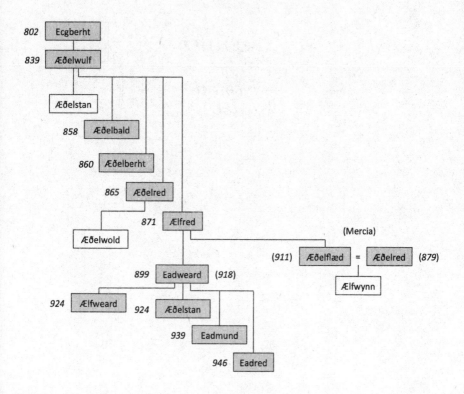

RULERS OF YORK

867–955

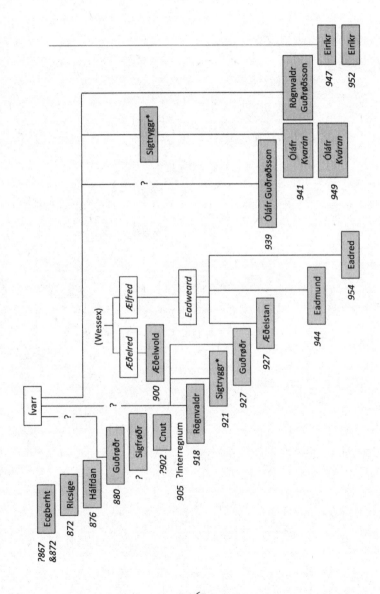

RULERS OF MERCIA
757–924

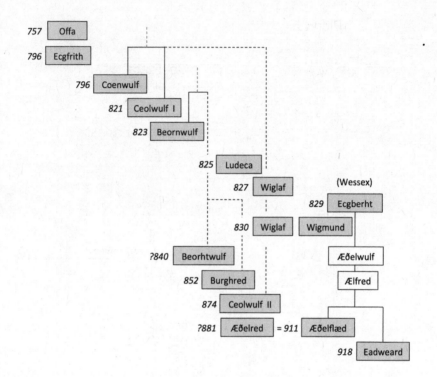

RULERS OF PICTAVIA; DAL RIATA; ALBA
839–955

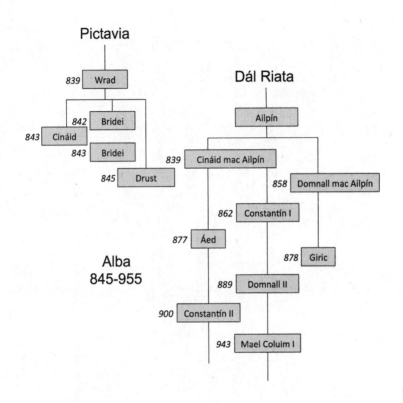

Pictavia

Dál Riata

839 Wrad

842 Bridei

843 Cináid

843 Bridei

845 Drust

Ailpín

839 Cináid mac Ailpín

858 Domnall mac Ailpín

862 Constantín I

877 Áed

878 Giric

Alba
845-955

889 Domnall II

900 Constantín II

943 Mael Coluim I

RULERS OF THE WELSH
808–950

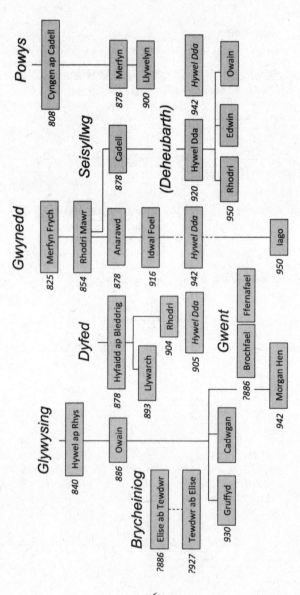

ABBREVIATIONS, SOURCES
AND REFERENCES

Original sources and the editions used
in the text and timelines:

AASB – *Acts of the abbots of St Bertin
by Folcwin*. EHD Secular narrative
sources 26, Whitelock 1979.
AC – *The Annales Cambriae*. Morris
1980.
AClon – *Annals of Clonmacnoise*.
https://www.ucc.ie/celt/transpage.
html
Æðelweard – *Chronicon*. Campbell
1962.
AFM – Annals of the Four Masters.
https://www.ucc.ie/celt/online/
T100005A
Alcuin Ep – *The epistolae of Alcuin*.
Allott 1974.
APF – *Armes Prydein Fawr*. Isaac 2007.
ASB – *The Annals of St Bertin*. Nelson
1991.
ASC – *Anglo-Saxon Chronicle*.
Garmonsway 1972.
Asser – Life of King Alfred. Keynes and
Lapidge 1983.
AU – *Annals of Ulster*. http://www.ucc.
ie/celt/online/T100001A.
CKA – *Chronicle of the Kings of Alba*.
Woolf 2007.
Egil's Saga – Scudder and Óskarsdóttir
2004.
EHD – *English Historical Documents
volume 1*. Whitelock 1979.
FoW – *Florence of Worcester : the reigns
of the Danish kings of England*. EHD
Secular narrative sources 9. Whitelock
1979.

Fragmentary Annals – Wainright 1975b.
GRA – *Gesta Regum Anglorum* –
William of Malmesbury. Giles 1847
and EHD Secular narrative sources 8.
Whitelock 1979.
HE – *Bede's Historia Ecclesiastica*.
Colgrave and Mynors 1969.
Historia Abbatum – Webb and Farmer
1983.
HR – *Historia Regum*. EHD Secular
narrative sources 3. Whitelock 1979.
HSC – *Historia de Sancto Cuthberto*.
South 2002.
LDE – *Symeon's Libellus de Exordio*.
Stephenson 1993.
Liber Eliensis – Fairweather 2005.
Nithard's Histories – Scholz 1972.
Orkneyinga Saga – Pálsson and Edwards
1981.
Poetic Edda – Larrington 2014.
Prose Edda – Bycock 2005.
RFA – *Royal Frankish Annals*. Scholz
1972.
RoW – *Roger of Wendover: Flores
Historiarum*. Giles 1849.
VC – *Vita Colombae. Adomnán's Life of
St Columba*. Sharpe 1995.
VW – *Eddius Stephanus's Vita Wilfridi*.
Webb and Farmer 1983.

Charters are referenced by their S-
(Sawyer) number, which can be used to
search for them in the online resource
called the Electronic Sawyer: http://
www.esawyer.org.uk/about/index.html.

NOTES

Author's note

1 http://www.pase.ac.uk; http://www.esawyer.org.uk/about/index.html.

Introduction

1 In his famous Letter to Bishop Ecgberht. Colgrave and Mynors 1969, 343ff.
2 The Seeress's prophecy, from the *Poetic Edda*. Larrington 2014, 9.

PART I
....
The tiger in the smoke

1

1 799: Pope Leo, RFA; Alcuin, *Alcuin Ep* 184; 800: Charlemagne, RFA; Godfrið king *c.* 800—he is first mentioned in the RFA under 804; Tynemouth and Hartness, R. W; 801: Lundenwic, HR; Æðelheard, *Alcuin Ep* 232; earthquake, RFA; Eardwulf, HR; 802: elephant, RFA; Hwicce, ASC; Iona, AU.
2 From the *Prosopography of Anglo-Saxon England* at http://www.pase.ac.uk/index.html.
3 RFA 807.
4 Retrieved from http://www.bbc.co.uk/news/uk-scotland-highlands-islands-38730046, January 2017.
5 RFA 804.

6 RFA 808.
7 Forte et al 2005, 10.
8 AU 795; some editors have interpreted the non-existent Latin form *scri*, a copying error by the original scribe, with *Sci*, and hence Skye; Woolf 2007, 45 and others argue for the 'shrine' translation.
9 Lowe 2008.
10 ASC 'E' 794 but correctly 796 in Garmondsway 1972, 57.
11 Translated by Whitelock 1979, 845, from Alcuin's letter to Higbald, 793.
12 Woolf 2006.
13 Carver 2008.
14 AU 839.
15 Whitelock, EHD 202, p. 854. Alcuin writing to Mercian Ealdorman Osberht in 797.
16 HRA 798.
17 Alcuin: *Alcuin Ep* 184.
18 For Wulfred's expansions Charter S1264; For Æðelheard's visit to Rome, ASC; for Pope Leo and successors RFA; for the Synod at Chelsea *Cotton Vespasian A xi*.
19 Blair 2005, 130.
20 Noted by Blinkhorn 1999, 19.
21 Charters S1434, S1436; S165.
22 Old English translation retrieved from http://asc.jebbo.co.uk/a/a-L.html, March 2016. Parker MS 'A' Chronicle. Garmondsway 1972, 60.
23 Dolley 1970, Plate VII.
24 Bede HE II.5.

2

1 Bede HE II.3. Colgrave and Mynors 1969. Wulfhere seems the most likely royal sponsor, according to Cowie et al 2012, xxviii.

2 Cowie et al 2012.

3 Cowie et al 2012, 5–7.

4 See Morton 1999 and Samson 1999 for the virtues and risks of using the terms *wic*, emporium and port.

5 See Whitelock 1979, section 197 for the conciliatory end to this episode.

6 ASC; NHF; ASB.

7 Watts 2004.

8 ASB 839. Nelson 1991, 43.

9 Fortriu: AU; Woolf 2007, 56; Louis: ASB; Ecgberht ASC.

10 Griffiths 2010.

11 ASB 844, 845.

12 Bede HE V.23; Bede, Letter to Ecgberht, AD734 in Colgrave and Mynors 1969, 343ff.

13 Foot 2011 133; Charters S1164; S1258: EHD 55, 79.

14 South 2002.

15 O'Brien 2002; Adams 2013.

16 South 2002, 47–51.

17 Tamworth: Rahtz & Meeson 1992; Ebbsfleet: Buss 2002; Nendrum: McErlean 2007; Adams 2015.

18 Charter S12: Oswine, King of Kent, grants one *sulung* on which iron is mined to the monastery of St Peter and Abbot Hadrian.

19 *Historia Abbatum* chapter 17: Webb and Farmer 1983.

20 Wright 2015.

21 Potts 1974.

22 Blair 2005, 255.

23 Blinkhorn 1999.

24 Blinkhorn 1997; 1999.

25 *Orkneyinga Saga*, chapter 105. Pálsson and Edwards 1981, 214–15.

26 Bannerman 1974.

3

1 O'Nolan 1962 for this online translation; Somerville and McDonald 2014 for an alternative translation; Barrett 2003 for discussion and context.

2 O'Nolan 1962, 156.

3 Anderson 1922, 263.

4 Roberts 2010.

5 Woolf 2007.

6 Woolf 2007, 87ff.

7 Cowley 2007. The relics that were 'rediscovered' in the thirteenth century are certainly not those of the historical David. The picture is complicated by the extreme decline in the fortunes of St David's during the eleventh century.

8 ASC 850 (851). The 'present day', so far as the chronicler was concerned, was about 893.

9 S 208.

10 Anglesey (Môn): AC 853 (properly 856); Wrekin S 206.

11 AU 856.

12 *Asser* chapters 12 and 17.

13 HSC 10, 11, 12.

14 Chase 1997.

15 Æðelweard *Chronicon* for 866. Campbell 1962, 35; Chase 1997.

16 *Fragmentary Annals*; Downham 2007.

17 Under the entry for 878.

18 Nelson 2013, 418.

19 ASC Parker MS 'A'. Garmonsway 1972, 68.

20 The *Anglo-Saxon Chronicle*; the *Historia de Sancto Cuthberto*; Asser's *Life of Ælfred*; Symeon's *Tract on the church of Durham*, and an eleventh-century Scandinavian tradition preserved in a poem by Sigvatr Þórðarson and in the Story of the sons of Ragnarr. See Townend 2014, 25–7.

21 From an entry in Symeon of Durham's *Tract on the church of Durham*, quoted by Townend 2014, 26.

22 HSC 10.

23 Hadley and Richards 2016.

24 Carr et al 1988.

25 The 'F' version of the *Chronicle*. Garmonsway 1975, 71.

26 Abbo of Fleury: *The martyrdom of St Edmund*. Retrieved from https://legacy.fordham.edu/Halsall/source/870abbo-edmund.asp, April 2016. Abbo spent time in England in about 985, just over a century after the events of which he writes and citing local tradition.

27 Blackburn and Pagan 2002.

28 ASC Laud MS 'E' under 870.

29 Keynes and Lapidge 1983, 80.

4

1 *Book of Revelation* 6:8–17 (King James Bible).

2 The Seeress's Prophecy, stanza 54, from Larrington 2014, 11 in the *Poetic Edda*.

3 From the Prose Preface to Gregory's *Pastoral Care*, translated with notes by Keynes and Lapidge 1983, 125.

4 Brooks 1979, 15–16.

5 Anderson 1908, 61.

6 AU 870.

7 AU 872.

8 AC 871.

9 Lavelle 201, 14.

10 Hadley 2006, 167; Hadley and Richards 2016 (quoting Peter Sawyer from a 1998 volume on Anglo-Saxon Lincolnshire).

11 Giles 1849, 206. I have altered the name spellings for consistency.

12 ASC Parker MS 'A' Chronicle 874 (for 873).

13 ASC Laud MS 'E' Chronicle 874 (for 873).

14 Stroud 1999; the excavations have never been fully published.

15 Richards 2004.

16 Richards 2004.

17 Charles-Edwards 2014, 491, quoting a Worcester king list.

18 http://www.britishmuseum.org/about_us/news_and_press/press_releases/2015/viking_hoard_found.aspx, June 2016

19 Naismith 2012, 165.

20 Laud MS 'E' Chronicle 875 (for 874).

21 AU 875; Woolf 2007, 111.

22 HSC 12; HSC 14.

23 Bede HE III.21, 22; Adams 2013, 282.

24 Townend 2014, 124.

25 Townend 2014, 103.

26 Adams 2015, chapter 9.

27 Townend 2014, 113ff.

28 Townend 2014, 119; Hadley 2006, 92ff.

29 HSC 12.

30 Garmonsway 1972, 75.

31 Campbell 1962, 41.

32 ASC 876.

33 ASC Parker MS 'A', Garmonsway 1972, 74.

34 Rahtz et al 1979.

35 Asser, *Life of Ælfred* 52.

36 Whitelock, EHD 100, 542: S362.

37 Asser, *Life of Ælfred* 54. Keynes and Lapidge 1983, 83–4.

38 ASC Parker MS 'A'. Garmonsway 1972, 76.

39 Æðelweard *Chronicon* 878. Campbell 1962, 42.

40 Æðelweard *Chronicon* 878. Campbell 1962, 42.

41 Bede, HE III. 23, writing of Cedd's foundation at Lastingham.

42 Colgrave 1956, 87.

43 *Beowulf* lines 83–5. Tolkien 2014, 16.
44 Gowland and Western 2012.
45 HSC 15, 16.
46 Edwin: HE II.12; Oswald: VC I.1.
47 Yorke 1999; Joy Rutter, in conversation with the Bernician Studies Group.
48 *Gesta Regum*, II, chapter 4. Giles 1847, 114.
49 Asser, *Life of Ælfred* 55. Keynes and Lapidge 1983, 84.
50 Parker MS 'A' *Chronicle* 878. Garmonsway 1972, 76.
51 Asser, *Life of Ælfred* 56. Keynes and Lapidge 1983, 84–5.
52 Asser, *Life of Ælfred* 56. Keynes and Lapidge 1983, 84–5.
53 Nelson 1986, 60.

PART II
Newton's cradle

5

1 HSC 12. South 2002, 53.
2 Woolf 2007, 79.
3 Hadley 2006, 41.
4 HSC 19. South 2002, 53.
5 HSC 20. For a commentary see South 2002, 96.
6 Rollason 1987. There is also a useful discussion of the context of the Guðroðr episode in Hadley 2006, 37ff.
7 Roberts 2008, 131–2.
8 ASC Parker MS 'A'. Garmonsway 1972, 76.
9 Æðelweard *Chronicon* 878. Campbell 1962, 43.
10 Two copies survive in Corpus Christi College Cambridge MS 383. Translation from Whitelock 1979, 416.
11 Whitelock, EHD 34, 416–17.

12 Davis 1955, 34.
13 Asser, *Life of Ælfred* 80. Keynes and Lapidge 1983, 96. Charles-Edwards 2014, 491.
14 Asser, *Life of Ælfred* 81. Keynes and Lapidge 1983, 96.
15 ASB 882. Nelson 1991, 225–6.
16 Noted by Æðelweard *Chronicon* 880. Campbell 1962, 43.
17 Recorded by Abbo, a monk of St Germain des Prés. Somerville et al 2014, 224.
18 Asser, *Life of Ælfred* 91. Keynes and Lapidge 1983, 101–2.
19 Whitelock, EHD 99, 540–1.
20 S346. A charter of 889 issued by Ælfred and Æðelred.
21 Asser, *Life of Ælfred* 83. Keynes and Lapidge 1983, 97–8.
22 As Bodleian Hatton 20.
23 ASC Parker MS 'A'. Garmonsway 1972, 80.
24 Clark 1999; Haslam 2010, for example. The 'Queenshythe charter' is S1628, dated generally to 898–899.
25 Æðelweard *Chronicon* 878. Campbell 1962, 46.
26 Hill 1981, 47.
27 Walker 2000, 76ff.
28 Blunt at al 1989, 21.
29 For a general overview, Hadley 2006 is invaluable.
30 Asser, *Life of Ælfred* 30. Keynes and Lapidge 1983, 77.
31 Hadley 2006, 158–9.
32 Dunmore and Carr 1976.
33 Andrews and Penn 1999.
34 King 1978; Hadley 2006, 104–5.
35 Campbell 2001, citing and acknowledging Dr Tom Williamson's pioneering work on the Norfolk Broads.
36 Hadley 2013a, 110–11.
37 Retrieved from http://www.english-heritage.org.uk/visit/

places/wharram-percy-deserted-medieval-village/history, April 2017.

38 *Annales Cambriae* 875.

39 Bruce-Mitford 1997. The excavations took place during the 1950s and 1970s. The published report is problematic and much evidence was either poorly recorded or is not available for the contemporary archaeologist to analyse or critique.

40 Loveluck 2007, 104.

41 Loveluck 2007, 127. Perhaps the most useful concise introduction of the role of such sites in trade, production and consumption in this period is Paul Blinkhorn's influential paper 'Of cabbages and kings...'. Blinkhorn 1999.

42 Campbell 2001.

43 Loveluck 2007, 28.

44 Loveluck 2007, 82.

45 Watts 2004.

6

1 ASC Parker MS 'A', 890.

2 ASC Parker MS 'A'. Garmonsway 1972, 83–4.

3 Forte et al 2005, 63; otherwise, the account comes from the ASC of 889–891.

4 Nelson 1986, 46.

5 Æðelweard *Chronicon* 878. Campbell 1962, 49. The remains of a defended enclosure at Castle Toll, north-east of the small village of Newenden where the River Rother once flowed past the Isle of Oxney, has been suggested as the site of the fort. For example Abels 1998, 287.

6 Yorke 2001.

7 ASC 893.

8 ASC Parker MS 'A'. Garmonsway 1972, 84.

9 Æðelweard *Chronicon* 878. Campbell 1962, 49.

10 ASC Parker MS 'A'. Garmonsway 1972, 85.

11 ASC Parker MS 'A', 893.

12 For example, the collection called *The worm forgives the plough* (1973).

13 ASC Parker MS 'A'. Garmonsway 1972, 89–90.

14 Asser, *Life of Ælfred*, 76.

15 Old English Text from Sweet's *Anglo-Saxon Reader in Prose and Verse*. Translation from Whitelock 1979, 539.

16 Stowe Charter XX. Whitelock 1979, 537.

17 From the prose preface to Gregory's *Pastoral Care*, loosely translated by Ælfred.

18 One manuscript of the Orosius translation survives with the Ohthere account intact: British Museum MS Add. 47967. For a full translation and detailed discussion of the geography and navigational aspects of both accounts, see Lund et al 1984.

19 Text and translation from Lund (ed) 1984, 18ff.

20 Crumlin-Pedersen 1984.

21 Sawyer 1984, in the same volume edited by Niels Lund.

22 Asser, *Life of Ælfred* 76. Keynes and Lapidge 1983, 92.

23 Campbell 2001, 16.

24 Hinton 1977, 11ff; 63ff; Biddle 1976.

25 Yorke 2001, 32.

26 Woolf 2001, 99.

27 Æðelweard *Chronicon* 901.

28 Keynes 2001, 48.

29 Nelson 2008.

30 Woolf 2007, 137; and see below, p. 261.

31 AU 902.

7

1 AU 902: retrieved from http://www.ucc.ie/celt/online/ T100001A, August 2016.
2 Griffiths 2010, 42.
3 Wainright 1975b.
4 Wainright 1975b, 80. The importance of the *Fragmentary Annals* was demonstrated by F. T. Wainright in the 1940s, despite several reservations about their authenticity. The consensus is that the framework of the Ingimundr story is sound; but that the detail, some of it embellished beyond credibility, must be treated with caution.
5 Wainright 1975b, 81.
6 HSC 22: South 2002, 61. The entry is firmly placed in Eadweard's reign by both earlier and later entries in the *Historia*.
7 *Fragmentary Annals*: Wainright 1975b, 81.
8 Wainright 1975a, 98.
9 Redknap 2004; Griffiths 2004; 2010.
10 Redknap 2004.
11 Owen and Morgan 2007. The name Llanbedrgoch, the 'red church of Pedr', suggests that an early ecclesiastical site lay in the vicinity.
12 Charles-Edwards 2013, 467ff.
13 Wilson 2008, 52–3.
14 Somerville et al 2014, 274ff; Alexander 1973, 150ff.
15 Wilson 2008, 28–32.
16 Wilson 2008, 38ff.
17 Sharples et al 2016; Graham-Campbell and Batey 2011.
18 Graham-Campbell and Batey 2011.
19 *Orkneyinga Saga* 6: Pálsson and Edwards 1981, 29.
20 Carver 2008, 145.
21 *Orkneyinga Saga* 8: Pálsson and Edwards 1981, 32. The deal may reflect more contemporary arrangements struck by earls in Iceland in the twelfth century. Nevertheless, this more pragmatic element in the saga may well reflect the sort of colonial arrangements that kings struck with their overseas governors to ensure fidelity and an increase in the royal coffers.
22 Woolf 2007, 122.
23 CKA quoted by Woolf 2007, 127.
24 CKA. Woolf 2007, 126.
25 Woolf 2007, 136.
26 Blunt 1985.
27 Blackburn and Pagan 2002. The location of the mints is unknown. The Christianized message invoking a saint with local affiliations is paralleled on the Continent, and in Scandinavian York, also issuing a saintly coinage in St Peter's name in the early tenth century.
28 Campbell 2001, following Dorothy Whitelock.
29 ASC 904.
30 Lyon 2001.
31 EHD I 101: Whitelock 1979, 543.
32 ASC Parker MS 'A'. Garmonsway 1972, 94.
33 ASC Peterborough MS 'E'. Garmonsway 1972, 95.

8

1 Foot 2011, 205, quoting a letter of Alcuin.
2 ASC Parker MS 'A'. Garmonsway 1972, 94–6.
3 Heighway 2001; Blair 2005, 342ff.
4 Foot 2011, 204ff.
5 Bede HE III.12.

6   ASC Peterborough MS 'E'.
    Garmonsway 1972, 95.
7   Lyon 2001. Eadweard's coins
    did not carry the names of
    moneyers, but each moneyer used
    diagnostic characteristics that
    later, in Æðelstan's reign, were
    accompanied by names allowing
    the identification of many of the
    minting sites with some confidence.
8   ASC Worcester MS 'D':
    Garmonsway 1972, 97.
9   ASC Worcester MS 'D':
    Garmonsway 1972, 99.
10 ASC Parker MS 'A' under the
    corrected year 916.
11 ASC Parker MS 'A', Garmonsway
    1972, 101.
12 ASC Parker MS 'A', Garmonsway
    1972, 102. Original Old English
    transcription retrieved from
    http://asc.jebbo.co.uk/a/a-L.
    html, September 2016. The identity
    of the Danish king is not known
    but see p. 299.
13 ASC Mercian Register MS 'C':
    Garmonsway 1972, 101, 105.
14 For example, Wainright 1975d.
15 ASC Parker MS 'A'. Original Old
    English transcription retrieved from
    http://asc.jebbo.co.uk/a/a-L.
    html, September 2016.
16 Blinkhorn 2013.
17 Boyd 2013.
18 Hall and Kenward 2005, 395ff.
19 Hall 2004, 287.
20 Stocker 2013.
21 Ten Harkel 2013.
22 Hadley 2006, 119ff.
23 Symonds and Ling 2002.
24 See also the definitive early paper
    on perception, effort and time
    surfaces (PETS) by Stead 1995.
25 S396: AD 926. King Athelstan to
    Ealdred, minister; confirmation of
    5 hides (*manentes*) at Chalgrave

and Tebworth, Beds., formerly
purchased from the Danes for 10
pounds of gold and silver. And
S397: AD 926. King Athelstan to
Uhtred; confirmation of 60 hides
(*manentes*) at Hope and Ashford,
Derbys., formerly purchased from
the Danes for 20 pounds of gold
and silver. Source: http://www.
esawyer.org.uk/browse/
ch_date/0900.html, retrieved
September 2016.
26 Original Old English transcription
    retrieved from http://asc.jebbo.
    co.uk/a/a-L.html, September
    2016. ASC Parker MS 'A',
    Garmonsway 1972, 104–5.
27 Bailey 2001.
28 By Wainright 1975c. Wainright,
    in the same paper, makes a case
    for two battles at Corbridge, the
    first in 914 and the second in 918.
    The current consensus, argued by
    Woolf (2007) and South (2002),
    is that the Cuthbert chronicler was
    confused and that there was a single
    battle at Corbridge in 918.
29 HSC 23. South 2002, 61. The
    narrative is partly reinforced and
    partly confused by the entry in
    HSC 24, which records another
    estate lost by St Cuthbert to
    Rægnald's men and confuses the
    story of the Corbridge battle with
    a second account that has taken
    the efforts of several historians to
    unravel.
30 AU 917.1.
31 HSC 24 South 2002, 63.
32 HSC 23 South 2002, 61–3.

PART III

Going native

9

1 HSC South 2002: see the maps after p. 118.
2 South 2002. Sections 22–24 of the HSC carry the narrative for the Rögnvaldr episodes.
3 Hadley 2006, 153; Hall 2000.
4 Molyneux 2011, arguing for a later tenth-century date. An English translation can be found in Noble 1983.
5 Noble 93, 105; original transcription by Felix Liebermann, Die Gesetze der Angelsachsen, 3 volumes, Volume 1, 374–8. Halle 1903–16.
6 Attenborough 1922, 121.
7 ASC Parker MS 'A', Garmonsway 1972, 100.
8 A much-cited example from the *Liber Eliensis* may provide evidence of such a case, later contested. Sharp 2001, 138.
9 ASC Parker MS 'A', Garmonsway 1972, 104.
10 Ritchie 2011.
11 Woolf 2007b.
12 Blackburn 2004.
13 Blackburn 2004, 332–3.
14 Rollason 2004.
15 Blackburn 2004.
16 *Gesta Regum Anglorum:* EHD Whitelock 1979, 305.
17 Sharp 2001, 82.
18 *Gesta Regum Anglorum II, 5:* Giles 1847, 124.
19 *Gesta Regum Anglorum:* EHD Whitelock 1979, 308.
20 Coatsworth 2001, 301.
21 *Gesta Regum Anglorum:* EHD Whitelock 1979, 305.
22 ASC Parker MS 'A', Garmonsway 1972, 104.

23 ASC Worcester MS 'D', Garmonsway 1972, 105.
24 HSC 25. South 2002, 65.
25 S395; Foot 2011, 73.
26 S394 Foot 2011, 75.
27 Nelson 2008, 125.
28 Foot 2011, 115–16.
29 Adams 2013; Tolkien 1936; 2014.
30 ASC Worcester MS 'D', Garmonsway 1972, 105.
31 Rahtz and Meeson 1992.
32 AU 927.
33 ASC Worcester MS 'D', Garmonsway 1972, 107.
34 Charles-Edwards 2012, 512. See also below, Chapter 11, on the Laws of Hywel Dda.
35 Lapidge 1980, 83–4.
36 Lapidge 1980, 98.

10

1 Lavelle 2005.
2 Attenborough 1922, 134.
3 Attenborough 1922, 135 (for the Old English); EHD 35, Whitelock 1979, 421 for the translation.
4 Blunt 1974.
5 Blunt 1974, 114.
6 From the *Acts of the abbots of St Bertin* by Folcwine the deacon. EHD 26, Whitelock 1979, 346. See also Woolf 2007, 163.
7 Under 933. EHD: Secular Narrative Sources 3. Whitelock 1979, 278.
8 *AClon* 933 (corrected from 928). Murphy 1896, 149.
9 S425.
10 S407: 930 for 934. EHD 104: Whitelock 1979, 548–50. Doubts about its authenticity are addressed by Whitelock.
11 EHD 104: Whitelock 1979, 548.
12 Ekwall 1922.

13 ASC MSS 'B' and 'C' *Mercian Register* under 911. Townend 2014, 67. It is possible, though unproven, that Agmundr is an alternative for Ingimundr, the invader of Anglesey in 902.

14 Eddius Stephanus: *Vita Wilfridi*, chapter 17.

15 Higham 2004.

16 S456–7.

17 HSC 26: South 2002, 65.

18 HSC 27: South 2002, 65.

19 S407.

20 HR 934: EHD Whitelock 1979, 278.

21 Foot 2011, 88. The charter was copied into the archives of the monastic community at Glastonbury and the witness list seems to have been abbreviated: we cannot declare the Welsh kings absent.

22 S1792. Translation courtesy of The electronic Sawyer, retrieved from http://www.esawyer.org.uk/charter/1792.html#, November 2016.

23 Blair 2005, 126–7.

24 *Gesta Regum Anglorum:* Giles 1847, 134.

25 Isaac 2007 for a discussion of the date and a full English translation. The text is contained in the *Book of Taliesin* in a manuscript catalogued as NLW Peniart 2.

26 APF 107–9. Isaac 2007, 177.

27 APF 72. Isaac 2007, 175.

28 APF 31. Isaac 2007, 171. The original story is preserved in the Kentish Chronicle belonging to the *Historia Brittonum* often attributed to Nennius. Morris 1980.

29 APF 40. Isaac 2007, 173.

30 APF 5–7. Isaac 2007, 171. *Caer Wair* is unidentified, despite a tempting association with the River Wear and Durham.

31 APF 55–60. Isaac 2007, 173.

32 AC under 919, corrected to 920. The *Annals* say that he was 'killed'.

33 APF 88–91. Isaac 2007, 175.

34 S434: a grant to the *familia*, the community at Malmesbury Abbey of 60 hides at Bremhill, Wiltshire.

35 EHD, Secular narrative sources 24. Whitelock 1979, 344, footnote 5.

36 *Gesta Regum Anglorum:* Giles 1847, 134.

37 Foot 2011, 54.

38 EHD 25. Whitelock 1979, 345.

39 Townend 2014, 63–4. The entry from the Portable Antiquities Scheme can be found at: https://finds.org.uk/database/artefacts/record/id/198978

40 Townend 2014, 64.

41 Rollason 2004, 311.

42 Townend 2014, 114–16.

43 *Prose Edda.* Bycock 2005, 63–5.

44 Townend 2014, 125–6.

11

1 *Annals of Ulster* 937. Retrieved from http://www.ucc.ie/celt/online/T100001A, November 2016.

2 EHD, *Secular narrative sources 3.* Whitelock 1979, 279.

3 ASC Parker 'A' Chronicle, retrieved from http://asc.jebbo.co.uk/a/a-L.html, November 2016; translated in EHD, Secular narrative sources 1. Whitelock 1979, 219.

4 Whitelock 1979, 220.

5 Woolf 2007a, 169.

6 *Gesta Regum Anglorum* 132; 135. EHD Secular narrative sources 8. Whitelock 1979, 305; 309ff.

7 Campbell 1938, 58; 147.
8 *Annals of the Four Masters* 935 for 937. Downham 2007, 241.
9 Downham 2007, 150–1.
10 Wood 2013, in which he opts for the second of these possibilities.
11 Adams 2013, 285–7.
12 Cavill 2014.
13 Cavill, Harding and Jesch 2004.
14 Cavill 2014; Breeze 2016.
15 Lavelle 2010, 299–300.
16 *Egil's Saga* chapter 48, verse 14. Scudder 2004, 84.
17 Campbell 1970.
18 *Egil's Saga* chapter 55, verse 19. Scudder 2004, 100–1.
19 Flodoard *Annals* 21(d). Fanning and Bachrach 2004, 31.
20 *II Æðelstan*. EHD 35. Whitelock 1979, 420.
21 *VI Æðelstan*. Attenborough 1922, 156ff; EHD 37. Whitelock 1979, 423ff.
22 *VI Æðelstan*. EHD 37. Whitelock 1979, 424.
23 *VI Æðelstan*. EHD 37. Whitelock 1979, 425.
24 *VI Æðelstan*. EHD 37. Attenborough 1922, 163.
25 ASC Worcester MS 'D', Garmonsway 1972, III.
26 ASC Worcester MS 'D', Garmonsway 1972, III. The *Chronicle* records this episode under 943.
27 Hadley 2007, 212.
28 Blackburn 2006, 217.
29 *S513* King Eadmund to his minister Æðelgeard, a grant of 7 hides at Tisted in Hampshire.
30 Rahtz 1976; 1979; Adams 2015, chapter 5.
31 Rahtz 1976; Rahtz, Anderson and Hirst 1979.
32 Stenton 1971, 446.
33 Giles 1849, 250.
34 S466.
35 Stenton 1971, 447ff; Blair 2005, 350.
36 According to an entry in the *Historia Regum*.
37 ASC Parker 'A' Chronicle, retrieved from http://asc.jebbo.co.uk/a/a-L.html, November 2016; I have used Alex Woolf's translation. Woolf 2007, 181–2.
38 Beresford 1987.
39 There is much useful information and analysis at http://www.early englishlaws.ac.uk/laws/texts/rspger; the text and translation appear online at: http://www.earlyenglishlaws.ac.uk/laws/texts/rspger/view/#edition,I_0_c_29/translation,I; see Crossley-Holland 1984, 257ff for a modern translation in print of the bulk of the text.
40 See, for example, the arguments in Williamson 2013, chapter 5.
41 Downham 2007, 109; and Peter Sawyer cited by Downham. Downham, imposing sense on some of the confusion of annalistic entries for these years, has Eadmund's taking of the Five Boroughs before the Tamworth and Leicester raid, following a straight reading of the *Chronicle*. 'D' version for 943. I have not been able to reconcile the conflicting accounts in that way. It seems to me that the Norse campaign in Danish Mercia must come first.
42 Evidence for the expulsion is discussed in Charles-Edwards 2013, 508. Iago made a comeback in the 950s, as shown by his attestation of a charter, S566, in 955.
43 Dykes 1966.
44 Jenkins 1990; Charles-Edwards 2013, 267ff.
45 Jenkins 1990, xxix.

46 Jenkins 1990, 45–6.

47 Campbell 1962, 54.

48 The first charter is S442 which records a gift of 6 hides in Devon from King Æðelstan to his *comes*, and namesake, Æðelstan. The last is S666 issued by King Eadwig in 956, witnessed by the *dux*. The epithet 'half-king' is recorded by Byrtferth of Ramsey, biographer of Archbishop Oswald of York, around the turn of the eleventh century. He offers considerable detail on the family, which enjoyed various links with the West Saxon dynasty.

49 HSC 28. South 2002, 67.

50 *Flores Historiarum* under 946; EHD Secular narrative sources 4: Whitelock 1979, 283; Woolf 2007, 183.

51 ASC Worcester MS 'D'.

12

1 Stevenson 1993, 681.

2 AU 865; Carver 2008, 144.

3 Carver 2008, 145.

4 Ritchie 2011, 16.

5 *Asser*, chapter 81. Keynes and Lapidge 1983, 996–7; I have followed Blair's (2005, 325) selection.

6 EHD Secular Narrative Sources 8. Whitelock 1979, 307.

7 Foot 2011, 200ff.

8 *Liber Eliensis* Book I, 41. Fairweather 2005, 75.

9 *Liber Eliensis* Book II, 32. Fairweather 2005, 128.

10 Hill 1981, 133; 143.

11 See Sawyer 1981 for a developed discussion of the phenomenon.

12 Stocker 2013, 120ff.

13 See Hill 1981, 127 for distribution maps and much more.

14 Sawyer 2013, 95.

15 Hill 2001.

16 Thornton 2013 for the most coherent and up-to-date summary of the institution.

17 Stenton 1971, 507.

18 Stenton 1971, 511.

19 S520. EHD Charters and laws 105. Whitelock 1979, 551–2.

20 ASC Parker MS 'A', Garmonsway 1972, 112.

21 Anderson 1922, 411.

22 Downham 2007, 115ff; Woolf 2007, 187–8.

23 Woolf 2007, 177ff.

24 ASC Worcester MS 'D'.

25 *Egil's Saga*, chapter 60 (verse 32). Scudder and Óskarsdóttir 2004, 124–5.

26 *Egil's Saga*, chapter 61. Scudder and Óskarsdóttir 2004, 128ff.

27 *Egil's Saga*, chapter 62. Scudder and Óskarsdóttir 2004, 132.

28 EHD Secular Narrative Sources 4. Whitelock 1979, 284.

29 Williams 1984.

30 Jarlshof underwent several campaigns of excavation in the early twentieth century, the records of whose work have caused considerable problems for later archaeologists trying to understand its tremendously complex occupation sequence. For a recent summary see Graham-Campbell and Batey 2011, a work which also includes summaries of the other major excavated sites of the period in Scotland, Portmahomack aside.

31 For the theory that Haraldr Bluetooth created the first centralized authority on Orkney, see Woolf 2007, 308.

BIBLIOGRAPHY

ABELS, R. P. 1988 *Lordship and military obligation in Anglo-Saxon England.* London: British Museum Press

ABELS, R. P. 1998 *Alfred the Great: war, kingship and culture in Anglo-Saxon England.* London: Longman

ABRAMS, L. 2001 Edward the Elder's Danelaw. In Higham, N. J. and Hill, D. H. (eds) *Edward the Elder 899–924,* 128–43

ADAMS, M. 2013 *The King in the North: the life and times of Oswald of Northumbria.* London: Head of Zeus

ADAMS, M. 2015 *In the Land of Giants: journeys through the Dark Ages.* London: Head of Zeus

AIRD, W. M. 2013 Northumbria. In Stafford, P. (ed) *A companion to the Early Middle Ages: Britain and Ireland c.500–c.1100,* 304–21

ALCOCK, L. 2003 *Kings and warriors, craftsmen and priests in Northern Britain AD 550–850.* Edinburgh: Society of Antiquaries of Scotland

ALEXANDER, M. (trans) 1973 *Beowulf.* Harmondsworth: Penguin Classics

ALLOTT, S. 1974 *Alcuin of York, c. AD 732 to 804. His life and letters.* York: William Sessions

ANDERSON, A. O. 1908 *Scottish annals from English chroniclers AD 500 to 1286.* London: David Nutt

ANDERSON, A. O. 1922 *Early sources of Scottish history.* Edinburgh: Oliver and Boyd

ANDERTON, M. (ed) 1999 *Anglo-Saxon trading centres: beyond the emporia.* Glasgow: Cruithne Press

ANDREWS, P. 1995 Excavations at Redcastle Furze, Thetford, 1988–9. *East Anglian Archaeology 72.* Dereham: Norfolk Museums Service

ANDREWS, P. and Penn, K. 1999 Excavations in Thetford, north of the river, 1989–90. *East Anglian Archaeology 87.* Dereham: Norfolk Museums Service

ARNOLD, T. (ed) 1885 *Symeonis monachi opera omnia.* London: Longman

ATTENBOROUGH, F. L. 1922 *The laws of the first English kings.* Cambridge University Press. Facsimile edition

BAILEY, M. 2001 Ælfwynn, the second Lady of the Mercians. In Higham, N. J. and Hill, D. H. (eds) *Edward the Elder 899–924,* 112–27

BAILEY, R. N. 1980 *Viking Age sculpture in Northern England.* London: Collins

BAKER, J. and Brookes, S. (eds) 2013 *Beyond the Burghal Hidage: Anglo-Saxon civil defence in the Viking Age.* Boston: Brill

BANNERMAN, J. 1974 *Studies in the history of Dalriada,* Edinburgh: Scottish Academic Press

BARRETT, J. H. 2006 Christian and pagan practice during the conversion of Viking Age Orkney and Shetland. In Carver, M. (ed)*The cross goes north: processes of conversion in northern Europe, AD 300–1300,* 207–26

BATTISCOMBE, C. F. 1956 *The relics of St Cuthbert.* Oxford University Press

BENGTSSON, F. G. 1954 *The Long ships: a saga of the Viking Age.* Trans. Michael Mayer. London: Harper

BERESFORD, G. 1987 Goltho: the development of an early medieval manor *c.* 850–1150. *English Heritage Archaeological Report 4*. Historic Buildings and Monuments Commission for England

BHREATHNACH, E. 2014 *Ireland in the Early Medieval world AD 400–1000: landscape, kinship and religion.* Dublin: Four Courts Press

BIDDLE, M. 1976 Towns. In Wilson, D. M. (ed) *The archaeology of Anglo-Saxon England*, 99–150

BLACKBURN, M. 2004 The coinage of Anglo-Scandinavian York. In Hall, R. A. et al (eds) *Aspects of Anglo-Scandinavian York*, 325–49

BLACKBURN, M. 2005 Presidential address 2004. Currency under the Vikings. Part I: Guthrum and the earliest Danelaw coinages. *British Numismatic Journal* 75, 18–46

BLACKBURN, M. 2006 Presidential address 2005. Currency under the Vikings. Part 2: The two Scandinavian kingdoms of the Danelaw, *c.* 895–954. *British Numismatic Journal* 76, 204–29

BLACKBURN, M. and Pagan, H. 2002 The St Edmund coinage in the light of a parcel from a hoard of St Edmund pennies. *British Numismatic Journal* 72, 1–14

BLACKMORE, L. 2002 The origins and growth of Lundenwic, a mart of many nations. In Hårdh, B. and Larsson, L. (eds) *Central Places in the Migration and Merovingian Periods*: Papers from the 52nd Sachsensymposium, Lund, August 2001, 273–301. Almqvist & Wiksell International

BLAIR, J. 2005 *The church in Anglo-Saxon society.* Oxford University Press

BLAIR, J. (ed) 2007 *Waterways and canal-building in Medieval England.* Oxford University Press

BLINKHORN, P. 1997 *Stranger in a strange land: Middle Saxon Ipswich ware.* Paper presented to the *Pottery in the making* conference. British Museum

BLINKHORN, P. 1999 Of cabbages and kings: production, trade and consumption in Middle Saxon England. In Anderton, M. (ed) *Anglo-Saxon trading centres: beyond the emporia*, 4–23

BLINKHORN, P. 2013 No pots please, we're Vikings: pottery in the Southern Danelaw, 850–1000. In Hadley, D. M. and ten Harkel, L. (eds) *Everyday life in Viking towns: social approaches to towns in England and Ireland c.* 800–1100, 157–71

BLUNT, C. E. 1974 The coinage of Athelstan, 924–939. *British Numismatic Journal* 44, 36–160

BLUNT, C. E. 1985 Northumbrian coins in the name of Alwaldus. *British Numismatic Journal* 55, 192–4

BLUNT, C. E, STEWART, B. H. I. H. and LYON, C. S. S. 1989 *Coinage in Tenth-century England.* Oxford University Press

BONNER, G. 1989 St Cuthbert at Chester-le-Street. In Bonner et al (eds) *St Cuthbert, his cult and his community to AD 1200*, 387–395

BONNER, G., STANCLIFFE, C. and ROLLASON, D. (eds) 1989 *St Cuthbert, his cult and his community to AD 1200.* Woodbridge: Boydell Press

BOYD, R. 2013 From country to town: social transitions in Viking-Age housing. In Hadley, D. M. and ten Harkel, L. (eds) *Everyday life in Viking towns: social approaches to towns in England and Ireland c.* 800–1100, 73–85

BREEZE, A. 2016 The Battle of Brunanburh and Cambridge, CCC, MS 183. *Northern History* 53:1, 138–45

BROOKS, N. 1964 The unidentified forts of the burghal hidage. *Medieval Archaeology* 8:4, 74–90

BROOKS, N. 1979 England in the ninth century: the crucible of defeat. *Transactions of the Royal Historical Society* 29, 1–20

BROOKS, N. 1984 The early history of the church of Canterbury. *Studies in the early history of Britain*. Leicester University Press

BRUCE-MITFORD, R. 1997 Mawgan Porth: a settlement of the late Saxon period on the north Cornish coast. *English Heritage Archaeological report* 13

BUSS, B. 2002 Ebbsfleet Saxon mill. *Current Archaeology* 183, 93.

BYCOCK, J. (ed and trans) 2005 *Snorri Sturlusson: The Prose Edda*. Harmondsworth: Penguin

CAMBRIDGE, E. 1989 Why did the community of St Cuthbert settle at Chester le Street? In Bonner et al (eds) *St Cuthbert, his cult and his community to AD 1200*, 367–86

CAMBRIDGE, E. 1995 Archaeology and the cult of St Oswald in pre-Conquest Northumbria. In Stancliffe, C. and Cambridge, E. (eds) *Oswald: Northumbrian king to European saint*, 128–63

CAMPBELL, A. 1938 *The battle of Brunanburh*. London: William Heinemann

CAMPBELL, A. (ed) 1962 *The Chronicle of Æthelweard*. London: Nelson and Sons

CAMPBELL, A. 1971 Skaldic verse and Anglo-Saxon history. *The Dorothy Coke Memorial Lecture in Northern Studies*, delivered at University College, London, March 1970. University College London

CAMPBELL, J. 2001 What is not known about the reign of Edward the Elder.

In Higham, N. J. and Hill, D. H. (eds) *Edward the Elder 899–924*, 12–24

CARR, R. D., Tester, A. and Murphy, P. 1988 The Middle-Saxon settlement at Staunch Meadow, Brandon. *Antiquity* 62:235, 371–7

CARVER, M. 2006 *The cross goes north: processes of conversion in northern Europe, AD 300–1300*. Woodbridge: Boydell Press

CARVER, M. 2008a Post-Pictish problems: the Moray Firthlands in the 9th–11th centuries. *The Groam House Museum Annual Academic Lecture*. Rosemarkie: Groam House Museum

CARVER, M. 2008b *Portmahomack: monastery of the Picts*. Edinburgh University Press

CARVER, M. and LOVELUCK, C. 2013 Early Medieval, AD 400–1000. In Ransley, J., Sturt, F. and Dix, J. (eds) People and the sea: a maritime archaeological research agenda for England. *Council for British Archaeology Research Report* 171, 113–37

CAVILL, P., HARDING, S. and JESCH, J. 2004 Revisiting Dingesmere. *Journal of the English Place Name Society* 36, 25–38

CAVILL, P. 2014 The battle of Brunanburh in 937: battlefield dispatches. In Harding, S. E., Griffiths, D. and Royles, E. *In Search of Vikings: interdisciplinary approaches to the Scandinavian heritage of North-West England*, 95–108

CHADWICK, N. K. (ed) 1964 *Celt and Saxon: studies in the early British Border*. Cambridge University Press

CHARLES-EDWARDS, T. M. 1979 The distinction between land and moveable wealth in Anglo-Saxon England. In Sawyer, P. H. (ed) *English medieval settlement*. London: Edward Arnold

CHARLES-EDWARDS, T.M. 2014 *Wales and the Britons 350–1064*. Oxford University Press

CHASE, C. 1997 *The dating of Beowulf.* University of Toronto Press

CLARK, J. 1999 King Alfred's London and London's King Alfred. *London Archaeologist* 9:2, 35–8

COATSWORTH, E. 2001 The embroideries from the tomb of St Cuthbert. In Higham, N.J. and Hill, D.H. (eds) *Edward the Elder 899–924*, 292–306

COLGRAVE, R.A.B. (ed and trans) 1956 *Felix's Life of St Guthlac*. Cambridge University Press

COLGRAVE, B. and MYNORS, R.A.B. (eds) 1969 *Bede's Ecclesiastical History of the English People*. Oxford World Classics

COUPLAND, S. 1991 The fortified bridges of Charles the Bald. *Journal of Medieval History* 17, 1–12

COUPLAND, S. 2002 Trading places: Quentovic and Dorestad reassessed. *Early Medieval Europe* II: 3, 209–32

COWIE, R. and BLACKMORE, L. (eds) 2012 *Lundenwic: excavations in Middle Saxon London, 1987–2000*. Museum of London Archaeology Monograph 83

COWLEY, F.G. 2007 The relics of St David: the historical evidence. In Wyn Evans, J. and Wooding, J.M. *St David of Wales: cult, church and nation*, 274–81

CROSSLEY-HOLLAND, K. (trans) 1984 *The Anglo-Saxon world: an anthology.* Oxford World Classics

CRUMLIN-PEDERSEN, O. 1984 Ships, navigation and routes in the reports of Ohthere and Wulfstan. In Lund, N. (ed) *Two voyagers at the court of King Alfred*, 22–9

DARK, P. 2000 *The environment of Britain in the first millennium* AD. London: Duckworth

DAVIDSON, M.R. 2001 The (non) submission of the northern kings in 920. In Higham, N.J. and Hill, D.H. (eds) *Edward the Elder 899–924*, 200–11

DAVIS, R.H.C. 1955 East Anglia and the Danelaw. *Transactions of the Royal Historical Society* 5, 23–39

DOLLEY, M. 1970 *Anglo-Saxon pennies*. London: British Museum

DOLLEY, M. and MOORE, C.N. 1973 Some reflections on the English coinages of Sihtric Caoch, King of Dublin and York. *British Numismatic Journal* 43, 45–59

DOLLEY, R.H.M. 1955 A neglected but vital Yorkshire hoard. *British Numismatic Journal* 28, 11–17

DOWNHAM, C. 2007 *Viking kings of Britain and Ireland: the dynasty of Ívarr to AD 1014*. Edinburgh: Dunedin

DOWNHAM, C. 2009 The Viking slave trade. *History Ireland* May/June 2009, 15–17

DUMVILLE, D.N. 1992 *Wessex and England from Alfred to Edgar*. Woodbridge: Boydell Press

DUMVILLE, D.N. 1997 The churches of North Britain in the first Viking Age. *Fifth Whithorn lecture*. Friends of the Whithorn Trust

DUNMORE, S and CARR, R. 1976 The late Saxon town of Thetford. *East Anglian Archaeology Reports* 4. Dereham: Norfolk Archaeological Unit

DYKES, D.W. 1966 Seventeenth-century Glamorgan trade tokens. *Morganwwg* 10, 31–51

EDWARDS, J. F. 1987 The transport system of medieval England and Wales: a geographical synthesis. Unpublished PhD thesis, University of Salford. Retrieved from file:///C:/Users/Admin/Desktop/travel%20in%20med%20England%20PhD.pdf, November 2015

EDWARDS, N. 1996 *The archaeology of Early Medieval Ireland*. London: Routledge

EKWALL, E. 1922 *The place-names of Lancashire*. Manchester University Press

FAIRWEATHER, J. 2005 *Liber Eliensis: a history of the Isle of Ely from the seventh century to the twelfth*. Woodbridge: Boydell Press

FANNING, S. and BACHRACH, B. S. (ed and trans) 2004 *The Annals of Flodoard of Reims, 919–966*. Readings in medieval civilisations and cultures 9. Plymouth: Broadview Press

FINBERG, H. P. R. (ed) 1975 *Scandinavian England: collected papers by F. T. Wainwright*. Chichester: Phillimore

FOOT, S. 2011 Æthelstan: the first King of England. New Haven and London: Yale University Press

FORTE, A., ORAM, R. and PEDERSEN, F. 2005 *Viking empires*. Cambridge University Press

FOSTER, S. M. 2014 *Picts, Gaels and Scots: early historic Scotland*. Edinburgh: Birlinn

GARMONSWAY, G. N. 1972 *The Anglo-Saxon Chronicle*. London: Dent

GILES, J. A. (trans) 1849 *Roger of Wendover's Flowers of History*. London: Henry G. Bohn

GILES, J. A. (trans) 1906 *Old English chronicles*. London: George Bell

GOOCH, M. L. 2012 Money and power in the Viking kingdom of York, *c*. 895–954. Unpublished PhD thesis, Durham University

GOWER, G. 2002 A suggested Anglo-Saxon signalling system between Chichester and London. *London Archaeologist* 10:3, 59–63

GOWLAND, R. L. and WESTERN, A. G. 2012 Morbidity in the marshes: using spatial epidemiology to investigate skeletal evidence for malaria in Anglo-Saxon England (AD 410–1050). *American Journal of Physical Anthropology* 147:2, 301–11.

GRAHAM-CAMPBELL, J. and BATEY, C. E. 2011 *Vikings in Scotland: an archaeological survey*. Edinburgh University Press

GRAHAM-CAMPBELL, J. 2013 *The Viking world*. London: Frances Lincoln

GRIFFITHS, D. 2004 Settlement and acculturation in the Irish Sea region. In Hines, J., Lane, A. and Redknap, M. (eds) *Land, sea and home*, 125–38

GRIFFITHS, D. 2010 *Vikings of the Irish Sea*. Stroud: The History Press

HADLEY, D. M. 2006 *The Vikings in England: settlement, society and culture*. Manchester University Press

HADLEY, D. M. 2013a Viking raids and conquest. In Stafford, P. (ed) *A companion to the Early Middle Ages: Britain and Ireland c. 500–c. 1100*, 195–211

HADLEY, D. M. 2013b Scandinavian settlement. In Stafford, P. (ed) *A companion to the Early Middle Ages: Britain and Ireland c. 500–c. 1100*, 212–30

HADLEY, D. M. 2013c Whither the warrior in Viking-Age towns? In Hadley, D. M. and ten Harkel, L. (eds) *Everyday life in Viking towns: social approaches to towns in England and Ireland c. 800–1100*, 103–18

HADLEY, D. M. and RICHARDS, J. D. 2016 The winter camp of the Viking Great Army, AD 872–3, Torksey, Lincolnshire. *Antiquaries Journal* 96, 23–67

HADLEY, D. M and RICHARDS, J. D. (eds) 2000 *Cultures in conflict: Scandinavian settlement in England in the ninth and tenth centuries.* Turnhout: Brepols

HADLEY, D. M. and TEN HARKEL, L. 2013 (eds) *Everyday life in Viking towns: social approaches to towns in England and Ireland c. 800–1100.* Oxford: Oxbow

HALL, R. A. and KENWARD, H. 2004 Setting people in their environment: plant and animal remains from Anglo-Scandinavian York. In Hall, R. A. et al *Aspects of Anglo-Scandinavian York,* 372–426

HALL, R. A. 2000 Anglo-Scandinavian attitudes: archaeological ambiguities in late ninth to mid-eleventh century York. In Hadley, D. M. and Richards, J. D. (eds) *Cultures in conflict: Scandinavian settlement in England in the ninth and tenth centuries,* 311–24

HALL, R. A. 2001 A kingdom too far: York in the early tenth century. In Higham, N. J. and Hill, D. H. (eds) *Edward the Elder 899–924,* 188–99

HALL, R. A. 2004 *Jórvik*: a Viking Age city. In Hines, J., Lane, A. and Redknap, M. (eds) *Land, sea and home,* 283–96

HALL, R. A. 2007 *Exploring the world of the Vikings.* London: Thames and Hudson

HALL, R. A., ROLLASON, D. W., BLACKBURN, M., PARSONS, D. N., FELLOWS-JENSEN, G., HALL, A. H., KENWARD, H. K., O'CONNOR, T. P., TWEDDLE, D. and MAINMAN, A. J.

2004 *Aspects of Anglo-Scandinavian York.* York: Council for British Archaeology

HAMEROW, H. 2012 *Rural settlements and society in Anglo-Saxon England. Medieval History and Archaeology.* Oxford University Press

HART, C. 1982 *Byrhtferth's Northumbrian Chronicle. English Historical Review* 97, 558–82

HASLAM, J. 1987 The second burh at Nottingham. *Landscape History* 9, 45–52

HASLAM, J. 1997 The location of the 10th century burh of *Wigingamere*: a reappraisal. In Rumble, A. R. and Mills, A. D. (eds) *Names, places and people: an onomastic miscellany in memory of John McNeal Dodgson,* 111–30. Stamford: Paul Watkins

HASLAM, J. 2009 *Planning in Late Saxon Worcester.* Retrieved from https://jeremyhaslam.files.wordpress.com/2009/12/planning-in-late-saxon-worcester.pdf, April 2017

HASLAM, J. 2010 King Alfred and the development of London. *London Archaeologist* 12:8, 208–12

HAYWOOD, J. 1999 *Dark Age naval power: a re-assessment of Frankish and Anglo-Saxon seafaring activity.* Hockwold-cum-Wilton: Anglo-Saxon Books

HEIGHWAY, C. 2001 Gloucester and the New Minster of St Oswald. In Higham, N. J. and Hill, D. H. (eds) *Edward the Elder 899–924,* 102–11

HERBERT, M. 1988 *Iona, Kells, and Derry: the history and hagiography of the monastic familia of Columba.* Oxford: Clarendon Press

HIGHAM, N. J. and HILL, D. H. (eds) 2001 *Edward the Elder 899–924.* London: Routledge

HIGHAM, N.J. 2004 Viking-Age settlement in the north-western countryside: lifting the veil? In Hines, J., Lane, A. and Redknap, M. (eds) *Land, sea and home.* Society for Medieval Archaeology Monograph 20, 297–311

HILL, D. 1981 *An atlas of Anglo-Saxon England.* Oxford: Blackwell

HILL, D.H. 2001 The shiring of Mercia – again. In Higham, N.J. and Hill, D.H. (eds) *Edward the Elder 899–924,* 144–59

HILL, D. and COWIE, R. 2001 *Wics: the Early Medieval trading centres of Northern Europe.* Sheffield Archaeological Monographs 14. Sheffield Academic Press

HINDLE, P. 2001 *Roads and tracks for historians.* Chichester: Phillimore

HINES, J., LANE, A. and REDKNAP, M. (eds) 2004 *Land, sea and home. Society for Medieval Archaeology Monograph* 20. Leeds: Maney

HINTON, D.A. 1977 *Alfred's kingdom: Wessex and the South 800–1500.* London: J.M. Dent

HINTON, D.A. 1999 Metalwork and the emporia. In Anderton, M. (ed) *Anglo-Saxon trading centres: beyond the emporia,* 24–31

HODGES, R. 1982 *Dark Age economics.* London: Duckworth

HODGES, R. 2000 *Towns and trade in the Age of Charlemagne.* London: Duckworth

HUNTER-BLAIR, P.H. 1964 Some observations on the *Historia Regum* attributed to Symeon of Durham. In Chadwick, N.K. (ed) *Celt and Saxon: studies in the early British border,* 63–118

ISAAC, G.R. 2007 *Armes Prydein Fawr* and St David. In Wyn Evans, J. and Wooding, J.M. *St David of Wales: cult, church and nation,* 161–81

JAMES, E. 1988 *The peoples of Europe: the Franks.* Oxford: Blackwell

JENKINS, D. 1990 *The law of Hywel Dda: law texts from medieval Wales.* Welsh Classics 2. Llandysul: Gomer Press

JOLIFFE, J.E.A. 1926 Northumbrian institutions. *English Historical Review* 161, 2–42

JONES, G. 1973 *A history of the Vikings.* Oxford University Press

KEYNES, S. and LAPIDGE, M. 1983 *Alfred the Great: Asser's* Life of King Alfred *and other contemporary sources.* Harmondsworth: Penguin

KEYNES, S. 2001 Edward, king of the Anglo-Saxons. In Higham, N.J. and Hill, D.H. (eds) *Edward the Elder 899–924,* 40–66

KING, A. 1978 Gauber high pasture, Ribblehead – an interim report. In Hall, R.A. (ed) 1978 *Viking Age York & the North.* CBA Research Report 27, 21–5

KIRBY, D.P. 2000 *The earliest English kings.* London: Routledge

LACEY, B. 2013 *Saint Columba: his life and legacy.* Dublin: the Columba Press

LAPIDGE, M. 1980 Some Latin poems as evidence for the reign of Athelstan. *Anglo-Saxon England* 9, 61–98

LAPIDGE, M. 1982 Byrhtferth of Ramsey and the early sections of the *Historia Regum* attributed to Symeon of Durham. *Anglo-Saxon England* 10, 97–122

LARRINGTON, C. (ed and trans) 2014 *The Poetic Edda.* Oxford World's Classics

LAVELLE, R. 2005 Why Grately? Reflections on Anglo-Saxon kingship in a Hampshire landscape. *Proceedings of the Hampshire Field Club and Archaeological Society* 60, 154–69

LAVELLE, R. 2010 *Alfred's wars: sources and interpretations of Anglo-*

Saxon warfare in the Viking Age.
Woodbridge: Boydell Press

LEWIS, C.P. and THACKER, A.T.
(eds) 2003 Early Medieval Chester
400–1230. In *A history of the County
of Chester* Volume 5 Part 1, the City
of Chester: General History and
Topography. London: Victoria
County History

LOVELUCK, C. 2007 Rural settlement,
lifestyles and social change in the later
first millennium AD: Anglo-Saxon
Flixborough in its wider context.
Excavations at Flixborough Volume 4.
Oxford: Oxbow

LOWE, C. 2008 *Inchmarnock, an
early historic island monastery and its
archaeological landscape.* Edinburgh:
Society of Antiquaries of Scotland

LOYN, H.R. 1984 *The governance
of Anglo-Saxon England 500–1087.*
London: Edward Arnold

LOYN, H.R. 1992 The church and the
law in early Anglo-Saxon England.
*Tenth Brixworth Lecture: Vaughan
paper 37.* University of Leicester

LUND, N. (ed) 1984 *Two voyagers at the
court of King Alfred.* York: William
Sessions

LYON, S. 2001 The coinage of Edward
the Elder. In Higham, N.J. and Hill,
D.H. (eds) *Edward the Elder 899–924,*
67–78

MCERLEAN, T. 2007 *Harnessing
the tides: the Early Medieval tide
mills at Nendrum Monastery,
Strangford Lough.* Northern Ireland
Archaeological Monographs 7.
Norwich: HM Stationery Office

MCGRAIL, S. 2014 *Early ships and
seafaring: European water transport.*
Barnsley: Pen and Sword

MAINMAN, A.J. and ROGERS, N.S.H
2000 Craft, industry and everyday
life: finds from Anglo-Scandinavian
York. *The Archaeology of York* 17: The

small finds. York: Council for British
Archaeology

MAITLAND, F.W. 1911 Northumbrian
tenures. In Fisher, H.A.L. (ed) *The
collected papers of Frederic William
Maitland, Volume 2.* Cambridge
University Press

MARCUS, G.J. 1980 *The conquest of the
North Atlantic.* Woodbridge: Boydell
Press

MIDDLETON, N. 2005 Early medieval
port customs, tolls and controls on
foreign trade. *Early Medieval Europe*
13:4, 313–58

MILNE, G. 1990 King Alfred's plan for
London. *London Archaeologist* 6:8,
206–7

MOLYNEUX, G. 2011 The Ordinance
concerning the Dunsaete and the
Anglo-Welsh frontier in the late 10th
and 11th centuries. *Anglo-Saxon
England* 40, 249–72

MORRIS, C.D. 1977 Northumbria and
the Viking settlement: the evidence
for land-holding. *Archaeologia
Aeliana* Series 5:5, 81–103

MORRIS, J. 1980 *Nennius: British
History and the Welsh Annals.* History
from the sources. London: Phillimore.

MORRIS, R.K. 1989 *Churches in the
landscape.* London: Phoenix

MORTON. A. 1999 Hamwic in its
context. In Anderton, M. (ed) *Anglo-
Saxon trading centres: beyond the
emporia,* 48–62

MURPHY, D. 1896 *The Annals of
Clonmacnoise.* Dublin University Press

NAISMITH, R. 2012 *Money and power
in Anglo-Saxon England: the southern
English kingdoms 757–865.* Cambridge
Studies in medieval life and thought.
Cambridge University Press

NELSON, J.L. 1986 'A king across the
sea': Alfred in Continental perspective.
*Transactions of the Royal Historical
Society* 36, 45–68

NELSON, J. L. 1991 *The Annals of St Bertin*. Ninth century histories 1. Manchester Medieval Sources

NELSON, J. L. 2008 The first use of the second Anglo-Saxon *Ordo*. In Barrow, J. and Wareham, A. *Myth, rulership, church and charters*, 117–26

NELSON, J. L. 2013 Britain, Ireland and Europe *c.*750–*c.*900. In Stafford, P. (ed) *A companion to the Early Middle Ages: Britain and Ireland c.500–c.1100*, 232–48

NEWTON, R. 1972 *The making of the English landscape: the Northumberland landscape*. London: Hodder and Stoughton

NOBLE, F. 1983 Offa's Dyke reviewed. *British Archaeological Reports, British Series* 114, ed. Gelling, M.

O'BRIEN, C. 2002 The Early Medieval shires of Yeavering, Breamish and Bamburgh. *Archaeologia Aeliana* Series 5:30, 53–73

O'NOLAN, K. (trans) 1962 *The Life of St Findan*. CELT Corpus of electronic texts. Cork: University College. Retrieved from http://www.ucc.ie/celt/published/T201041/text001.html, April 2016

O'SULLIVAN, D. and YOUNG, R. 1995 *The English Heritage Book of Lindisfarne: Holy Island*. London: Batsford

OWEN, H. W. and MORGAN, R. 2007 *Dictionary of the place names of Wales*. Llandysul: Gomer.

PÁLSSON, H. and EDWARDS, P. (eds) 1981 *Orkneyinga Saga: the history of the earls of Orkney*. Harmondsworth: Penguin

PEDDIE, J. 1999 *Alfred, warrior king*. Frome: Sutton Publishing

POTTS, W. T. W. 1974 The pre-Danish estate of Peterborough Abbey. *Proceedings of the Cambridge Antiquarian Society*, 65:2, 13–27

PRATT, D. 2007 *The political thought of King Alfred the Great*. Cambridge University Press

PYE, M. 2014 *The edge of the world: how the North Sea made us who we are*. Harmondsworth: Penguin

RAHTZ, P. A. 1976 Buildings and rural settlement. In Wilson, D. M. (ed) *The archaeology of Anglo-Saxon England*, 49–98

RAHTZ, P. A., ANDERSON, F. W. and HIRST, S. M. 1979 The Saxon and medieval palaces at Cheddar: excavations, 1960–62. British Archaeological Reports British Series 65

RAHTZ, P. A. and MEESON. R. 1992 An Anglo-Saxon watermill at Tamworth. *Council for British Archaeology Research Report* 83

RANDSBORG, K. 1980 *The Viking Age in Denmark*. London: Duckworth

RANSLEY, J., Sturt, F., Dix, J., Adams, J. and Blue, L (eds) 2013 People and the sea: a maritime research agenda for England. *Council for British Archaeology Research Report* 71

REDKNAP, M. 2004 Viking Age settlement in Wales and the evidence from Llanbedrgoch. In Hines, J., Lane, A. and Redknap, M. (eds) *Land, sea and home*, 139–76

REDKNAP, M. 2007 St Davids and a new link with the Hiberno-Norse world. In Wyn Evans, J. and Wooding, J. M. *St David of Wales: cult, church and nation*, 84–9

RICHARDS, J. D. 2004 Excavations at the Viking barrow cemetery at Heath Wood, Ingleby, Derbyshire. *Antiquaries Journal* 84, 23–116

RICHARDS, J. D., NAYLOR, J. and HOLAS-CLARK, C. 2009 *Anglo-Saxon landscape and economy: using portable antiquities to study Anglo-Saxon and Viking Age England*.

Retrieved from http://intarch.ac.uk/
journal/issue25/2, March 2016

RITCHIE, A. 2011 *Govan and its carved
stones*. Govan: Friends of Govan Old

ROBERTS, B.K. 2008a The land
of Werhale – landscapes of Bede.
Archaeologia Aeliana, Series 5:37,
127–59

ROBERTS, B.K. 2008b *Landscapes,
documents and maps: villages in
Northern England and beyond AD 900–
1250*. Oxford: Oxbow books

ROBERTS, B.K. 2010 Northumbrian
origins and post-Roman continuity:
an exploration. In Collins, R. and
Allason-Jones, L. (eds) *Finds from the
frontier: material culture in the 4th
and 5th centuries*. York: Council for
British Archaeology, 120–32

ROBINSON, C.H. 1921 *Anskar, The
Apostle of the North, 801–865, translated
from the Vita Anskarii by Bishop
Rimbert his fellow missionary and
successor*. London: SPCK

ROLLASON, D.W. 1987 The wanderings
of St Cuthbert. In Rollason, D.W.
(ed) *Cuthbert, saint and patron*, 45–61

ROLLASON, D. 1989a St Cuthbert and
Wessex: the evidence of Cambridge,
Corpus Christi College MS 183.
In Bonner, G., Stancliffe, C. and
Rollason, D. (eds) *St Cuthbert, his cult
and his community to AD 1200*, 413–24

ROLLASON, D. 1989b *Saints and relics
in Anglo-Saxon England*. Oxford:
Wiley-Blackwell

ROLLASON, D. 2003 *Northumbria
500–1100: creation and destruction of a
kingdom*. Cambridge University Press

ROLLASON, D. 2004 Anglo-
Scandinavian York: the evidence of
historical sources. In Hall, R.A. et al
Aspects of Anglo-Scandinavian York,
305–24

ROLLASON, D.W. (ed) 1987 *Cuthbert,
saint and patron*. Durham: Dean and
Chapter

ROWLEY, T. 2001 *The Welsh Border:
archaeology, history and landscape*.
Stroud: The History Press

SAMSON, R. 1999 Illusory emporia
and mad economic theories. In
Anderton, M. (ed) *Anglo-Saxon
trading centres: beyond the emporia*,
76–90

SAWYER, P.H. 1977 Kings and
merchants. In Sawyer, P.H. and
Wood, I. (eds) *Early medieval
kingship*, 139–58

SAWYER, P.H. 1981 Fairs and markets in
Early Medieval England. In Skyum-
Nielsen, N. and Lund, N. (eds)
Danish Medieval History: new currents.
Copenhagen: Museum Tusculanum
Press, 153–68

SAWYER, P.H. 1984 Ohthere and
Viking Age trade. In Lund, N. (ed)
*Two voyagers at the court of King
Alfred*, 43–55

SAWYER, P.H. 2013 *The wealth of Anglo-
Saxon England*. Oxford University
Press

SAWYER, P.H. (ed) 1979 *English
medieval settlement*. London: Edward
Arnold

SAWYER, P.H. and WOOD, I. (eds) 1977
Early medieval kingship. University of
Leeds

SCRAGG, D. 2008 (ed) *Edgar, King of
the English 959–975: new interpretations*.
Woodbridge: Boydell Press

SCUDDER, B. (trans) and
ÓSKARSDÓTTIR, S. 2004 *Egil's Saga*.
Harmondsworth: Penguin

SCHOLTZ, B.W. (trans) 1972
*Carolingian Chronicles: Royal
Frankish Annals and Nithard's
Histories*. University of Michigan Press

SHARP, S. 2001 The West Saxon
tradition of dynastic marriage: with

special reference to Edward the Elder. In Higham, N. J. and Hill, D. H. (eds) *Edward the Elder 899–924*, 79–88

SHARPE, R. (ed and trans) 1995 *Adomnán of Iona: Life of Saint Columba*. London: Penguin

SHARPLES, N. et al 2016 The Viking occupation of the Hebrides: evidence from the excavations at Bornais, South Uist. In Berrett, J. H. and Gibbon, S. J. (eds) *Maritime societies of the Viking and medieval world*. Society of Medieval Archaeology Monograph 37. London: Maney, 237–58

SHEEHAN, J. 2008 The *Longphort* in Viking Age Ireland. *Acta Archaeologica* 79, 282–95

SIMPSON, L. 1989 The King Alfred/St Cuthbert episode in the *Historia de Sancto Cuthberto*: its significance for mid-tenth-century English history. In Bonner, G., Stancliffe, C. and Rollason, D. (eds) *St Cuthbert, his cult and his community to AD 1200*, 397–412

SMYTH, A. P. 1984 *Warlords and Holy Men: Scotland AD 80–1000*. Edinburgh University Press

SNEDDON, D. and STRACHAN, D. 2014 The turf longhouses of Glenshee. *Northern Archaeology Today*, Issue 5, 9–13

SOMERVILLE, A. A. and MCDONALD, R. A. (eds) 2014 *The Viking Age: a reader*. Readings in medieval civilisations and cultures XIV. 2nd edition. University of Toronto Press

SOUTH, T. J. (ed.) 2002 *Historia de Sancto Cuthberto: a history of Saint Cuthbert and a record of his patrimony*. Anglo-Saxon Texts 3. Cambridge: D. S. Brewer

STAFFORD, P. 2013 *A companion to the Early Middle Ages: Britain and Ireland c. 500–c.1100*. Chichester: John Wiley

STANCLIFFE, C. and CAMBRIDGE, E. (eds) 1995 *Oswald: Northumbrian king to European saint*. Stamford: Paul Watkins

STEAD, S. D. 1995 Humans and PETS in space. In Lock, G. and Stancic, Z. (eds) *Archaeology and Geographical Information systems: a European perspective*. London: Taylor and Francis, 313–18

STENTON, Sir F. M. 1971 *The Oxford History of England: Anglo-Saxon England*, 3rd edition. Oxford: Clarendon Press

STEVENSON, J. 1993 *Simeon's History of the church of Durham*. Facsimile reprint. Felinfach: Llanerch

STEWART, I. 1967 The St Martin coins of Lincoln. *British Numismatic Journal* 36, 46–54

STOCKER, D. 2013 Aristocrats, burghers and their markets: patterns in the foundation of Lincoln's urban churches. In Hadley, D. M. and ten Harkel, L. (eds) *Everyday life in Viking towns: social approaches to towns in England and Ireland c. 800–1100*, 119–43

STROUD, G. 1999 *Derbyshire extensive urban survey archaeological assessment report: Repton*. English Heritage. Retrieved from: http://archaeologydataservice. ac.uk/archiveDS/archive Download?t=arch-881-1/ dissemination/pdf/EUS_Texts/ Repton/Repton.pdf, May 2016

SYMONDS, L. A. and LING, R. J. 2002 Travelling beneath crows: representing socio-geographical concepts of time and travel in early medieval England. *Internet Archaeology* 13.1 Retrieved from: http://intarch.ac.uk/journal/ issue13/1/toc.html, September 2016

TALBOT, C. H. 1954 *The Anglo-Saxon missionaries in Germany*. London: Sheed and Ward

TAYLOR, C. 1979 *Roads and tracks of Britain*. London: J. M. Dent

THACKER, A. 1995 *Membra disjecta*: the division of the body and the diffusion of the cult. In Stancliffe, C. and Cambridge, E. (eds) *Oswald: Northumbrian king to European saint*, 97–127

THOMAS, C. 1971 *The early Christian archaeology of North Britain*. Oxford University Press

THORNTON, D. E. 2013 Localities. In Stafford, P. (ed) *A companion to the Early Middle Ages: Britain and Ireland c.500–c.1100*, 446–58

TOLKIEN, J. R. R. 1936 *Beowulf; the monster and the critics*. British Academy: Sir Israel Gollancz memorial lecture

TOLKIEN, J. R. R. 2014 *Beowulf: a translation and commentary*. Edited by Christopher Tolkien. London: Harper Collins

TOWNEND, M. 2014 *Viking Age Yorkshire*. Pickering: Blackthorn Press

VINCE, A. 1984 New light on Anglo-Saxon pottery from the London area. *London Archaeologist* 4:16, 431–9

WAINRIGHT, F. T. 1975a North-west Mercia. In Finberg, H. P. R. (ed) *Scandinavian England: collected papers by F. T. Wainwright*, 63–130

WAINRIGHT, F. T. 1975b Ingimund's invasion. In Finberg, H. P. R. (ed) *Scandinavian England: Collected papers by F. T. Wainwright*, 131–62

WAINRIGHT, F. T. 1975c The battle at Corbridge. In Finberg, H. P. R. (ed) *Scandinavian England: Collected papers by F. T. Wainwright*, 163–80

WAINRIGHT, F. T. 1975d Aethelflæd, Lady of the Mercians. In Finberg, H. P. R. (ed) *Scandinavian England: collected papers by F. T. Wainwright*, 305–24

WAINRIGHT, F. T. 1975e The submission to Edward the Elder. In Finberg, H. P. R. (ed) *Scandinavian England: collected papers by F. T. Wainwright*, 325–44

WALKER, I. W. 2000 *Mercia and the making of England*. Stroud: Sutton Publishing

WATTS, V. 2004 *English place-names*. Cambridge University Press

WEBB, J. F. and Farmer, D. H. (ed and trans) 1983 *The Age of Bede*. Harmondsworth: Penguin

WICKHAM-JONES, C. 2015 *Orkney: a historical guide*. Edinburgh: Birlinn

WHITELOCK, D. 1979 *English Historical Documents Volume I: c.500–1042*. 2nd Edition. London: Eyre Methuen

WILLIAMS, G. 2013 Towns and identities in Viking England. In Hadley, D. M. and ten Harkel, L. (eds) *Everyday life in Viking towns: social approaches to towns in England and Ireland c. 800–1100*, 14–34

WILLIAMS, J. 1984 From 'palace' to 'town': Northampton and urban origins. *Anglo-Saxon England* 13, 113–36

WILLIAMSON, T. 2013 *Environment, society and landscape in Early Medieval England: time and topography*. Anglo-Saxon Studies 19. Woodbridge: Boydell Press

WILSON, D. M. 2008 *The Vikings in the Isle of Man*. Aarhus University Press

WILSON, D. M. (ed) 1976 *The archaeology of Anglo-Saxon England*. Cambridge University Press

WILSON, D. M. (ed) 1980 *The Northern World*. London: Thames and Hudson

WOOD, M. 2013 Searching for Brunanburh: the Yorkshire context of the 'Great War' of 937. *Yorkshire Archaeological Journal* 85:1, 138–59

WOOLF, A. 2001 View from the west: an Irish perspective on West Saxon dynastic perspective. In Higham, N. J. and Hill, D. H. (eds) *Edward the Elder 899–924*, 89–101

WOOLF, A. 2006 Dún Nechtain, Fortriu and the geography of the Picts. *Scottish Historical Review* 85: 2: 182–201

WOOLF, A. 2007a From Pictland to Alba 789–1070. *The New Edinburgh History of Scotland*, Volume 2. Edinburgh University Press

WOOLF, A. 2007b Where was Govan in the Early Middle Ages? *The Govan Lecture*. Glasgow: Friends of Govan Old

WOOLF, A. 2009 *Mdal: imagining Shetland before the Vikings*. Paper delivered to the Island cultures and Shetland identity conference, Lerwick 2009. Retrieved from https://www.academia.edu/22127847/Imagining_Shetland_before_the_Vikings, February 2016

WRIGHT, D. 2015 Early Medieval settlement and social power: the Middle Anglo-Saxon 'Home Farm'. *Medieval Archaeology* 59, 24–46

WYN EVANS, J. and WOODING, J. M. 2007 *St David of Wales: cult, church and nation*. Woodbridge: Boydell Press

YORKE, B. 1999 Alfred the Great: the most perfect man in history? *History Today* 49, Issue 10

YORKE, B. 2001 Edward as atheling. In Higham, N. J. and Hill, D. H. (eds) *Edward the Elder 899–924*, 25–39

ZALUCKYJ, S. 2001 *Mercia: the Anglo-Saxon kingdom of central England*. Logaston: Logaston Press

PICTURE CREDITS

All images are by the author except:

1   Stromness: Sarah Annesley.
3   Inchmarnock hostage stone: Headland Archaeology Ltd/Chris Lowe; Wikimedia Commons.
9   *Sea Stallion of Glendalough*: photo by Frank Spiers.
11 Norse runes at Maes Howe: Sarah Annesley.
23 Treaty of Aelfred and Guthrum: Corpus Christi Library, Cambridge.
27 The Stockholm *Codex Aureus*: Wikimedia Commons.

28 The Alfred jewel: Ashmolean Museum, University of Oxford, UK /Bridgeman Images.
32 The Cuerdale hoard: JMiall; Wikimedia Commons.
38 Fierce beast from St Oswald's Priory: Fae; Wikimedia Commons.
46 Frontispiece of Bede's *Life of St Cuthbert*; Wikimedia Commons.
50 Raven penny of Óláfr Guðrøðsson, king of York: Arthur Bryant Coins Limited. www.bryantcoins.com

ACKNOWLEDGEMENTS

THERE IS NOW an overwhelming amount of literature on the Viking Age in Britain. In acknowledging the debt I owe to all those scholars on whose work I have leant, I apologize for any errors of interpretation or fact. Any omission of credit on my part is inadvertent. I am grateful to Professor Sam Turner of the University of Newcastle Department of History, Classics and Archaeology, for affording me invaluable research facilities as a Visiting Fellow. I would particularly like to thank the following for their help or advice along the way: Werner Karrasch, the brilliant photographer at Roskilde Ship Museum; my cousin Anya, who introduced us; my old friend Jacqui Mulville; colleagues and friends in the Bernician Studies Group; Professor Diana Whaley for all sorts of help with language and place names; Peter Fitzgerald, for kindly showing me Ecgberht's stone in Penselwood; and Paul Blinkhorn for acting as a ceramic fact-checker. My thanks also go to Dr Lynne Ballew for reading the text and making many invaluable suggestions for improving it. My editor, Richard Milbank, has been unfailingly encouraging, sympathetic and sharp-eyed. A book is only half a book until it has been through its publisher's hands. The designers and production staff at Head of Zeus and Pegasus Books are similarly owed a great debt of gratitude for bringing *The Viking Wars* to life with style. Finally, a thank you to the diggers: the archaeologists who tough it out in the field, who give us hope of drawing back the veil that hides our ancestors from us.

INDEX

A

Aachen, 57

Abercorn, 165, 166

Acleah, battle of, 93, 220

Adulf mcEtulf, 361

Æbbe (sister of King Oswald), 117

Æðelbald, king of Mercia, 33, 41, 121, 126

Æðelbald, king of Wessex, 93, 95

Æðelberht, king of Kent and Wessex, 94, 95

Æðelflæd, Lady of the Mercians (Ælfred's daughter), 273

  builds fortress at *Bremesburh*, 279

  plan to conquer Danish Mercia and East Anglia, 161

  captures Derby, 287, 299–300

  dies at Tamworth, 302

  grants land to Ingimund, 239–44

  refortifies *vill* at Kingsholm, 275–76

  takes Leicester, 287

  marries Ealdorman Æðelred, 187, 239

  rules Mercia, 239

  acquires Oswald's relics from Bardney, 274

  builds forts at *Scergeat* and Bridgnorth, 282–84

  refounds burh at Worcester, 185

  treaty with York, 302

Æðelgifu, 233–34

Æðelheard, archbishop of Canterbury, 10, 34, 35

Æðelnoth, ealdorman of Somerset, 143, 218

Æðelred (d.871), king of Wessex (Ælfred's brother), 94, 95, 96, 102, 109–10, 112

Æðelred (d.911), ealdorman of Mercia (Ælfred's godson), 176, 178, 186, 188, 209, 210, 211, 212, 214, 215, 228

  loyalty to Ælfred, 213

  submits to Ælfred, 177

  control of Cheshire, 190

  surrounds Roman fort of Chester, 215

  dies, 279–80

  campaign against Gwynedd, 177

  incapacitated, 240

  refortifies *vill* at Kingsholm, 275–76

  marries Æðelflæd, 187, 239

  acquires Oswald's relics from Bardney, 274

  Warwickshire Avon and Great Ouse, 189

  refounds burh at Worcester, 185

Æðelred II, 198, 436, 449

Æðelstan (Ælfred's brother), 75, 76, 94, 95

Æðelstan (Ælfred's grandson),

  purchases Amounderness, 362–65

  assemblies, 352–54

  Brunanburh, battle of, 388, 390, 392, 396, 398–9

  treatment of Constantine of Alba, 393

  expansion of royal residence of Cheddar, 407

  coinage, 405

  death, 400

  fostered at Æðelred's court in Mercia, 239, 335

  and Hywel Dda, 417

  invades Alba, 369–70

  and Louis of West Francia, 400

  buried at Malmesbury, 400

  sends embassy to Óláfr proposing battle, 397

  patronage of Oswald cult, 276, 368

  enacts 'peace guild', 401, 412

  recognizes Eadmund cult, 267

  Rex Totius Britanniae, 351, 357, 358, 360, 457

B